SOL

REFIGURING AMERICAN MUSIC

A series edited by Ronald Radano and Josh Kun

Charles McGovern, contributing editor

SOUNDS OF
CROSSING

MUSIC, MIGRATION, AND THE AURAL POETICS OF HUAPANGO ARRIBEÑO

ALEX E. CHÁVEZ

Duke University Press
Durham and London   2017

Printed and bound by CPI Group (UK) Ltd, Croydon, CR0 4YY
Designed by Heather Hensley
Typeset in Arno Pro by Westchester Publishing Services

Library of Congress Cataloging-in-Publication Data
Names: Chávez, Alex E., [date] author.
Title: Sounds of crossing : music, migration, and the aural
poetics of Huapango Arribeño / Alex E. Chávez.
Description: Durham : Duke University Press, 2017. |
Series: Refiguring american music | Includes bibliographical
references and index.
Identifiers: LCCN 2017028529 (print)
LCCN 2017041721 (ebook)
ISBN 9780822372202 (ebook)
ISBN 9780822370093 (hardcover : alk. paper)
ISBN 9780822370185 (pbk. : alk. paper)
Subjects: LCSH: Huapangos—Social aspects—United States. |
Mexican Americans—Songs and music—Social aspects—
United States. | Mexican Americans—United States—Social
life and customs. | Mexico—Emigration and immigration—
Songs and music. | United States—Emigration and
immigration—Songs and music.
Classification: LCC E184.M5 (ebook) | LCC E184.M5 C438 2017
(print) | DDC 305.868/72073—dc23
LC record available at https://lccn.loc.gov/2017028529

Duke University Press gratefully acknowledges The Institute for
the Scholarship in the Liberal Arts, College of Arts and Letters,
University of Notre Dame, which provided funds toward the
publication of this book.

Cover art: *Huapangueros* wait out the mountain fog (La Florída,
Querétaro). Photo by Alex E. Chávez.

For María del Refugio and Catalina

Hoy brillan nuestro senderos
lo digo en mis verserías
yo con estos violineros
las noches las hago días . . .

Today our paths are radiant
I say this in improvised verses
in the company of these violinists
I turn nights into mornings . . .
—CACHO

CONTENTS

ACKNOWLEDGMENTS

The focus and scope of scholarship are often deeply shaped by meaningful life experiences. My artistic work beyond the academy has profoundly influenced my theoretical and methodological praxis, and the worlds of performance in which I have taken part for most of my life have been most instructive in guiding my understanding of how race, gender, and citizenship continue to shape my existence and the lives of those in this book. This highly personalized relationship between art, politics, family, and academic research makes the text now before you possible—it is the product of shared knowledges and collective efforts that have sculpted my quest to apprehend the human experience through forms of cultural expression. A great many people who have shaped me and my scholarship are all an inspiration. I cannot possibly thank all of them here.

I thank first my late mother, María del Refugio Esquivel, forever my best friend and voice of reason; my father, José Chávez, who gave me the gift of music; my younger sister, Cathy, and my late older sister, Catalina, whose memory I cherish. I am indebted to both the Chávez and Villeda families of Querétaro and Mexico City for their unending support throughout my many years of music and research in their midst. I also thank Jennifer Kotting—the writing of this book would not have been possible without her contributions and ceaseless encouragement.

I owe an intellectual debt of gratitude to my dissertation committee, who guided the very first iteration of what would become this book: Martha Menchaca, Robin Moore, Joel Sherzer, and, especially, Richard R. Flores and José E. Limón. As your student, I now count myself among a rich intellectual tradition of Chicana/o anthropology pioneered by don Américo

Paredes. I humbly aspire to be the type of scholar whose work inspires others, just as you have done for me.

I express my deepest appreciation for the care and mentorship of my senior colleagues Richard Bauman, Charles L. Briggs, Gilberto Cárdenas, Alejandro Lugo, Olga Nájera-Ramírez, Daniel Sheehy, and Nena Torres. Your guidance and example have been a source of strength for me.

The ideas expressed in this book also developed with the nurturing aid of time and intellectual community, particularly during my postdoctoral appointments. I am grateful for Daniel and Jessica Martínez and the wonderful staff of the Institute for Latino Studies at the University of Notre Dame; the Department of Latina/Latino Studies at the University of Illinois at Urbana-Champaign, where I reconnected with my *compañero* Gilberto Rosas and found another brother-in-arms, Francisco Baires—you, Sarah, the university YMCA, the Champaign-Urbana Immigration Forum, and the ethnic studies postdoctoral fellows became family; and the Latin American and Latino Studies program at the University of Illinois at Chicago—Nena, your belief in me helped me in ways you can't imagine, and I am likewise grateful for the opportunity to work alongside esteemed colleagues Amalia Pallares, Alejandro L. Madrid, and Ralph Cintron. In this capacity, both the Ford Foundation family and the Association of Latina and Latino Anthropologists have been wonderful support systems that constantly remind me that we academics of color are not alone and that our voices are important.

I thank the Advanced Seminar in Chicano Research at the University of Texas at Austin, in particular Estevan Azcona, Alan Gomez, Pablo González, Veronica Martínez, Russell Rodriguez, and Cristina Salinas, for your friendship and mentorship. I also thank my graduate school companions, Santiago Guerra, Ken MacLeish, Courtney Morris, and Raja Swamy. Years later, now as an assistant professor, I am proud to call both the Department of Anthropology and the Institute for Latino Studies at the University of Notre Dame my home—a heartfelt thanks to all of my colleagues.

I thank various individuals and institutions that invited me to share portions of this material over the years, including Aaron Fox at the Center for Ethnomusicology at Columbia University; the Latin American and Latino Studies Program at the University of Illinois at Chicago; the Department of Folklore and Ethnomusicology, the Department of Anthropology, and the Center for Latin American and Caribbean Studies at Indiana University; the Newberry Library Seminar in Borderlands and Latino Studies; and the Folklore Student Association at Ohio State University.

I greatly appreciate the manuscript reviewers' careful readings and insightful suggestions, all of which strengthened this work. And I am especially grateful for the wisdom and guidance of Ken Wissoker, Elizabeth Ault, and Josh Kun at Duke University Press; thank you for believing in this project and for shepherding me through the process of transforming what was once a manuscript waiting to be a book into the text now before you. The final stages of this book also benefited from the beautiful translation work of Cristina Cabello de Martínez and the musical genius of Grey Larsen.

Portions of the research that informs this book were supported by the National Science Foundation, the Ford Foundation, the Center for Mexican American Studies and the College of Liberal Arts at the University of Texas at Austin, and the Institute for Scholarship in the Liberal Arts, College of Arts and Letters at the University of Notre Dame.

Among those who supported me along the way with wonderful friendship and creative energy were Dolores García and Roger Reeves, all the University of Texas Chicanada, and my extended musical families in Austin, Texas, and Chicago, Illinois—our work together has been vital to my survival.

Finally, I recognize with the utmost gratitude and respect those whose lives are chronicled in these pages. I thank them for their trust, generosity, and patience. From the Sierra Gorda to Texas, from the Zona Media to Mississippi and back, our time together in friendship and learning is why this work exists. Although I have altered names in most cases to protect identities and privacy, I am forever grateful to Graciano, Guillermo Velázquez, María Isabel "Chabe" Flores Solano, Proceso Sánchez, Doña Rosa, Valentín, Homero, Salomón, Ricardo, Xavi, Zeferino, Daniel, Don Lencho, Vincent Velázquez, Pascual, Cacho, Flavio, Claro, Isaías and the families of El Refugio, San Luis Potosí, for their generosity and life lessons. Last, I thank those who did not live to see the publication of this work but whose memory is inscribed in these pages: Senovio, Sebastián Salinas, Franco González, Mauro González, Fortunato Ramírez, Benito Lara, and Purísima Villeda—*presente*.

AMERICAN BORDER/LANDS

And since there is no crossing that is ever undertaken once and for all,
this ontological imperative of making the world intelligible to ourselves is,
of necessity, an enterprise that is ongoing.
—M. JACQUI ALEXANDER, *PEDAGOGIES OF CROSSING*

Sound, then, is a substance of the world as well as a basic part of how
people frame their knowledge about the world.
—DAVID NOVAK AND MATT SAKAKEENY, INTRODUCTION TO
KEYWORDS IN SOUND

Their stories seem impossible, nearly tragic. But the truths they hold are undeniable. My mother crossed the border in Juárez in the trunk of a car when she was thirteen. She left her home in rural Zacatecas, arriving at the border weeks later—the details of that journey remain unknown to me. After she crossed, she worked for some months as a domestic in El Paso, labor for which she was never compensated. Her sister, who was living in a small red-dirt town northeast of there, came for her late one night: "Pack your things. It's time to go." My mother had no belongings.

My father crossed near Ojinaga, Chihuahua. He had walked the brush—open chaparral dense with cacti, ocotillo, mesquite, and cenizo just west of Big Bend National Park. For nearly a week, he and two cousins traced old Apache trails in the dead of winter. For a sixteen-year-old from the steamy mountains of the Huasteca queretana in north-central Mexico, the snow and bitter temperatures seemed alien. They trekked north toward the so-called Davis Mountains (more like hills compared to back home, he thought) that hug Fort Davis, past Marfa. There was no hip artist colony then, just desert.

These stories defined much of who my mother was and who my father continues to be today. They have given meaning to their work, their undertakings, their failures, their accomplishments, their children's lives. I was born years later, after they had crossed, after they had met and married, after they had found steady jobs and gone on to their second or third, and after they had begun to feel at home in West Texas—a place not so welcoming to undocumented migrants and their children. These stories circulated even after the greatest difficulties had passed; portions of them were mentioned offhandedly in daily conversation, whispered softly when imparting words of wisdom and care, and exhaled through gritted teeth when they confronted yet other borders—cultural, social, and otherwise—or were forced to deal with life's tragedies. I've pieced together their telling; I've found meaning in them, too. They've become a part of me, so that all the smaller borders—the soft ones, the institutional ones, the cultural ones we sometimes experience more like deep chasms—are familiar to me, despite my educational and professional achievements. Some feel as dangerous as they do familiar, everyday encounters that thrust me into an uneasy space where my nerves come alive with anger and fear . . . as in northern Indiana, not too long ago . . .

I'm performing *huapango* at a wedding reception where a group of *mexicanos* has congregated to celebrate the marriage of two of their own. Held at a local VFW hall in a small town, this gathering is being watched all evening long by a crowd of Anglo veterans who are drinking at the bar located on the opposite side of the building; a heavy velvet curtain covered the single doorway between the two spaces. At first, I am unaware of this. Then I hit the restroom, and my two huapango bandmates come in after me. A rather intoxicated Anglo man twice my age, presumably a veteran, is at the sink, washing his hands. He notices us, turns, and approaches me, standing a little too close, eyeing me up and down. His body sways. I edge back. I'm alien to him. My boots, sombrero, and guayabera are regalia from another world. He begins to speak slowly and loudly, making sure we can understand English, though the liquor in his system impairs his speech: "You know, I tell them you all paid good money for this place, and they shouldn't get upset about it. It's good business." "Them," I realize, means a group of agitated veterans on the other side of the building who are protesting the Mexican presence, surveilling the dancing wedding guests (who paid "good money" to rent the space), sneaking an occasional peek around the velvet curtain. I notice them out of the corner of my eye.

My fellow performers didn't initially catch the gist of the man's comments, his underlying threat, but I could imagine the conversation on the veterans' side of the hall. They were none too pleased with the foreign music shaking the walls of the building and seeping into *their* evening, with the mexicanos claiming space, with their brown children playing outside in the darkness. The threat of some unimaginable violence being plotted next door to us loomed, at least in my mind. Why not? Hours south of here, in Indiana's capital city, debates rage on among lawmakers over provisions in the proposed anti-immigrant law S.B. 590. Most lawmakers agree with it in principle. Concerns are largely about its feasibility. Northern Indiana is a beating center of these xenophobic politics, not to mention Second Amendment fervor, which gives me pause in the context of the ongoing rise in mass shootings. And yet here they are, a group of migrants in celebration, carving out a place for themselves amid these various tensions—huapango music is being played even this far north, and improvised poetry is in the offing on this midwestern American night.

The man reaches for the door, mumbling something unintelligible as he steps out into the hall, where he's met with the celebratory sounds of hard-stomped zapateado dance echoing in the corridor. He goes back to the veteran bar. His words continue to echo in my head, "It's good business."

The specter of immigration reform and border walls, mounting deaths along the U.S.-Mexico border, and growing controversy over executive orders and harsh immigration laws across the country saturate the popular media and political discourse in the United States, fueling both heated debate and public anxieties.[1] This politicized terrain is undergirded by a much larger concern with the future-tense "Story of America" (Stewart 1996), as groups of U.S. citizens grapple with the browning of "their country" amid the cultural and demographic realities linked to expanding transnational political-economic ties with Latin America—the often-cited majority-minority question plays itself out at the local level in places far from the border, in places like northern Indiana. While a palpable enthusiasm emerged during the presidential election of 2012 with regard to Latina/o issues and their potential rise to the top of the national agenda, this excitement left unchallenged nativist sentiments that cast so-called illegal immigrants as a racialized source of criminality, sentiments that have ushered in proposed state-level legislation targeting migrants across the country.[2]

National appeals to the Latina/o community ring hollow, as the call for change in politics has at times been cast as a need for a change in tone—a political tokenism bereft of any genuine dismantling of this racist worldview, for racism is not deemed wrong, merely inconvenient when too audible in national politics. In other words, the supposed change of heart—that is, to see Latin American migrants as human beings—is anything but heartening, particularly when talk surrounding a revision in how the United States deals with undocumented migration remains committed to border militarization and considers the policing of Latina/o communities writ large as a necessary part of the equation. Unfortunately, in the Obama era of mass deportation and with its intensification after the 2016 presidential election, the underlying social location of Latin American migrants, specifically, remains entrenched in the racialized logics of disposability with little concern for the complex cultural adjustments and adaptation processes they live out in their attempts at integrating into the highly stratified American social order. Indeed, migrant detention and border buildup are quite profitable—"it's good business."

Beyond the realm of immigration policy, the business of othering communities of color is framed alongside visions of a "real" America, a politics of culture that has prompted the gradual defunding of the public sector and an abandonment of urban areas over the past four decades in the face of demographic shifts and civil rights movements. Racial conservatives refuse to invest in a brown American "underclass" they don't see as part of their cultural legacy. In a self-fulfilling prophecy, the breakdown of social institutions that is so often blamed on "immigrants" and minorities is the result of white retrenchment, not the imagined cultural dysfunctionality and pathology projected onto these racialized populations. Yet, ironically, in the aftermath of recent election cycles, "real" Americans are left asking, "How do we create constituents out of people we have utter contempt for?" while simultaneously wielding nostalgic narratives of an idyllic (and racially segregated) past in response to the perceived displacement of white privilege.[3] "Make America Great Again" rings falsely in my ears. In the America I have described here, stories abound of those who cross its borders—literal and figurative. As in my childhood, these stories are whispered, but as this book reveals, they are also sounded out and improvised in loud all-night performances in the presence of hundreds of dancing migrant bodies, stomping, moving, and being *moved*.

THE VOICE

The enduring dilemma of how the United States has historically defined social membership along the lines of race reveals how expressive culture is often where the symbolic borders of American belonging are reconfigured. Presently, this is occuring in a context of mass expulsion, loudly voiced xenophobia, and daily violence with regard to Latina/o communities across the continental United States. This book argues that transnational music making in everyday Mexican migrant life, specifically, positions itself at the tensive center of this volatile discursive terrain, where certain sounds—as expressive indices of a supposedly deficient culture metonymically linked to the corrosion of America—both symbolically and materially claim a place in the space of the U.S. nation-state, refiguring the borders of citizenship and alienage through embodied and agentive forms of cultural expression. In other words, for performers, "auditory perception is intimately enmeshed with bodily action" (Berger 2009: 13). Therefore, the corporeality of these performative enactments is understood in these pages as aesthetic labor, the materiality of which—just like "the subjectivity of migrant labour"—attains a "subversive potential" given that the economic subordination of migrant workers within the space of the U.S. nation-state is inseparable from the structures of immigration law, policy, and the juridical nature of illegality (De Genova 2009: 461). My specific focus is the performance of Mexican *huapango arribeño*—an understudied musical form—as a lens with which to understand the cultural and spatial contours and politics of this transnational migrant world.

A music little known outside its region of origin in the Mexican states of Guanajuato, Querétaro, and San Luis Potosí, huapango arribeño takes its name from the Nahuatl word *cuahpanco*, derived from *cuahuitl* (wood), *pan* (atop), and *co* (place), thus signifying "atop of the wood." This refers to the *tarima* (wooden platform) atop which people dance zapateado (patterned footwork) in various styles of vernacular Mexican music (G. Saldívar 1937). The term *arribeño* (highlander) refers to the mountainous regions of Guanajuato and Querétaro—*arriba* means "above"—and also to the midregion of San Luis Potosí, which sits higher (*más arriba*) in altitude than the Huasteca portion of the state.[4]

This book represents the first extended study of huapango arribeño, a topic otherwise absent from scholarship on Mexican music. Although ethnomusicologists, folklorists, and linguistic anthropologists will be able to glean the details of its formal musico-poetic properties—particularly its extensive use of the Spanish *décima* (ten-line stanza) and its relation to the Mexican stringed-music genre often referred to as *son*—this book follows the moments of this music's lush and improvisational performance within the lives of both audiences and practitioners, from New Year's festivities in the highlands of Guanajuato to backyard get-togethers along the back roads of Central Texas. In doing so, it provocatively uses *sounds of crossing* as a graphic model to map the bindings and cultural adjacencies produced through the enactment of huapango arribeño's music and poetics across this transnational geography

MAP I.1 Map of Mexico highlighting *huapango*'s region of origin

in the late twentieth and early twenty-first centuries. In this way this book traces the contemporary pathways, or crossings, of moving bodies and bodies of musical and poetic discourse to reveal the ways in which migrants both give voice to and respatialize the oscillations of their existence in Mexico, their clandestine treks across the border, and the workaday problems of unauthorized social life in the United States. Significantly, the focus here is on how these performative contexts—which exhibit music, poetry, and dance—give rise to what huapango arribeño practitioners, or *huapangueros*, commonly refer to as *el destino* (the calling). Far more than a term for an artistic vocation, el destino constitutes a vernacular theory of aesthetic production predicated on intimate bonds of sociability between audiences and huapangueros, or *compañeros del destino* (companions of the calling). Put another way, the quotidian (understood as both a spatial and a temporal designation) necessarily begins and ends with the body, and huapango arribeño's constellation of embodied aesthetic practices gives voice to stories of ordinary living. This reflexivity is central to the fluidity of the "poetic function" (Jakobson 1960), that is, in animating social categories (e.g., race, citizenship, geography, history) in textual praxis (Dent 2009).

I mobilize the concept of aural poetics to refer to this dialogic interplay between embodiment and aesthetics. In doing so, I rely on José E. Limón's designation of cultural poetics as "acts of cultural interpretation focused on aesthetically salient, culturally embedded textualities and enactments" (1994: 14). While my position overlaps with Limón's situated renderings of vernacular performance—dancing, verbal art, and oral legend—I augment his formulation with the term *aural* to lend further specificity to the field of aesthetic cultural production that concerns this book. Specifically, I explore musico-poetic textualities made legible through a relational process of sonic enactment and reception, a process that possesses its own social aesthetic sensibility, or poetics. Therefore, this book lends huapango arribeño an "ethnographic ear" (Erlmann 2004). It is a story (broad)cast through the perceptual field of voicing, a concept that collapses the border-binary—as it has been articulated through the epistemological "project central to Euro-Western modernity" (Weidman 2015: 234)—between the material or sonorous aspects and the immaterial, agentive, or political meanings of sound.[5] The material textures of sounds (the voice included) may be conceptualized only in culturally specific—and therefore subjectively affective—terms. We hear (literal) voices as warm, sweet, velvet, haunting, and so on, ideas that simultaneously inform that very experience. We are *moved* by them. Philosopher Don Ihde extends this intervening logic and suggests that to listen to the "surfaces" of sounds is to "be aware in the process of the pervasiveness of certain 'beliefs'" (2007: 49) as we hear and construct the social life of sound phenomenologically. In this way sound is heard through culturally and historically situated forms of listening, that is, through aural modes of attention that circulate within social fields of meaning and experience contoured by power, politics, and economy. To claim (as this book does) that voicing *matters*—resonates both materially and immaterially—is to account for embodied musico-poetic performance as a form of communication attuned to interaffective states of attachment, of living, of solidarity within a field of U.S.-Mexico social and economic relations and all that that entails. To invoke my intellectual precursors, people "sing with their heads thrown back" (Paredes 1958: 34) and "mumble damn-foolishness into microphones" (Limón 1994: 94) to voice their presence in a world that otherwise silences their place in it. Whether carefully crafted verse or guttural *grito* (a cry of emotional release), both embody the social anatomy of discontent with the politics that encode the dominated conditions of ethnic Mexicans (Flores 2002). This is how voicing *takes place*—its material enactment constructs mattering maps that represent the ways social actors move through the world, or desire to do so (a process I refer to as *self-authorization* in chapter 5). In more conventional theoretical terms, I am politicizing what Mikhail Bakhtin (1981) has elsewhere termed *dialogism* as a way of understanding how the voices of individual actors are constitutive of their engagements with a much broader social horizon. Aaron A. Fox's comments on the expressive centrality and power of the voice in Texas white working-class culture are instructive: "The voice stands for the embodied, socially embedded self; it stands also for a communal identity in which that self has a particular and irreducible dignity. The fragile but necessary living human voice, in all its individual embodied thought and felt particularity, and in all its iconic social symbolism and situational indexicality, is the vigorous poetic entextualization . . . of a cherished *critical* 'ordinariness'" (2004: 42–43). To a similar end, Limón anticipates Fox in his work on the folkloric practices of marginalized working-class Mexican-Americans in South Texas as expressive forms that voice "a critical difference of consciousness in antagonistic contradistinction" to the "fragmentary pressures" of an alienating dominant Anglo culture (1994: 117).

This concern with voicing edges toward recent work in the field of sound studies.[6] While this sonic turn attends to an array of topics, including ethnographies of emplaced auditory landscapes, sound production, technologies of sonic circulation and inscription, and the politics of listening, there remains an opening for the continued application of this theoretical predisposition to questions of music and migration.[7] Indeed, Frances R. Aparicio and Cándida F. Jáquez (2003) took up the theme of "musical migrations" over a decade ago in an edited volume that bears that very name. However, in their analysis, migration operates largely as a metaphor for the transnational movement and interplay of folk and popular musics across Latin America. The actual physical movement of people across geographic distances is not an ethnographic concern, such that music making in the everyday expressive lives of migrants remains somewhat unexamined. Migration in this and other works is primarily a shorthand for the sonic proliferation embedded in the globalizing music industry, with an emphasis on the various forms of circulation and resignification that constitute what Ana María Ochoa Gautier (2006, 2014) has subsequently termed the "aural public sphere" in Latin America. Ochoa Gautier's formulation is continuous with R. Murray Schafer's ([1977] 1994) "soundscape" in her attention to the material dimensions of language, music, and the voice, while also remaining phenomenologically attuned to embodiment and the senses as central to the socially and culturally positioned forms of listening that constitute modern personhood and political subjectivities. With attention to nineteenth-century Colombia, Ochoa Gautier's work demonstrates the continued challenge of integrating analytical attention to both the sonic qualities and the ephemeral dimensions of sound, which requires an anthropology capable of contextualizing the deliberate intentionality of listening as an ethnographic modality centered in auditory perception.[8] In the present case, ethnographic alertness to huapango arribeño's sonic nexus of music and poetics foregrounds the role aural immediacy plays in articulating selves and subjectivities in relation to others. With this in mind, I return throughout this book to the notion of el destino—the calling—as a communicative modality, or voicing, that generates auditory intimacies of "enduring social resonance" across time and space among migrants (Faudree 2013: 18). This necessarily opens the door to metadiscursive analysis, or focused attention to the critical reflexivity emergent from the domain of music, for el destino is a potent local theory that attends a constellation of abstract concerns regarding life, livelihood, personhood, performance, community, and aesthetics, all of which are brought together through the deep sociability—or intimacy—engendered in the course of music making.

Yet, while I explore this singular musical genre, I am equally concerned with the cultural scriptings that frame the practice of vernacular Mexican musics. These framings are centrally about the sounds of national belonging and alienation on both sides of the U.S.-Mexico border. I take specific interest in these sonic emplacements and displacements in the present neoliberal era of transnational integration between the two countries. How do "Mexican sounds"—as a locus of aesthetic behaviors, performative acts, and signifying practices—resonate across physical, aural, and cultural borders, and what do they reveal about transnational migrant lives lived across them? Indeed, "traditional" sounds—amplified through the loudspeaker of *mexicanidad*—ring out as calcified sonic artifacts of cultural patrimony across the aural border of the U.S. nation-state in ways that brace attitudes about "Mexican culture" as a distortion that is polluting "American" national identity and cultural homogeneity. This particular sonic envelope offers one—and certainly the most pervasive—way of perceiving Mexican musics, which in a U.S. context are signified as foreign Spanish-language noise. The term *noise*, while admittedly referring to a generalized material aspect of all sound, operates as an evaluative category for sounds that are, at best, considered culturally incomprehensible or, at worst, deemed to possess unassimilable and alien meanings thought to be of no social value. David Novak elaborates, "[Noise] becomes the discursive *borderline* that separates one kind of person, or sound, or place absolutely from another and ultimately reduces all of the 'noncultural' elements that cannot be folded into normative systems of meaning" (2015: 133; emphasis added). Discursive borders are similarly produced through linguistic processes of social differentiation and exclusion operative in the juridical and cultural discourses that construct the so-called illegal Mexican migrant as not only a subject outside the American polity but a racially inferior and linguistically deficient outsider. This latter stigmatization is shaped by institutionally sanctioned forms of listening that hear race and class difference when encountering the Spanish language and associated expressive practices (Rosa 2010; Rosa and Flores 2015). Following the cultural logic outlined above, this is how, similar to music, certain forms of speaking among Latinas/os and ethnic Mexicans are marked as disordered sound: noise (Attali 1985: 6).

Nevertheless, Mexican migrants practice their own situated forms of listening amid the aural gaze of everyday Americans and state surveillance, as Dolores Casillas (2011) demonstrates with respect to the ways in which Spanish-language radio listeners who live below the radar use the airwaves to subvert *la migra* (immigration authorities) through live alerts that track, monitor, and outwit the U.S. Immigration and Customs Enforcement (ICE). This "inverse surveillance" is also contingent on communication among listeners—on sounds that create connections and form the basis for imagining communities (Casillas 2011). Samuel K. Byrd's recent volume *The Sounds of Latinidad: Immigrants Making Music and Creating Culture in a Southern City* (2015) gestures toward such a focus, as he explores how music became a vehicle for community formation among Latina/o migrants in Charlotte, North Carolina, amid the "graying skies" that resulted from the economic recession and the failure to pass comprehensive immigration reform in the 2000s. As his argument goes, creative expression functioned as a way of claiming cultural citizenship through "[synthesizing] disparate elements—nationalities, class backgrounds, ages, and migration experiences"—into a form of southern *Latinidad* (5). Despite the title, however, Byrd's work omits an analysis of how sound ideologies and ideologies of sound are instructive in understanding the ways migrants live in and hear the world. In other words, how and why does sound matter—materially and immaterially—when one is examining multiple experiences of migration? With this query in mind, the present work understands sound as "reveal[ing] social space as an artifact of material practices complexly interwoven with semiotic processes" (Eisenberg 2015: 202) and therefore significant in recognizing how embodied expressive affiliations are axial to *voicing* one's place in the world, that is, claiming space across the physical divides of nations and the cultural divides of politics.

BORDERS AND BORDERLANDS

Although the scholarly field of border studies and the metaphorical use of the borderlands are often conflated, they are distinct. Border studies typically examines the material conditions of the U.S.-Mexico border as a concrete physical place, largely from the perspective of the social sciences (R. Alvarez 1984; Bustamante 1983, 1992; Bustamante et al. 1992; Davidson 2000; De León 2015; Dunn 1996; Nash and Fernández-Kelly 1983; O. Martínez 1994, 1996, 1998; Mattingly and Hansen 2006; Nevins 2002; Rosas 2012; Ruíz and Tiano 1991; Sadowski-Smith 2002; Segura and Zavella 2007; Téllez 2008; Vélez-Ibañez 1983, 1996, 2010; Vila 2000). The borderlands are used metaphorically to speak of a liminal state of in-betweenness in work in the humanities, largely cultural studies (Anzaldúa 1987; Elenes 2011; García Canclini 1990; Keating 2005; Rosaldo 1989; J. Saldívar 1997; Stephen 2007).[9] A seminal figure in the development of the latter theoretical framework, Gloria Anzaldúa, also distinguished between "a dividing line" (or border) and "the emotional residue of an unnatural boundary" (borderland) (1987: 3). Nevertheless, while the borderlands are often considered the symbolic divides among various social groups, the former, more concrete geopolitical perspective is equally undergirded by a broader consideration of the boundary work implicit in social and cultural ideologies of difference making. One cannot fully understand the physical presence of the U.S.-Mexico border as a result of U.S. imperialism without accounting for the racial ideologies that drove westward expansion in the nineteenth century (De León 1983; Paredes 1958, 1961). Centered on illegality and border inventions/inspections/crossings, respectively, the contemporary work of Nicholas De Genova (2005) and Alejandro Lugo (2008) explores how the materiality of U.S.-Mexico border policies extends across the continental United States and subsequently shapes cultural logics that produce and restrict citizenship in everyday life, inspecting, monitoring, and surveilling "what goes in and out in the name of class, gender, race, and nation" (Lugo 2008: 115). Indeed, social relations are always shifting and embedded in much broader and more complex cultural conflicts that are historical in scope, and thus the racialization of ethnic Mexicans in the United States is inseparable from the U.S.-Mexico border as a concrete physical site (of crossing and inspection) that in turn operates as an (invented) allegorical social divide in the U.S. American imagination that renders ethnic Mexicans "policeable subjects" (Rosas 2006). This critical and ethnographically grounded integration of geographic/physical and cultural/conceptual perspectives is what Robert R. Alvarez Jr. (1995) termed an "anthropology of borderlands."

I would add, as an implicit aspect of the project of modernity, that the deepening political-economic relationship between Mexico and the United States throughout the twentieth century has only further inscribed these imagined social differences. Here, I refer specifically to transnational migration in the devastating wake of the Mexican Revolution; U.S. labor demands extending through World War II and the Cold War era, contractually managed through the Bracero Program (1942–1964); the era of structural adjustment in the 1980s alongside an imagined moral panic surrounding undocumented migration that resulted in heightened border militarization; the dissolution of both protectionism with regard to domestic industry and the foundations of agrarian reform law in Mexico in the 1980s; and, finally, the signing of the North American Free Trade Agreement (NAFTA) a decade later. The work of U.S.-Mexico borderlands scholarship across the spectrum of social sciences and humanities has been to trace the "transnational dialogues that have informed culture and life" within this set of historical circumstances (Madrid 2011: 2). Indeed, Américo Paredes long ago identified the U.S.-Mexico border region as a generative site of cultural praxis and social struggle for those subjects marginalized in the U.S. national construction. Others have since conceptualized the U.S.-Mexico borderlands as an epistemological zone of liminality and encounter. Additional and more territorialized understandings of the borderlands as geographic area or cultural region have concentrated on folkloric items and social processes, producing no shortage of ethnography (Dorsey and Díaz-Barriga 2011; Flores 1995; Garza Villarreal 2014; Guerra 2011; Limón 1994; Nájera 2015; M. Peña 1985, 1999). This book engages, augments, and integrates this body of border studies, border ethnography, and borderlands theory, particularly that which has been critically informed by the framework of transnationalism. I build on the bifocal orientation of Nicholas De Genova (2005), Nina Glick Schiller et al. (1992), Gina M. Pérez (2004), Roger Rouse (1991, 1992), and Patricia Zavella (2011), who have taken transnational theory into social spaces in which familial, economic, and political moments are offset by conflicts and constraints.[10] I share these concerns and considerations with regard to the multiplicity of the lived experiences of Mexican migrants and focus on music making as a location where they shape and live with political-economic forces that are seemingly distant.

Given the existing body of borderlands music scholarship in particular, I am preceded by many, most notably Paredes's (1958, 1976) seminal work on the *corrido* (Mexican ballad) of border conflict. Borderlands in this body of work refers to both music whose practice is geographically proximate to the U.S.-Mexico border and Mexican music whose transnational audience and listenership exceeds the political and cultural boundaries of both the United States and Mexico. This scholarly corpus has been augmented most recently by those elaborating on commercial forms ranging from Tejano (Tex-Mex music) (M. Peña 1999; Vargas 2012) to the Mexican brass *banda* (Simonett 2001), accordion-driven *norteña* (Ragland 2009), the corrido of drug trafficking (Edberg 2004), Chicana/o punk (Habell-Pallán 2005), mariachi (Sheehy 2006), *pasito duranguense* (Hutchinson 2007), and *Nor-tec* (Madrid 2008). Attentive to the complicated cultural exchanges within the purview of the broader Latin American social formation, much of this work has offered insightful perspectives on these forms, often drawing on Néstor García Canclini's (1990) notion of hybrid cultures in theorizing the consumptive politics of popular culture and the transnational flows of musico-symbolic formations therein. While music typically deemed folkloric circulates alongside "what historically has been considered mass music" (Ochoa Gautier 2006: 808), huapango arribeño's own circuits of circulation are in many ways distinct from those of popular music, presenting us with a different, though complementary, perspective surrounding performance, migration, and political economy. Moreover, expressive culture in borderlands studies has largely been treated as an epiphenomenal manifestation or symbolic token of lived realities. The objects of such analysis have typically been elite literary forms, film, and mass-mediated music with little ethnographic grounding. In contrast, my argument going forward as it pertains to huapango arribeño privileges the materiality of vernacular performance, and I do so with an ethnographic focus on sound and aesthetic embodiments.

It is not a Southern Californian shantytown (Chavez 1992), nor buried in Chicago's urban sprawl (De Genova 2005), nor a long-established New York barrio (Dávila 2004), and it also differs from a small town in the midwestern heartland (Vega 2015). *Aquí*, along the narrow strips and steep edges of the city, is where these locals live.[11] It is not quite country, not quite suburban, just far enough out but still close. On the outskirts? You jump on the six-lane highway, escape the city limits, speed past low-built office parks and strip malls flanked by big-box chain restaurants, past shooting ranges and hunting outfitters, past colossal outlet stores and Cineplexes. Keep driving. The jagged blur of neon signs and concrete is softened by the blurry heat haze rising from the sea of parking lot asphalt baking in the sun. Gated subdivisions and megachurches come into view. You're almost there. You exit and reach a maze of farm-to-market roads encumbered by the earthmoving equipment being used for construction on the stretch of highway half a mile up from where you exited. You pull over and turn off your car, then get out and walk onto the gravelly edge between the road and dirt. At first, it seems quiet, almost silent. But then you tune in to the constant rush of wind from the never-faraway highway, the low rumble of eighteen-wheelers carrying vegetables, merchandise for the big-box stores, packaged foods, and equipment for oil drilling out west. If you listen closely enough, you hear construction; there's always something going up. It's not as quiet as it would seem, but everything is muffled and distant. Is a new overpass being built? Are they performing routine road maintenance? Whatever the case may be, the shoulders of these small roads serve as open-air storage yards for materials and machinery. Besides, the landfill is nearby, too. You climb back in and drive a little further. Greasy-spoon Tex-Mex diners and BBQ joints, dilapidated mobile home parks, and overpriced and overstocked convenience stores dot intersections that lead to other intersections, which take you to yet other roads and intersections, and so on. This maze eventually circles back to the highway, back to the bustling sea of concrete, the extravagant homes, the rush of commerce.

The spaces in between these monuments of American economic prosperity are filled with rolling bluestem grassland and wind, a backdrop that reminds you that you are in Texas. Otherwise, the manicured corporate landscape visible from the highway could be mistaken for anywhere U.S.A. There is also a human landscape to consider, one that speaks to the nativist politics of migration and labor subordination at play. Many of the people who sustain the service, construction, and agricultural sectors necessary for this world to exist call this bizarre interstitial space—not quite country, not quite city— home. Just down the road, the menacing threat of deportation towers in the form of private migrant-detention centers—in some cases they are only a few miles away, in others a few hundred miles away: Hutto, Dilley, Laredo. The people who cook and serve the food in the restaurants and outlet food courts, who clean the office parks and chain stores, who build the subdivision homes, who construct, quarry, and design the items essential to the rustic Hill Country–meets–Southern aesthetic—in all of its handcrafted woodwork, its rusted-steel and limestone chic—are Mexican migrants who live here, too, surrounded by the structures they build but alienated by the economies they sustain, ostracized by the larger society they make possible. Their labor is valued but not their lives.

These places are becoming all-subsuming sprawls of commerce and development extending out from the city—Austin, Dallas, Houston, San Antonio, Waco. More important, these migrants are at the center of an economically prosperous America made possible by transnational labor, much of which is undocumented. From within that center, if you look a little closer, past the shade of cedar, elms, and live oaks, over the tall bluestem and mesquite, beyond the broken-down trucks and rusted-out metal fences, up the driveways and cluttered patios, into the kitchens and living rooms, you'll peer into the intimate lives of migrants who are otherwise rendered invisible. They stay, they leave, they return, and they live their lives along the way. And if you listen—at these homes and ballrooms and rodeos where they congregate— you'll get wind of stories that will tell you all you need to know. If you listen, you'll realize that these homes, these patios, these spaces of congregation, are powerfully tethered to far-off places, too, forming part of a palimpsest of time and space that tells the story of transnational living and belonging—of America's borders and borderlands.

Doña Rosa keeps beer in the fridge for afternoons like this.[12] People show up, a certain kind of relaxed conversation starts to *take place*, and before you know it so does huapango arribeño. Senovio, her husband, quit drinking some time back. Diabetes. Still, Doña Rosa keeps the fridge modestly stocked for guests. Today, I am a guest, so naturally, she offers me a frosty twelve-ounce can.

I grew up in homes like this. Small two-bedroom ranch-style houses with shag carpeting, eggshell-colored hawk-and-trowel drywall, popcorn ceilings, oversized furniture wrapped in plastic and stuffed into a tiny living room. You walk in and make your way around the dusty mountain of work boots, sneakers, cowboy hats, and baseball caps piled by the front door that belong to the company that's gathered. You step into the steady wind generated by the swamp cooler in the window, bellowing out its motorized cadence, struggling to cool the space. The door closes behind you, and your eyes take a moment to adjust to the darkness—thick maroon curtains block out the sun, and only the white glow of a television set and fluorescent bulbs in the kitchen offer a sort of mood lighting. You scan the scene and find that every inch of the walls and surfaces is covered in an effusive array of home decor: the obligatory ceramic angels and elephants, artificial flowers, mirrors in faux-gold frames, family pictures, and Catholic paraphernalia including a cheap print of Leonardo da Vinci's *Last Supper* that hangs lopsided in the kitchen, eyeing you. You maneuver around tightly squeezed bodies, say a series of hellos, shake calloused hands—you see that Homero, Valentín, Daniel, Salomón, Ricardo, and Graciano are all here (you'll make their acquaintance in the pages ahead). You settle into the plastic-wrapped loveseat, crack open the cold one you've been handed, and drift into the flow of things—the conversation, the laughter, the tuning of instruments, utterances nested within a soothing aural thicket of clanking kitchen pans, the high-frequency whine from the muted television set, the swamp cooler's hum, the far-off thuds of activity in other rooms, no doubt children playing.

It's damp in here—the sound, that is . . . The clutter of artifacts and the cushion of soft, flat surfaces and bodies deaden the attack of voices and instruments, their timbre slightly dulled and their direction tightened—strumming, singing, and talk shoot straight into the ears, sharp, like an arrow . . . a sound engineer's dream. You focus on Doña Rosa's voice: "¡Todavía, cuando se casó la hija de mi tío, eran las ocho de la mañana y la gente bailando!" (Even still, when my uncle's daughter got married, it was eight in the morning, and people were still dancing away!). Talk swells at moments and dips down to near silence at others, with a paced and jagged layering of musical sounds underneath—the attenuated strumming and plucking of strings, the soft phantom mouthing of words, half sung, half spoken, all in preparation for music soon to be played. As often happens in a gathering of musicians like this, talk hovers around memorable huapango arribeño performances, and, unavoidably, the topic of particular musicians comes up—the uniqueness of their playing, their personalities, unforgettable dances they performed in, and so on. This collective remembering takes the form of paused statements and sparse dialogue, winding down and picking up at different moments like a breeze that won't make up its mind, perhaps hinting of an approaching rain shower in the form of music and poetry.

The cadence of the exchanges of Doña Rosa and her husband, Senovio, is musical; their utterances dance across our ears as they trade memories of one veteran musician and note how he no longer plays through the dawn because of his age. She interjects and makes note of other veterans who still do, and do it well. She's recalling one performance close to Victoria, Guanajuato, where her family is from. It was at a wedding.

> ¡A las diez sirviendo el desayuno a toda la gente—menudo y todo—y los músicos tocando! Esa boda fue en Álamos. . . . Ahí se hacen las bodas y se acostumbra que en la mañana se les da desayunar a la gente—el menudo y barbacoa que sobró, lo que haiga.

> (At ten in the morning, everyone was being served breakfast—menudo and everything—and the musicians were still playing! That wedding was in Álamos. . . . At those weddings it is customary to serve people breakfast in the morning—the leftover menudo and barbecue, whatever is left.)

She pauses her story, glances toward the kitchen, and offers those present something to eat. The talk of food and social obligation must have prompted this gesture. Most of us pass for now but will likely take her up on her offer later.

As the conversation resumed, Senovio named this practice: "¡El recalentado!" I chimed in, "La tornaboda." The *tornaboda* refers to a feast held the day after a wedding in which family and friends celebrate the newlyweds with a meal that may consist of leftovers, though not always. Senovio stresses, "Nosotros pa' allá le decimos el recalentado" (Over there we say *recalentado*). The timbre of his words changes slightly; he shifts his body and elevates the pitch of his voice, as if calling out to someone across a distance: "¡Vamos al recalentado allí on' ta' fulano!" (Let's go to the recalentado where so-and-so is at!). Senovio momentarily inhabits the voice of a person presumably from the region in question to demonstrate the sociability that surrounds the recalentado as a community event, much like the wedding celebration and huapango arribeño performance that preceded it. This fragment of his speech is a type of other-voiced direct discourse, or "reported speech purportedly in the voice of another but unmistakably inhabited by the polemical presence of the speaker" (A. Fox 2004: 120). We listen and momentarily imagine ourselves calling out to a neighbor across a dusty street in Álamos, eager to feast and perhaps just as eager to nurse a hangover from the festivities the night before.

As if Senovio's performance might have pulled us further into Mexico, Doña Rosa pivots—like any good dancer—and swings us back around. The talk of large celebrations and convivial partying triggers a memory of her equally large family in and around Álamos, now spread all over the United States. She says proudly, "Dondequiera que escuches ese apellido—Ibarre—es de la misma familia." (Wherever you hear that last name—Ibarre—it's all the same [my] family.) Senovio follows her lead and extends these bonds of kinship further into specific places in the United States: "Vas pa' Dallas y hay de esa familia." (You go to Dallas, and there are members of that family.) A muted chuckle from someone follows the mention of this first city.[13] Doña Rosa and Senovio continue listing off places, carefully mapping out for us the people they are connected to. They begin in unison with giant grins:

> **DR AND S:** Vas pa' Houston, San Antonio—Ibarre. (You go to Houston, San Antonio—Ibarre.)
>
> **S:** Vas pa' Florida, vas pa' Chicago, vas pa' Austin, vas pa' San Antonio—Ibarre. (You go to Florida, you go to Chicago, you go to Austin, you go to San Antonio—Ibarre.)
>
> **DR:** En Seattle. ¡En California! San Francisco, Los Ángeles—Ibarre! (In Seattle. In California! San Francisco, Los Angeles—Ibarre!)
>
> **S:** En San Rafael. ¡Ooohh . . . ahí está la mata! (In San Rafael. Ooohh . . . that's where the taproot is!)

This prompts laughter from everyone. Doña Rosa and Senovio's back-and-forth is a meaningful recognition of bonds between family and friends that extend across the U.S.-Mexico border. The chorus of laughter following Senovio's final statement, however, marks a shared realization that transnational Mexican migrants are deeply rooted in the space of the U.S. nation-state despite being unwanted—this defiant reality represents a victory that animates a type of communal jocularity. These connections among people and between places are on this occasion expressed through talk as a sort of prelude to the music and poetry that followed. To that end, music making, as this book demonstrates, takes on a special significance among this community, for it refigures the sociopolitical and economic terms of migration through aesthetic means. Huapango arribeño voices the intimacy and connection at stake in the experiences of Mexican migrants—a phenomenological consideration that has no distinct essence or cohesion, as it were, but rather is in motion, always.[14]

SOUNDS OF CROSSING

The indignant policing of migrant bodies in everyday moments is indicative of the cultural and racializing logics that restrict Mexican migrant life across the continental United States, of the ways the boundaries of America are intensely present in "informal managements" (Rosas 2006) at the vernacular level. In turn, the spaces convened by and through huapango arribeño performance emerge as politicized moments of congregation amid the vulnerabilities of transnational living in this post–Great Recession era, or, as huapango arribeño troubadour Guillermo Velázquez puts it in the following verses:

Hay inquietud en la raza
porque en los U.S.A. hoy día
como que la economía
no anda de muy buena traza

———

Mexican folks are anxious
because today in the U.S.A.
it seems like the economy
is practically in disarray

The space of huapango arribeño performance is entangled with politics, mobility, and emplacement, and it is a goal of this book to demonstrate how the microelements of huapango arribeño music and poetics—as overlapping communicative resources—are the creative embodiments of social and individual engagements with the U.S.-Mexico transnational social and political-economic formation, engagements that speak directly to the uncertainties and anxieties of the troubled U.S. economy in which migrant livelihoods are positioned, as Velázquez voices above. This requires an ethnographic ear attuned to how the musical and poetic minutiae of a long-standing traditional repertoire index present-day realities concerning the boundaries of race and nation as they relate to Mexican migrants. Therefore, the *sounds of crossing* refers to, on the one hand, (1) sonic invocations—a calling to mind through music and poetics—that are centrally about people and places and tell how both travel and, on the other, (2) the ways such invocations themselves exceed their space-time situatedness, or *sounding across place*, both metaphysically and physically. A full understanding of both senses within the purview of Mexican migrants' social lives requires attention to the embodied dimensions of performance in contexts where migrant bodies are subject to various forms of structural and cultural violence. In other words, to follow these sounds is to trace how this community's own chosen form of expression is projected out as a way of binding lives and geographies across the dense, lingering, and knotted dissonance of class, race, politics, and transnational mobility as key dimensions of the Mexican migrant experience.[15] This formulation is not the same as a materially emplaced acoustic environment (or soundscape), nor is it equal to—although perhaps adjacent to—an audiotopic construction (Kun 2005), but this book's major contention is that sound claims space physically and culturally in ways that rebuke politically motivated nationalist and segregationist epistemologies. At last, huapango arribeño is treated in these pages not as a cultural artifact—unearthed from a substratum of authentic (and necessarily fetishized) Mexican culture—but as a complex and contingent voice heard across localities. In the words of Jacques Attali (1985), "music is more than an object of study: it is a way of perceiving the world" (4).

This book centers on the world of transnational migration and, more important, the sounds, social lives, and cultural real that flow through it. Many of the borderlands music scholars previously mentioned have relied also on García Canclini's (2001) extension of Gilles Deleuze and Félix Guattari's (1972, 1987) notions of deterritorialization and reterritorialization to discuss the relocation of displaced sounds and their symbolic productions. I, too, look in this direction, with particular interest in the politics surrounding the transnational movements of Mexican migrants. I ask, how do the transnational political-economic contours of human mobility generate stories subsequently voiced through embodied music and poetics? How do these forms of expression circulate and in turn generate subjectivities? This final consideration opens up discussion of the political—that which animated laughter in Doña Rosa and Senovio's living room in Texas, that which prompted the intoxicated Anglo man in northern Indiana to accost me in the bathroom, and that which is woven throughout most of the stories you will encounter in this book. Fundamentally, the political is a question of inclusion and exclusion, of class, of belonging, and of citizenship, a concept that scholars have augmented socially (Del Castillo 2007; Gálvez 2013) and culturally (Rosaldo 1994). Both social and cultural citizenship extend the sense of belonging beyond the political rights accorded by the state and instead privilege everyday practices and dimensions of identity through which people create community, fashion subjectivities, and perceive their world. It is among these practices that I locate huapango arribeño as an aesthetically salient cultural form that binds and gives voice to the multiple places that constitute transnational living.[16] *Voicing*, therefore, refers to the textual interplay between (1) musical expression, (2) ritual poetic discourse, and (3) bonds of sociability expressed through ordinary conversation among the practitioners and people in question and, furthermore, the ways in which this nexus constructs and advances vernacular theories for understanding space, time, emplacement, and personhood. Attention to these theories requires an ethnography of performance—a conceptual framework centered on the discursive action, artistic activity, and social interactive dimensions that constitute aesthetic enactments. In this regard, I rely also on Richard Bauman and Charles L. Briggs's definition of poetics as "the artful use of language in the conduct of social life" (1990: 79) as a way of conceptualizing the culturally situated moments of composition and creative exchange where huapango arribeño music and décimas sound out and braid themselves to build a loud, felt, and circulating interaffective dialogue. With this approach in mind, I call attention to (1) the conventions and structural rules that govern live performance, referred to as *reglamento*; (2) the recurring grammar and rhetorical logics of composition, referred to as *fundamento*; and (3) the reflexive theory linking the domains of aesthetics and sociability, referred to as *el destino.* Empirically, these aspects of performance are represented with the aid of transcriptions and descriptions of naturally occurring music and poetics. Theoretically, I turn my attention to the semiotic constructions of copresence (or the poetics of affect) and the metapragmatic discourses emerging from performance that mediate the relative social distance between audiences and practitioners, both of which brace an analysis linking the social resonance of huapango arribeño performance to phenomenological fields.

Finally, I follow De Genova's lead and consciously employ the term *migrant* to "[disrupt] the implicit teleology of the more conventional term *immigrant*," which connotes "a one-directional and predetermined movement" (2005: 2).[17] De Genova suggests that transnational migration is primarily a spatialized experience where social relations not only transcend distances but also form a conjunctural space that comprises innumerable places that are home to everyday practices of meaning making. These makings, moreover, do not carve out an "idyllic Mexican cultural space" apart from the nation-state; rather, they are forged at the very intersection of transnational migration, labor subjugation, and social inequality at the nation-state's heart (111). I would further add that the flows of everyday life that achieve such bindings are at their most fundamental level manifest through embodied acts whose enactment in space and time—in this case across the "treacherous geographies" (Rosas 2006) crucial to the U.S.-Mexico border formation—necessarily becomes a politicized mode of creative and generative social exchange.[18] By way of this conceptual move as it pertains to the conjunctural space of transnationalism, I deploy *trans* in the sense of active *crossing* and thereby attend also to the correlative social decentering of the space of the nation-state. This paradigmatic shift bypasses nationalist and essentialist models that cling to an "originary Mexican space" (De Genova 2005: 99–100): José Vasconcelos's *México de afuera*, Américo Paredes's (1958) Greater Mexico, and the primordial Aztlán within the Chicana/o nationalist paradigm all come to mind. Nevertheless, transnationalism is not a paradigmatic solution that neatly frames the experiences of the communities in question but, rather, a problem to be engaged with, as migrants must do in daily life. Therefore, in these pages *belonging* is not a catch-all appeal for juridical citizenship. Going forward, I use the term as a phenomenological address to account for the embodied affects that coalesce around the complicated relationship between immaterial and material registers of experience—in this case, sound and place—which in turn generate bonds of sociability that reveal the contingency between inclusion and exclusion in everyday life. To belong is "an enterprise that is ongoing" (M. Alexander 2005: 6).

ENCOUNTERS

M. Jacqui Alexander (2005) calls for a grounding of theory in everyday life, drawing on personal experience in her explorations of race, modernity, and colonialism, an epistemological project to be sure. Inspired by her work and that of others—namely, Gloria Anzaldúa, Américo Paredes, and Renato Rosaldo—I too rely on my life experiences, on the memories that both haunt and make possible my entanglement with huapango arribeño music. Like verses and melodies that hang in the air, my ethnography too is coated with a "broad brushed phenomenology" (A. Fox 2004: 30). As a researcher, ethnographer, and participant, I attempt ethnography in the same spirit of poetic telling and retelling that one finds in huapango arribeño. My interlocutors' knowledges, in this regard, hold an equally important space in my rendering; in fact, the dialogic and transpersonal exchanges among us, sharing our perspectives, are a major part of the process of tracing how meanings, feelings, and resonances are conveyed culturally. Fixated on the spaces between those phenomena, my ethnographic process thus acknowledges the lack of division between the subjectivity of the ethnographer, ethnographic writing, and the world itself (Deleuze and Guattari 1987). The space of ethnography is boundlessly conducive to (and not analogically restrictive of) meaning and ought not be contained within the "single, static plane of analysis" (Stewart 2007: 3). It is built on the affirmation that *this is happening* or occurring or existing. This is best represented by what D. Soyini Madison (2011) refers to as the labor of reflexivity, a space of contingency built on sociality and alliance, manifest in the spatiotemporality of the story itself, where one's presence laboriously spreads out as an intrinsic part of ethnography. True, our entextualized observations are relatively stable constructions of what exemplifies the systemicity of social processes—exemplars. However, we are always inside the phenomenon itself, and central to these pages, then, is the embodied moment of intersubjective encounter—a back-and-forth connection with others that is admittedly difficult to measure, or quantify, yet is undeniable, even unavoidable, a reflexivity that huapangueros consistently draw on for their own musico-poetic labor, a key point that is explored throughout and that inspires both the content and the style of my writing (in particular, see chapter 6, "Huapango sin Fronteras," for a discussion of interaffectivity).

This book connects performance to everyday life, but it does not keep to a linear chronology so much as form an assemblage of moments, remembrances, and dialogic encounters that ultimately create an incomplete picture (like a social theory) that disturbs the desire to know "Mexican culture."[19] It reveals the space of performance to be full of bundled relationships to be disarticulated; this space is not an already constituted form but rather a "porous array of intersections where distinct processes crisscross from within and beyond its borders" (Rosaldo 1989: 20). *Sounds of Crossing* traces the web of aesthetics, politics, sensate experience, past histories and social memory, and anticipated events, moving through space and time to reveal their forceful coming together within the context of a twenty-first-century transnational U.S.-Mexico social formation. The viability of ethnography in this approach, however, exists away from the realm of so-called *objective* proof and instead acknowledges the many voices of migrants and their importance in ways that "confidently resist the slings and arrows of positivism's obsession with evidence" (Madison 2011: 130). I treat personal stories and poetics as social histories in their own right. In this way I perform ethnography that is an undeniably personal and private act made both public and plural (Berry 2011). Reflexive ethnography, Rosaldo (1989) maintains, signifies a postmodern skepticism, an intellectual dismantling of regimes of objectivity and the mythic charter of distanced ethnography (Stocking 1983), an erosion of the categorical legacy of anthropology, which now competes "with the truths of case studies that are embedded in local contexts, shaped by local interests, and colored by local perceptions" (21). It is here—embedded in the U.S.-Mexico borderlands—that we find native ethnographers Anzaldúa, Limón, and Paredes, for instance, whose exemplary positioned accounts offer unique and critical perspectives central to the paradigm of an anthropology of borderlands as a whole. This brand of native ethnography has challenged conventional intellectual wisdom regarding people of Mexican origin, their culture, and anthropology's conceptual formulations. Still, a rejection of objectivity doesn't mean that the embrace of one's own situated subjectivity is without its complications. Subjectivity itself, James Clifford (1988) suggests, is more often than not beyond the control of the ethnographer, such that the cultivation of an ethnographic science must always be understood vis-à-vis more political debates regarding representation. As anthropologists, we tend to want the ever-elusive patterns of culture to be clear and defined, and we wish for interpretation itself—the drawing out of meaning and significance—to possess a degree of clarity. Embracing one's own subjectivity does not guarantee this. Instead, that embrace requires that one enact particular strategies of representation that ought to take into account not only one's own positionality but also that of our interlocutors, who are equally positioned. As Paredes (1993) reminds us, the informant always speaks to us from *somewhere*. My own "somewhere"—with its overlapping transnational spatial and temporal dimensions—is where I have often come face-to-face with my grandfather.

In February 2012 I had just finished playing a *huapango huasteco* performance at the Old Town School of Folk Music in Chicago with my previously mentioned huapango trio.[20] As is customary, we waited outside the hall to greet the audience members, shake hands, and discuss various facets of the music and performance. Two people who looked to be my age approached me and said they were delighted to have heard huapango huasteco live onstage. They introduced themselves as sister and brother and explained how they'd recently discovered that their great-uncle had been a well-known musician in Mexico, but who had played a different style of huapango in Querétaro. He was heralded as an influential *trovador* (troubadour, or poet-practitioner), they said. I looked into their faces and saw myself for a moment. I asked the man's name. "Mauro," they replied without hesitation. I embraced each of them and said, "Now I know I have cousins in Chicago because he was my grandfather." It appeared Mauro was following me again.

Traces of Mauro's memory have circulated within me as deeply as my parents' stories of crossing. I met him only once, but even if I had little direct knowledge of him, the familial connection still holds meaning in the poetic world in which he moved and in which I now move and am inscribed. His place in my life is beyond my control, except to the extent to which I can embrace him, however tentatively. I tell my single story of him, the sobering moment when, on a visit to Querétaro, Mexico, I, for the first and only time, encountered my grandfather.

Entre sueños (amid dreams), we took an afternoon trip with my parents and several paternal relatives to a tiny community in the mountains above my father's hometown in northern Querétaro, Mexico. We all piled into an old fifteen-passenger van—a rusty, battered mammoth relic of the 1970s—and noisily turned onto the dirt road that led the way, leaving clouds of dust in our wake. I was seven years old.

In the company of aunts, uncles, and cousins, I was on my way to meet Mauro, my father's father. The community wasn't too far away, about a thirty-minute climb up mountainsides, just enough time for a child's mind to ponder, though not resolve, vexing questions concerning his family. I was told very little about him. I overheard that he was a musician of some kind. That's all. Up until that day even my father had not seen him in close to thirty years.

The trip was brief. We arrived at a small cluster of homes perched on a hillside, some made of concrete, others mere wooden shacks. Our parents inquired where the old man lived. They found him. We children followed.

I recall timidly walking up to a tired, stoic old man as he sat warming his bones in the afternoon sun. I introduced myself and shook his dry, calloused hand, and someone explained to me that he was my grandfather. As I shyly observed him, standing next to him, I could sense a chorus of wisdom in his touch, his demeanor.

A year later, he passed away. As time went on, I began to ask questions. I often overheard family, friends, and musicians speak of Mauro with great ceremony: "Trovador, músico, huapanguero . . ." (troubadour, musician, huapango practitioner), they would say. I suspect that these conversations had already been happening earlier, but after his passing I took a deeper interest in them. What exactly is a *trovador*?, I asked. Who was my grandfather? Why do people recall his memory so? These questions have occupied my mind for some time.

Yearly family trips to Querétaro throughout my childhood and countless conversations with relatives and huapango musicians left me with scores of stories about Mauro, his life and his craft. Those varied accounts partially answered my embryonic queries. In a sense, these pages are in part the reflection of a search kindled long before I arrived at the University of Texas at Austin, where I began my formal research around huapango arribeño as a doctoral student in anthropology, encountering Mauro's memory time and time again. Though I never had a relationship with the man, I came to know him through those who remembered him on both sides of the border. This collective remembering has traveled with me. My engagements with communities and huapangueros alike have been mediated in varying degrees by it. Ethnography, for me, has thus been a dynamic process embedded with an inescapable personal history, a struggle to understand and negotiate my entanglement with this powerful precursory cultural memory. I recall the words of Guadalupe Reyes, a veteran troubadour from Querétaro who had performed across from Mauro numerous times in the all-night musical and poetic marathon encounters referred to as *topadas*:[21]

> Él [Mauro] fue un elemento; no estaba fácil para derrotarlo. . . . Allá en Arroyo Seco fue donde lo acabé de plano que ya no tenía con qué. Luego él empezaba y decía, "Apagaste esta lumbre, pero todavía queda el bracero." ¡Era terco! Hasta Don Antonio García me decía, "¡Oyes, ese Mauro está demonio! ¡No lo acaba uno muy fácil!"

(He [Mauro] was elemental; defeating him was no easy task. . . . It was in Arroyo Seco, where I had outright finished him and he had nothing left. But still he went on, "You've put out the fire, but the coals still remain." He was stubborn! Even Don Antonio García would tell me, "That Mauro is a devil! You can't finish him easily!")

Reyes composed a *poesía* to speak of his most memorable topadas with various troubadours.[22] He mentions Mauro first:

DE MIS TRIFULCAS VOY A TRATAR
DE AQUELLOS GÉRMENES DE POESÍA
CUANDO JUGABA EN LA VERSERÍA
Y AHORA MARCHITO EN UN DELIRAR

Topé con Mauro y Don Emeterio
con Don Bartolo y Antonio García
el superior en la versería
y mucha fama por su criterio
yo me quedaba pensando en serio
pero con ánimo de triunfar
con Antonio Escalante y Asención Aguilar
Asención Mesa y Isabel Ibarra
conferenciando con mi guitarra:
DE MIS TRIFULCAS VOY A TRATAR[23]

———

I AM GOING TO TELL OF MY BATTLES
OF THOSE POETIC SEEDLINGS
WHEN I PLAYED IN VERBAL DUELING,
AND NOW I WITHER IN DELIRIUM

I clashed with Mauro and Don Emeterio,
with Don Bartolo and Antonio García.
he was the best in the way of verses
and gained much fame for his judgment
I remained serious in pensive thought
with the righteous fortitude to triumph
in front of Antonio Escalante and Asención Aguilar
Asención Mesa and Isabel Ibarra,
conferencing with my guitar:
I AM GOING TO TELL OF MY BATTLES

Even now, though Mauro passed long ago, his still-warm coals continue to glimmer and flare up in moments of movement and encounter—from Guanajuato to Texas and back—much like the oscillations that mark the transnational lives of those featured in this book, lives who shadow my recollections as I write.

I am traveling from Houston to West Texas, my cousin Amador in tow, recently arrived from Querétaro via northern Florida. Curiously, he asks me to keep playing the old tape of vinuetes (dirges) I keep in my car. He stares out the window. "A la vez tristes y alegres. Como que escucho la chilladera de la gente en el velorio." (Both sad and happy. I can hear the people crying at the wake.). He was picked up by ICE and deported a few months later.

A trip to the Austin bus station—Humberto and a friend, both hua-pangueros, have asked me for a ride. They're headed back to Guanajuato (voluntarily). Humberto has been coming to Texas since 1980: working as a ranch hand, working in construction, doing landscaping. He was thirteen the first time he crossed.

I am taking the long bus ride from Rioverde, San Luis Potosí, to Ciudad Acuña, Coahuila . . . First-time crossers are on board. The bus made a quick stop in the town of Cerritos to pick up passengers. It was late. A few souls climbed on—five men, one woman. One sits next to me, a few years younger than me; Rubén was his name. He tells me he and the others are crossing. They're all friends, headed for Houston. The coyote will be waiting for them on the outskirts of Ciudad Acuña. Hours later, the bus stops, as a deep mauve hangs in the sky like a blanket—night turning into day, Acuña in the distance, frost on the ground. It's January. I hand Rubén my number, and he rushes to meet the others outside. I never hear from him.

"Perhaps we'll run into each other at a huapango arribeño performance," I say to myself months later. Perhaps an improvised greeting in his honor will alert me to his presence. Perhaps. After all, it is Rubén and his companions who make these performative moments possible. Huapango arribeño musicians are *their* musicians, and the poetics that bloom belong to *them*. They too claim the American night for themselves. Huapango arribeño lives loud, carrying memories of people and place, telling of the experiences that bind, the things that one can't control, reaching out to people who are close or far away, or who were gone before one was ready to see them go, and voicing the politics that govern many of these happenings.

HOW IT ALL PLAYS OUT

This book begins in the 1970s, though it necessarily attends to a cursory history of huapango arribeño before that time—more as a point of reference than as a matter of focused inquiry. Seminal years considered along the way include 1982, which marks the beginning of the Mexican debt crisis; 1986, when the Immigration Reform and Control Act passed; 1994, the year of the ratification of NAFTA, in addition to a groundswell of heightened U.S.-Mexico border militarization and anti-immigrant laws across the United States; 2001, which brought the events of September 11 and the ensuing conflation of the issues of terrorism, border enforcement, and undocumented migration; and 2006, when massive mobilizations occurred throughout the United States in support of migrant rights.

These moments also mark meaningful chapters in my own life as a child of Mexican migrants: my mother and father crossed into the United States in the early 1970s and I was born years later; they were both granted amnesty through the Immigration Reform and Control Act, and I witnessed the arrival of family from Mexico in the wake of NAFTA; I began my research not long after September 11, and I was deeply embedded in the huapango arribeño community on both sides of the U.S.-Mexico border amid the groundswell of protest in 2006 and witnessed firsthand how the subsequent political backlash impacted their daily lives as individual states responded with anti-immigrant laws, deportation campaigns, and migrant-detention efforts on the part of the federal government with programs like the 287(g) program and Secure Communities (which later became the Priority Enforcement Program). Fieldwork and real life have overlapped in ways beyond my control. Creatively, my role as a musician granted me access that was crucial in developing my understanding of this expressive world. Politically, my unrestricted mobility as a U.S.-born citizen brought into relief the brutal reality of the entitlements of citizenship—it was easy for me to cross the physical border, while many of the individuals who populate these pages came close to dying in their attempts.

The people in this book make up part of the Mexican diaspora in the United States—35.3 million people in 2016, according to the Pew Research Center.[24] Some are among the estimated 5.6 million unauthorized Mexican migrants.[25] They come from mission towns and rural communities nestled in the Sierra Gorda municipalities of Atarjea, Doctor Mora, San Luis de la Paz, Santa Catarina, Tierra Blanca, Victoria, and Xichú in Guanajuato and Arroyo Seco, Jalpan de Serra, Landa de Matamoros, and Pinal de Amoles in Querétaro. Others come from the midregion of San Luis Potosí—or the Zona Media—in particular, the municipalities of Cerritos, Ciudad Fernández, Rioverde, San Ciro de Acosta, San Nicolás Tolentino, Villa Juárez, and Armadillo de los Infante, which borders the region.[26] But, for them, home is also in Central and East Texas and along the Gulf coast, from Houston to northern Mississippi. And while these places are the focus of this book, this community extends to California, Florida, Tennessee, and many other places where I did not conduct formal research—recall Doña Rosa and Senovio's mapping.

Over the years I witnessed huapango arribeño music and poetics grow more sharply political, most deeply from their sheer embodied voicing. This and other realizations emerged out of formal ethnographic fieldwork carried out over the course of a decade among huapangueros on both sides of the U.S.-Mexico border. These individuals have diverse migratory histories and various legal statuses—some are long-term legal residents, others undocumented recent arrivals. During my research I conducted interviews as a way to contextualize the experiences of my interlocutors as both huapangueros and migrants; I attended social gatherings where I observed huapango arribeño performances firsthand in both Mexico and the United States; I engaged in ethnographic performance—that is, as a musician myself, I also participated in music making alongside huapangueros. Finally—from the standpoint of formal analysis—I retrospectively examined the musical and poetic discursive workings generated in these contexts with critical attention to their aesthetic design, thematic structuring and propositional content, and pragmatic use as highly situated and interactive modes of representation that accomplished social ends. Along the way, I time and again found myself at gatherings before and after huapango arribeño performances: before performances, practitioners, families, and friends informally inspired the poetry and music to be played, and afterward they slowly relinquished the nearly euphoric gravity of hours of listening or dancing. In fact, I arrived at this project as a musician in these very settings, first observing and then actively performing alongside musicians.

Much like my experiences, the chapters of this book perform when and where huapango arribeño itself lives and breathes, spreads out, and inscribes social lives. The ensuing chapters establish themes like the *planta* (base quatrain) that guides a set of improvised décimas before venturing into the airy territories of aesthetics and experience (this reference to poetics will make more sense as you read on). Inspired by the aesthetic framework of huapango arribeño, I am guided by this community's own reflexive theorizing regarding the social contexts in which performance is positioned. To speak of el destino, reglamento, and fundamento—and all that these vernacular theories entail— is to recognize the aesthetic sensibilities that not only produce huapango arribeño performance but tether it meaningfully to social lives en route. This book is carried along in this manner, and along the way the following themes emerge at singular and compounded moments: impermanence, reflexivity, movement and mobility, counternarratives, presence and resonance, and the politics of home and belonging.

Chapter 1, "Aurality and the Long American Century," examines the cultural relationship between Mexico and the United States through the landscape of Mexican music and the politics of aurality. Huapango, I argue, is burdened by the semiotics of national authenticity in dual senses: (1) it participates in a U.S. racial markedness structure as a sonic index for a derided Mexican otherness, and (2) it is also the soundtrack to a powerful antimodernist Mexican national sentiment. In order to demonstrate this transnational cultural linkage, the "ranchero chrono-trope" is introduced as a way of understanding (1) the spatiotemporality of essentialist representations of Mexican culture and (2) the specific sterotypes—or tropes—embedded in the space-time construct. The second chapter, "Companions of the Calling," familiarizes the reader with the musico-poetic design and performance of huapango arribeño. I describe how huapango arribeño's dynamic performance produces the shared sentiment of being compañeros del destino among huapangueros. From this standpoint, I argue that back-and-forth movement—at the levels of migration, the dialogic topada performance style particular to huapango arribeño, and the cultural syncretism central to the historical making of Mexican vernacular stringed music in general—is crucial to this music. This discussion challenges conventional narratives that immobilize huapango as calcified tradition by arguing that polyphony and intertextuality—as dialogic components—are at the heart of huapango arribeño.

In "Verses and Flows at the Dawn of Neoliberal Mexico," hip-hop is discussed as a familiar musical model as a way of introducing the relationship between poetics and politics (or verses and flows), with a focus on a brand of post-NAFTA transnational hip-hop among Chicanas/os-Latinas/os. I then pivot and similarly situate the topada performative dynamic in the real-life context of neoliberal structural adjustment; that is, I consider how huapangueros from the 1980s on have reimagined this performance style through new geographies of cultural transmission catalyzed by neoliberal migration flows from Guanajuato to Mexico City and to the United States. To illustrate this, I center on the New Year's Eve topada in Xichú, Guanajuato, with attention to its recent history as a grassroots festival site.

In "Regional Sounds: Mexican Texas and the Semiotics of Citizenship," I then detail how huapango arribeño performance in Texas complicates the symbolic construction of ethnic Mexican musics as regional styles, Tejano and Regional Mexican, respectively. While the marketing around these musics ties them to unique and homegrown regional identities that take precedence over homogenizing national or pop styles, they ultimately coat themselves with the use value of traditional iconography undergirded by American and Mexican nationalisms, pitting one against the other. Huapango arribeño is caught in the middle, and its expressive domain carves out a transnational space for itself, indeed reimagining the horizons of its own region of origin as listeners and practitioners put huapango to use in constructing their lives beyond central Mexico and in the United States amid heightened and pervasive xenophobia.

"From Potosí to Tennessee: Clandestine Desires and the Poetic Border" applies Michel de Certeau's (1984) concept of the *poetic*—in which everyday inhabitations run against the grain of the official intentions of built space—to the U.S.-Mexico border, particularly how huapango arribeño performance as an aspect of transnational life unfolds according to its own logic and possesses its own rhetoric, poetics, and desires, making ambiguous the official legible order of the border. This sociolinguistic and embodied critique of presumed illegality is made clear by detailing an ethereal vector existing between San Luis Potosí and Tennessee, as improvised verses are sung across the border to a person long gone from Mexico. The lyrical greeting that may never be heard draws a wistful and poetic line of desire between those places, grounding the argument that the impermanence of performative moments can powerfully negate the supposed boundaries and politics of geography.

"Huapango sin Fronteras: Mapping What Matters and Other Paths" begins with a huapango arribeño performance at an immigrants' rights rally in 2006 and ends at a newly established huapango festival. We visit the home of Doña Rosa in between. Along the way I argue that interaffectivity and intimacy between people also connect to place, such that migrants form "mattering maps" that transcend national boundaries. While advocating for an ethnographic approach that seeks to learn how that mapping occurs in the everyday lives of migrants, I offer a critique of texts that neglect to do so and that reify the attitudes reflected in musical discourses concerning the Mexican character—sounds and sentiments succinctly expressed in the famous *canción ranchera* (country song) "Camino de Guanajuato," which I analyze. I suggest that these received narratives are metapragmatic mattering maps that impose their own models of circulation and of the meaning of Mexican culture. Huapango arribeño, I conclude, provides a mapping of its own that traces the paths and flows of daily life across borders, beyond Mexico, and outside, but always in intimate relation to, the nation-state, such that we can ascribe meanings to *Mexico* and *Mexican music* that comprise a multitude of places and sounds.

With these arguments in mind, the title of this book reflects the ultimate purpose I have in writing. Huapango arribeño is, of course, a type of Mexican music that is largely unexplored through ethnography. When I invoke *Mexican music*, I mean simply a musical style performed by people from Mexico—I do not lean on ontology about what is Mexican or what Mexican expressive culture is. As I discuss the transnational contours of contemporary migrant life, it will also become clear that *Mexican music* refers to the people who are performing rather than the location of performance. I argue that people carry locations with them, here and there, so a town in Mexico can be imaginatively invoked at a performance in Texas, and vice versa. In thinking through this dynamic, the concept of crossing, also part of the title, illustrates how lives are bordered by assumptions, expectations, and tropes as much as by physical boundaries, walls, and policing. My understanding of the border is not ahistorical, however, but rather necessarily informed by a broader perspective on how its meanings and material conditions have shifted continuously over time in accordance with changing political, economic, and social circumstances within the context of the "power struggles at the core of the societies that use it [the border] to define themselves" (Madrid 2011: 2). Presently, the difference making that is operative in the material and semiotic work performed by the U.S.-Mexico border produces a subjugated, so-called illegal immigrant subject. Finally, within this context, I consider migrant aural productions, which exceed predetermined notions of who Mexicans are and where they belong, as the "sounds of crossing"— sounds that cross the boundaries of both cultural and legal rationalities tethered to nation-states.

In the end, these pages are about Mexican migrant artists who go on living and creating, pushing and pulling at the real and metaphorical edges of nation-states. In these pages an opening emerges where everyday people give form to a tactile and fleeting expressive world that erupts in moments of congregation—dramatic and everyday. This is what rests behind the music; this is what is potentially left out of supposedly definitive accounts of the ethnohistorical variety and what likewise escapes studies that gaze on everyday life from a distance. This is what's at stake: attention to "people's own theorizing of their conditions" and the ways these insights can engender a type of "emancipatory reflexivity" that may "challenge present-day regimes of veridiction, including philosophical universals," ranging from hegemonic truths about ethnic Mexicans and migrants to armchair readings that silence the arts of living from below (Biehl 2013: 575, 583). Huapango arribeño, in this sense, is not the object of study in these pages so much as it provides an analytical lens in to the contemporary experiences of Mexican migrants.

ONE

AURALITY AND THE LONG
AMERICAN CENTURY

A mild and enervating climate and their constant intercourse with the aborigines, who were and still are degraded to the very lowest class of human beings, all contributed to render the Mexicans a more ignorant and debauched people than their ancestors had been.
—JOEL POINSETT, *LETTER TO SECRETARY OF STATE MARTIN VAN BUREN (1829)*

Now sounds the march of new conquistadors in the American Southwest. . . .
Their movement is, despite its quiet and largely peaceful nature, both an invasion and a revolt.
—JOHN S. LANG AND JEANNYE THORNTON, "THE DISAPPEARING BORDER" IN
U.S. NEWS & WORLD REPORT (1985)

Nothing connects us all but imagined sound.
—BENEDICT ANDERSON, *IMAGINED COMMUNITIES*

In beginning to explore the contemporary politics that surround Mexican migrants' musical expression within the cultural space of the U.S. nation-state, we must first historicize the aural constructions of Mexican culture as a nationalist project in Mexico and a racializing discourse in the United States. While twentieth-century cultural constructions in Mexico have positioned Mexican vernacular musics as authentic expressions of the national soul, to be found in the space of the idealized (though socially backward) countryside, narrative constructions in the United States have braced primitivist claims with regard to Mexican culture in the service of the projects of white racial hegemony and imperialism—or, in other words, a well-documented anti-Mexican xenophobia (Chavez 2008; Santa Ana 2002). I introduce the phrase *the long American century* to help frame the historical linkage between these ideological scriptings, which are central to both countries' nation-building projects.

Writing of the rise of industrial capitalism and the modern nation-state, British Marxist historian Eric Hobsbawm coined *the long nineteenth century* to refer to the period from the French Revolution to the start of World War I (1789–1914) in his striking trilogy *The Age of Revolution, 1789–1848* (1962), *The Age of Capital, 1848–1875* (1975), and *The Age of Empire, 1875–1914* (1987). We can identify similar processes of political and economic development in North America—in Mexico and the United States, specifically—from the mid-nineteenth century through the late twentieth century, beginning with the Mexican-American War (1846–1848), continuing through the Mexican Revolution (1910–1920), and lasting up through the passage of NAFTA (1994). While Hobsbawm's sequel, *The Age of Extremes: The Short Twentieth Century, 1914–1991*, makes the case for a short twentieth century—which according to him ends with the failure of state communism in 1991—I call on *Time* publisher Henry Luce's infamous moral endorsement of the rise of U.S. hegemonic influence in global politics after World War II, which he terms the "American century." In other words, for ethnic Mexicans, the "American century" of U.S. political and economic domination began long before World War II—nearly a century earlier, to be precise. With this temporal frame in mind (1848–1994), two questions emerge for the purposes of this chapter: historically, how has the United States come to hear Mexico? And, indeed, what does Mexico sound like?

TRACK ONE: A MEXICAN SOUND?

The sonic landscape of Mexico is expansive, including everything from the popular regional Mexican stylings of contemporary banda and norteña to the electronic global chic of Nor-tec, the folk-inspired rock-hybrid sounds of Mexico City band Café Tacuba, and the vernacular afromestizo stringed music of Veracruz. However, more emblematic styles that have been deemed the sounds of a presumed national tradition—mariachi, for instance—come with their share of cultural baggage, always in need of disarticulation. Huapango is no exception.

The etymology of *huapango* is debated. To restate, Gabriel Saldívar (1937) maintains it is of Nahuatl origin, from the word *cuahpanco*, signifying "atop of the wood," a reference to the stomped zapateado dance performed atop a wooden platform. This seems to indicate that huapango refers explicitly to dance, and in part it does, for it may be seen as synonymous with the fandango social gathering centered around dance and music making in eighteenth-century New Spain, later banned during the Spanish Inquisition (G. Saldívar

1937; Sheehy 1979).[1] Yet, over time, *huapango* has come to identify the musics played at such gatherings, particularly the huasteco and arribeño varieties. In music scholarship, within popular culture, and among practitioners of Mexican musics, the term *huapango* is, nevertheless, usually invoked as a reference to the galloping 6/8 rhythm that is typical of the style but has been interpreted across genres. This and other musicological features make it familiar and recognizable—many ethnic Mexicans and appreciators of Mexican music know huapango when they hear it in all of its variations, from *huapango norteño* to its echoes in the work of tribal DJs and its bel canto performance by the immortal stars of Mexican cinema. The last example is what sounds in the ears of many as a type of classic or authentic huapango. While the popularity of the form outside of its region of origin—along the Gulf coast and in the central states of Guanajuato, Hidalgo, Puebla, Querétaro, and San Luís Potosí—owes much to the silver screen, this stylized representation is, ultimately, a complicated one that reveals much about the knotted relationship between performance, the semiotics of authenticity, and the sonic borders of national identity.

A life lived in a sepia film—smoky mountains tower in the distance, endless plots of lush farmland roll out from the foothills, and a Spanish-tiled hacienda glows beneath a big, open sky dotted with giant feathery clouds. Impeccably dressed *charros* (horsemen) on horseback patrol caliche-paved streets flanked by primitive jacal dwellings as women sheepishly dash from one abode to the next, their heads down, tugging firmly at their rebozos. Swells of ambiguously folkloric music suddenly flood the landscape, flowing in diegetically from beyond. The atmosphere is now sonically poised for men (and rarely women) to croon heartfelt serenades beneath picturesque balconies or cry out passionately in crowded cantinas, projecting out in the full-throated *estilo bravió* (bold style). This is the visual and sonic scaffolding of a Mexico artfully constructed by the *comedia ranchera*, the most commercially successful genre of Mexican national cinema in the twentieth century, popularized the world over. Indeed, this space-time dream world is a vital component of the first film of this kind, *Allá en el Rancho Grande* (*Out on the Big Ranch*). Directed by Fernando de Fuentes and released in 1936, this pastoral drama starred Tito Guízar and Esther Fernández and featured the music of Lorenzo Barcelata, an actor and composer. Like most films of this type, its plot involves a love triangle, and subsequent twists and turns (involving revenge and betrayal) play themselves out amid the webs of unbridled patriarchy, beneath the surface of which we find a highly stratified race- and class-inflected hierarchy integral to the hacienda political economy. Hailed as the film that marks the beginning of what many term the golden age of Mexican cinema, *Allá en el Rancho Grande*'s music deserves as much attention as its visual lexicon, for its scoring plays a crucial role in authenticating certain ideas concerning Mexican identity through the sounds of tradition—a formula that would be re-created time and again in this genre of film.

Music is the expressive form that rings loudest in *Allá en el Rancho Grande*'s folkloric collage. In some of the film's pivotal scenes, music serves as a powerful vehicle for sonically illustrating sentiments crucial to the narrative plot; this not only bestows on the featured sounds an air of ideal-typical Mexican music culture but, more important, casts the feelings conveyed through them as authentically Mexican—a true window into mexicanidad (Mexican cultural nationalism). And while certain *canciones típicas* (traditional songs) and canciones rancheras (country songs) are overtly melancholic, with expressions of pastoral longing ("Canción Mixteca," for instance), the featured huapango performances most densely embody a near-cartoonlike Mexican aesthetic of machismo, particularly given their placement in presumed masculine spaces: the *palenque* (cockfighting arena) and cantina. In the former, an eager crowd of men with a few scattered *chinas poblanas* (women in traditional Chinese Pueblan dress) welcomes two huapango guitar trios who ready themselves for a musical duel, symbolically anticipating the cockfight about to take place between the rival haciendas, Real Minero and Rancho Grande. The two groups, Trío Murciélagos and Trío Tariácuri, are introduced as "los meros cancioneros del alma nacional" (the bona fide singers of the national soul) by the ring announcer, presenting their performance—and the message it conveys—as a true expression of the Mexican spirit. Wearing wide-brimmed sombreros and starched charro costumes (one ensemble is dressed in white, the other in black), with *zarapes* (shawls) draped carefully over their shoulders, the musicians each rest one leg atop a chair placed in front of them as they assume a boastful stance and prepare to face off in this choreographed bout of musical flyting.

Both ensembles proceed to interpret huapango-esque songs authored or arranged by Barcelata that retain the galloping 6/8 styling but with added musical and vocal flourishes.[2] The first trio performs "Lucha María," a song that depicts a male fairgoer as a fearless gamecock requesting the company of a woman, comparing her beauty to that of a mermaid.[3] "La Presumida" (the presumptuous gal) is performed by the second. Its lyrical stanzas describe an apple bird that calls out longingly for the attention of his fickle loved one, who is all too eager to find love with another.[4] This portrayal of huapango-crooning charros is indeed seductive, inscribing a sexual charisma on huapango performance that positions it as an apt vehicle for casting romance—or, more appropriately, the conquest of a woman—as a battle, a confrontation between men, where the winner is the one who displays superior skills, or in this case musical talents, symbolically representative of male virility. While no winner is declared in the film, it is clear that the aesthetic nexus of traditional song, image, and performance is meant to offer a glimpse into the essence of the Mexican character (*el alma nacional*), which, when examined closely, is bound to an idealized masculinity: true Mexicans are machos who boast and successfully win a woman's favors.[5]

Later, we are folded into yet another bout of huapango dueling in the immediate wake of the film's namesake ranchera performance—the climactic aesthetic act of the entire feature—as the main protagonist, José Francisco (played by Tito Guízar), performs the song "Allá en el Rancho Grande" in a crowded cantina. After a bit of coaxing, he asks those present what song they want to hear; an anonymous voice offscreen answers emphatically, "Rancho Grande!" José Francisco agrees and is swiftly handed a guitar from behind the bar. As he performs in the forceful bel canto style, the end of each of his verses is punctuated by carefully scripted gritos and jeers from the bar's patrons, who joyfully sing along during the ranchera's refrain. However, the convivial mood generated by this communal hymn is suddenly compromised by the huapango duel that follows, after an individual in the bar calls out for a "huapango retachado" (huapango challenge), a request seconded by another, who wants one "de mucha contestación" (with back-and-forth responses). José Francisco accepts and baits the audience, asking who will exchange verses with him. Martín, played by Barcelata, takes up the challenge. He works under José Francisco and has also fallen in love with Cruz, José Francisco's sweetheart. However, while José Francisco has just announced that he intends to marry Cruz, Martín and everyone present know that the hacienda boss, Felipe, has made advances toward her. Angered by this and jealous of José Francisco, Martín reveals this public secret during the musical duel, and the scene becomes one of restrained violence, as José Francisco's manhood is threatened. Authored by Barcelata, the ensuing *coplas de huapango* (huapango couplets) articulate a poetics of macho one-upmanship that culminates in this final verse:

Vale más saber perder
y guardar bien el honor
con la mujer que uno quiere
no hay que hacer combinación;
si pierdo revancha tomo
y a la cruz de mi pasión
por un caballo palomo
no se la cambio al patrón

———

You must be graceful in defeat
and steadfastly keep your honor
the woman that you love
you must not share;
if I lose, I take revenge
and the passion for Cruz
for a white stallion
to the boss, I shall not exchange

What begins as a series of witty jibes between the two men quickly descends into heteronormative claims in defense of Cruz's virginity.[6]

The world's introduction to huapango arrives with a healthy dose of machismo, a casting that passes with ease into officialized academic accounts that further treat this musical form as a prototypical vehicle for masculinist aggression. Octavio Paz's treatise in *The Labyrinth of Solitude: Life and Thought in Mexico* echoes this, also making references to popular music—no doubt that diffused through the folklore of national cinema—to brace his own claims: "Narcissism and masochism are not exclusively Mexican traits, but it is notable how often our popular songs and sayings and our everyday behavior treat love as falsehood and betrayal. . . . The Mexican conceives of love as combat and conquest" (1961: 41). A long list of intellectuals—from Paz to Samuel Ramos and Jorge Portilla—have simultaneously chastised the perils and extolled the virtues of machismo to exaggerated heights that would make it seem that violence and fatalism are a uniquely Mexican condition. Scholars, including both Américo Paredes (1993) and Olga Nájera-Ramírez (1997), have called this psychoanalysis into question. Nájera-Ramírez (1997), in particular, has examined how the embodiment of these macho notions in the constructed figure of the singing charro as an emblem of cultural patrimony powerfully (en)genders a highly masculinist mexicanidad. In other words, the above-described visual and aural lexicon has authenticated a specific type of maleness subsequently enfolded into commonsense notions of Mexican culture and identity, notions that have also informed academic accounts. For instance, in the article "The Huapango: A Mexican Song Contest" (1942), Jean B. Johnson describes a coastal music from southern Veracruz characterized by the "noisy jarana" (small Mexican chordophone) and the fandango dance space, in which singers interrupt the performance with recited verses, typically original compositions, ranging from barbs to declarations of love. While he identifies the style as huapango, it is clear that the music, which he suggests retains a close affiliation with Caribbean song, is *son jarocho*. And the contest he refers to is in fact the practice known as *florear la tarima*, or adorning the tarima with décima verses. This practice opens up the gathering for dancing before experienced practitioners adorn the platform with their patterned footwork. These recitations indeed provoke pauses in the music such that the audience members enter into an evaluative role as they judge the skill of the décima performer. Irrespective of these nuances in performance or the differences between what are entirely distinct musical styles, Johnson manages to voice a matter-of-fact claim that derisively caricatures these poetics: "It is hardly necessary to add that these contests frequently become heated, and often end tragically in a flash of daggers beside the river" (234). Paredes's influential essay "On Ethnographic Work among Minority Groups: A Folklorist's Perspective" (1993) comes to mind for the misguided representations of this music as tragically violent are "somewhat unreal" (74).[7] While Johnson provides no evidence to support the above assertion of habitual violence provoked by huapango, one may assume that he was influenced by the popular media of the day, indeed by films like *Allá en el Rancho Grande* and the dueling displays of aggression they featured. Similar contests dramatized on the silver screen worth mentioning include those between Luis Aguilar and Cuco Sanchez (*El Gallo Giro* [The Game Rooster], 1938), Pedro Infante and Blanca Estela Pavón (*Los Tres Huastecos* [The Three Huastecans], 1948), and Pedro Infante and Jorge Negrete (*Dos Tipos de Cuidado* [Two Careful Types], 1953).[8] Set in a utopian world where heavy drinking, womanizing, and violence are as natural as the landscape, the traditional huapango sound transcribed onto that world has become metonymically linked to the trope of the Mexican character.

While these sonic images are integral to the racial project of Mexican culture in the early twentieth century (a topic taken up in the next section), they also constitute an aural space where others (specifically its North American neighbor) have come to hear Mexico as well. In *Audiotopia: Music, Race, and America* (2005), Josh Kun makes a case for how the American racial imaginary has been generated in part through experiences of music and sound. The power of selective listening, he suggests, has constructed an aural harmony in the service of the project of U.S. white racial hegemony, which has silenced the (presumed) dissonance that racial and ethnic difference introduce. Within this context Kun argues that such difference ultimately sounds out against the constraints of monocultural American citizenship, disturbing the national aesthetics of unisonance. I extend Kun's argument and suggest that the construction of "the American audio-racial imagination" (Kun 2005: 26) is not only about *how* America hears itself domestically but equally about *what* it hears itself against (which sounds from outside its national borders). In other words, the policing of American national culture is a segregationist project that necessarily extends its aural gaze beyond the physical space of the nation. Although muting the audible resonance of sonic cultural flows and formations across national borders is an impossible task, emergent transnational musical geographies that reach into any and all nation-states are often resignified and appropriated to effect social silences in the service of broader nationalist projects. The "Mexican sound" discussed thus far has bled into the space of the U.S. nation-state in dialectical fashion throughout the twentieth century as an audible signifier of an otherness against which the United States has defined its own racial project (see chapter 4 for an extended discussion). Among other things, Mexican music in the American mainstream appears as a racialized index that connotes (1) primal festivity, (2) carefree and unserious expression, and (3) pastoral backwardness—all of which brace parallel beliefs about ethnic Mexicans as a whole. This aural construction owes, however, much of its ideological weight to the project of Mexican musical nationalism, a large component of which has been the Mexican media industry. Huapango is thus burdened by "the national" in dual senses: (1) it participates in a U.S. racial markedness structure as a sonic index for a derided Mexican otherness, and (2) it is also the soundtrack to a powerful antimodernist Mexican national sentiment.

> Somos indios mestizos es cierto
> pero no con un cactus a un lado
> mucho menos jorongo embrocado
> ni dormidos allá en el desierto
> somos pueblo y aún no hemos muerto

somos arte, color, poesía
tradición convertida en porfía
tinta, letra y mil versos unidos
y en batallas también decididos:
¡VIVA EL ARTE DE LA POESÍA!

————

We are Indian mestizos, it is true
but not with a cactus at our side
much less draped in a zarape
nor asleep out there in the desert
we are a vibrant people, and we have not perished
we are art, color, poetry
tradition transformed into struggle
ink, lyrics and thousands of woven verses
and determined also in battles:
LONG LIVE THE ART OF POESÍA!

—Graciano

TRACK TWO: SILENCE AND THE NATIONAL SPACE

The political legitimacy of the nation as an imagined community is the result of a constellation of ideological discourses, some of which take artistic forms that citizens come to feel are representative of a unique national identity. The cultural work of this powerful symbolism—which includes music and ideas about music—socializes citizens to feel a sense of national sentiment. To put it another way, modern nation-states rely on the power of tradition to establish a genealogical basis for an assumed shared identity (Lomnitz 2001: 132). And as Alexander Sebastian Dent elaborates in reference to Brazilian country music, "Components of this dialogic between forward and backward-looking have been mediated musically" (2009: 1). Thomas Turino (2003) refers to this particular semiotics as "musical nationalism" and cites as examples military songs and national anthems, folkloric tradition, and songs appropriated for political purposes (e.g., Bruce Springsteen's "Born in the U.S.A."). In the Mexican case, over time various regional sounds have come to form part of a musical canon that appeals to a deep and tacitly shared national sentiment of *lo mexicano*. This results in part from a broad range of nationalist cultural policies—including the efforts of the Secretaría de Educación Pública (Ministry of Public Education)—in the wake of the Mexican Revolution and the decades that followed.[9] Nevertheless, as the previous section revealed, the project of Mexican musical nationalism has situated the essence of Mexican music in a particular geographic landscape—*el rancho*, or the idealized countryside.

In the Spanish vernacular, the term *rancho* typically refers to a small rural hamlet. The rancho as a symbolic cultural construction, however, is a repository for an assumed collective heritage rooted in expressive cultural practices tied to subsistence ranching and horsemanship—much as the figures of the gaucho and *llanero* (plainsman) invoke a romanticized pastoralism in Argentina and Venezuela. The result is a "memory bank"—as Yolanda Broyles-González (2006) terms it—that fashions imagined connections to the countryside. Marcia Farr (2006) traces the history of the term *rancho* back to the Germanic family of northern European languages. She writes, "Although situations in which the word *rancho* was used were plentiful in sixteenth-century America, it was mostly used en *el hablar vulgar* (folk language), not by the educated and literate. . . . Those literary uses that do exist, however, indicate that this word meant improvised housing, midway between more stable dwellings and more transient ones. Moreover, several such ranchos constituted a pueblo or small village. Finally, *rancho* . . . also came to mean a part of land that is farmed" (35). Indeed, ranching and agriculture existed as important modes of organizing regional economies for most of New Spain and Mexico's history up through the twentieth century, at which point Mexico experienced accelerated processes of industrialization and urbanization that transformed its geopolitical landscape. Rural migration to Mexico's urban centers also has a long and complicated history but occurred on a particularly massive scale in the wake of the devastation caused by the Mexican Revolution, itself a popular uprising in opposition to the displacement associated with Porfirio Díaz's modernization of Mexico's subsistence economies in the late nineteenth century. This political-economic transformation, Olga Nájera-Ramírez (1997) suggests, subsequently found expression in the Mexican canción tipica (traditional song), soon labeled the canción ranchera (country song) as its themes became increasingly pastoral in scope, symbolically indexing the failed promises of the Revolution. The rancho symbol complex that emerged at the cultural crossroads of early twentieth-century Mexico—and was articulated through its musical canon—speaks of a nation struggling to both define itself and reimagine its past in the wake of centuries of institutional racism (certainly during the Porfiriato) that marginalized or even criminalized homegrown musical expressions like the son jarocho, for instance (Sheehy 1979; Díaz Sanchez and Hernández 2013). As communities, musicians, and music making were reconstituted in urban environments like Mexico City, a blurring of regional stylistic distinctions occurred, giving rise to a more-or-less uniform ranchera song by the mid-twentieth century. Its standardization was the result of dissemination via the emergent technologies of radio, film, and audio recordings—a media alliance that would subsequently serve as the cornerstone of Mexico's powerful and government-supported entertainment industry (Gradante 1982; M. Peña 1985).[10]

In the early twentieth century, the circulation of this assumed pastoral heritage was integral to the growth of national awareness among the masses, a sentiment previously "diffuse and . . . associated precariously with an intellectual elite" (Schmidt 1978: 21). This is not to suggest, however, that beneath the layers of invented tradition there rests a transcendental premodern cultural substrate à la Guillermo Bonfil Batalla's (1996) "Deep Mexico." Quite the opposite, this ontological distinction between "deep" and "imaginary" is false, as Claudio Lomnitz (1992) explains in his critique of Bonfil Batalla's binary formulation: "Both ideologies are linked to sets of real practices and . . . both ideologies are products of the collective imagination. In other words, they are both 'deep,' and they are both 'imaginary.' In attributing 'reality' to one and 'illusion' to another, Bonfil is merely returning to the nationalist drawing board of the Mexican Revolution without having fully confronted the reasons why the 'imaginary' Mexico has become so very real" (248). The reasons are multiple and include the power of the Mexican media. Whether this "visual operation" (García Canclini 1995: 118) represented (1) a romantic nostalgia for something lost—recently arrived migrants from the countryside longing for a mythologized rural innocence in an alien urban environment (Monsiváis 1995; Nájera-Ramírez 1997)—or (2) a conservative response to the progressive social policies of President Lázaro Cárdenas, it undoubtedly broadcast the rancho as a protonational space-time when/where authentic Mexican culture dwells. This imagining is what I term the *ranchero chrono-trope*.[11]

Drawing on Mikhail Bakhtin's (1981) concept of the chronotope as an optic with which to explore the space-time relational dimensions that contour narrative representations of cultural systems, I propose the ranchero chrono-trope as a way of understanding (1) the spatiotemporality of essentialist representations of Mexican culture and (2) the specific stereotypes—or tropes, as described in the previous section (machismo, fatalism, defensiveness)—embedded in that space-time construct. In other words, this concept helps frame how the space of the rancho becomes charged, how its time thickens with the flesh of a ruralized cultural poetics (Bakhtin 1981: 84).[12] Indeed, the rhetorical force of tropes—understood here as figures of thought in social life—lies in their aesthetic effects, in their capacity to align subjectivities, space, and time (Fernandez 1991); this is to say, they often function as chronotopes in their own right. In problematizing the micro-macro distinctions often found in studies of language, Jan Blommaert (2015) makes a case for the usefulness of the chronotope as a way of understanding the dialectical relationship between the two. He writes:

> I propose to see chronotopes as the aspect of contextualization through which specific chunks of history (understood here in the Bakhtinian sense as spatiotemporal) can be invoked in discourse as meaning-attributing resources or . . . as historically configured and ordered tropes. In addition, I propose to see scales as defining the scope of communicability of such tropes. . . . Both concepts are useful to distinguish between two dimensions of context and contextualization: that of the availability of specific contextual universes for invocation in discursive work (chronotope), and that of their accessibility for participants and audiences involved in discursive work (scale). (111)

The rancho—as a spatiotemporal construct—is an elaborate frame whose interpretive work invokes a specific "tropic [chunk] of history" (111) that brings pastoral social types, actions, landscapes, and political worlds into meaningful view. In other words, this potent motif lends credence to an idyllic agrarian world where the national soul dwells—at the spatial periphery of modernity and always in a temporal past tense. However, with respect to the scale of communicability, these narrative plot elements have become recognizable owing to an institutionalized discourse that not only blends space and time but *bends* them as a means of conditioning a specific set of cultural semiotics. These semiotics engender simultaneous (and thus conflicting) feelings of both admiration for an authentic former poetic world and also pejorative condescension toward that very world. Speaking of the ongoing transnational circulation and consumption of such pastoral nostalgia in popular music and film, Farr observes, "These cinematic representations persist even today in the collective imagination (both in Mexico and in the United States) as the somehow authentic and true Mexico of the past, even though they are juxtaposed quite paradoxically in the public mind with the disdainful attitude toward rancheros as uncultivated and uneducated peasants" (2006: 39). As such, if the essence of Mexico is in the rancho, this pastoral backdrop positions Mexico as antimodern and in turn braces derisive claims that Mexicans are backward and their "culture" primitive.[13] This chrono-tropic imagining elides the reality that the political and economic marginality of Mexico—like much of the underdeveloped and developing world—is at the center of the project of modernity.[14]

The rise of the rancho (and its associated musical folklore) in the Mexican imagination occurs alongside racial ideologies, specifically *mestizaje* (mixed ancestry), or the origin myth of a unique racially mixed identity. These claims to racial harmony and consolidation—perhaps best typified by José Vasconcelos's *raza cósmica*—veil the brutal realities of the colonial project, constituting what Peter Wade considers "racist and even ethnocidal practices of whitening" (2003: 263).[15] In the 1930s *indigenismo* (indigeneity) also emerged as a rhetorical validation of indigenous identity that reinforced racist assumptions of essentialized primordialism in the guise of the familiar archetype of the noble savage. This institutionalized cultural and intellectual milieu becomes widespread in Mexico at the moment when a dominant media alliance begins to carve out a mass market of consumer citizens, resulting in a rancho symbol complex, which at its core reinscribes the dominant racial order. In doing so, it also legitimizes various forms of ongoing marginalization. With respect to music, this ruralized cultural poetics is integral to the project of Mexican musical nationalism—it displaces sounds from their historical, temporal, social, and placial contexts in favor of a romanticized space-time located somewhere out there, or the mythical realm of *allá* at the periphery of modernity. Allá (perhaps most poetically "on the big ranch"), however, is quite materially the hacienda.

Returning to the scene at the start of this chapter, perhaps you can picture it in its old glory, seen through the glow of film. Despite its romantic representation, the hacienda was a brutal place, the heart of the colonial project. When examined critically, its folklorized musical overtures that are woven into this dreamlike landscape play a role, ironically enough, in silencing the history of empire building in the guise of a simpler "social structure where everyone knew their place, where certain privileged men ruled" (Nájera-Ramírez 1997: 25). This appropriation of vernacular forms of expressive culture amounts to an "aural epistemology of purification" (Ochoa Gautier 2006). Women are marginalized (Carter Muñoz 2013; Nájera-Ramírez 1997), blackness is erased (A. González 2010), and regional specificity is flattened (Turino 2003). And this is likely why cultural theorists such as Roger Bartra (2002) ultimately ask of this process of signification: does it mean anything to be Mexican? An adjacent line of inquiry, perhaps, might lead us to explore the relationship between the experiential texture of daily lives and the "stereotyped genre-bound exemplars" of the rancho "making their way across the pages and grooves and screens of mass-mediated popular culture" (A. Fox 2004: 82). These questions require us to listen to the many and particular worlds that make up Mexico, beyond received notions of a harmonious sphere of national culture in the context of space, as Lomnitz (1992) suggests. Or, rather, we must account for multiple spatialities in localized settings and the frames of interaction among diverse groups of people in those settings; otherwise, we are complicit in the project of "a historical sociology of the silence that has characterized the relationship of certain sectors of the Mexican population and state institutions" (Lomnitz 2001: 284). As opposed to a deep Mexico, this silent Mexico—or "the various populations that live beyond the fractured fault line of Mexico's national public sphere"—exists at the very heart of the project of modernity, the failure of democracy, and the contemporary transnational politics of the neoliberal state. To mitigate the conditions of their marginalized lives, large portions of this silent Mexico migrate across the U.S.-Mexico border. The question arises, then, how do their voices sound out in the space of the U.S. nation-state?

> Gente del rancho que un día emigró
> y que venciendo la adversidad
> logra niveles de calidad
> que otro no alcanza ni aunque estudió
> gente muy jóven que potenció
> habilidades y hoy da en que hablar
> porque produce, tiene un lugar
> y hasta es a veces patrón de gringos
> en un "big bisnes" ya no hay distingos:
> ES UNA COSA MUY DE ADMIRAR

> ———

> Folks from rural hamlets who long ago emigrated
> upon overcoming adversity
> have achieved levels of success
> that others do not reach, even if they are educated
> these are young people who focused
> their talents and today have much to show for it
> because they produce, they have a place
> and at times they are the gringos' boss

ethnic distinctions fall away in matters of business:

IT'S QUITE A BEAUTIFUL SCENE

—Guillermo Velázquez

TRACK THREE: ECHOES OF MODERNITY

It is possible to hear the historical feedback of the ranchero chrono-trope in the space of the U.S. nation-state, beginning even before its full initiation. Writing a century before the rancho's rise as a spatiotemporal envelope of national identity, Joel Poinsett ([1829] 2002) acknowledged the hacienda as one major cornerstone of the Spanish Empire. His admission is not without its own contradictions, however, given that he was writing at a time when rumbles of war with Mexico were building audibly in the United States. In the 1820s Poinsett served in various political and authorial roles in relation to Mexico, which positioned him to publicize severely racist generalizations that have remained largely intact to this day.[16] In a strange twist, after leaving his post as special envoy to Mexico years later, Poinsett suggested in a letter to then secretary of state Martin Van Buren that the "recurring oppression" of the hacienda system was to blame for the "ignorant and debauched" status of the Mexican people. Although he made racist claims, he managed to contextualize the social turmoil that followed the Mexican War of Independence (1810–1821), suggesting it was a direct result of the oppressive political economy "under which [the Mexican people] formerly laboured." Driven largely by the racial ideology of Manifest Destiny, North American encroachment into Mexican territory during the nineteenth century was part of the broader project of American expansion, strengthened by the belief that God had made Anglo-Americans the custodians of democracy in the Western hemisphere. Walt Whitman had this to say at the dawn of the Mexican-American War: "What has miserable, inefficient Mexico—with her superstition, her burlesque upon freedom, her actual tyranny by the few over the many—what has she to do with the great mission of peopling the new world with a noble race? Be it ours, to achieve that mission!" (editorial, *Brooklyn Daily Eagle*, July 7, 1846). The Mexican-American War—an imperialist war—violently introduced the socioeconomic restructuring of a geographic expanse previously belonging to Mexico. It was a war of modernity waged against a supposedly barbarous people and justified as an integral part of God's will to make the geographic expanse of America fruitful and free. The ideological construction of a singular barbarous threat has gone hand in hand with historical material processes—that is, the "Mexican other" is the outcome of not merely a discursive exercise in sociosemantics but a materially lived project of negation. Whitman's sentiments persist as contemporary concerns over the browning of America regularly spark loud debates that resort to racist depictions of who belongs in the United States and who it belongs to, claims that often draw on the ranchero chrono-trope in inflammatory ways. In July 2013, for instance, as Tea Party activists rallied against so-called illegal immigration on the U.S. Capitol grounds in Washington, D.C., Ken Crow, cofounder of the Tea Party Community, emphatically howled:

> I'm from Texas, and one of the things about being from a ranch in Texas is that you learn about breeding. You learn about breeding livestock, you learn about breeding horses. And believe it or not I'm here to talk to you about your breeding. You are American patriots. You came from those incredible blood lines of Thomas Jefferson and George Washington and John Smith. And all these great Americans, Martin Luther King. These great Americans who built this country. You came from them. And the unique thing about being from that part of the world, when you learn about breeding, you learn that you cannot breed Secretariat to a donkey and expect to win the Kentucky Derby. You guys have incredible DNA and don't forget it. You've got the breeding, you've got the DNA, you've got the patriotism and you've got the sacrifice. And I'll be damned if I'm going to give my country up to a bunch of people who do not deserve to be here.[17]

The rally hosted the likes of Senators Ted Cruz (R-TX) and Jefferson Beauregard Sessions (R-AL), national figures who, like those in attendance, considered themselves to be far from that "other" part of the world, from out there, from allá—a place where people possess the culture/heritage/DNA of donkeys (a stereotypical fixture in the Mexican rancho landscape, to be sure). Leo R. Chavez considers discourse of this ilk central to what he terms the "Latino threat narrative," an ideological scripting that "posits a neo-evolutionary scenario but in reverse, the devolution of society" (2008: 45). Mexican culture, in this regard, is viewed as a contaminating threat to American national identity—it is backward (subhuman even, donkey-like) and thus incapable of positively "[influencing] the larger society in any appreciable way" (45). Poinsett's racism echoes loudly into the present, for if the geographic border between Mexico and the United States is the result of an imperialist war (of maneuver) that Poinsett anticipates, Crow's speech represents the ongoing social war (of position) that Poinsett discursively pioneered.[18]

In an era of increased economic integration with Mexico, labor migration flows into the segregationist space of the United States continue to animate such reactions. With this in mind, recent music scholarship has tasked itself with tracing how flows of music take shape within this exceedingly xenophobic context. Drawing on Arjun Appadurai's (1996b) theorizing in the wake of what he suggests is a crisis of modernity and a collapsing of hegemonic national identities, scholars contend that music shared across the boundaries of nation-states reveals not only how identities are forged and performed in a context of transnational economies (or the complicated relationship between the local and the global) but also how borders themselves are ultimately "fluid, give-and-take areas where complexity, negotiation, and hybridity are everyday constants" (Madrid 2008: 3–4). In his work on Nor-tec electronic dance music, for instance, Alejandro L. Madrid makes a case for understanding localized music making from Tijuana, Mexico, as a postnational project of territorial resignification, writing, "As the experiences of many citizens at the border suggest, a postnational condition should not refer to the viability of the nation-state as a political entity but rather to its necessary restructuring according to the real needs of its citizens. Such re-signification entails recognition of the local diversity that is often homogenized by nationalist discourses. This type of reevaluation is necessary if the nation-state is to be reconsidered a feasible form of political organization within the globalized postnational constellation" (2008: 197). While Madrid is speaking of Mexico specifically, I have transitioned my focus to the United States. To apply his insights to this context requires that we recognize how contemporary discourses of homogeneity—or DNA and bloodlines—are voiced in response to the perceived threat posed by transnational migration, such that the language of national identity (and belonging) is also that of juridical identities (alien, illegal, undocumented) tied to national borders. To imagine postnational identities within this broader U.S.-Mexico perspective is, therefore, to recognize the types of subjectivities fashioned beyond the exclusionary juridical practices of the nation-state, subjectivities that gesture toward its reimagining so that it may be more inclusive—as is argued in the present discussion—of undocumented migrants.

Embedded in this point is a critique of what is perhaps a common meaning *postnationalism* has taken on in Latina/o music scholarship, becoming a gloss for *transnationalism*. Within contemporary processes of globalization, people and identities are constantly moving, crossing borders, as are practices of music making. To account for the ways in which musics are increasingly geographically diffuse isn't necessarily the same as providing an understanding of how these practices go beyond the politics of the nation-state. The spatial movement of Mexican folk-derived popular musics across national boundaries, for instance, certainly speaks to the transnational growth of their respective markets for production and consumption, given labor migration between the United States and Mexico. But how do these musics speak to the racialized politics of illegality and to people's needs to fashion expressive practices of self-valorization within this context? How do everyday practices of music making *play* a part? Accounting for how music in everyday life becomes politicized in relation to border logics is necessary in deepening our understanding of how migrants disarticulate—in homegrown expressive ways—the materiality of the brutal juridical-economic logics administered by nation-states and corporate interests in their ruthless management of human and capital flows. Though attentive to the transnationalization of political economies in the post-NAFTA era, I cannot accept this interpretation as postnational without reservations or qualifications, for in my estimation flows of music cannot serve as a stand-in for flows of people—or, in the words of Lawrence Grossberg, "dissemination as 'immigritude'" (1996: 103)—particularly those who labor under the dehumanizing realities of the nation-state's renewed militarization of the U.S.-Mexico border and policing efforts in the continental United States. Herein looms a spectacle braced by racial ideologies that produce the commonsensical notion of illegality, at the center of which rests an exploitable Mexican other whose identity is a bordered one—tethered to the primitivism of the ranchero chrono-trope.

While scholarship focused on Mexican musics at times celebrates the invocation of ranchero iconography in a U.S. context as an assertion of a subaltern subjectivity against the normative claims of American white identity (J. Saldívar 1997), analysis rarely goes beyond the surface of *lo ranchero* itself.[19] In other words, the challenge is to grapple with the contradictions of how Mexican national identity is constructed in relation to modernity. By *modernity*, I mean a project that epistemologically and scientistically rejects the "normalizing functions of tradition"—a movement guided by "reason" and the liberating promise of progress, of which the consolidation of nation-states and the rise of industrial capitalism form part (Habermas 1983: 5).[20] In both Mexican and U.S. contexts, such material transformations are undergirded by deep histories of racial subjugation—from the colonial hacienda to westward expansion, respectively—that have inscribed a "distance-mediated relationality . . . based on . . . cultural alterity" (Elie 2013: 220). In the present transnational moment, perceived racial difference casts Mexicans as a criminalized source of transnational labor in the space of the U.S. nation-state. Understanding difference, however, is a contextual process of comprehending racial tradition as both a part of and a response to modernity. Opposed to an essentialist master narrative of race that supposes that racial communities are "autonomous, homogeneous, integrated, and essentially authentic," W. Lawrence Hogue (1996: 3) argues that racial tradition is marked by interaction with, rather than isolation from, modernity. In fact, its roots spring from groups who are targeted for appropriation, labor, and economic marginalization, such that individuals in those groups participate in the projects of modernity but do not receive its fruits. Alternately, the collectivity and resistance made possible by racial tradition (in a rhetorical or discursive rather than objective or biological sense) also bear witness to a desire to be distant from the oppressions of modern capitalism, to abide within a different conception of space and time, and therefore alternative subjectivities, opening up a space of countermodernity (Grossberg 1996).[21] Nicholas De Genova's interpretation of counterpublic slogans like "¡Aquí estamos, y no nos vamos!" (Here we are, and we're not leaving!) is useful in conceptualizing this final point, for such slogans represent an incorrigible, irreversible presence of migrants in the space of the U.S. nation-state whose politics "both identifies and is committed to the impossibility of inclusivity" (2010: 105). The performance of these and other expressions embodies a rejection of the state's dehumanizing categories and the ruthless subjugation of migrant life (Rosas 2012), for "the human activity from which [performance] is produced is founded on a process that accentuates the social relations that constitute it" (Flores 1994: 278). In other words, expressive enactments are fundamentally social acts that stake claims of belonging through a vitality and conviviality otherwise severed or denied. Thus, the purpose of discussing parts of a racial tradition, in this case one that is also vernacular, is not to solidify the notion of a premodern, authentic specimen that retains at its core idealized markers of the past (allá)—much as the legacy of Robert Redfield's (1930, 1941, 1950, 1953, 1956) work posits a fundamental contrast between isolated Mexican folk culture and modern urban civilization. Rather, the aim of this discussion is to identify how a performative practice, as part of a racial tradition, operates as part of and in response to the pressures and circumstances of modernity, how it is used to forge collectivity, how it changes and moves as people change and move, how it carries a different kind of power with it that is conceived against imposed and limiting notions of space and time. Huapango arribeño, I argue, is crucial in meeting everyday needs for intimacy, place, and belonging in this regard—beyond culture, beyond illegality, and irrespective of geography; through it, postnational subjectivities are fashioned and necessary, *aquí* (here), not allá.

> Saludar es muy preciso
> para poder comenzar
> hoy que he venido a chambiar
> y a cumplir un compromiso
> porque mi destino quiso
> traerme como un huapanguero
> y andando sobre el sendero
> para cumplir mis labores
> sí, señoras y señores:
> AQUÍ ESTÁN SUS HUAPANGUEROS

> ———

> Greetings are in order
> to be able to commence
> now that I have come to labor
> and to fulfill a commitment
> because el destino wanted
> to bring me as a huapanguero
> and as I travel along the path
> to fulfill my duties
> yes, ladies and gentlemen:
> HERE ARE YOUR HUAPANGUEROS

> —Pánfilo

TRACK FOUR: VERNACULAR THEORIZING

Nonethnographic works that rely on the mass media in sourcing symbolic interpretations can at times straddle a fine line, particularly when calling out for the voices of the oppressed while largely leaving silent the people spoken of. Indeed, there exists a present trend in which, most notably, the U.S.-Mexico border is disembodied through an elaborate semiotics in which things crossing borders substitute for the cultural real of the lives lived across that border. However, capital moves much differently than migrant bodies, and, unfortunately, this fact often serves only as a prefatory note in work that focuses on *mediascapes* that enjoy the same privilege (Heyman 1994; Limón 1998; M. Martínez 2002). Such a focus potentially exploits the meanings of "the border," for if we are to intervene in its discursive formation and the axial role it plays in reproducing social and spatial divisions that are materially lived— illegalized migrant personhood being perhaps the most salient example—then we need to speak about the people who tread across that border. Ultimately, "concepts must be experienced, they are lived" (Massumi and Manning, quoted in Shaviro 2009: vii). Nonethnographic analysis is hardly as problematic when this question of the subaltern speaking is not at play. Indeed, such approaches in their sole reliance on discourses of representation to the detriment of material realities, favor notions of identity—which itself assumes a self-defined constituency where "every individual is a representative of the totality"—rather than the phenomenal field of subjectivity, which opens up the possibility for understanding the multiple and differentially valued points of attachment that articulate experiences in the world, itself "contextually produced epistemological value" (Grossberg 1996: 87, 98). Nevertheless, there remains a question of how scholarship on expressive culture can provide "opportunities to engage directly with" *communities themselves*, to *hear* them, particularly within the context of incessant *criminal*-ization and illegalized personhood, as Arturo J. Aldama attempts to do elsewhere.[22] Undoubtedly, the consumptive flow of popular culture across borders in the Mexican case is itself constitutive of multiple practices of production, both ideological and material, as Stuart Hall (1973) proposes.[23] The present work takes this opportunity to engage in an alternative to the interpretive turn in cultural analysis, which has so far provided more metacommentary than poesis (Taussig 1993: xvii).

In his recent exposé of Américo Paredes's life's work, José E. Limón juxtaposes what he deems a situated Mexican-American folkloristics with the project of cultural studies more broadly, observing the latter's efforts to be less concerned with "face-to-face forms of everyday expressive culture, especially in methodological terms" (2013: 133). Utilizing my ethnographic work on huapango arribeño as a point of reference, he attends to the "more culturally specific matter of . . . contemporary Chicano/Chicana cultural studies," suggesting that "the evasion of everyday vernacular expressive culture as a subject of inquiry and discipline has much less warrant" given the rich history of Mexican-American folkloristics (133).[24] With incisive and Paredes-like wit, Limón warns against speculation by asking (and denying) a series of wildly rhetorical questions that, without close reading, can appear to be his own speculations, when in fact they are admonishments against a certain type of scholarly guesswork that forgoes the vernacular and instead substitutes a semiotics of popular culture. When it comes to huapango arribeño, popular culture is less crucial to the issue than the vernacular and the everyday, leaving ethnography the best (I would argue, only) option.

Nevertheless, there exists a major difference between the cultural poetics of my precursors and the ethnographic work I embark on in these pages. Most prominently, both Paredes and Limón consider the experiences of Mexican-Americans, not Mexican migrants in the United States. This is a crucial distinction. Writing of the folklore of Mexican-origin groups in the United States—a community which constitutes México de afuera (the Mexican community outside the borders of national Mexico)—Paredes makes the case for three distinct bodies of vernacular expressive culture, while also offering a corrective to the shortcomings of previous hispanophile, diffusionist, and regionalist paradigms. His taxonomy identifies the folklore of (1) regional groups whose ancestors are the early settlers of the U.S. Southwest; (2) rural or semirural migrants, largely recently arrived agricultural workers who share a body of expressive culture with the regional groups and enrich their corpus with material from Mexico; (3) urban groups that borrow from those previously mentioned and fashion their resulting expressive practices in enclave communities. Despite these distinctions and the problems they pose, Paredes's research, to be truthful, focused almost exclusively on the regional folklore of Texas-Mexicans native to the Lower Rio Grande Valley. Similarly, the subjects of Limón's major ethnographic work, *Dancing with the Devil: Society and Cultural Poetics in Mexican-American South Texas* (1994), are native-born ethnic Mexicans of South Texas. In contradistinction, this book concerns the musical and poetic practices of Mexican migrants in the United States and Mexico. In this regard, my ethnography requires an augmented cultural poetics that is postnational in scope. I deploy postnationalism, however, not in reference to mere transnational cultural flows—historical or otherwise—but as a means of looking toward the ways in which vulnerable and marginalized communities fashion identities beyond the nation-state altogether, as mentioned previously. For contemporary music scholarship that seeks to attend to the Latina/o migrant experience in particular, this requires an ethnographic focus on how migrants stake a claim in the space of the U.S. nation-state through embodied aesthetic acts in contexts where their bodies are subject to dehumanizing forms of violence: the risks of border crossing, unlawful detention, racial profiling. This requires that we listen . . .

In this regard, my work expresses similarities to Patricia Zavella's (2011) recent ethnography in that it also examines behaviors, actions, and stories that spring from the experiences and perspectives of everyday life; in this case, the experiences and perspectives are those on which a lush and creative musico-poetics pivots, offering an embodied critique of the ruthless subjugation of migrant life. However, as part of rejecting melancholy as a typical Mexican trait, I diverge from the placelessness within the poetics of her title, *I'm Neither Here nor There*. Zavella and other transnational theorists suggest that migrants are constantly negotiating their identity based on a lack of belonging, a lack of place; in the case of ethnic Mexicans, they feel "as if they do not fully belong in social worlds in Mexico or the United States" (189).[25] In conversation with her ethnographic observations, I articulate through this book that migrants also often experience much more than feeling unwanted; they experience wholeness instead of lack, wherein they claim the agency and reject the exclusions that have been put on them. Migrants and their families are not perpetually in mourning, as Ricardo Ainslie (1998) argues, no more than we are perpetually anything. To say so is to fall wittingly or unwittingly into the aforementioned essentialist melancholic tropes. Ethnic studies scholars, myself included, are apt at disarticulating the problematic, invented narrative of American exceptionalism. We recognize it as an invention, or an "origin myth," as Elizabeth Martínez (1998) terms it—the idea that the United States is not an imperial nation. Yet some still latch onto other equally essentialist discourses about Mexicanness and attach them to migrants—characteristics and conditions like melancholy, mourning, fatalism—notions that should be available for deeper critical reflection and disarticulation rather than common use. Bartra supplies one set of tools to do so. In *The Cage of Melancholy: Identity and Metamorphosis in the Mexican Character* (1992), he describes how the invention of the nation of Mexico has been an othering process in which the Mexican peasant becomes inextricable from the image of the nation along with a whole range of characterizations. This othering is racial, classist, and entirely ahistorical, despite claims to critical historicity, and the final result is the invention of a form of institutional culture that obfuscates the actual workings of power. By essentializing deficiencies as entirely cultural, inequality becomes depoliticized, which was not always the intention of some of the more left-leaning literati who participated in building these stereotypes. This set of associations also connotes isolation—a *jaula* (cage), as it were—especially from progress, and through dualistic thinking this flips to "primordial savagery" (Bartra 1992: 32). Even further, indifference to death (and therefore life as well) is an invention that trails also into a miserable kind of heroic fatalism, as is apparent in the ranchero chrono-trope (61, 65). These narratives have spread through folkloristics, ethnomusicology, and anthropology and into other theoretical realms, whether delicately or in full bloom.

A good portion of this book acknowledges that cultural and spatiotemporal negotiations exist among migrants but does not qualify them as mourning or melancholic as a rule. While recognizing the fluid and ambiguous interstices that exist between dominant national and cultural systems and that challenge nationality as the primary category of identity, I nevertheless stray from the liminality of concepts like *nepantla* and third space (Anzaldúa 1987; Rouse 1991) to speak of senses of collective identity and in turn look to the vernacular analytics at hand in my ethnographic work. Therefore, this book does answer Zavella's query regarding "how and where [migrants] find the means to overcome the rifts" (2011: 189) by offering some celebratory expressive examples through huapango arribeño and storytelling. The hope is that my contribution will both enrich the field with new poetic data and encourage a wider range of approaches to music as both a medium and a part of everyday life. People's lives unfold relative to a Mexican state that habitually marginalizes them, across a border that criminalizes them, within a host nation that accepts them as laborers and little else (or a transnational capitalist enterprise interested in the migrant body as a disposable commodity), and—in the present case as it pertains to listeners and practitioners of huapango arribeño—within the arch of a *moving* expressive practice that both draws on and builds itself vis-à-vis the most present-tense currency of the here and now. I offer examples of self-authorization, instead of self-negotiation. I offer ways migrants bring each other close against the odds in moments of performance, instead of mourning those who are far away. I show how people take their places with them, both here and there (*aquí y allá*), instead of being without home or place. As Alexandra T. Vazquez suggests with respect to the culturally scripted idea of Cuban music, when we move beyond the convenient image of hermetically sealed tradition and its concomitant cultural tropes, beyond the essentialist representations of sound readily available for study or consumption, at the vernacular level "what we're really talking about is people: how they came to be a part of, what they contributed to, how they made it sound, and what directions they took it" (2013: 8).[26]

> Voy a trovarles según mi estilo
> con mi guitarra y mis compañeros
> pero aquí broto versos primeros
> porque yo siento no dar el kilo
> pero este verso yo lo perfilo

con este canto que le he pensado
en que el momento que se ha llegado
y de cantarles así sería
y hoy les entrego mi versería
MUY BUENAS NOCHES PÚBLICO HONRADO

———

I am going to improvise for you in my style
with my guitar and with my companions
but composed verses must spring forth first
because I feel I might not be capable
but this verse I have outlined
to this melody that I have composed
for this very moment, which has now arrived
to sing for you, for it was to be so
and today I give you my verses:
A VERY GOOD EVENING HONORABLE PUBLIC

—Xavi

TRACK FIVE: AURAL POETICS

Very little work has been done on huapango arribeño, except to define and preserve it, which is a typical response to a form of music deemed traditional (Olmos 2003; Cardona 2007; Parra Muñoz 2007; Jiménez de Báez 2008; Gómez-Ullate García de León 2011). It can be tempting to label huapango arribeño tradition or folklore, in part because it possesses formal performative and poetic properties that might lend it such a designation. This is particularly the case when it comes to the exclusive use of the décima and the topada performance setting, which is an encounter between two ensembles where they engage in musical and poetic flyting for hours at a time. Briefly, the décima is practiced throughout Latin America, as are forms of verbal dueling.[27] In the Mexican case, the décima is also part of the vernacular jarocho, huasteco, and Tierra Caliente traditions, though versions of it were also incorporated into the corrido.[28] Nevertheless, these very features are always breathing, and formulaic treatments are often uninterested in these shifts, save for plotting them onto a historical-geographic cartography. Although folklore and ethnomusicology in the United States have long since abandoned trait lists (Feld 1984) in favor of ethnographically grounded studies of performance (Sherzer 2002), most recently inspired by the experimental moment in anthropology (Clifford and Marcus 1986), their counterparts in Mexico have been less inclined to do so. That body of work still echoes the approach of music histories written in the post-Revolutionary period. We will explore this contention further in the next chapter. Nevertheless, I turn away from an ideologically entrenched conventional *folclor* (folklore) and instead follow the dense textures of performance. I follow an aural poetics that disrupts the peripheralizing tendencies of modernist ideology (Bauman and Briggs 2003) and dislodges the master narratives of mexicanidad reliant on the reification of vernacular forms as premodern vestiges of a former poetic world. In treating huapango arribeño just as it is—improvisational, changing, traveling—I offer instead ethnographic glimpses of how music and performance take shape within, and are shaped by, everyday people, social actors in everyday life. Performance traces eruptions of storied lives and the lives of stories, whose dispersals illuminate breaches in the "abbreviated shorthand account of nationalist myth" (Stewart 1996: 3), such that these pages are "an interaction with, rather than a comprehensive account of," huapango and Mexican music (Vazquez 2013: 9).

Let's prepare, then, to step into the gap of the unfamiliar within the most familiar of spaces. We begin with the opening where the layers of culture and society ramify, where they mount up within a social imaginary and are then aesthetically voiced into something that *moves* (physically, cognitively, and emotively). What stories are being told? What makes them possible? How do they exist as sites of cultural struggle and connection? The question of Mexico and its people has nearly always leaned on the immovable structures and monuments of national identity, as so many intellectuals have ruminated on in the past and continue to. This self-referential loop—to draw on Kathleen Stewart, Brian Massumi, and Gilles Deleuze and Félix Guattari—encircles and animates an allegorizing master narrative of mexicanidad. The challenge, then, is to speak of expressive cultural production in relation to Mexican migrant personhood in a way that does not source material from a distance or lean on assumptions about culture and identity (oftentimes entrenched in the ranchero chrono-trope) but rather draws on people and listens to their stories, an argument that cannot be made without their voices, for this is where the connections between everyday life and performance are intensely felt, where they move around like a body through crowded Mexico City streets, rushing out of the Rio Grande and past the thicket of South Texas brush, meandering slowly in between calm patches of yard in rural Mississippi . . . Huapango arribeño readily connects with these intensely storied experiences amid dense somatic moments where individuals use their creative capacities to enable sites for aural textualizations of their otherwise silenced voices and marginalized bodies.[29] Rendered neither a disembodied data set nor the once-removed subjects of cultural translation, the voices that speak confront us with the hard reality that expressive culture often circulates under brutal circumstances. It plays a vital role in refiguring lived subjectivities and geographies—a "daily framing of life" (Stephen 2007: 5) that, in the case of huapango arribeño, comprises interwoven music and verses.

Sounds of Crossing informs a material understanding of the border through bordered lives where creative moments are the inception of very real possibilities, a series of disruptive proliferations. Unexpected and aparallel movements challenge the assumed linearity of migration, of assimilation, as well as the calcified walls of culture, of the border, of America. Here, intimacies take off into other things—reflections, life paths, explorations, loss, renewal—back-and-forth and back again. Here, expressive practices comprise movements that deride border logics. They explode into intimate moments spent with others in the present, in the past, across geographies; into intensities that are felt, that expand out—the residues that cross and stick.[30] Rather than a series of discontinuous, deterritorialized absences from state and homeland, I present the movements of Mexican migrants through huapango arribeño, offering a perspective that takes into account how multiple presences, homes, intimacies, and relationships figure into processes of tethering-while-untethering, the adjacency between places seemingly distant—the *doing* in any claim of undoing. The locational movements of huapango arribeño certainly matter, but so does its embedded expression in a U.S. context, that is, the way it lends credence to subjectivities articulated through music and poetry that stake claims of belonging, that voice solidarities across borders in daily life and thus connect people to the space of the U.S. nation-state in ways that ascribe new meanings to citizenship. These new meanings are indeed postnational, not because they exceed the physical and cultural confines of Mexico, but because with each huapango in the offing beneath the arch of illegality, migrants assert their right to exist and know themselves beyond the structural violence enacted at the level of the nation-state. Here, performance is a necessity, it is ongoing, it is an act of becoming. This is what twenty-first-century American life sounds like in places where huapango arribeño is thriving during afternoon fiestas and all-night performances. These are the sounds of crossing: sonic and performative transgressions across the territorial borders of the two nations and beyond the essentialist boundaries of Mexican and American national identities, imagining new ways of existing against the grain of history. Let us take up the call and listen.

TWO

COMPANIONS OF THE CALLING

The poetic voice is the most flexible of voices.
—DON IHDE, *LISTENING AND VOICE*

Since intimate feeling is a burn-off, it is burning-off that expresses it,
not the thing, which is its negation.
—GEORGES BATAILLE, *THE ACCURSED SHARE*

Son cosas de la vida, cosas del destino.
(They are matters of life, matters of the calling.)
—HOMERO, TEXAS

I heard the phone ring. I didn't recognize the number, but I answered the call. The muted voice on the other end sounded familiar; its cadence drew me in— Homero. My face lit up (as I was later told by the people I was with). We hadn't spoken in months, since my move to the Midwest from Texas. He updated me on life back home, his job situation (always precarious given his undocumented status), and the oppressive heat—sure, the muggy weather, but more so *la migra*. He dovetailed this with news of Valentín, another huapanguero: "Lo echaron pa' México hace un poquito. Según lo paró la policía y vieron que no tenía papeles. Lo encerraron por un tiempo y luego lo echaron." (They deported him to Mexico not too long ago. The police supposedly stopped him and saw that he didn't have papers. They locked him up for a while and then deported him.) Shocked, I asked Homero for details—when, where, how Valentín is doing, where he is—none of which Homero could answer with any certainty. As we both struggled to trace the sequence of events, he finally sighed as if offering a kind of solace: "Son cosas de la vida, cosas del destino" (They are matters of life, matters of the calling). In colloquial Mexican Spanish, *destino* (destiny) means "life path" or "fate." Among huapangueros, *el destino* also serves as a referential gloss for their artistic vocation—musicians "siguen el destino" (follow a calling). They give themselves to the art of huapango arribeño. However, there is also an augmented meaning at play that exceeds music making as a life path. More important, *el destino* expresses a connective resonance with a multiplicity of intimacies produced through performance and in everyday life. Take Homero's pairing: "matters of life" and "matters of *el destino.*" If one didn't know this adjacent meaning, his statement might seem redundant: "matters of life, matters of a life path." However, his specific reference to el destino enacts a semantic distinction from *life path* that simultaneously signals a tangled connection between matters of living and matters of performance, where music making is necessarily shaped by the unfolding trajectories of living itself. Huapangueros speak of el destino with great ceremony, a reverence for the intensity and responsibility wrapped up in the act of aesthetic engagement alongside fellow huapangueros. The energy expended in performance reverberates; it enacts an aesthetic mode of sociality with those listening. Audiences expect to be fully engaged musically and poetically, taking on an evaluative role, and practitioners must fully adhere to this responsibility, which gives their craft the utmost associational resonance, particularly when they attend to matters of everyday life. This social surround—or dialectical expressive relationality—opens up the auditory field of huapango arribeño, making it legible across temporal and spatial settings (Ihde 2007: 73). This overflowing of performance and sociality explains the common address musicians use with one another: *compañeros del destino*—companions in life, companions of the calling—something reminiscent of Mark Slobin's affinity groups, or "charmed circles of like-minded music-makers who are drawn magnetically to a certain genre that creates strong expressive bonding" (1993: 98).

In what follows, I detail the musico-poetic design and performance of huapango arribeño and the ways in which it produces this shared sentiment. As a way of revising conventional narratives that would otherwise fix huapango "tradition" in place, I argue that back-and-forth movement is integral to huapango arribeño at the levels of migration, the dialogic topada performance, and the cultural syncretism central to the historical making of Mexican vernacular stringed musics.

ENCOUNTERS

Anduve de sheetrockero
también en la construcción
a veces de jardinero
con diferente patrón

yo soy derecho y sincero
les digo de corazón.

En mi mente está grabado
siempre recuerdo ese día
por ser indocumentado
me aprehendió la policía
en mi troca Silverado
a mi casa conducía.

Carretera ochenta y tres
que corre de sur a norte
todo me salió al revés
por no tener pasaporte
a declarar con el juez
me llevaron a la corte.

———

I went about as a sheetrock worker
likewise laboring in construction
sometimes as a gardener
working with different bosses
I am trustworthy and sincere
I say this from the heart.

Engrained in my mind
I always recall the day when
for being undocumented
the police apprehended me
in my Silverado truck
as I was driving home.

Highway 83
that runs from south to north
everything ended in misfortune
for not having a passport
to stand before the judge
they hauled me off to court.

Valentín wrote these *sextillas* (six-line stanzas) while he was being held in an immigration detention facility in central Texas awaiting his deportation proceeding. The federal Secure Communities initiative—replaced by the nearly identical Priority Enforcement Program in July 2015—enlisted local law enforcement in implementing the federal mandate of identifying and removing all criminal aliens who posed a threat to public safety. Over two million people had been deported as of September 2011. In time between being arrested and being deported, individuals like Valentín are subject to the humiliations of extralegal detention, a highly profitable enterprise outsourced to the likes of Halliburton, Geo Group, and the Corrections Corporation of America (recently renamed CoreCivic) (Akers Chacón and Davis 2006).[1] Unlike other spheres of social life, which have witnessed the retraction of the neoliberal state, this restructured security framework has grown exponentially.[2] "It's good business . . ." Valentín feels lucky, however. He was held for only two weeks:

> Me echaron a [Nuevo] Laredo. Y llegué con cuarenta dólares que tenía en el bolsillo. Y dije, "¿Qué hago?" A las once de la noche, ahí me soltaron en el puente, dije, "¿Qué hago?" Y bien peligroso. Pero traía mi celular y con una rayita [de recepción]. Me acordé que traía el número de un primo que tengo en [Nuevo] Laredo. Dije, "Ojalá que ande aquí." Y que le habló y que contesta, le dije, "Aquí estoy, primo." "No te muevas de ahí, ahorita mando por ti," me dijo, "no te preocupes." Me llevó a su casa. Me estuve una semana ahí.

> ———————————

> (They deported me to [Nuevo] Laredo. And I arrived with forty dollars in my pocket. I thought to myself, "What do I do?" At eleven o'clock at night, they let me go there at the bridge. I thought to myself, "What do I do?" It was dangerous. But I had my cell phone, and it had one bar [of reception]. I remembered that I had the number of a cousin of mine who lives in [Nuevo] Laredo. I thought, "Hopefully he's around." So I called him up, and he answered, I told him, "I'm here, cousin." "Stay where you are, I'll send someone over to get you," he said. "Don't you worry." He took me to his house. I stayed there a week.)

Valentín was working in construction in San Antonio at the time he was apprehended and commuted from where he was living outside of Austin by way of Highway 83—east of the more heavily trafficked and policed I-35. This alternate route seemed safer, but, as it turns out, a minor traffic violation landed him in jail and subsequently in ICE custody—a recurring story for many undocumented migrants held in detention for nonviolent offenses.

After a week in Laredo, he made it back to his hometown in northern Querétaro before settling across the state line in Guanajuato. That region—the Sierra Gorda—is where Valentín grew up. He never went to school, working the *milpa* (cornfield) with his father instead. He later began making a living playing huapango arribeño, learning to play the violin at the age of fourteen. He remembers, "Oía unas cuerdas y se me enchinaba el cuero" (I would hear the sound of strings, and I would get goose bumps). He began playing professionally in the late 1970s and had his first topadas shortly thereafter.

His life as a huapanguero is not separable from his life as a transnational migrant. After arriving in the United States for the first time at the age of seventeen, he picked oranges in Florida, then labored in construction in Nashville, and, just before being deported, was working for a masonry company in San Antonio, though he also did drywall from time to time. Equally versatile in matters of huapango, he also dabbles in poetry, although a violinist by trade. His stanzas above voice the story of countless migrants who work hard, negotiate everyday geographies, and often encounter (sometimes violently) the state.

After speaking with Homero, I tried to reach Valentín. I acquired the phone number of a *caseta* (public phone stall) in the rural community in Querétaro he was supposedly living in. Anticipating an upcoming trip to nearby Xichú, Guanajuato, I thought I might be able to see him. I called before and during my trip. No luck. Within hours of arriving in Xichú, however, just as I was making my way to the local caseta there to phone family back in Texas, surreally, as if we'd anticipated each other's presence, I saw Valentín walking toward me on the sunny street. He called out. I paused in near disbelief. We embraced and walked down the hill to the modest room he was renting. He immediately filled me in about his moves: his forcible removal from the United States and then his move from Querétaro to Guanajuato. He settled in Xichú a few months back.

We whisked through details so as to attend to what was really on both of our minds—the huapango arribeño performance taking place the following evening. Every year in the mountains of northeastern Guanajuato, the town of Xichú celebrates the coming of the New Year with a festival surrounding a climactic topada performance (more on the festival in the next chapter). There, two huapango arribeño ensembles—made up of two violins (the lead and second fiddle, or *primera* and *segunda vara*), a *guitarra quinta huapanguera* (larger modified eight-string bass guitar, similar to the more common six-stringed version), and a *vihuela* or *jarana huasteca* (different types of small five-stringed chordophones)—face each other across the central plaza, engaging in a musical and poetic encounter that lasts for hours, beginning late on the night of December 31 and lasting through the next morning. The days leading up to the topada are filled with townwide gatherings centered around music and art. People from all over the region and beyond attend, nearly tripling the town's population. This is why I was there, and what Valentín and I were nearly giddy about. We wondered what dynamic would emerge between the two ensembles set to encounter one another. The music and poetics that bloom during topadas often surprise not only the audience but the huapangueros themselves. Valentín has been in plenty of topadas and knows this well. We imagined the intensity of performance, reaching a fever pitch as thousands of people dance at midnight and continue to stomp their feet through the dawn, finally stopping at noon the next day.

Indeed, that night of the performance, at its edges, just before the light of dawn, both Valentín and I paused, speechless. We locked eyes as one ensemble unveiled a new musical overture—the simultaneous life and death of this melody oscillated between major and minor keys, a dizzying arrangement that baited the other ensemble across the way to respond in kind. I shivered, beginning in my feet and up through my skin. As the moment came alive, the thousands around us were shaking the ground beneath us with every patterned stomp, a vigorous current that prompted shouts of elation despite the bitter cold. Our bodies followed along with the physical waves of sound and thundering energy into a state of alertness. That moment became an hour, ten hours, seemingly eternal, before it was suddenly over.

When I describe a topada to those unfamiliar with it, they are often amazed at the thought of an eight-, ten-, or twelve-hour back-and-forth, at that level of intensity, on the part of both the performers and the audience. The excessive nature of the time and energy spent is unlike so many other performance styles. In that very excess lies the conviviality, the tones and tensions, and the laborious explorations that I have come to know as crucial to huapango as an intertextual and polyphonic locus of aesthetic enactments and responses. Pulses of dialogic engagement align and spiral out, touching those present and performing—a type of hanging on to every word, every note, ever conscious of the risks taken at each turn. Think of huapango arribeño as a dense, musical architecture that yields a rhythmic and poetic complex. It has jagged, sharp edges in structure, timbre, and tone. There is gravity behind the sudden drops and shifts between verses and melodies. You become attentive to these modulations; they snag the ears—extreme changes that move you, catch you, confront you.

Listening, Charles Briggs suggests, is not merely the act of assessing how "what is said" is an accurate "reflection of what is 'out there'" but also an engaged moment of communicative exchange where we interact with our social surroundings and likewise contribute to their construction (1986: 3). Listening is an active and continuous negotiation of the "out there" or the building of context—"an agentive process" (Berger 2009: 13). The body listens along with the ears. The mind listens to the environment, not just the most highly symbolic content. To listen, then, is to participate in a communicative unfolding in which sound is shared as a "subject of all 'subjects'" (Nancy 2007: 41). Here, the body is "a resonance chamber or column of beyond-meaning" that opens up both presence and sense (31, 25). This understanding applies to all manner of discursive interactions, most certainly huapango arribeño's dramatic topada performance. This beckons attention to the construction of sounds between practitioners and listeners across this interactional space of discursive encounter. Harris M. Berger's concept of stance is useful in conceptualizing the layered meanings brought into performance, or the "affective, stylistic, or valual quality" of the subject's (intentional) social engagement (or "grappling") with items of performance and the manner in which performance is subsequently brought into experience (2009: 21). Berger distinguishes between the performer's approach to the performative text (compositional stance) and the way the listener "actively constitutes the music in her experience through perceptual practices" (audience stance) (13).

Listening also pertains to my own subject position in relation to the *words* and moments voiced linguistically throughout this chapter, specifically, and the book more generally—my stance. As researchers, we play a key role in generating data from our interlocutors, placing ourselves in circumstances where we coax and/or witness verbal interactions. Unfortunately, the interview, the methodological approach we rely on most, often impedes us from gaining competence in speech repertoires and modes of communication particular to the communities in which we do our research, depriving "the researcher of an adequate sense as to how the information she or he obtains fits into broader patterns of thinking, feeling, and speaking" (Briggs 1986: 2).[3] This conventional metacommunicative routine veils its own performative capacity. This concern, however, offers the possibility for critical reflection on how our present-tense social entanglement has the capacity to change the balance of politics, to short-circuit the authorial flows of power, in the hopes that we can discover how the self is dialogized. This is where one's embodied presence (voice) enters an entanglement between our storied selves and others' stories. And this is where ethnography becomes "a point of impact, curiosity, encounter" (Stewart 2007: 5). These realizations are drawn from my presence alongside practitioners and listeners alike, principally as a student and performer of these musics, in moments that preceded and extended beyond the supposed bounds of the methodological science of fieldwork. One can write so-called ethnography without experiencing these communicative frames in the guise of objectivity, but such an approach forcefully diverges from this listening I have described and in doing so reinscribes the distance between ethnographer and subject. I keep this polemic in mind to demonstrate next how huapango arribeño fits into the landscape of Mexican vernacular musics.

A TROUBLED GENRE

Drawing on Charles Briggs and Richard Bauman's (1992) work on intertextuality, the remainder of this chapter makes a case for huapango arribeño as a multivoiced participatory aesthetic that exceeds received understandings of national folklore. I draw on their critique of the limitations of genre—particularly the classificatory perspective—and apply these insights to the category of Mexican vernacular stringed music referred to as *son*. To return to a point made in previous chapters, the diverse variants identified as types of Mexican music have been historically constituted by shifting sociocultural processes and interrelationships of encounter. Often viewed through a primordialist lens, those deemed traditional are homologized with culture in ways that essentialize them as authentic practices of assumed heritage, fixed in time and space (Madrid 2008: 52). Interestingly, while the officialized narratives that surround son as a musical genre tip their hat to processes of cultural hybridity—typically noting the indigenous, European, and African mestizaje at play in the musics' formation—they simultaneously position particular variants of son as closed musical domains, thus deeming certain forms to be authentic representations. Taken to its logical end, this position considers all other sounds to be outside the borders of tradition. In other words, in fashioning ideal types, this teleology denies the very hybridity celebrated on the surface. This conflict of perspectives surrounding authenticity, tradition, cultural patrimony, autonomous expression, folklorized spectacle, and the state with regard to both performance and scholarship is robust and well represented in the literature (Alonso Bolaños 2008; Chamorro 2000; Meierovich

1995). Moreover, this tension is presently playing itself out in the grassroots transnational practice of son jarocho among U.S. Latinas/os, largely those of Mexican descent, in places like Los Angeles, Chicago, Austin, and New York City. The practicing of son jarocho outside of Veracruz, Mexico, has raised questions of authority, repertoire, and the uses of tradition in new social spaces. While some practitioners and scholars would hold onto fixed notions of form and performance, a host of young scholars—many of them also jarocho musicians—are exploring how an emergent crop of transnational *jaraneros* (son jarocho practitioners) are challenging, living out, and resignifying the meanings of that music as part of the ongoing flux and change so much a part of the transformative story of son jarocho (Balcomb 2012; Bearns Esteva 2011; Díaz-Sánchez 2009; M. González 2009; Loa 2005; Loza 1992; Sánchez-Tello 2012).[4] Similarly, the mariachi world has grappled with this debate for decades with respect to the circuits and politics of its practice outside Mexico (Rodríguez 2006; Sheehy 2006).

The questions raised through these intertextual tensions center around what tradition is and who gets to define it. In agreement with the above scholars, I too argue that the everyday practice of these musical forms exceeds the borders of essentialism and idyllic typologies. Ultimately, the myth of authenticity is a simulacrum, as Alejandro L. Madrid argues with respect to Mexican folk-derived popular styles like norteña (accordion-based music from northern Mexico, specifically the states of Tamaulipas, Nuevo León, and Coahuila) and banda (brass music from Mexico's Pacific coast; the state of Sinaloa is a primary site), now grouped under the regional Mexican category—authenticity is "a discourse that occupies the place of reality in the imagination of those who adopt it" (2008: 17). Reality, however, is not an essentialist bedrock of the real that exists behind myth but, rather, a recognition of the processes of resignification crucial to the construction of all expressive practices over time.[5] On closer inspection, the supposedly immovable sonic monuments on which rigid musical identities are constructed are anything but. Musical forms and practices are always in flux; they are the site of multiple and competing struggles for the construction of identity in shifting social contexts—a process perhaps most recognizable as the ongoing dynamic between maintenance and innovation.

To return to huapango arribeño, it, like many other regional forms, falls outside of the official cartographies of Mexican folk musics, most notably in studies chronicling the son genre, which it most closely resembles (Mendoza 1956; Moreno Rivas 1979; Reuter 1992; G. Saldívar 1934; Sheehy 1998;

Stanford 1972, 1984). From Gabriel Saldívar's *Historia de la música en México (épocas precortesanas y colonial)* (1934), through the mid-twentieth-century décima scholarship of Vicente T. Mendoza, to more contemporary accounts offered by Thomas Stanford (1984) and Jas Reuter (1992), huapango arribeño is not mentioned.[6] This elision comes into relief if we consider the problematic character of the son typology itself and the expressive cartography it privileges. The term *son* in the Spanish-speaking world has existed as a reference to music making since the seventeenth and eighteenth centuries.[7] Its use to denote a genre-specific music type in Mexico, however, materialized in the early twentieth century in tandem with that country's modernist ideologies of mexicanidad and its racial discourses of mestizaje. At this historical juncture, educators, intellectuals, and state officials began the work of emplotting grassroots expressions into a newly constructed master narrative of Mexican ethnoracial identity that deemphasized localized and pluriethnic cultural practices and subjectivities.[8] Thus, in the first music histories written in the post-Revolutionary period, the term *son* is utilized to enfold a cluster of regional music forms—similar in style—into an officialized discursive field operative in promoting a singular national music culture (Turino 2003). This strategy is one outcome of a much larger debate among intellectuals shaping what would become the chief expressive manifestations of Mexican nationalism, an ensemble of symbols to brace the iconography of the national character, in which the idea of an assumed and shared folklore would be touted as the emblematic core of Mexican identity (Bohlman 1988: 54). While some sought to craft a nationalist aesthetic in the image of high Enlightenment tradition, others were more attuned to vernacular *criollista* (creole), indigenist, and populist forms that would enable essentialist claims to mexicanidad (Madrid 2009).[9] In some ways, the expressive scaffolding we have inherited is a product of both. Here, the emergence of state-sponsored education programs and staged festivals featuring sanitized "folkloric" performances of select *aires nacionales* (national anthems)—primarily of the jarocho and Tierra Caliente varieties (Campos 1928; Jáuregui 2007; Madrid 2009: 117)—were central to canonizing particular folk musics to "be inflicted upon their citizens" (Corona and Madrid 2008: 6).[10]

While formal musical particularities were less detailed in earlier music studies, a number of the musics placed beneath the arch of what is considered son do exhibit common musicological features, as Daniel Edward Sheehy points out, that lend the term a certain utility. Son variants, music scholars have come to suggest, are typified by the following: (1) they are played almost exclusively using stringed instruments (though percussive elements may be found in certain types); (2) Spanish poetic forms are the primary lyrical conventions; (3) they are predominantly performed in triple meter; and (4) they are associated with terpsichorean practices.[11] To a degree, these traits distinguish these forms from other genres of Mexican musics—the corrido (Mexican ballad), the canción ranchera (country song), the accordion-driven norteña of northern Mexico, and the brass and woodwind banda of the Pacific coast region (Sheehy 1998). When considering the aforementioned attributes as defining musical contours, scholars and musicians alike identify a number of son variants, including (1) *son de la Tierra Caliente*, from the states of Guerrero, Michoacán, and portions of Jalisco, Colima, and Nayarít, whose types include the *planeco, calentano, abajeño*, and *jalisciense*; (2) *son de la Costa Chica*, in the states of Guerrero and Oaxaca, where the Mexican version of the South American *cueca*, known as the *chilena*, is practiced—although its inclusion in the genre is contested; (3) son jarocho of Veracruz; and (4) *son huasteco*, which is practiced along Mexico's central Gulf coast in the huasteca regions of Hidalgo, Puebla, Querétaro, San Luís Potosí, and Veracruz. Rather than flatten the complexities of this expressive corpus by deeming it evidence of a musical mestizaje, the genesis of these formal properties should be interrogated as an expansive political economy of historical influence, encounter, cultural violence, and acculturation among indigenous, African, and European (largely Spanish) populations across Mexico. To treat the origins of huapango arribeño is to understand it as part of a similarly conceived process of syncretic exchange and building through which a diverse set of peoples carved out ways of life and means of expression under extreme circumstances.

Again, huapango arribeño's region of origin is where the states of Guanajuato, Querétaro, and San Luís Potosí come together. Presently, the huapango arribeño four-member ensemble consists of two violins, a vihuela (also utilized in the son de la Tierra Caliente) or a jarana huasteca (commonplace in the son huasteco), and the guitarra quinta huapanguera (also used in the son huasteco).[12] However, the ensemble's configuration has changed over time. For instance, while the core instrumentation of six-stringed guitar and violin seems to date to the late nineteenth century, a sundry of other instruments have been featured along the way, according to oral accounts, including the clarinet, *requinto* (a lead guitar or perhaps mandolin), *bajo quinto/sexto* (an instrument used in the accordion-based norteña music), and *guitarrón* (a bass instrument used in mariachi). Mentions of both the vihuela's and the jarana huasteca's inclusion date to the 1930s, though widespread usage did not occur until the late 1960s. The vihuela had dominated over the jarana until recently, but the latter is now becoming popular again. Similarly, the guitarra quinta huapanguera, while also mentioned as early as the 1930s, did not become widely used until the late 1960s and 1970s. It is not known exactly when the décima made its way to the Sierra Gorda, nor is it clear exactly when huapango arribeño became consolidated into the musical form we come to recognize. Collective memory in the region, nonetheless, extends back to the mid-nineteenth century, when a number of troubadours and musicians were alive and performing in precursory *controversias* similar to the topada—these early troubadours and those performing at the turn of the twentieth century include Eugenio Villanueva, José Torres, José Ceballos, Tranquilino Méndez, Pancho Berrones, Pantaleón Rodríguez, Antonio López, José Rosales, and Mauro's father. Those born during the social upheaval of the Mexican Revolution include Eleuterio López, Agapito Briones, Antonio García, Antonio Escalante, Ernesto Medina, Nico Montalvo, and Mauro himself. The following generation, mostly born between World Wars I and II (during the Global Depression of the 1930s), includes Guadalupe Reyes, Asención Aguilar, Adrián Turrubiartes, Juan Rodríguez, Miguel González, Ismael Orduña, and Teodoro Ruiz. The more notable troubadours born in the 1940s and 1950s, who then emerge as practitioners in the 1960s and 1970s, are Cándido Martínez, Ángel González, Asención Meza, and Guillermo Velázquez. The subsequent cohort largely populates the pages of this book; many of them are referred to using pseudonyms.

As far as violinists are concerned, some of the noted deceased practitioners include Román Gómez, Ceferino Juárez, Lorenzo López, Eusebio "Chebo" Méndez (the son of Tranquilino Méndez), Simón Castillo, and Otílio Villeda.[13] Though ostensibly part of the older generation, Lorenzo Camacho, Franco Rivera, and Los Cucos (Isidro Rodríguez and his son, Refugio Rodríguez) are still living and occasionally perform.[14]

The little research that exists on huapango arribeño has brought together a diverse set of perspectives, including those of academics, lay folklorists, and native scholars (Carracedo Navarro 2000, 2003; Olmos 2003; Velázquez 2004; Cardona 2007; Parra Muñoz 2007; Jiménez de Báez 2008; Gómez-Ullate García de León 2011; González-Paraíso 2014). As of late, the voice of ethnohistorian Rafael Parra Muñoz seems to ring loudest in this intertextual exchange. Mostly concerned with detailing the historical formation of huapango arribeño, his bachelor's thesis, "Tradición y sociedad: El devenir de las velaciones y el huapango de la Zona Media y la Sierra Gorda" (2007), paradoxically erects a fixed understanding of what this musico-poetic practice ought to be. This leads him to dismiss its most contemporary practitioners and their craft as inauthentic.[15] When discussing huapango poetic renderings of labor migration, he diminishes them as a peripheral brand of "politicized poesía" inimical to tradition and then—as a self-proclaimed arbiter—gives us the final word on the ideal role of the troubadour: "Si bien el trovador puede informar, criticar, educar, su función principal es la de divertir" (Sure, the troubadour may inform, critique, educate, [but] his principal function is to amuse) (71). Parra Muñoz's blasé flattening perhaps emerges from his absentee approach, in which, as Kathleen Stewart warns, "it is acceptable (even politically correct) to 'explain' another culture by rewriting its story from a distance with the help of external metanarrative themes" (1991: 402).[16] The reification of vernacular practices as premodern tradition, in this regard, ignores the unfolding dynamic of tradition as an actively shaping and transformative cultural force that expressively handles time and space in relation to social institutions and formations. Rather than approaching "associations of place, people, and culture [as] social and historical creations to be explained, not given natural facts" (Gupta and Ferguson 1997: 4), portrayals of "other cultures" as *dwelling*, in the words of James Clifford (1997), carry on the much-critiqued isolated-totality perspective that is indisposed to "ethnography beyond cultures" (Gupta and Ferguson 1997). In contrast, throughout this book I position huapango arribeño as a living and breathing, expressively structured vehicle through which people voice their concerns and perspectives across the shifting topographies of social and political life.

Leaping into the gap of the unfamiliar, into the space of performance alongside my interlocutors, I've come to recognize huapango arribeño as a connective throwing together, an entangled compositional moment constituted by intimate "modes of knowing, relating, and attending to"—acts of listening (Stewart 2008: 73). This is never more audible than in moments like those described by Abel, a troubadour from Guanajuato, as he speaks of this shared entanglement within the topada performance:

> El poeta tiene que recibir a el otro pa' que vaya la cosa pareja. . . . La topada es cuestión de armonía, no es ofensiva o defensiva. Comoquiera uno se tiene que estar cuidando para que la gente esté captando el tema de que se trate. Entre dos músicas se encadena y florece. . . . La gente está entusiasmada para escuchar a uno y uno recibe el cariño que ellos le están mandando.

(The poet must receive the other [poet] so that things are on an even keel.... The topada is a question of harmony; it's not about offense or defense. No matter what, one has to be cautious so that the audience is cognizant of the poetic theme that is being attended to. Between the two ensembles there is a linking, and [performance] blooms.... The people are excited to hear you, and you receive the affection they give you.)

To return to Briggs and Bauman (1992), given its musicological features, huapango arribeño may be linked to an abstracted model of music, son in this instance. To do so without critical reflection, however, is to passively accept the nationalist sentiments indexically connected to this genre, as described above. If we recall, the previous chapter explored the modernist distancing embedded in the ranchero chrono-trope that is so much a part of the sonic iconography of mexicanidad. However, when taken intertextually, the simultaneous ordering and disordering aspects of genre become evident. Consequently, huapango arribeño may be viewed as both necessarily ordered—it possesses certain conventions that link it generically to similar sounds deemed to be son—and open-ended, for it necessarily extends beyond its "present setting of production or reception" and is thus connected to other times, places, and communities and certainly to sounds that fall outside of the son typology (147–148). Given this dynamic, no generic scheme can provide a final, consistent, or all-encompassing systemic account. The challenge is to follow the moves and flows of performance across physical and metaphysical borders— the inherent tension in its simultaneous cohesion and nonfixity—for the relationships within and across expressive forms necessarily produce order and disorder. Intertextuality, or the construction of relationships among texts (in this case, musical variants) that produce generic links, also results in gaps between them. These gaps may be minimized or highlighted, and the strategies for doing so are implicated in ideological motives necessarily connected to broader social, political, economic, and historical circumstances crucial in producing genres and their uses.

Nevertheless, to suggest that changes in music culture and/or the ways in which musics are framed parallel changes in society is hardly a world-shattering revelation. In the body of music scholarship on Greater Mexico, I am preceded by, most notably, Américo Paredes (1958) and his groundbreaking work on the corrido of border conflict.[17] Still, given the troubled perspective offered by scholars like Parra Muñoz, I am motivated to make this argument as it pertains to the multiple voicings of huapango arribeño. To be sure, in his interrogation of the genealogies of folkloristics, Briggs attends "to the way Paredes simultaneously created a critical model of how the circulation of folklore shapes and is shaped by politics of culture and cultures of politics, including how cultural forms move and how such movements become objects of representation" (2012: 94–95). Along these lines, vernacular performance is "actively made through the circulation of social representations and aesthetic forms through time and space," and its enactments endeavor to map the ways in which these multiple knowledges and communicative practices circulate (96). In parallel fashion, other institutionalized cultural forms (i.e., media accounts, legal discourses, popular culture) also offer particular renderings of events and everyday life. However, these representational practices usually claim that their models of circulation and communicable cartographies constitute authoritative accounts. Similarly, folkloristics is guilty of reifying its own selective metapragmatic projections of circulation as definitive "reflections of how cultural forms are actively circulating" (97). And, as a modernist project, the son paradigm is complicit in domesticating vernacular expressive practices, that is, in mapping them allá (out there), suspending them in time, while both heralding them as the essence of the national soul and necessarily reinscribing them as backward. Given its absence in the genre's construction, huapango arribeño rests at the periphery of this othering language space.[18]

Taking a more nuanced approach, the remainder of this chapter attends to the structural anatomy of the improvisational style with regard to its poetic conventions, musical elements, and the context and rules guiding the nexus of performance. I consider this a necessary task, as most readers will be unacquainted with what this music sounds like and no other major source exists on the topic. Still, I do not mistake description for critical thinking. I trace a host of dynamic intertextual becomings such that any hoped-for or relied-on categories fall apart instantly. On this very point, Guillermo Velázquez succinctly summarizes the changes in huapango arribeño over time: "Se van consensando maneras sin hablarse" (One reaches an unspoken consensus). Musicians are always "searching for handles on cultural domains and [they] share these with one another in an effort to coarticulate their horizons of focused consciousness" to produce performance through performance itself (McDowell 2010: 128). As such, ethnographic moments attentive to acts of (music) making have, in my experience, yielded more important insights into the implications of huapango arribeño than the setting up of categorical arguments based on generic taxonomies (and forms), or, worse yet, textual dichotomies that define what is ideal-typical huapango arribeño and what is not, for these are insufficient means to understand the stances both practitioners and listeners take in coconstituting the atmosphere of performance.

FUNDAMENTO: POETICS, SEMIOSIS, AND SOCIALITY

The wind whips around everyone's faces, dancing furiously across bodies struggling to warm themselves against the autumn chill. It's dusk, and the sky is wide, loud, clamoring with huapango melodies and church bells above. It's Victoria, Guanajuato, and the musicians are at the northern end of the town's central plaza, surrounded by dancers and onlookers. In momentary pauses, in between violins and patterned steps, a raspy, labored voice belts out verses, casting them out into the wind. The voice belongs to the troubadour Amador. I walk up in the company of Gabino, a musician who is to perform later that evening. In the meantime, he grabs something to eat from a vendor and takes in the sights and sounds. I join him.

Amador spots Gabino through the crowd and begins to improvise a decimal—a base quatrain glossed by a corresponding set of four décimas. Distracted while greeting others, I miss the beginning but am quickly pulled in by the rest.

APRECIABLE DON GABINO
PORQUE ASÍ YO LO REQUIERO
COMO DIGNO COMPAÑERO
COMPAÑERO DEL DESTINO

(1) a—
b—
b—
a—
a—
c—
c—
d—honorable compañero
d—lo saludo y lo estimo y lo quiero
C—APRECIABLE DON GABINO

(2) En hacerle reverencia
aquí con la melodía
conmemorando este día

hoy día de la Independencia
hoy que Don Gabino está a la presencia
porque lo estimo y lo quiero
y yo como un guitarrero
saludos le quiero dar
porque es digno de apreciar
PORQUE ASÍ YO LO REQUIERO

(3) Mis intenciones son mías
y es muy digno de apreciar
tocando con Don Pilar
las noches, las agonías
y al trovar mis verserías
con estímulo sincero
yo como un versero
a usted lo quiero elogiar
permítame el apreciar
COMO DIGNO COMPAÑERO

(4) Al hallarme conversando
en esta fecha del mes
porque anda con Andrés
pues dondequiera tocando
de las fiestas disfrutando
sufrir lluvia, remolino
decirlo se me aprevino
porque así yo lo requiero
Gabino, apreciable compañero
COMPAÑERO DEL DESTINO

———

ADMIRABLE DON GABINO
FOR I DEMAND THIS OF MYSELF
AS A DIGNIFIED COMPANION
COMPANION OF THE CALLING

(1)a—
b—
b—
a—

a—

c—

c—

d—honorable companion

d—I greet him, and think highly of him, and care for him

C—ADMIRABLE DON GABINO

(2) As I pay him homage

here with this melody

commemorating this day

Independence Day[19]

today that Don Gabino is present

because I think highly of him and care for him

and I as a guitarrero

I want to greet him

because he is worthy of praise

FOR I DEMAND THIS OF MYSELF

(3) My intentions are mine

he is worthy of praise

as I play with Don Pilar

through agonizing nights

and as I improvise my versings

with sincere energy

I, as a poet,

want to praise you

allow me this gesture

AS A DIGNIFIED COMPANION

(4) As I find myself conversing

on this day of the month

because he goes about with Andrés[20]

well, performing anywhere,

immersed in festive gatherings

suffering rain and windstorms

it dawned on me to say this

for this is how I call on you

Gabino, admirable companion,

COMPANION OF THE CALLING

I listen and instantly feel the trembling of the sensing hairs within my ears, caught by verses that describe the changes we can all sense, spatially, bodily. "Suffering rain and windstorms"—we feel the whipping of air on our faces, wet and heavy, the music tells us, though the present darkness above is dry and frigid. Who knows which feet are stomping, and which are still?

Intimacy, Georges Bataille (1991) describes, is achieved by surpassing the self, where one's own body engages in ecstatic communication with another or many others, allowing for a type of communion, often realized along unknown paths that release the self from the enclosures of scarcity and utility.[21] This unbinding, as Jürgen Habermas and Frederick Lawrence (1984) illustrate in their own reading of Bataille, is a process though which alienation dissipates through moments of unmitigated closeness with the other, surrendering subjectivity; in the present case, this is where individuals stand and lean on each other's shoulders in the act of performance and how that transformative experience of self-transcendence is paradoxically a resonant point of surrender that binds "us" in order to "retrieve those experiences exposed in ecstasy," where the performative moment is one of transition—intense and labored— through which musicians become *companions of the calling*. This helps understand why, upon seeing Gabino from afar, Amador is overcome with the desire to express this very sentiment, where his poetics tells everyone that "I" am here, "we've" been there—companions recalling, knowing, imagining, and creating all at once with words and notes soon lost to the night, but for memory.

Huapango arribeño's most salient feature is perhaps its poetics, a dense and textured act of transmission that pieces together social narratives, remembrances, and imaginings that interpolate intensely and signify (Vansina 1985). This aspect is guided by what troubadours refer to as *fundamento*— the foundational ground on which poetic claims are raised, loosely akin to worldly *experientia*, though better thought of as reflexive cultivations of a specific social-locational affinity based in situated knowledges. These renderings describe events (contemporary and historical), places (near or far), social concerns that touch everyday life (i.e., U.S.-Mexico migration), individuals deemed important (i.e., genealogies of huapango arribeño practitioners), and so on. Troubadours accumulate a vast corpus of material appropriate for an array of occasions—ranging from weddings, to baptisms, to birthdays, the New Year, and so on—during which they debate and engage one another with any number of thematic formulations. Ángel González, a troubadour native of Palomas in the municipality of Xichú, Guanajuato, declares:

LOS POETAS TROVADORES TENEMOS LA MISIÓN
DE INFORMAR A LA GENTE LO QUE ESTÁ SUCEDIENDO
DE TANTAS OTRAS COSAS QUE ESTÁN ACONTECIENDO
Y ALEGRARLES LA VIDA, TAMBIÉN EL CORAZÓN

———

WE TROUBADOUR POETS BEAR THE MISSION
OF INFORMING THE PEOPLE OF WHAT IS OCCURRING
OF THE MANY THINGS THAT ARE TRANSPIRING
AND BRIGHTEN THEIR LIVES, ALSO THEIR HEARTS

Décima poetics are typically less mythologizing than epic poetry. The themes of the décima highlight the workaday and aspects of cultural memory in a manner that escapes the moralistic motifs often found in corridos, for instance. Audiences desire (and thus make real and necessary) the laborious performative enactment of these bursts of discursive energy rendered in the décima poetic form—an octosyllabic ten-line stanza of Spanish origin whose most widely used variant is credited to Vicente Gómez Martínez Espinel (1550–1624), an acclaimed Spanish writer and musician of the *siglo de oro* (golden age), or the period of artistic and literary florescence in Spain that generally is considered to begin in 1492 with both the completion of the Reconquista (the Christian recapturing of the Moorish-controlled Iberian Peninsula) and the voyages of Christopher Columbus to the New World. Although ten-line stanzas of different design were used and performed with some frequency as early as the fifteenth century—including those commonly referred to as *copla real* (some of which took the general form of ABAABCDCCD)—the *espinela*, as a broad empirical and performative category, ultimately triumphed over these variants.

The *décima espinela* (ABBAACCDDC) has been popular throughout Latin America since the dawn of the colonial period. Sources suggest that its diffusion occurred by means of the Catholic Church's evangelical efforts and labors, as clergy attempted to Christianize indigenous populations with the aid of song and poetry, and as a result of colonial aristocratic popularization, as the cosmopolitan sensibilities of Spanish soldiers, conquistadores, and colonial officials gained favor (Paredes 1993). Presently, the décima espinela is the typical poetic form used in huapango arribeño and thus imposes certain structural constraints on the music's textual production.[22] It is the primary orienting framework for the production and reception of poetic discourse. Its emergent verbal products—always conceived in practice-based terms—take on the configuration of either a *poesía* or a *decimal* (explained in detail later), forms whose infrastructural elements and compositional formation are generically intertextual, meaning that they iterate situational frames that index past, present, and anticipated experiences, places, and social relationships, as the vernacular axiom of *fundamento* indicates.

Fundamento enables types of claiming, but these claims are to be dialogued, challenged, debated. This situated and dialogic production of what Richard Bauman refers to as generically informed discourse "indexes prior situational contexts in which the same generic conventions have guided discursive production" and whose associational links may invoke any of the constituent elements of those settings—including place, participant roles, and social scenarios, thus "[transcending] the bounded, locally produced speech event" (2004: 5). Huapango arribeño augments Bauman's position to a degree, for although oftentimes informed by such prior contexts, iterability does not rely exclusively on the past nor on moments when the "same generic conventions have guided discursive production," in this case décima performance (5). There exists a balance between new and old that shapes huapango arribeño poetics, a constant negotiation between their reliance on a fixed form and their improvisatory newness. Of necessity, they are always new and always old. Philipa Rothfield describes this productive tension with the aid of Alfred North Whitehead: "There is a kind of rhythm to this perpetual oscillation between emergent newness and ongoing establishment. The rhythmic shift between old and new is not merely the relentless pursuit of the new. The process of becoming past also enters that which becomes, connecting with the process of becoming itself. In that sense, a certain reverence is maintained for the old. It partners the agency of the new via that which is called the creative advance" (2008: 2). "Creative advance," in a manner of speaking, then, is illustrated in the vernacular fundamento, which signals the act of poetic coordination to be a deeply socially constructed and informed practice. In Bakhtinian terms, huapango arribeño's poetics are generated in relation to other discursive structures—poetic, institutional, everyday—evincing Bauman's conception of "social life as discursively constituted, produced and reproduced in situated acts of speaking and other signifying practices that are simultaneously anchored in their situational contexts of use and transcendent of them, linked by interdiscursive ties to other situations, other acts, other utterances" (2004: 2). The ongoing process of huapango arribeño poetic production and reception is not a regurgitation of form—despite the rigidity of the décima—but rather a transposable frame of social reference that many have a hand in making. The meanings embedded in social life are intertextually constructed and subsequently recontextualized amid the in-the-moment signification and alignment of huapango arribeño poetics. This sense of the democratic construction of performative discourse will be explored further in chapter 5 with specific focus on the *saludado*, or improvised greeting.

To return to Berger, his discussion of compositional stance is appropriate in considering how in the emerging process of composition "every note stipulated develops a partial autonomy, and the composer develops a relationship to that piece as it is being created" (2009: 12). In other words, not only does the troubadour's approach to the poetic composition in performance—as a form of stance—result in a determination of word and note choice from a variety of possibilities, but this very grappling "is also a constitution of the music in experience," where the processes of "production and constitution are locked in a complex and very intimate dialectic" (12). Take Amador's decimal from earlier. His compositional effort is made possible through referencing Gabino's lifeworld as an artist, a huapango arribeño musician, a compañero del destino. The unfolding verses index an intimate associational linking, in this case, how Amador and Gabino have come to (and continue to) know each other as artists. Further, the direct mention of "agonizing nights" and "festive gatherings" is an evocative calling to mind of the constituent elements of huapango arribeño performance as a (past, present, and future) form of sociality—celebratory, labored, intense, and embodied. All of these elements speak to Amador's relationship to the unfolding material, or his stance, which further reinforces how huapango arribeño hinges on the ubiquitous presence of a generic intertextuality as a means to align the experiential horizons of performers and audiences and thus achieve remarkable results that connect, satisfy, and *move*—physically (in the form of dance) and emotively (in the form of evalual social engagement)—and thus become socially legible.

With regard to formal structuring, the term *poesía* refers to the lyrical content of the first portion of the huapango arribeño musical piece, which is organized in the following manner:

(1) poesía
(2) decimal/*valona*
(3) *jarabe* or *son*[23]

I will term this musical piece the *pieza arribeña* for analytical purposes, although it does not have a formal name among huapangueros. Its tonal cadence follows the familiar I–IV–V (root, subdominant, dominant) diatonic three-chord circle progression in Western music and is nearly always played in major keys, D, A, and G being the most common. The poesía is anchored by a *planta*—a quatrain rhyming ABAB or ABBA—and a series of corresponding décimas. This configuration is composed and memorized beforehand, forming part of the troubadour's repertoire. When performing, the troubadour begins the poesía by singing the planta (most often it is sung twice at the beginning); the shape of its melody is chosen from a set of preestablished and commonly shared *tonadas* (melodies), though troubadours embellish it to suit their aesthetic preference or to meet the needs of their vocal range. Some uniqueness is displayed in the rhythmic expression of the tonadas—primarily irregular shifts in pulse—which are performed at midtempo in either the 6/8 Mexican huapango style or asymmetrical time signatures. In the case of irregular or complex times, the planta melody is subdivided into triple and quadruple meters—for instance, in some cases three measures of the latter in 3/4 with a final measure in 4/4, giving the unique sense of 13/4, or one measure of each, giving the feeling of 7/4.

Once the troubadour begins singing the planta and strumming along on the guitarra quinta huapanguera, the remaining musicians in the ensemble immediately follow. The violins restate the planta's melody and loop it until the troubadour decides to stop and begin reciting the first décima in the corresponding set that makes up the poesía, at which point the entire ensemble halts. This pause does not happen abruptly; rather, troubadours slowly decrease the intensity of their strumming, signaling to the others that they are about to stop. During this silence, the troubadour recites a décima, of which the tenth line is the first of the original planta. This structuring is called *pie forzado* (literally, forced foot, referring to the adherence to a poetic base) throughout Latin America, and it describes the practice of anchoring the final line of each décima (abbaaccddC) with the first of the base quatrain (Abba or Abab), whereby each décima coincides with the planta both syntagmatically (completing the base quatrain) and paradigmatically (expanding on the initial theme established by the quatrain). Accordingly, in the poesía's structure only the first nine lines of the décima are recited, while the tenth is sung, for it is the first line of the planta which is sung again, at which point the music and singing resume. This sequence is repeated no fewer than four times and typically no more than seven. Below is a sample poesía authored by the troubadour Isaías:

A: ¡VIVA, QUE VIVA LA VIDA!
B: ¡VIVA MIENTRAS LA GOZAMOS!
A: ¿QUÉ TIESOS Y BOCA ARRIBA?
B: ¿PA' QUE LA NECESITAMOS?

(1) A: Nuestro paso es por el mundo
B: un relámpago fugaz
B: es un instante nomás
A: es lo breve de un segundo
A: y en ese pensar profundo
C: que se reconcentra y anida
C: el disfrute sin medida
D: la vivencia que perdure
D: y aunque muy poquito dure:
C(A): ¡VIVA, QUE VIVA LA VIDA!

(2) Que sea la familia el centro
el motor que hace que gire
la existencia que no expire
el sentimiento de adentro
que acudamos al encuentro
de una relación florida
y que la familia unida
goce, piensa, sufre y ría
y aunque dure como un día:
¡VIVA, QUE VIVA LA VIDA!

(3) Si ha habido errores pensemos
en lo que ya sucedió
y si se deterioró
la relación renovemos
lo valioso que tenemos
en la pareja querida
buscando y dando salida
eso suplico a esa cruz
y rauda como la luz:
¡VIVA, QUE VIVA LA VIDA!

(4) ¿Qué caso tiene gastar
energías en lo indeseable
si en un rato es muy probable
todo llega a terminar?
Por eso hay que valorar
la existencia recibida

que entrando la despedida
estando uno en el ataúd
y mientras haya salud:
¡VIVA, QUE VIVA LA VIDA!

(5) Que siempre sea primavera
gozo y dicha por evento
y disfrutar el momento
como si el último fuera
después de que uno muera
todo culmina y se olvida
dimensión desconocida
la que se vive después
y por eso de una vez:
¡VIVA, QUE VIVA LA VIDA!

———

A—LIVE! LONG LIVE LIFE!
B—MAY IT LIVE WHILE WE ENJOY IT!
A—FOR ONCE WE'RE RIGID AND FACE-UP[24]
B—WHAT NEED DO WE HAVE FOR IT?

(1) A—Our journey on this earth
B—is a fleeting flash
B—it is only an instant
A—it is the brevity of a second
A—and in this profound realization
C—deep and nestled within
C—is unmitigated enjoyment
D—may life's experiences endure
D—and although it doesn't last long:
C(A)—LIVE! LONG LIVE LIFE!

(2) May family be the center
the engine that makes one run
may existence not expire
the deep feeling
we discover when we find
a relationship in full bloom
and may the tight-knit family

enjoy, ponder, suffer, and laugh
and though it may last only a day:
LIVE! LONG LIVE LIFE!

(3) If there have been mishaps, let us consider
what has already transpired
and if things fell apart
let us renew our relationship
the valuable thing we have
as a beloved couple
as we search and forge ahead
this is what I beg of the cross
and swift as a light:
LIVE! LONG LIVE LIFE!

(4) What good is it to waste
energies in the undesirable
for it is probable that at any moment
everything will come to an end?
This is why we must cherish
our received existence
for when our farewell approaches
and one is in the coffin
rejoice now in good health:
LIVE! LONG LIVE LIFE!

(5) May it always be spring
joy and good fortune on every occasion
and delight at every moment
as if it were the last
for after one has died
everything concludes and is forgotten
an unknown reality
is what the afterlife brings
and that's why at once:
LIVE! LONG LIVE LIFE!

The décimas used in huapango arribeño poesías can be anywhere from
eight to sixteen syllables. Those with ten syllables or fewer are known as
sencillas (simple/single), and those with more than ten as *dobles* (double). In

the parlance of Spanish poetry, octosyllabic verses are referred to as *versos de arte menor*, and those with nine or more syllables are considered *versos de arte mayor*. While the recitation of poesías and the singing of the corresponding plantas are forceful and invoke a sense of high drama, this vocality cannot be confused with the type of storytelling that is unfolding; in other words, while performers convey the phonaesthetic sentiment of epic poetry, the poetics are not epic in scope. (See appendix A, example 1.)

After the planta of the poesía section is sung for the final time, the violins, as expected, continue to play the tonada of the planta, while the troubadour begins to mentally grasp at the skeletal form of the décimas they are about to release as part of the second portion of the pieza arribeña. The lyrical component of this second portion is referred to as the *decimal*, while its musical structuring is known as the *valona*.[25] The threshold of this transitional moment is fluid, richly involved, and occupied by a focused contemplation of the anticipated flourishes about to unfold. This attenuated rehearsal is muted, subdued, phantomlike, with the performer's eyes usually closed, lips softly mouthing words, while the music in waiting is subtly coaxed by the violinists as they lightly bow their instruments (McDowell 2010). Then, suddenly, instead of pausing to recite yet another décima as part of the poesía, the troubadour launches into an entirely new planta, also in the form of a quatrain (usually ABBA, seldom ABAB), formally commencing this second portion—decimal/valona. This planta anchors the decimal; however, unlike in the poesía, the planta is sung only once at the beginning of this section and never returned to.

Although the primary poetic form utilized in this portion is also the décima, here they are sung (not recited), are typically octosyllabic, and are entirely improvised in glossed form such that the final line of the first décima mirrors the first line of the decimal planta, the final line of the second décima mirrors the second line of the decimal planta, and so forth, until the entire planta has been glossed with a total of four improvised décimas. The sung melody that accompanies both the decimal planta and the décimas in this portion is standard, though, again, troubadours embellish according to their preference and needs. These melodies exhibit a free rhythmic style and thus are performed *a capriccio*, a free approach to the tempo in cadenza-like fashion as the troubadour strums along with the guitarra quinta huapanguera.[26]

Unlike in the poesía portion, the music never pauses during the decimal/valona—the strumming of the guitarra quinta huapanguera and vihuela con-

EXAMPLE 2.1 *Decimal planta* "Don Roberto" by Pánfilo

tinually accompanies as each décima is delivered in sparse, focused utterances that shift in volume and intonation. The underlying rhythmic pulse of the strumming can be counted in 2/4, although the stresses in the accompanying singing and violin melodies (discussed in the next section) can often shift and disguise the rhythm as triple meter. Meanwhile, the troubadour's unique cadence takes on a chantlike quality in which the final word in each line is often subject to syllabic lengthening—consonants in particular undergo this phonological stressing whereby (as in the first line of the decimal planta example below) words like *ser* are sung *serrrrr*. This pacing organizes the flow of improvisation prosodically. Here is a decimal example by the troubadour Graciano:

LA POESÍA DEBE SER
FUERZA, MENSAJE, Y RAZÓN
Y LIBERTAD DE EXPRESIÓN
QUE SIEMPRE HA DE FLORECER

(1) Hay que trovarle al amor
y a los problemas sociales
a los pueblos desiguales
al arte, gusto, y folclor
a la noche, su resplandor
la luz y el atardecer
como un nuevo amanecer

EXAMPLE 2.2 Glossed *décima* "Don Roberto" by Pánfilo

que renace con el día
enojo y algarabía
LA POESÍA DEBE SER

(2) La mente con su poder
va forjando un pensamiento
y así se forma un cimiento
que se debe de ejercer
y después es un deber
que se expresa con razón
se agiganta el corazón
dando sus palpitaciones
se juntan las emociones
FUERZA, MENSAJE, Y RAZÓN

(3) Todito lo que se expresa
con una fe verdadera
da frutos en la carrera
de la alegría o la tristeza
quien llora, quien canta o reza
pero en fin es la expresión
lágrimas, risa, o emoción
la lluvia o la sequía
la pobreza o jerarquía
Y LIBERTAD DE EXPRESIÓN

(4) Contra todo el imperialismo
o a favor de la alegría
que viva la poesía
y que viva el optimismo
para cerrar un abismo
ver el campo florecer
la poesía debe ser
fuerza, mensaje, y razón
y libertad de expresión
QUE SIEMPRE HA DE FLORECER

———

POETRY MUST BE
STRONG, THOUGHTFUL, AND REASONED

FREEDOM OF EXPRESSION
THAT MUST ALWAYS FLOURISH

(1) We must sing verses to love
and to social problems
to the world's inequality
to art, pleasure, and folklore
to the resplendent night
to the first day's light and dusk
like a new dawn
that is reborn with the day
anger and rejoicing
POETRY MUST BE

(2) The mind with all its strength
goes about forging thoughts
and this is how a foundation is formed
that is necessary to exercise
and then it becomes a duty
that is expressed with reason
the heart grows larger
beating its palpitations
emotions gather
STRENGTH, MESSAGE, AND REASON

(3) Everything that is expressed
with a true faith
bears fruit along the way
of happiness or of sadness
for those who cry, sing, or pray
but in the end it is expression
of tears, laughter, and emotion
rain or drought
poverty or power
FREEDOM OF EXPRESSION

(4) Against all imperialism
or in favor of happiness
long live poetry
and long live optimism

so that it may close the abyss
and see the fields bloom
poetry must always be
strong, thoughtful, and reasoned
freedom of expression
THAT MUST ALWAYS FLOURISH

The phonaesthetic entanglement of poetics, melody, and voice pro-duces the texture of creating in-the-moment, where acoustic rises, sustained pitches, and rhythmic arranging create an intersection of sonic surfaces. This layering—of musical and phonological (stanzaic) parallelisms—is how im-provisational performance is managed and organized by the troubadour, but violinists in executing their own harmonic labyrinths also coordinate similar types of maneuvering.

POLYPHONIC EXCESS

Two middle-age women sit next to each other, a single blanket stretched over their laps, huddled together, not too far from where Gabino and the other musicians are positioned here in Victoria, Guanajuato. The performance is in full swing, and I've set up camp just beside Gabino's ensemble. Gabino now sits high up on the *tablado*, or the raised bench huapango arribeño ensembles straddle during topada performances.[27] These structures tower above the au-dience, one at each end of the dancing area, with the public in between and the ensembles physically facing each other across this distance, above a sea of heads bobbing rhythmically just below in between them, stomping and dip-ping up and down.[28]

Tonight's topada is between troubadours Flavio and Isaías, each accom-panied by three other musicians. It's still early on in the engagement, one o'clock in the morning or so, and both ensembles are performing in the key of D major, as is customary at this time of night. One of the women next to me is nodding off; she leans on the other, who is wide awake. Gabino, who is accompanying Flavio, is performing at the moment. Subtly, during the deci-mal/valona portion of their intervention, they play a *remate* (violin melody) with a modulation in the key of A. I perk my ears up. Isaías and the musicians atop the tablado across the way take the bait and during the third portion of their own subsequent intervention respond with a jarabe that includes a remate modulation in the key of A as well. On the next go-around, Gabino and Flavio offer up a jarabe of their own also containing a similar modulation.

This dynamic coaxing suddenly animates the crowd. Bodies and minds begin latching on to this elaborate swerving: something is about to change. Indeed, the woman who is fully awake nudges the snoozing one, giving her a sharp elbow to the ribs, warning her not to go to sleep: "No te duermas, cabrona, que van a tocar en LA mayor!" (Don't you go to sleep, bitch, they're about to play in A major!). She senses it, too—listening, sensing, watching, evaluating, anticipating, grappling. In the subsequent intervention, Isaías's ensemble shifts from D to A major. She was right.

This exchange and others like it are wrapped up in the tripartite pieza arribeña, the musico-poetic arrangement with which huapangueros engage and improvise. To a degree, it serves as the primary vehicle that guides the emergence of a collectively informed discourse that is necessarily polyphonic, both in terms of music structure and in the dialogic sense. The heterogeneous musical and poetic elements that constitute the pieza arribeña serve as meta-signals and strategies that carefully coax a multitude of voicings. And orchestrating this relational orientation of voices (musical and poetic texts) to other voices is a virtuosic act of control, of situated and active musicianship that powerfully highlights the dense aesthetic strategies at work in the moment, in dialogue, that animate a certain aural saturation. In musical terms, this, once more, includes the use of asymmetrical time signatures (and the oscillations between simple and compound meters therein), the a capriccio improvisation of glossed décimas, and, finally, the complex bundling of cascading violin melodies.

For instance, during the decimal, after the initial planta is sung and in between each subsequent glossed décima, the violins play a series of remates, of which there exists a vast corpus from which to choose. These constitute the valona. One in particular is referred to as the *valoneado*, and it serves as the anchor of this melodic bundling. It is always played immediately after the decimal planta and repeated as many times as needed; the violinists loop this melody while troubadours ready themselves to sing their first improvised décima, at which time the violinists stop playing. Thereafter, the primera vara decides what remate is to be played after each improvised décima, and the segunda vara follows. These subsequent remates are typically played twice, after which both violins return to the valoneado, which again is looped until the troubadour decides to sing the ensuing glossed décima. This process is repeated three times, that is, in between the four décimas glossed by the troubadour as part of the decimal.

These musical interludes consisting of remates and valoneado are intensely syncopated and incorporate fast trilled notes reminiscent of baroque-style movements. Also, as a counterpoint—during the spaces in which the troubadour sings each décima and the violins fall silent—the *vihuelero* or *jaranero* ornately strums around the troubadour's recitation, also in a syncopated manner. With respect to the shapes of the violin melodies, they are diatonic to the key of the piece and make liberal use of arpeggios in line with the overall harmonic movement within. Where nondiatonic notes are introduced, they tend to be a flattened seventh over the tonic chord before a movement to the subdominant chord. Downbeats tend to contain strong chord tones—root third or fifth—with the weaker upbeats filling out the shape of the melodic line. Some exhibit a development of motifs that crescendo toward the end of the remate. The harmonic relationship between the two violins tends to be based around thirds and sixths, which stray into fourths and fifths where necessary to maintain the flow of the melodic line, both of which exhibit liberal use of mordents, giving the sense of a harmonically pleasing sonic filigree. The musical accompaniment can generally be felt in a 2/4 time signature.

Other remates, however, loop in a way that displaces the 2/4 downbeat pulse, meaning that the melody can begin on beat 1 the first time around and then on beat 2 the second time around (see appendix A, example 2). Still others are a bit more intriguing from a metric standpoint. For instance, a remate can shift back and forth from a compound triple meter (9/8) to a simple duple meter (2/4) in a very fluid way (see appendix A, example 3). The 9/8 sections are almost reminiscent of Scandinavian fiddling traditions.

After the fourth décima, the troubadour abruptly strums the guitarra quinta huapanguera three to four times to signal that the decimal has concluded and to simultaneously introduce the third and final section of the pieza arribeña: the jarabe or son, options which are always played in 6/8. This final section features the violinists with minimal lyrical participation on the part of the troubadour. Here, the primera vara chooses what jarabe or son is to be played, and the segunda vara follows. In the case of a son, Mario González, a violinist from Guanajuato, elaborates, "Los sones son conocidos porque son de una intensidad mas lenta y mas baja" (Sones are recognizable because they are less intense). Some of the more common include "Presumidas," "Rositas Arribeñas," "Vaivenes," "Conchitas," "Pajarillos," "Diablitos," "Cuervitos," "Frijolitos," and "Tecolotitos."[29] Each son consists of a base melody (*entrada*), which is played immediately after the decimal/valona concludes. The guitarra

EXAMPLE 2.3 *Valona* violin *remate*, key of D

quinta huapanguera and vihuela join in quickly as soon as they recognize the entrada. This son base melody is looped as many times as the primera vara sees fit and is then followed by the *paseado* portion, which establishes the vocal melody for the corresponding son verse. Sones feature two to three short sung verses in sextilla form, a six-line stanza rhyming ABABAB, though usually the first two lines are repeated (at times mirroring each other), resulting in an eight-line verse: A(1) B(2) A(1) B(2)—A(3) B(4) A(5) B(6). A verse for a "Rosita Arribeña" might go something like:

A(1) Florecita de rosal
B(2) del jardín de Guanajuato
A(1) florecita de rosal
B(2) del jardín de Guanajuato;
A(3) Vamos hablando formal
B(4) ay mamacita del alma, para platicar al rato
A(5) nos vemos en el corral
B(6) ay mamacita del alma, afuerita del curato

Usually the vihuelero sings these sextilla verses, though the troubadour may do so at times. This sequence—entrada, paseado, verse—is repeated two to three times; after the final verse is sung, however, the violins proceed to play a closing remate to end with, which is a derivation of the entrada. Mario González comments, "El remate es parecido al son, pero no es el son natural, ya es otra cosa muy independiente pero esta emparentado y hermanado con el son" (The remate is similar to the son [base melody], but it is not the original son; it is something else all its own, but it is related to the son). After the closing remate has been looped a number of times, the son is finally concluded with a brief and standard closing melody that sways back and forth referred to as a *vaivén*, which is used for all sones and jarabes. (See appendix A, example 4.)

As should be apparent by this point, the pieza arribeña increases in intensity with each passing section, and this is particularly the case if a jarabe is played during the final climactic portion.[30] In fact, during the topada performance, ensembles often begin the engagement by playing sones and gradually shift to jarabes. Mario González explains, "El jarabe es mas arrebatado con una intensidad y música mas alegre" (The jarabe is more unruly with a greater intensity and a more uplifting melody). Another violinist from San Luis Potosí, Salomón, admits, "Cuando escucho los remates de jarabe, has de cuenta que me estoy comiendo un dulce de guayaba" (When I hear jarabe melodies, it's as if I'm eating a guava sweet candy). I know just what he means. In some of the melodic bundles in a jarabe, especially the *re-ti-que-teo* (a highly ono-matopoetic word that refers to a melodic figure employed as part of the ja-rabe), the music takes flight. In the moment, you hear a wave of whistles and cheers erupting, feet pounding even harder. These moments loop and seem to go on forever as the music widens and people dig their heels in hard while they stomp out the zapateado.

This is how the jarabe plays out. The primera vara also begins the ja-rabe with a planta, which is then followed by a series of *remates de jarabe*, which are variations on the melodic theme established by the planta. This bundling of planta and corresponding remates requires immense skill on the part of the violinists and, when done seamlessly, sweetly, in Salomón's words, showcases a heightened virtuosic ability to provide multiple and variant voicings on the same musical theme, over and over. For instance, violinists may play the jarabe planta and adjoin a single remate and repeat this particular coupling one to three times. Or they may adjoin two to three remates de jarabe to the planta (thereby lengthening this grouping) and not repeat the bundle at all. At other times a planta and remate are repeated and then topped off with a final closing remate. (See appendix A, example 5.) The sequencing possibilities seem endless here. After having played a particular bundle, however, the violins always close with the standard vaivén, which signals to the troubadour to sing a verse in the form of either a quatrain or a sextilla, again, a capriccio. The violins rest during this brief moment. This sequence—bundles of remates de jarabe with an adjoined verse—is repeated at least three times (though it can be done as many times as the en-semble wishes), but with entirely different melodic bundles each and every time.[31]

Though there exist a myriad of other possibilities, violinists' virtuosity is perhaps best expressed in their ability to incorporate subtle modulations within the series of bundled remates de jarabe. The more ornately and seam-lessly the threads are woven together, the more the audience is aware of the skill they are witness to because it's directly translated into the ability to re-ceive corporeally and dance. In the heat of a topada, if the musicians are locked in and thus able to stretch the music, the people present are equally locked in, equally in it. Their patterned steps provide a type of percussive dimension, a response, and the energy of their pounding feet is excessive and reciprocal. Violinists will be inclined to loop melodies longer when dancers are giving off

EXAMPLE 2.4 *Jarabe remates,* key of G

steam. In addition, the ability to shift the tonal center of a jarabe serves a very basic function within the topada setting—to signal a change in musical key to the other ensemble, or petition for one, and thus move the tonal structuring of the topada. (See appendix A, examples 6, 7, and 8.)

Typically, ensembles commence the topada in the key of D major, then shift to the key of A major two to three hours after midnight (assuming that the topada began two or three hours before midnight), and finally switch to G major at first light, or typically around six in the morning. These shifts may be subtle or abrupt. In the case of the former, violinists utilize modulations, referred to by most as *piquetes*—"little pricks," or nudges to ease the transition. "Uno de primera vara tiene que negociar. ¿Cambiamos de tono? Se consulta uno con el trovador, pero uno lleva esa responsabilidad. Los piques son pa' decir, 'Ya es momento.'" (If one is the lead violinist, you have to negotiate. Do we change keys? You consult with the troubadour, but one ultimately has the responsibility. The *piques* are used to tell the other ensemble, "It's time to change."). Valentín explained this to me and has guided me in this way during performances. However, as is sometimes the case, this tonal structure may be entirely ignored, and ensembles may opt to engage each other in musical keys that are less commonplace—the key of E or F, for instance. Further, included among a violinist's repertoire are also modulations in minor keys, often referred to as "Peteneras," a reference to the huapango huasteco and son jarocho of the same name whose most salient feature is its modulation between E minor and G major.[32] At times, this musical play may dominate the tone of the topada, whereby ensembles laboriously (re)contextualize prior and anticipated musical statements, as in the example between Flavio and Isaías's ensembles in Victoria, Guanajuato, which we began this section with.

REGLAMENTO: PERFORMANCE, POESIS, AND THE DIALOGIC

Although huapango arribeño is performed on any number of occasions (both religious and secular), it blooms most intensely during the topada performance, the all-night performative encounter between two huapango arribeño ensembles where they engage in both musical and poetic flyting.[33] The name *topada* comes from the verb *topar* (to collide with) and signifies the heightened reciprocity and intensity that constitute the performative excesses of such encounters. Distinct from what Américo Paredes (1966) refers to as the *contrapunto*—the informal and secular form of décima flyting that took place along the Texas-Mexico border in the mid-nineteenth century—the topada is a highly formalized marathon event lasting anywhere from seven to twelve hours. In this way, it also differs from other Latin American décima traditions, including the paya in Chile and punto in Cuba, for instance, most of which are highly impromptu.

Becoming a huapango arribeño practitioner requires one to enter the rigorous world of heightened performance practice and dialogic exchange and the topada is the aesthetic cradle that nourishes the talents demanded of musicians. Troubadour Guillermo Velázquez explains:

Es [la topada] el espacio donde verdaderamente el que quiera ser músico o poeta se forja y lo demuestra porque tiene el elemento de la confrontación, el elemento del combate, el elemento de la emulación, donde se plantea un nivel de exigencia que no se da cuando uno está tocando solo. . . . Tener físicamente en frente a otro músico o a otro poeta significa ya un desafío. . . . Sería el espacio privilegiado de la formación de un trovador y un músico, por la sabiduría misma de la tradición. Ese es el espacio donde se demuestra la vocación, donde se demuestra si verdaderamente uno asume el destino de ser lo que quiere ser y donde se gana o se pierde en cuanto reconocimiento de la gente. Y no solo en una topada, tiene que ser a lo largo de muchas topadas y de muchos años. . . . No puedes asumirte como poeta o como músico si no has estado en ese crisol.

(It [the topada] is truly the space where the person who wants to be a musician or a poet is forged and has to prove it because it entails the element of encounter, the element of combat, the element of rivalry, where a heightened level of practice and competitiveness is exercised that is not present when one is performing alone. . . . To have another musician or poet physically in front of you signifies a challenge. . . . It is the privileged space in the formation of a troubadour or musician because of the knowledge of the tradition that it requires. It is the space where one proves this vocation, where one truly proves the desire to follow this calling, and where one wins or loses the favor of the people. And not only in one topada, it requires a number of topadas over a number of years. . . . You cannot become a poet or musician if you haven't been in that crucible.)

This crucible is the generating force that transforms novice musicians into competent practitioners. Troubadour Xavi shares, "Esas regañadas si eran bonitas, fíjese" (Those scoldings were pretty). He continues:

Cuando apenas empezaba llegue a enfrentarme con los grandes. Una vez don Agapito Briones, créamelo que me dio mi buena desplumada, todavía me acuerdo de una de sus plantas." (When I first started out, I went up against the legends. One time [against] Agapito Briones, believe me that he gave me a good trouncing, I still remember one of his plantas [base quatrains]):

POR UN RESPETO DE DISCIPLINA
VOY A MOSTRARTE MI EDUCACIÓN

A VER SI EN ESTA CONTRADICCIÓN
LOGRES QUE EL PUEBLO TE DÉ PROPINA

———

SO YOU MAY SEE THE DISCIPLINE REQUIRED
I'M GOING TO SHOW YOU MY TALENT
LET'S SEE IF IN THIS CHALLENGE
YOU CAN ATTAIN THE ACCOLADES OF THE PEOPLE

Xavi was born in 1966, a native of Cerritos in San Luis Potosí. At the age of nine he began playing the jarana alongside his father, a famed veteran troubadour, and at times he also accompanied troubadours Asención Meza and Antonio García. By the mid-1980s, he was playing his first engagements as a troubadour in his own right with noted violinists like Tacho Ruiz, Tacho Hernández, and Eusebio "Chebo" Méndez. By the early 1990s, both he and Méndez had become members of Los Leones de la Sierra de Xichú—Xavi on the vihuela (for more on this group see the following chapter). He recalls another scolding he received as he was starting out, this one from his father:

> Estaba en una topada frente a don Guadalupe Reyes en San Luis Potosí. Me bajé del tablado a bailar un ratito. Y ahí andaba mi papá esa vez y que me ve y me dice, "Vienes a trabajar o a bailar? Fíjese lo que le está diciendo el señor!" Estaba chavo yo.

———————————————

> (I was in a topada facing Don Guadalupe Reyes in San Luis Potosí. I stepped down from the tablado to dance for a little while. And my dad was in the audience that time, and he saw me and scolded me, "Did you come to work or to dance? Listen to what that man is saying to you!" I was young.)

Joel Sherzer describes verbal dueling as a type of intertwined and interactional "grammatical and lexical play" that creatively displays "the relationship between and among language, culture, society, and the individual" (2002: 69)—a description that may apply to all aspects of huapango arribeño's poetics and musicality as intertextually and polyphonically constructed utterances. There are spatial and material aspects to how the performance plays out. When performing (in any context, not only the topada), musicians position themselves in the following manner: the vihuelero or jaranero is seated to the troubadour's immediate left, the primera vara is seated to the troubadour's immediate right, and the segunda vara to the troubadour's far right. Throughout the topada, ensembles take turns performing the pieza arribeña: as soon as one finishes, the other commences. This back-and-forth usually begins in the early evening and lasts until midmorning.[34] The winner, so to speak, is never formally announced, although audience applause, cheers, and zapateados may offer an indication of who has come out ahead. Still, there is no official decision declaring who has been vanquished, nor is there a moment when a victor is announced.

Nevertheless, how do I begin to describe the tense oppositions within the topada performance without giving a false impression of antagonism or a pecking order? How do I portray some sense of collaborative making rather than fighting, winning, and defeating? First, *in tension*, the mutually oppositional and yet creative forces on each tall, wooden tablado exist in a material space while constructing something experiential and ephemeral. Second, *intentioned* collaboration exists long before the night of the performance. The two groups of four set out intentionally to build something together through musical and textual poesis, forcing, inviting, testing, and supporting each other upward in order to build an arch—an aural space made with purpose. The stability of performance lies inherently in the oppositional forces pressing against each other, hoisting one another up, gaining height together. And its structural integrity relies on *reglamento* (the performative protocol), the musico-poetic formal structuring of huapango arribeño, whose elements are the tools with which performance is enacted as a dynamic multivoiced dialogue of performative callings. The performance takes shape—it is brought forth, resting on this resolution, this joining, this arch, this intimacy. And before you know it, you're in it, under it, with it, and then, before you're ready, it's gone . . . Done. It was subtle at first: greetings called out carefully, slowly, but you sense what's coming. It is reaching a climax and then dissipating. When the performance is over, the scaffolding of the tablados disappears, but the arch of the shared aural experience remains and binds all sorts of things—people, poetics, places.

When musicians dig in and commit to taking aesthetic risks, they are necessarily engaged in the extensive exercise of listening—listening to the musicians sitting at one's side and across the way, to the people in attendance, and to the performance space as it slowly comes into full bloom. With each passing moment, with each alternating musical and poetic intervention performed, the act of listening increases in intensity—poesía, decimal, valona, son, jarabe, verse, remate, all gradually braiding themselves to produce an assemblage of statements, of claims, of voices in conversation, touching and passing through bodies. Again, reglamento—the detailed code of etiquette—guides this flow such that one ensemble among the two is responsible for bringing to bear an array of musical and poetic resources. This ensemble *lleva la mano* (literally, "has the hand"). Much like the notion of el destino, this meaning is augmented to mean far more than "an advantage," referring, rather, to being accountable to take the initiative; said ensemble is entrusted with a detailed set of responsibilities, including (1) commencing the engagement, that is, making the first musical intervention of the evening; (2) deciding when sones and jarabes are to be played, and what types; (3) establishing the topic of poetic debate; (4) initiating different portions of the topada; and (5) shifting between musical keys and setting the general musical pitch. The ensemble designated as having this responsibility is either that which first positions itself atop its tablado or the one chosen by the person(s) who have organized the topada, or at times the ensembles consult with one another just before the topada and decide this.

Ensembles negotiate within/through this performative protocol and call this to the other ensemble's attention, especially when one or the other strays or is inattentive. *La mano* can be ceded. Accordingly, it is within the parameters of these performative rules of engagement that musicians demonstrate their competence—they must be able to respond with sones and jarabes, perform in various musical keys, and attend to poetic themes and queries. Valentín outlines the means by which such engagement is sustained by violinists, in particular:

> Uno tiene que tener muchas plantas de jarabe y sones, que no toque el mismo, que sean diferentes y con diferentes remates. (One must have many jarabe and son base melodies. You can't repeat the same ones, they must be different, and with different remates.)

> Estar preparado pa' si estando en la topada con el contrincante poder darle respuestas a sus peticiones. (To be prepared to respond to the opposing musicians' requests within the topada.)

> Conocer los tonos. Si el contrincante te pide tonos, pues saber qué tono te está pidiendo y dar la respuesta. (To know the musical keys. So if the opposing musician asks that you shift musical keys, well, to know what musical key they are asking you to play in and be able to respond accurately.)

La mano assures a performative dialogue between the ensembles, and, as is becoming clear, the violinists, the primera vara in particular, guide the ensemble through the encounter. Valentín continues:

Estando un una topada, agarra uno temas también, tanto el violinista como el poeta. Uno se engancha en temas de son, de jarabe. Por ejemplo, "Las Presumidas", el tocarle varias "Presumidas" al contrincante, que es el mismo son pero diferentes. Yo le puedo tocar unas diez "Presumidas" al del frente sin cambiar. Y si él me toca una "Presumida", bueno pues yo le contesto con esta.

———————————

(When you are in a topada, one engages in themes as well; the violinist does so just as the poet [does]. One digs into son and jarabe themes. For instance, "Las Presumidas," you can exchange various "Presumidas" with the musicians in front, which is the same son but you play variants. I can play ten "Presumidas" in front of another violinist without switching to another son. And if he sends a "Presumida" my way, well, I'll answer with another.)

Mario González adds:

Dentro del complemento de los cuatro músicos, el varero es el que dirige musicalmente la orquesta. . . . También tiene sus cualidades el varero porque el varero se apoya del poeta y el poeta se apoya del varero también. Según como sea la capacidad de quién sea, el varero pues, tiene que estar seguro de lo que hace tanto el poeta como el varero. Y si el varero decae pues también el poeta se acaba. O' sea, el chiste es que hay que sobresalirle a lo que uno está haciendo. O' sea echarle todos los kilos. . . . El poeta va ordenando su letra y el varero lo va acompañando. Y también otra cosa, el varero también va ordenando su sonería, su música. . . . El poeta está cantando lo de él, pero no sabe con qué va salir el varero.

———————————

(Within the four-musician grouping, the violinist is the one who directs the ensemble musically. . . . The violinist also has his virtues because the violinist relies on the poet, and the poet also relies on the violinist. According to the abilities of whoever it may be, the violinist, well, has to be sure of what he is doing, as does the poet, so does the violinist. And if the violinist falters, well, the poet is also finished. Meaning, the point is to accomplish what you are engaged in. That is, to give it your all. . . . The poet is arranging his poetry, and the violinist is accompanying him. And also, another thing, the violinist is also arranging his sones, his music. . . . The poet is holding his own, but he doesn't know what the violinist is going to come up with.)

In other words, the violinist serves as the ensemble's chief musical guide, constructing a musical map that everyone follows.

Like violinists, troubadours must also have a varied repertoire and within it a few poetic resources that aspire upward like the mutual building of the arch. Among the more ingenious implements are *poesías encadenadas/enlazadas* and *poesías de esdrújula*. In the former, the lines that form the décima are chained together in such a way that each line begins with the word or words that ended the preceding one. Troubadour Cándido Martínez from San Luis Potosí, authored the following:

(encadenada)
¡QUÉ VIVA EL POETA QUE CANTA POESÍA!
POESÍA QUE DIFUNDE EN DISTINTOS SENDEROS
SENDEROS EL QUE DIOS LE CONCEDIÓ AL VERSERO
VERSERO EL QUE CANTA DE NOCHE Y DE DÍA

Cuántas epopeyas el poeta compone
compone su obra en tamaños distintos
distintos los versos de cuatro o de quintos
de cinco, de seis, o de nueve renglones
renglones que siempre el poeta dispone
dispone dispuesto si hay energía
si hay energía es que hay compañía
compañía observando lo que el poeta narra
narra entre violines, vihuela, y guitarra:
¡QUE VIVA EL POETA QUE CANTA POESÍA!

———

LONG LIVE THE POET WHO SINGS POESÍA!
POESÍA THAT SPREADS ALONG DISTINCT PATHS
PATHS THAT GOD HAS GRANTED THE POET
THE POET WHO SINGS NIGHT AND DAY

How many epics the poet composes
composes his work of distinct dimensions
of distinct verses of four or five
of five, of six, or of nine lines
lines that the poet always arranges

arranges gladly if there is energy
if there is energy, there must be an audience
an audience that observes what the poet narrates
narrates alongside violins, vihuela, and guitar
LONG LIVE THE POET WHO SINGS POESÍA!

Poesías de esdrújula also display a complex parallelism in their prosodic structuring. *Esdrújula* is a word whose pronunciation stresses the third-to-last syllable, for instance, the words *molécula* (molecule) and *décima*. Every line of each décima that makes up a poesía de esdrújula incorporates one or two such words, resulting in a distinct cadence that sits at near triple meter. Cándido Martínez again:

(esdrújula)
CON ESTA MÚSICA SE ALEGRA MÉXICO
SEGÚN LA PRÁCTICA DE CADA MÚSICO
EN ESTA FÓRMULA QUERIDO PÚBLICO
AQUÍ ESTÁ CÁNDIDO CON SU DIALÉCTICO

Si en nuestro México hay algo mágico
son los poéticos cantando décimas
unas fantásticas otras muy pésimas
pero con método algo automático
es nuestro símbolo tan sistemático
también científico, igual numérico
cuando hay un público siempre genérico
es que los músicos van afinándose
otros al baile van congregándose:
CON ESTA MÚSICA SE ALEGRA MÉXICO

———

THIS MUSIC BRINGS HAPPINESS TO MEXICO
ACCORDING TO THE PRACTICE OF EVERY MUSICIAN
IN THIS FORMULA DEAR AUDIENCE
CÁNDIDO IS HERE WITH HIS DIALECTIC

If there is something magical in Mexico
it is poetic practitioners singing décimas
some fantastic, some very awful
but with an intuitive method
it is our systematic symbol

it is scientific, also numerical

when there is a generous public

it's so because musicians are readying themselves

while others are congregating to dance

THIS MUSIC BRINGS HAPPINESS TO MEXICO

Both types of poesía showcase a degree of lyrical ingenuity, which coaxes opposing huapangueros to respond in kind.

The topada itself is a negotiated sequencing of distinct moments guided by those with la mano.[35] This assemblage, similar to the pieza arribeña, increases in intensity. Troubadours typically begin the engagement with poesías and decimales that introduce themselves and their accompanying musicians and greet those in attendance (the audience in general and also, though not always, the musicians situated across the way). Under the guise of fundamento, they then move on to speak thematically to the occasion in question. For instance, in the case of the celebration of an *ejido*, poesías and decimales often speak of the Mexican Revolution, the historical details of the community in question, agrarian reform, and the like. After having exhausted this portion, troubadours may then, though not always, move on to discuss a topic of their choosing—*tema de fundamento* (foundational theme)—that is not necessarily related to the occasion in question: the genealogical history of huapango arribeño musicians, migration, local history or regional geography, national politics, popular culture, changes in the region (political, cultural, economic, etc.), religion, and so on. This heightened lyrical dimension comes together at sharp and intersecting points where troubadours demonstrate their knowledge of poetic themes, present nuanced points of view, question and petition one another, and stake claims. Within the purview of the pieza arribeña, the poesía—which is composed beforehand and memorized—is where troubadours stake such positions; during the decimal a space is opened for dialogically improvised engagement.[36]

After the temas de fundamento have been exhausted, the *bravata* (boasting) portion commences. This is considered the climax of the topada; it is the moment when troubadours engage with one another in digs, banter with each other, question each other's musical competence, and often defame and ridicule one another in jest. However, this portion does not come without warning, or at least it's not supposed to. The troubadour with la mano petitions the other musicians across the way, in effect asking if they are feeling up to it. Managing this petition is always delicate, yet during this portion the engagement reaches a fever pitch and often reluctantly comes to a close, at which point troubadours give each other a reconciliatory greeting and make their final farewells. At times, ensembles might play assorted *piezas* (polkas) or huapangos huastecos to close out. Here are portions of poetic examples documented in the field representing each of these sections.

INTRODUCTIONS
ABEL AND DON LENCHO, DALLAS, TEXAS

SOY UN BRAZO DE LA RAMA QUE HA FLOREADO
COMO PLANTA VEGETAL ME CONSIDERO
DE LO FRESCO DE LA SIERRA Y EL VENERO
DE AGUA PURA CRISTALINA FUI REGADO

Ahora que ando en esta chamba me presento
con mi música de veras como puedo
con mi nombre Abel, frente a don Lencho
apoyado de mi orgullo y mi instrumento
complaciendo a ese nivel que tiene aliento
y agradezco a todo aquel que me ha invitado
serán angustias de un amor apasionado
por donde ando trabajando mi destino
serranista y sigo siendo campesino:
SOY UN BRAZO DE LA RAMA QUE HA FLOREADO

———

I AM A LIMB BORN OF THE BUDDING SPRIG
I CONSIDER MYSELF A FLOWERING PLANT
OF THE COOLNESS OF THE MOUNTAIN SPRING
NOURISHED BY CRYSTAL-CLEAR WATER

Now that I labor in the calling, I introduce myself
with my music, truly, as best I can
my name is Abel, in front of don Lencho
provisioned by my pride and my instrument
fulfilling my duty with the utmost energy
and I am grateful for all who have invited me
perhaps these are the throes of a passionate love
wherever I labor in my calling

I'm from the sierra and continue being a campesino
I AM A LIMB BORN OF THE BUDDING SPRIG

—Abel

ASÍ ES LA VIDA DEL CANTADOR
CRUZANDO PLANES Y SERRANÍAS
CANTANDO VERSOS, ¿CUÁNTAS POESÍAS?
CUÁNTOS LO ESTIMAN CON MAS AMOR

Yo desde niño ya me inspiraba
ni cuál estudio, tenía nociones
solo en oír las composiciones
en este oficio siempre pensaba
ya un poco a poco me preparaba
pero pidiéndole a mi Creador
en que me hiciera merecedor
llegar a un banco a cantar mis versos
lo fui logrando con mis esfuerzos:
ASÍ ES LA VIDA DEL CANTADOR

———

SUCH IS THE LIFE OF A POET
TRAVELING VALLEYS AND MOUNTAIN RANGES
TO SING VERSES, POESÍAS A PLENTY
HOW MANY VALUE HIM WITH GREAT LOVE

Since I was young I was inspired
I had no schooling, only intuition
as I heard the compositions
in this calling that I thought of always
then little by little I readied myself
but asking of my creator
to make me worthy
of scaling a tablado to sing my verses
I achieved it with my efforts:
SUCH IS THE LIFE OF A POET

—don Lencho

Iraq War / September 11

POR TODAS PARTES DE LA REGIÓN
SE CORRIÓ EL TEMA, NOTICIA Y RUIDO
QUE EN NUEVA YORK DE ESTADOS UNIDOS
HUBO UN DESASTRE Y UNA EXPLOSIÓN

Mes de septiembre, once la fecha
siendo en el año del dos mil uno
llegó la muerte de uno por uno
sin dar aviso, menos sospecha
por la mañana la cosa fue hecha
ese día martes fue la función
como a las ocho el primer avión
pegó en la torre donde había un gentío
esa mañana fue un desafío:
POR TODAS PARTES DE LA REGIÓN

———

ALL THROUGHOUT THE REGION
THE ISSUE, NEWS, AND SOUND CAME TO BE HEARD
THAT IN NEW YORK, IN THE UNITED STATES
THERE WAS A DISASTER, AN EXPLOSION

Month of September, 11th the date
it was the year 2001
death arrived, one by one
without warning, not even a suspicion
in the morning the deed was done
the happening was on that Tuesday
at around eight, the first plane
hit the tower full of people
that morning was one of adversity:
ALL THROUGHOUT THE REGION

—Abel

LLEGÓ LA GUERRA, DIO SU ZARPAZO
CAYÓ BAGDAD Y TODOS LO SABEN
PERO A SADDAM Y TAMBIÉN BIN LADEN
PUES, NO HAN PODIDO ECHARLES UN LAZO

Septiembre once no se me olvida
muchos murieron en Nueva York
cuánta catástrofe, cuánto dolor
la pena en mi alma no da cabida
miles y miles pierden la vida
bajo un presagio del cielo raso
esa tragedia no fue de paso
pues fue el principio y la realidad
de lo que pasa hoy en Bagdad:
LLEGÓ LA GUERRA, DIO SU ZARPAZO

_____

WAR IS UPON US WITH A BLOW
BAGHDAD HAS FALLEN AND EVERYONE KNOWS
BUT SADDAM AND ALSO BIN LADEN
WELL, THEY'RE STILL AT LARGE

I cannot forget September 11
many died in New York
what a catastrophe, what pain
the sorrow overwhelms my soul
thousands lose their lives
beneath the omen of a false sky
that tragedy was not in passing
well, it was the beginning and the reality
of what occurs today in Baghdad
WAR IS UPON US WITH A BLOW

—Graciano

DECIMALES TRANSITIONING INTO THE BRAVATA
ÁNGEL GONZÁLEZ AND CELSO, JALPAN DE SERRA, QUERÉTARO

HAY QUE CANTAR UN RATITO
PARA ALEGRAR A ESTA GENTE

ÉNTRALE POETA DE EN FRENTE
VAMOS HACIENDO EL RUIDITO

(2) El poeta vive al día
y siempre ha de estar atento
cualquier acontecimiento
un ciclón o carestía
como antes ya lo decía
yo lo expreso atentamente
oye, que habla tu sirviente
gracias por esa atención
comencemos el aporreón
PARA ALEGRAR A ESTA GENTE

———

WE MUST SING A LITTLE WHILE
TO ANIMATE THESE PEOPLE
JUMP IN, OPPOSING POET
LET'S MAKE SOME NOISE

(2) The poet lives day by day
and must always be attentive
to whatever occurence
a hurricane or poverty
as I mentioned before
I express this attentively
listen, your humble servant is speaking
thank you for your attention
let us begin the trouncing
TO ANIMATE THESE PEOPLE

—Ángel González

ÁNGEL, TE ESTOY ESCUCHANDO
Y CONTESTO A MI MANERA
AVIÉNTATE LA PRIMERA
YO AQUÍ TE ESTOY ESPERANDO

(2) Ante toda la reunión
no es que me sienta un fantoche

ya casi en la media noche
yo te doy contestación
si es que quieres aporreón
depende de mi manera
con mi quinta huapanguera
al público de esta gente
Ángel, hoy que estás en frente
TE CONTESTO A MI MANERA

―――

ÁNGEL, I AM LISTENING TO YOU
AND I ANSWER AS I PLEASE
YOU JUMP IN FIRST
I'LL BE HERE WAITING FOR YOU

(2) Before this audience
it is not that I feel like a braggart
it is nearly midnight
so I'll give you an answer
if you want to goad me
I'll accept on my terms
with my quinta huapanguera
in front of this public gathering
Ángel, today when you are in front
I ANSWER YOU AS I PLEASE

―Celso

BRAVATA

FIDEL AND HILARIO, SAN CIRO DE ACOSTA, SAN LUIS POTOSÍ

―――――――――――――――――――――――――――――――――――――

¿POR QUÉ TE ELEVAS ALLÁ A LA ALTURA?
SI TU DESTINO SE QUEDA ATRÁS
CONMIGO TIENES Y AHORA VERÁS
NOMÁS NO LLORES POBRE CRIATURA

Te digo y te hablo con la verdad
que yo te escucho y tú no me entiendes
tú no te acercas y no comprendes
aquellas frases de claridad

aquí que diga la humanidad
quién habla y dice con más finura
esto no es juego, ni es travesura
es un destino sabio y honrado
y tú no te hayas capacitado:
¿POR QUÉ TE ELEVAS ALLÁ A LA ALTURA?

―――――

WHY DO YOU THINK OF YOURSELF SO HIGHLY?
FOR YOUR TALENTS ARE SORELY LACKING
YOU'VE MET YOUR MATCH WITH ME
JUST DON'T GO CRYING, POOR CHILD

I speak to you with the truth
for I can hear you, but you don't understand
you don't come close to comprehending
the phrases I share with much clarity
let all those present tell it so
which of us speaks with greater talent
this is no game, nor an escapade
it is a wise and honored calling
and you are not in the least qualified:
WHY DO YOU THINK OF YOURSELF SO HIGHLY?

—Fidel

PARA SERVIRLE, MI SUPERIOR
VAMOS CUMPLIENDO CON LA TAREA
PARA QUE EL PÚBLICO EL PLEITO VEA
DÉME UNA PRUEBA DE SU VALOR

Aquí me tiene a disposición
buen puede entrarle a dicho combate
y si comete algún disparate
tendré que darle su reprochón
y si me ofende con más razón
el público siéndolo sabedor
aunque la pique de historiador
y como bardo de gran saber

esto prontito vamos a ver:
PARA SERVIRLE, MI SUPERIOR

———

I'M AT YOUR SERVICE, FORMIDABLE OPPONENT
LET US CARRY OUT THE TASK AT HAND
SO THE PUBLIC MAY BEAR WITNESS TO OUR QUARREL
GIVE ME PROOF OF YOUR COURAGE

I am here at your disposal
now you may enter into the present combat
and if you commit any mistake
I'll have to give you a bitter scolding
and, moreover, if you offend me
the public surely will bear witness
even if you consider yourself a historian
and a supposed wise bard
we'll soon be the judge of this:
I'M AT YOUR SERVICE, FORMIDABLE OPPONENT

—Hilario

RECONCILIATORY REMARKS AND FAREWELLS IN DECIMALES

GRACIANO AND PABLO, XICHÚ, GUANAJUATO

MUCHAS GRACIAS A ESTA GENTE
COMITÉ ORGANIZADOR
YA SE VA ESTE TROVADOR
LES DEJO UN VERSO EN LA FRENTE

(1) Yo me voy impresionado
de ver tanta algarabía
y se hace chiquito el día
porque estoy emocionado
pero el contrato ha acabado
y si no fui competente
pido perdón a la gente
me voy de esta región

los llevo en mi corazón
MUCHAS GRACIAS A ESTA GENTE

———

MANY THANKS TO THE PEOPLE
TO THE ORGANIZING COMMITTEE
THIS TROUBADOUR IS LEAVING
I LEAVE YOU WITH A VERSE IN MIND

(1) I walk away impressed
at having witnessed so much rejoicing
and the day becomes shorter
because I am thrilled
but the engagement has come to an end
and if I was not competent
I apologize to the audience
I leave this region
I carry you in my heart:
MANY THANKS TO THE PEOPLE

—Graciano

ADIÓS PÚBLICO HONRADOR
NOS VAMOS A RETIRAR
GRACIAS LE VAMOS A DAR
COMITÉ ORGANIZADOR

(1) Yo soy el Pablo Armendáriz
Mario, Gabino, desde ayer[37]
y hoy en este amanecer
les dejamos decimales
y con saludos cordiales
quiero dar un esplendor
a este pueblo observador
a esta bastante gente
les dice aquí su sirviente
ADIÓS PÚBLICO HONRADOR

———

GOOD-BYE, HONORABLE PUBLIC
WE ARE GOING TO DEPART
WE GIVE THANKS TO
THE ORGANIZING COMMITTEE

(1) I am Pablo Armendáriz
Mario, Gabino, since yesterday
and today at dawn
we leave you with decimales
and with cordial greetings
a splendid gift I want to impart
to this observant public
to so many people
your humble servant says to you:
GOODBYE, HONORABLE PUBLIC

—Pablo

Although I have mapped the structure of this music for the purpose of analysis, I do not consider taxonomical thinking to be the whole story so much as a way of imagining how everything comes together. Huapango arribeño is an act in the making, a vigorous negotiation that, although grasped through a general sense of form, takes shape beyond any sense of fixity. It enters into a span of broader polyphonic and intertextual processes of signification. This kind of lush, creative, and semiotic excess simultaneously emanates from and reinforces vernacular theories of performance practice that are crucial to its vitality—destino, fundamento, reglamento—and this "distinctive set of interpretive rules" comes together most dynamically during the topada, a field of intensities where musicians situate their music making in "wider contexts of personal association and collective memory" (McDowell 2010: 127, 147), for it is the music's social base that propels huapangueros toward one another. The competitive camaraderie at play comes in the form of poetic and musical jousting, where both ritualized speech and the sonic filigree of violins emerge in front of the audience's aural gaze, their pleasurable investment increasing with each passing moment. In this way the topada is sustained by those whose very subjectivities are constituted through the constellation of narratives that flourish within these performative contexts as an "arena of social process" (128). People seek out their musicians and enable the spaces for topadas to take place. Here, huapango arribeño—a collection of poesías, deci-males, valonas, sones, and jarabes—is coaxed into being through the com-municative exchanges between huapangueros (those next to you and those situated across the way); between musicians and the audience; between that which has previously been articulated, that which is anticipated, and all their varied recontextualizations. Indeed, this intertextual enactment is necessary to the production and reception of performance, where energy, technique, and sentiment enable musicians to elegantly communicate a sense of high drama—soaring notes, words, phrases, and melodies that wrap around everyone present. The arch of topada performance therefore pushes and augments the creative ho-rizons of performance (or creative advance), engendering an always moving and intimate dialogue between musicians, while dancers and listeners negotiate the space of poetic and musical narrative through their own participatory politics.

THE CALLING

Valentín looks up, listens intently as we both witness the topada in Xichú together. The troubadours are Celso of San Luis Potosí and Pablo of Xichú. Celso lleva la mano, and he and his ensemble have decided to forgo the key of A major entirely, shifting chromatically from D to E. Pablo and his musicians across the way follow, attempting to respond. As time passes, his violinists begin to struggle, however. Our friend Naro takes a break from dancing; he walks toward us, his sweaty body letting off steam. He grabs my shoulder and shakes me; we both look toward Pablo and his musicians, and he confesses, "No hombre, ni se baila a gusto. Uno anda zapateando pero con la cara toda torcida." (No way, man, you can't even dance comfortably. You're stomping your feet, but with your face all crooked.). The violinists on that end of the dance floor are not playing to his liking, it seems, and he can't help but react to the sonic dissonance, wearing his disapproval on his face—furrowed brow, sour look, twisted mouth. Naro is grappling with the performance, following melodies and poetics, registering virtuosic moments and misfires, attending to the huapangueros' stance—the "valual and affective quality" of his engage-ment is clearly influencing his overall experience of the meaning of the music, in turn constituting his own (audience) stance (Berger 2009). He rests for the moment, hoping the next time around things will sound better.

Cacho, Celso's primera vara, breezes through the engagement, however. The key of E seems to suit him quite well. The competitive camaraderie is now on full display, and the troubadours share in the following decimal exchange—a metalinguistic exercise that comments on each other's performance.

VERGÜENZA HAS DE TENER
OYE PABLO, CANTADOR
ME FIJO QUE EL "MI" MAYOR
TÚ NO LO PUEDES PONER

(1) La gente cuenta se ha dado
y el que trova esto te narra
para tocar la guitarra
Pablo, tú estás acabado
aquí y en cualquier poblado
esto yo te hago saber
te falta mucho que entender
las cosas se ponen graves
¿y de tonos tú que sabes?
VERGÜENZA HAS DE TENER

(2) Estando aquí en los tablados
Pablo, te digo en las pistas
yo veo que tus violinistas
tocan muy desentonados
te lo digo en versos trovados
ante un pueblo observador
Pablo, estás en un error
mas te quiero recalcar
primero ponte a estudiar
OYE PABLO, CANTADOR

(3) Aquí por esta ocasión
te sostengo lo que hablo
Guillermo enséñele a Pablo
como es un "MI" mayor
para que se oiga mejor
y así se gane el honor
lo admiro por su valor
ya sea en jarabes o sones
Pablo, tú si descompones
ME FIJO QUE EL "MI" MAYOR

(4) Pablo hoy que vengo a Xichú
te digo bueno y no borracho

me fijé que tu muchacho
es buen músico que tú
te crees la cu-rru-cu-cu
pero aquí vas a perder
aunque no lo quieras creer
oye Pablo trovador
el tono de "MI" mayor
TÚ NO LO PUEDES PONER

———

YOU SHOULD BE ASHAMED
LISTEN, PABLO, TROUBADOUR
I SEE THAT IN E MAJOR
YOU ARE UNABLE TO PLAY

(1) People have now taken notice
what this troubadour now narrates
in the ways of playing guitar
Pablo, you are washed up
here and in whatever place
this I am letting you know
you have a lot to learn
things have become serious
and what do you know of musical keys?
YOU SHOULD BE ASHAMED

(2) As we are here atop the tablados
Pablo, I tell you that in questions of music
I see that your violinists
are playing well out of tune
I tell you in improvised verses
before this observant public
Pablo, you are making a mistake
I want to stress this to you
first you should begin practicing
LISTEN, PABLO, TROUBADOUR

(3) Here on this occasion
I support what I have mentioned
Guillermo, please show Pablo[38]

how to play in E major
so that he may sound better
and regain his honor
I admire him for his courage
be it in jarabes or sones
Pablo, you make a mess of things
I SEE THAT IN E MAJOR

(4) Pablo, today that I have come to Xichú
I tell you sober, not drunk
I see that your compatriot[39]
is a better musician than you
you do think highly of yourself
but here you will surely fail
even if you refuse to believe it
listen, Pablo, troubadour
the key of E major
YOU ARE UNABLE TO PLAY

—Celso

CELSO, NO TE DE CORAJE
EN ESTA NOCHE MAÑANA
¡VIVA LA MUJER SERRANA!
HOY SE LE BRINDA HOMENAJE

(1) Celso, por acá está el tema
no le pudiste llegar
ya te fuiste hasta el mar
por mi parte no hay problema
bien sería la diadema
pero eso es de purito ultraje
¿y para qué te haces guaje?
yo en todito me fijo
¿qué? ¿Chalo no te dijo?
CELSO, NO TE DÉ CORAJE

(2) Celso, sin cortesías
autor es tema y de neta

y a llegar buen poeta
que te hagas poesías
pa' que andes de rancherías
y como dijo Quintana
tú me sirves de botana
tú no eres trovador
dice tu servidor
EN ESTA BELLA MAÑANA

(3) No cantas ni una siquiera
pienso que es lo que es vergüenza
de ser poeta piensa
y aquí en esta cabecera
piensa con esa manera
y en la tierra mexicana
te digo de la dama,
digo ya basta el ultraje
ya que ahora se hace un homenaje
¡VIVA LA MUJER SERRANA!

(4) Tú tienes tus vanidades
te digo sin más entonos
Celso, no se dicen tonos
se dicen tonalidades
consulta y son las verdades
¿y para qué te haces guaje?
hoy se brinde un homenaje
porque se debe de hablar
de la dama en el lugar
CELSO, HOY ES SU HOMENAJE

———

CELSO, DON'T BE ANGERED
ON THIS DARK MORNING
LONG LIVE HIGHLANDER WOMEN!
TODAY WE PAY TRIBUTE TO THEM

(1) Celso, the theme is out this way
you couldn't even come close
you've gone all the way out to sea[40]

as for me, I have no problem
such loving accolades are well and good
but what you've done is an insult
and why are you being so absent-minded
I take notice of everything
what, did Chalo not tell you?[41]
CELSO, DON'T BE ANGERED

(2) Celso, I'll speak plainly
an author attends to themes and is competent
and to become a good poet
go and write poesías
so you can perform in communities
and as Quintana said
you are merely an appetizer for me
you are not a real troubadour
your humble servant tells you
ON THIS BEAUTIFUL MORNING

(3) You haven't even sung one poesía
I think this is a shame
reflect on what it is to be a poet
and here in this municipality[42]
think along those lines
and on Mexican soil
I tell you of the respectable lady
I say enough with the insults
for today we pay tribute
LONG LIVE HIGHLANDER WOMEN!

(4) You certainly have your vanities
I say to you without modulating
Celso, you don't say tones
they are called keys
go and ask and you shall know the truth
and why are you being so absent-minded
today we pay tribute
because we must speak of

the women of this place
CELSO, TODAY IS A TRIBUTE

—Pablo

Each troubadour's decimal refers to and characterizes the unfolding debate with specific reference to prior iterations of the opposing troubadour's poetic discourse. This coconstituted reflexivity focused on each other's linguistic, poetic, and performative competences involves an assessment of how sound and well-informed instances of poetic discourse actually are, that is, how grounded they are in grammatical and performative patterns—fundamento and reglamento. Each troubadour is monitoring for aesthetic fit. Pablo claims Celso is not attending to temas de fundamento; topically, the thematic focus of the topada—in honor of *la mujer serrana* (the woman of the Sierra)—is the organizing theme of the Festival del Huapango Arribeño y de la Cultura de la Sierra Gorda in Xichú this year. And Celso claims Pablo is lacking in his ability to play in the key of E, thus not fulfilling the demands of reglamento. However, these metalinguistic enactments are themselves potential instances of object language. In other words, the unfolding poetic commentary focused on what décima poetics are accomplishing (or not) in this particular context is a metalinguistic objectification of language that is itself in the objectified décima form and therefore available for future objectification within the topada.[43] What we bear witness to in this instance is a reflexive account of the dialogic production of discourse and an in-the-moment assessment by both parties of the quality of one another's performance, of one another's participation in the coconstruction of the topada. According to both troubadours, each has misfired (Austin 1962).

By sunrise, Celso and Cacho finally move to the key of G major, though they manage to sneak in a few piquetes in E minor. I'm dancing close to Celso's tablado right as Cacho begins to modulate from G major to E minor. An older gentleman dancing not too far from me stops, listens, looks up at Celso's tablado, turns and looks in Pablo's direction, then loudly exclaims, "Oye nomás, cabrones!" (You hear that, bastards!). The debate continues.

(verso de jarabe)
Por mi parte no hay problema
Celso, yo soy buena reata

si no hallas ninguna del tema
cántante una de bravata

———

As for me, I have no problem
Celso, I am a good lasso
if you can't attend to the theme
sing one of bravata

—Pablo

(verso de jarabe)
Oye Pablo, en este rol
las cuerdas no me congojan
allí les va este SOL mayor
y a ver si así la despiojan

———

Listen, Pablo, in this role
the instrument strings don't distress me
here goes this G major
let's see if you can pull it off now

—Celso

"Performance rests on an assumption of responsibility to an audience for a display of communicative virtuosity," Bauman argues, a communicative dynamic that opens up the textuality in question to evaluate scrutiny by those listening and dancing, by those touched by the dialogic overflow of music and poetics (2004: 9). The social legibility of performance is contingent on aesthetic evaluation and vice versa, a feedback loop that animates and integrates ideological and embodied responses that draw together the affective qualities of aurality. In this outward coursing, this aural saturation, the ligatures of sociality are embodied aesthetically; in these moments life paths cross and occupy a space contoured by an intimately and laboriously produced musico-poetic arch of communicative exchange. This exchange is a calling—it is a vocation, competence in performance, an aesthetic commitment, but it is also a hailing forth, a voicing, a literal calling out to the other next to you, to those across from you, to the audience surrounding you. It's your throat growing raw from it, the urgency of it, and you simultaneously struggle to stay awake and stay patient as you wait to release your next décima; it is when you feel most viscerally that music making is your life path, and everyone is dancing, stomping, to hear you keep playing and jump wholly, mentally, physically, into what you are doing.

Calling out is a task performed by the body, taken in by the ears. To call out is to animate interpersonally, to reach with the voice, to share aloud stories that will circulate in that moment and beyond it, remaining legible, if only in memory. The calling happens internally and externally. Mario González—within the broader perspective of the topada—suggests that this performative dynamic, although always on the brink of toppling over, must necessarily be balanced harmoniously. It is called out, and the response is called back by listening, dancing, commenting, yelling, staying, and leaving. The calling is mutual. The practitioner is responsible to the audience, imploring the audience to be responsive. He comments:

> Uno transmite a los oyentes. Tienes que sacar tu mejor repertorio para que la gente te la jales para acá. . . . La gente ve de aquí pa' allá y dice, "Esta música se oye bonita" o "Aquellos no se dejan." Esto es el rebote, la contradicción. La gente es la que va a escuchar, a bailar.

> (One transmits to those listening. You have to display the best of your repertoire so that you gain the favor of the people. . . . The people look in both directions and comment, "This ensemble's music sounds beautiful" or "Those aren't giving in." This is the rebounding, the controversy. The people are there to listen, to dance.)

The resolution, then, is neither a win nor a loss but an interaction with the audience, he suggests, though on the surface the interaction is framed around two juxtaposed groups, calling out to one another. And we come full circle, from the augmented meanings of el destino—beyond life path and toward intimacy—to its palimpsestual overlay with the unembellished semantic resonance of *calling*, for the performative enactments that make up huapango arribeño are constituted through dialogue, through a continuously moving and negotiated reaching and calling out. Intimacy is embedded in performance, through poetic and sonic callings between the groups performing, but, more important, between the huapangueros and the audience. The kinesthetic burning of energy atop the tablados enables layers of material and immaterial expenditure through dancing, chatting, and partying to the point of exhaustion, and this excessive, glorious burning off—lasting past sunrise—is slathered over the entire space with music sounding off into distances, disturbing sleep, inviting consumption for the sake of excretion. We take in the sound; our feet tap and burn and hurt; we hold each other close; our sweat is slick and smells like *café de olla* (cinnamon-laced coffee) and beer. The musical key suddenly changes, and the boot heels around me hit harder. I'm thrust into the choreographed mass. A *borracho* (drunk) asks a woman to dance, and she wags her finger to signal "no"; he moves on, unfazed. He dozes, drinks, and then dances again. The sun peeks over the mountains; it rises, taking forever. Children join the crowd again after napping through the sonic filigree of A major. The dancing grows muted, but only for a moment—G major and the final *poesías de bravata* are on their way; you can feel it. I'm hungry, but I don't want to go; I know it's about to end. Suddenly, the air becomes damp, the sky overcast, and the morning is now steamy from the dew—daybreak. Sunlight slowly begins to wrap around everyone and everything.

The space of performance is, more than anything, a space of intimacy in which people, performance, and the space itself are unbound, surpassing the boundaries of one's own body. *Things*, which are so often closed off and fragmented into singular presencing, open up to conjoin, meld, and happen. From a Bataillean perspective, the excess of performance is a way of releasing humans (in particular, but not exclusively) from the enclosures established by the political economy—capitalist, from a Marxian viewpoint. Unbinding the singularity of being is necessary to the suturing of social fragmentation that happens through capitalism. By *unbinding*, I refer to Habermas, who defines it as a process through which the closed-off subject can regain intimacy with "a life-context that has become alien, confined, cut off, and fragmented" (1984: 81–82). Unbinding, here, happens through spontaneous sounded revelry through which the listener surrenders subjectivity, if only for a moment— "Oye nomás, cabrones!" (You hear that, bastards!). When we are faced with a lack of intimacy and sovereignty, being human means searching for those things that are lost, and doing so along unknown paths.

Kathleen Stewart describes this excess in different circumstances, but to a similar end: "Imagine the sense of being caught up and carried along in a poetic movement, how meaning lies emergent in the unfolding of events about which there is always something more to say, how stories not only allow but actively produce an excess of meaningfulness, a constant searching" (1996: 58). Musicians walk these unknown paths during topadas and watch the audience members do the same, ending up somewhere deeper; they are not sure where it's all going, yet are pushing to explore the simultaneously lush and airy territories of that experience, bearing witness to whatever happens. Huapangueros move forward in this space, always changed by it, changed by each other, companions existing between a polyphony of destinos: the presently lived moment (intimacy in the making), an aesthetic commitment (unfolding in the now and as a life path), and the sociality of life itself—neither isolated nor singular, they are all caught up and called out in one way or another. This extension of intertextuality into everyday life—all the way through society at large—harkens precisely to Homero's sentiment at the beginning of this chapter as he reflected on his day-to-day existence as a migrant laborer and Valentín's deportation, saying that all of these things qualified as "matters of life, matters of the calling" . . .

Mentions of troubadour poets echo out from precolonial Mexico (Ravicz 1970) and equally as far back as twelfth-century Occitania. The term *troubadour* is itself French, although it borrows from the Occitan *trobar*—to compose, discuss, and invent—at the core of which is a sense of the troubadour as a "finder," or, in the words of Michael Serres, a "producer of improbable novelty" (1997: 104). To search is to take up the call to elevate the ordinary through memorably structured music and language, to lend sounded significance to the everyday, to amplify through "dramaturgical voice" (Ihde 2007: 167). In this way the calling—el destino as vocation, as vernacular theory of aesthetic production, as intertextual voicing—is centrally about "sociable feeling" (A. Fox 2004). In sum, the calling ultimately puts on display a collective affinity that calls attention to the place of history, language, and culture in people's lives, both implicitly and explicitly. In the midst of this intertextual entanglement of aesthetics and society, situated knowledges are performed into being, often under duress and out of necessity as types of differential consciousnesses (Sandoval 1991). And this is where the next chapter moves us—to Guanajuato and Querétaro, to farming communities teetering on hillsides and sunken mining towns huddled on the ridges of towering mountains; to places filled up and emptied out with desire in the face of the drastic modulations that occurred in everyday life in Mexico in the 1970s and 1980s; to a culling of shared memories of seasonal migration—a heaping of polyphonic voicings regarding this transformative moment on top of a palimpsest of meanings already amassed, a moment that anticipates huapango arribeño's migration to the United States.

THREE

VERSES AND FLOWS AT THE DAWN OF NEOLIBERAL MEXICO

¿Quién cruzó el desierto? ¿Quién llegó al colegio?

¿Quién es empleado? ¿Quién abrió negocio?

¿Quién no tiene miedo de llegar al cielo?

¿Quién sabe luchar? ¡Nosotros!

¿Quién sale a protestar y sabe marchar?

¿Quién defiende sus derechos y sabe ganar?

¿Quién sabe vivir, sabe compartir, sabe convivir? ¡Nosotras!

Nosotras, nosotros, ya no somos "los otros."

Somos la razón del browning of America

———

Who crossed the desert? Who attended college?

Who is employed? Who opened a business?

Who isn't afraid to reach the heavens?

Who knows how to fight? We do!

Who goes out to protest and knows how to march?

Who defends their rights, knows how to win?

Who knows how to live, how to share, how to coexist? We [women] do!

We [women] do, we [men] do, we are no longer "the others."

We are the reason for the browning of America.

—OLMECA

Las manos diestras en construir

o ensamblar partes automotrices

manos que siembran, riegan raíces

o hacen andamios para subir

ojos capaces de discernir

ágiles mentes, dedos ligeros

de piscadores o de torneros

sin fin de gente cuya destreza
ha generado tanta riqueza:
¡VIVA EL TRABAJO DE LOS BRACEROS!

———

Dexterous hands that build
or assemble automotive parts
hands that sow, that irrigate roots
or assemble scaffolding to climb atop
eyes capable of discerning
agile minds and able fingers
of farmworkers or machinists
endless people whose skills
have generated so much wealth:
CHEERS TO THE WORK OF THE BRACERO MIGRANT LABORERS!
—GUILLERMO VELÁZQUEZ

"SWEET HOME CHICAGO"

Los Angeles–based hip-hop MC Olmeca took to the stage in Chicago in a fury, showcasing his English-Spanish bilingual flow, hypnotizing the predominantly Latina/o audience, heads bobbing in unison, fists in the air; they were fixated by the artist-activist-educator and the urgency in his lyrics. A son of migrant parents, Olmeca performs a brand of hip-hop that sounds of both inner-city U.S. America and Latin America, pulling from both wells of influence to rap introspectively about backyard family get-togethers over standard Caribbean *boleros* like "Reloj" in the style of the Chilean crooners Los Angeles Negros, harkening toward the Latina/o roots of hip-hop proper. His brand of politics has paired him with the likes of Dolores Huerta, Naomi Klein, Emory Douglas, and Zack de la Rocha at political rallies and in university settings. On this night he channels both personal history and activist spirit as he performs songs from his latest release, *Brown Is Beautiful* (2013), rockin' this small club in what used to be a Puerto Rican neighborhood—long since gentrified—just like on any other stage in Canada, Mexico, or Europe. Immigration and youth empowerment are the themes of *Brown Is Beautiful*, and they take hold this evening, resonating with the audience, many of whom are also children of migrants, Chicagoans through and through, who currently find their families the targets of ferocious xenophobic politics. In seeking out the extreme edge of this sentiment, one need look no further than Ann

Coulter's debate on immigration at the Conservative Political Action Conference just a month before Olmeca's performance. She also spoke about the "browning of America," and her argument moved gradually from diminishing the worth of brownness, particularly with regard to economic sustainability and health care, to making claims about "excessive fertility," equating the children of migrants with "litter" and trash. The transition from Latina/o reproduction to litter is far from accidental. It's a continuous narrative thread about people of color and their supposed pathological behavior. In contrast, Olmeca hailed forth these devalued brown youth—or trash, in the eyes of Coulter—invoking instead a dignified transnational working-class subjectivity: hard workers ("¿Quién es empleado?"), college students ("¿Quién llegó al colegio?"), entrepreneurs ("¿Quién abrió negocio?"), everyday people struggling in the city ("¿Quién sabe luchar?"). Theirs is a Chicago in motion, a daily grind and hustle, a space of dreams and labor flows tethered to Latin America, of friends and family close at hand and far away, coming and going, separated by borders, calling both places home. They are at the center of what Chicago is: a deeply segregated American city (like most) that isolates people of color and criminalizes migrants in daily life, pushing them to the margins, but a city, nonetheless, that they have built while incessantly challenging the stratified social order in which they are positioned, making a place for themselves in neighborhoods like Pilsen, Humboldt Park, and Little Village. Chicago is home . . . sweet home.

By now, Robert Johnson's "Sweet Home Chicago" may have come to mind, if only because this section bears its name. There exists an echo between the imagined diasporic connections of African-American migration north that Johnson's anthem of survival gives voice to and Olmeca's message of home among migrant families.[1] If one sets aside the lore surrounding Johnson's life, talent, and death, the literature on Johnson suggests that the torrid history of the South haunted the Mississippi blues man's desire for life beyond a racially segregated social order. The blues and its varied definitions are beyond the scope of the present discussion; however, it is worth noting that the genre's rise in popularity in the early to mid-twentieth century parallels what historians term the Great Migration, as African-Americans moved out of the rural U.S. South and into northern centers of industry. Searching for jobs and opportunity beyond the misery of racial oppression and poverty in the wake of failed Reconstruction and the rise of Jim Crow, African-Americans escaped to cities like Chicago, a place Johnson, as a traveling musician, was himself familiar with, having been there in addition to places like Texas, Canada, New York,

Kentucky, Indiana, Arkansas, and Memphis (Wald 2004). While his "Sweet Home Chicago" borrows from Kokomo Arnold's "Old Original Kokomo Blues," the shout-out to Chicago sets it apart, a poetics that imagines that city as a promised land of sorts—itself later home to a grassroots electric sound pioneered by African-American migrants just beyond Johnson's generation. To understand what Chicago as home meant to them in the 1940s and 1950s, we must similarly account for the realities of the day: lynchings, the murder of civil rights workers, church bombings, and of course, Emmett Till.

You, perhaps, are familiar with the story. The fourteen-year-old Till was murdered in the Mississippi Delta (home of the blues) in 1955 after purportedly flirting with an Anglo woman, Carolyn Bryant Donham (though it was recently revealed that her claims were fabricated). His killers shot him and mutilated his body, which they then disposed of in the Tallahatchie River, weighting it down with a cotton-gin fan. The versatile jazz and blues stylings of Nina Simone echo out a decade later:

Alabama's gotten me so upset
Tennessee made me lose my rest
And everybody knows about Mississippi Goddam[2]

While their acquittal and similar atrocities helped galvanize the civil rights movement of the 1950s and 1960s, the entire country was forced to face the barbarity of Till's murder, as his mother insisted on having an open-casket funeral service after his tortured, broken body was returned to his hometown. Till was from Chicago, a city that would produce a hard-hitting blues sound "at once urgently urban and country plain ... poised historically between different political, urban, and culture-industry orders, between Dwight D. Eisenhower and John F. Kennedy ... between an older industrial order and an oncoming postindustrial 'urban crisis'" (Lott 2011: 697–698). Another episode of racial violence, nearly thirty years after Simone's protest, was the brutal beating of Rodney King in Los Angeles, deep in the bowels of the so-called urban crisis.

In the wake of the rebellion sparked in response to the acquittal of King's Los Angeles Police Department assailants, black and brown artists also voiced their anger, telling the story of inner-city violence and injustice while also finding inspiration in their own communities' histories of resistance.[3] Perhaps the most well known are commercially successful hip-hop artists like Tupac Shakur and Dr. Dre. However, an entire generation of Latina/o and multiethnic performers emerged at this time, including the likes of Ozomatli, Quetzal, and Olmeca—all inspired by pre-Columbian cultures in naming their respective musical projects. Their musical voices also took shape in the wake of anti-immigrant hostility that swept across California during Governor Pete Wilson's tenure in office, the most immediate precursor to the present-day xenophobia targeting ethnic Mexicans. In response to the explosion of Mexican migration—or the browning of that state—California most famously passed the Save Our State voter initiative (1994), better known as Proposition 187, which aimed to exclude undocumented migrant children and their parents from virtually all public services.[4] Although it began in California, this trend went national and set the tone for the passage of the Illegal Immigration Reform and Immigrant Responsibility Act of 1996, which further militarized the U.S.-Mexico border and limited migrant eligibility for social service benefits at the local, state, and federal levels. These disciplinary policy measures were coupled with intensified border enforcement guided by the twin strategies of territorial denial and prevention through deterrence, which continue to utilize hazardous desert terrain to genocidally manage migrant bodies (Cornelius 2005; Hing 2004; Martínez et al. 2013; Nevins 2002). First implemented was Operation Hold-the-Line in El Paso, Texas in 1993; followed by Operation Gatekeeper in the San Diego area in 1994, Operation Safeguard in central Arizona in 1995, and Operation Rio Grande in South Texas in 1997. According to a report published in June 2013 by the Binational Migration Institute at the University of Arizona, between 1990 and 2012 the Pima County Office of the Medical Examiner in Tucson, Arizona, examined the remains of 2,238 migrants (Martínez et al. 2013: 11–12). "¿Quién cruzó el desierto?"

This order of things is a logical outgrowth of both a binational political-economic calculus between Mexico and the United States and a hard-line revival of U.S. Cold War politics in the 1980s. While the latter provided the geopolitical backdrop for an imagined moral panic surrounding undocumented migration and the subsequent border-security framework of low-intensity conflict (Dunn 1996), the former was spearheaded by Mexico's political class and industrial elite as they consented to industry deregulations in order to "circumvent the legal hurdles complicating access to the vast U.S. market" (Wise and Cypher 2007: 136). With the highly contested (if not entirely fraudulent) election of President Carlos Salinas de Gortari (1988–1994), neoliberal reforms dissolved much of Mexican protectionism of domestic industry in the name of stimulating foreign investment and paying off Mexico's debt. The answer was NAFTA. Ratified in 1994, the trilateral trade deal among Canada, Mexico, and the United States has been one of the largest and most lucrative in recent history. Although NAFTA was presented as an "antidote to emigration," Raúl Delgado Wise and James M. Cypher (2007: 120–121) argue that its "inner-rationality" was in fact an export of cheap labor achieved through both the disembodied export of labor via the *maquiladora* (assembly plant) industry (as imported materials are processed by low-skilled workers and then re-exported, overwhelmingly to the United States) and the direct export of transnational laborers. The crucial piece in this equation for Mexico, however, came three years earlier, in 1991, when de Gortari rewrote agrarian reform law, ostensibly doing away with article 27 of the Mexican Constitution and bringing an end to ejido land policy (which also included subsidies, price protections, and access to basic agricultural resources), thus making it easier for portions of low-producing lands to be used for large-scale commercial agriculture (Bohórquez Molina et al. 2003: 61). Because of this, combined with NAFTA provisions that allowed for imports of subsidized agricultural products from the United States, especially corn, it is no surprise that a Public Citizen report (2015) states that the number of undocumented migrants in the United States has increased 185 percent since NAFTA's signing (3.9 million in 1992 to 11.1 million in 2011).[5] Whereas Mexico had imposed import permits and tariffs (upward of 20 percent) on one-quarter of U.S. agricultural products before NAFTA, these levies were expunged; as a result, 1.5 million (others estimate twice as many) small-scale Mexican producers and their families were driven out of business (Stout 2008).

Increased migration flows across the U.S.-Mexico border in the 1990s may be linked to these neoliberal policies; however, the tumultuous 1970s and 1980s provide the appropriate context for understanding the emergence of these reforms. Economic shocks during these decades set the stage for Mexico's debt crisis in 1982 and subsequent policy responses during the de Gortari years. Huapango arribeño's most contemporary voicing, I argue, took shape at this moment in time, when literal and figurative flows—pre-NAFTA migrations and the poetics (in the spirit of hip-hop) that gave voice to these movements, respectively—emerged and catalyzed, for instance, a vibrant festival in Xichú, Guanajuato. Decades later, efforts to sustain this festival have taken hold among U.S. migrant communities, among the very people who have since navigated the post-NAFTA neoliberal border. So the browning of America that Olmeca celebrates is the result of migratory flows that were decades in the making, flows at the crossroads of transnational economic integration and border restrictions. This historical perspective allows us to pivot from the post-NAFTA world of the Los Angeles music scene via Chicago to huapango arribeño in the context of the dawn of neoliberal Mexico in the 1970s and 1980s. During this period, huapangueros reimagined their lives across this transforming social landscape—moving between rural areas and centers of industry. Amid an analogous time of economic crisis, they shaped dynamic and newly intelligible shifts in huapango arribeño's performance as a localized aesthetic negotiation of the global political and economic vicissitudes of the 1970s, a time when (1) post-Fordist labor flows were reconstituted in new and fluctuating arrangements—deskilled, mobile, and highly expendable (Giddens 1991)—and (2) U.S.-Mexico transnational economic integration began to develop into what would become neoliberalism.[6] The collapse of the Keynesian development strategy, the oil and monetary convulsions of the 1970s, and the appearance of structural adjustment throughout Latin America in the early 1980s are particularly relevant in locating huapango arribeño's expressive textures. This is to say, foregrounding the politics of global interconnectedness reveals how the "immediate experience of community is in fact inevitably constituted by a wider set of social and spatial relations" (Gupta and Ferguson 1997: 7).

In the remainder of this chapter, I illustrate this relationship between performance and labor migration, between poetics and political-economic realities (or verses and flows), by centering on the story of the emergence of Xichú, Guanajuato, as a grassroots huapango festival site. To lend specificity to this effort, I trace the life and work of one of its native sons, Guillermo Velázquez, a troubadour who came into the huapango arribeño tradition in the 1970s and played a pivotal role in founding Xichú's festival. Intensified migration from the region to the United States beginning in the 1980s—to California, Mississippi, Texas, and elsewhere—has contributed to his transnational popularity. He and his group, Los Leones de la Sierra de Xichú, have become a touchstone vital in strengthening community cohesion amid the tense politics and economic circumstances that surround the migrant experience. Together they have recorded and released nearly forty independently produced albums, and they continue to expand the horizons of tradition in ways that strengthen links between present-day realities and their aesthetic antecedents. Velázquez's story, in addition to the many other stories in this chapter, are not only of performance, or of coming to political consciousness, but most importantly they are stories of survival. I begin with Velázquez's early life, when his family left Xichú's mines for Mexico City.

THE GREAT METROPOLIS

Santa Fe y Real de Minas de Guanajuato was founded in the mid-sixteenth century after the Spanish discovered rich mineral seams in this portion of the greater Chichimeca region, making Guanajuato and its surroundings one of the most influential areas during the colonial period. Exploration and mining of the Sierra Gorda portion of northeastern Guanajuato began as early as the 1580s (Powell 1952).[7] Some of these mines remained active well into the twentieth century, including those of Xichú and Atarjea, Guanajuato, and the often-mentioned *minas del río colorado* and *minas del realito*, located in between the municipalities of Santa María del Río in San Luis Potosí and Victoria in Guanajuato. After World War II, countless Xichú natives were left jobless once the mineral wealth was exhausted in that township. Many subsequently migrated to labor in urban centers. Guillermo Velázquez's family was no exception. They traveled to and from Mexico City in the 1940s and 1950s within the context of embattled land claims—the legacy of Mexico's fraught history of post-Revolutionary agrarian reform, or lack thereof—and a waning local economy based on unproductive mines. Velázquez was subsequently born in the great metropolis in 1948 as his father and then-pregnant mother migrated from Xichú to Mexico City in search of work.

The interwar period just before Velazquez's childhood migrations was one of profound expansion in the state's role in determining monetary policy worldwide. Keynesian developmentalist strategies emerged on the world economic stage not only to replace the laissez-faire economics that contributed to the near collapse of capitalism during the Great Depression but also to guarantee state-managed growth and full employment as a way of curbing worker demands (Cleaver 1979). Seasonal migrants from the Sierra Gorda, like Velázquez's parents, encountered a transitioning industrial economy marked by a regimented logic of production in Mexico City's factories as the country's domestic industry fiercely reorganized work around a Taylorist logic of mass production to produce import substitutes (Buffie and Krause 1989; Lipietz 1997). This geographic oscillation between Mexico City and Xichú, as well as the precarious working conditions under which his parents labored, all influenced Velázquez's childhood—a life of travel from a mining province to an industrial metropolis.

In his late teens, Velázquez began to pursue a life in the clergy. He studied in seminaries in Querétaro and New Mexico before abandoning the priesthood quite suddenly years later, for which he cites the death of his father as the predominant reason. Soon after, he returned to Mexico City in search of work, just like his parents:

> En el 73 fue cuando estuve en una encrucijada de mi existencia. Me fui a México a buscar trabajo. Yo había estado en el seminario hasta ese momento. Decidí, a partir de la muerte de mi padre y otros factores, pues volver a cero. . . . Me costó mucho trabajo hallar empleo. Lo encontré en una fábrica de muñecas. . . . Estoy los tres años ahí.

> (In 1973 I was at a crossroads in my life. I went to Mexico City in search of work. I had been in the seminary up until that moment. After the death of my father and other circumstances, I decided to start over. . . . It took a lot of work to find employment. I found it in a doll factory. . . . I remained there for three years.)

Finding employment was a challenge, but he eventually managed to secure a factory job. He describes the routine he encountered:

> Al entrar yo a trabajar, a estar en contacto directo con el ambiente obrero, a tomar el camión en la mañana, a tomarme un licuado antes de chequar mi tarjeta, estar desde en la mañana hasta en la noche, regresar cansado, dormir unas horas y tener que levantarme muy temprano, también estar enfrentando al mismo tiempo una crisis depresiva en la que estaba y que fui remontando a base de agallas también—eso me abrió los poros a muchas cosas para las que yo no había sido suficientemente consiente.

> (To enter the workplace, to be emerged in factory life, to take the bus in the morning, to drink a milkshake before clocking in, to be there from morning to nightfall, to return home tired, sleep a few hours, only to wake up early again, all while suffering from a deep depression that took a great amount of willpower to overcome—all of that made me conscious of a number of things that I was previously unaware of.)

This consciousness, he goes on to describe, was the pivotal realization that his life in Mexico City was contingent on circumstances—social, political, and otherwise—impacting the world at large. The 1970s were marked by a global capitalist crisis in which the abandonment of the Bretton Woods system in 1971, the global food shortage of 1972–1974, the oil crisis of 1973, and the worldwide recession of 1974 all figured. David Harvey (1990) considers these shocks central to the post-Keynesian regime of flexible accumulation characterized by hyperaccelerated, fragmented, and dispersed systems of production. In Mexico the Luis Echeverría administration (1970–1976)—burdened by fiscal mismanagement, capital flight, and the deteriorating outcomes resulting from easing of protectionist policies on domestic industry—devalued the peso by 60 percent (Buffie and Krause 1989; Cardoso and Helwege 1992). These monetary convulsions and post-Fordist reorganizations of labor likely emerged in response to the resurgent radical movements of the postwar period and the revolutionary effervescence of the 1960s (Holloway 2002). This worldwide popular offensive was met by nation-states and multinational corporations with strategies that eliminated the social leveling afforded by the Keynesian management model, turning to the virtues of direct competition as a market control mechanism for social unrest. As Crozier, Huntington, and Watanuki (1975) argued, monetary instability was a direct result of too much democracy—the active participation of the masses in civic and political life had to be tempered with repressive rule.

Concurrent mobilizations of workers, women, students, the unemployed, intellectuals, artists, and activists also formed part of the popular movements and social rebellion during this time in cities like London, Paris, and West Berlin and in countries like Argentina, Brazil, Czechoslovakia, Italy, Jamaica, Japan, and the United States. In addition, 1968 also witnessed U.S. urban uprisings following the assassination of Dr. Martin Luther King Jr. and during the black and Chicano civil rights movements, the protests at the Democratic National Convention in Chicago, and global opposition to the war in Vietnam.[8] Political mobilizations in Mexico in 1968 echoed this cycle of social upheaval occurring the world over—indeed, the Tlatelolco massacre weighs heavily in the Mexican imagination to this day. Tlatelolco was but one incident in the Mexican government's dirty war against leftist elements, a secret scorched-earth campaign authorized under Presidents Gustavo Díaz Ordaz, Luis Echeverría, and José López Portillo. While visiting his brother in Mexico City, Velázquez unwittingly found himself in the immediate fallout of this most tragic episode: the Mexican military murdered hundreds (or thousands; the official body count is unknown) of students, demonstrators, and innocent bystanders on October 2, 1968, at a peaceful rally in the Plaza de Tres Culturas in Tlatelolco in the heart of Mexico City. Given this volatility, Velázquez comments with regard to his time living in Mexico City:

> Esos años fueron decisivos para mí porque por un lado alcancé a definir el rumbo de mi vida y por otro cobré conciencia de muchas cosas que estaban pasando en el país. Estamos hablando de la primera devaluación fuerte en el gobierno de Echeverría, estamos hablando de que en ese tiempo estaba gestándose todo lo que fue la guerrilla armada, que yo no sabía nada de eso, pero ahí estaba.

> (Those years were a turning point for me because, on the one hand, I was able to define my life path and, on the other, I became conscious of a number of things that were occurring in the country. We're talking about the first peso devaluation of the Echeverría administration, we're talking about a time when clandestine guerilla warfare was gradually unfolding, all of which I was unaware of, but it was all there.)[9]

He is but one of many Xichú natives who migrated to Mexico City during this frenzied time to work as day laborers and in factories.

In 1972, after having labored on the assembly line at an electronics manufacturing plant for three years with no pay increase, the late Sebastián Salinas—a huapango arribeño violinist also from Xichú, Guanajuato—participated in a three-month strike demanding a living wage and improved working conditions: "Tenía mi señora con una niñita y otra por venir y sin dinero, eso sí fue sufrimiento" (I had my wife with a little girl and another on the way and no money, that was suffering). Salinas's father, Miguel Salinas, a huapango arribeño troubadour, passed away when Sebastián was fourteen; from that moment on Salinas worked to help provide for his mother and siblings. He eventually migrated to Mexico City at the age of sixteen. He remained there for thirty-six years. And it was there that he reconnected with huapango arribeño. He came across a few huapangueros, befriended them, and slowly began to pick up the violin. He adds:

> Me dio por agarrar un instrumento en el estado de México. . . . Tocaba con otros músicos quienes andaban allá trabajando o que venían de la sierra a las tocadas. . . . Gente de la provincia que se iba a trabajar al DF, pues se llevaba la raíz y ahí se iba uno acoplando y trabajando.[10]

(I got the urge to pick up an instrument in the state of Mexico. . . . I would play with other musicians who were there working or who came from the sierra to play. . . . Folks from the province [i.e., countryside] who went to Mexico City to work, well, they would bring the tradition with them and in that way we would come together, working away.)

At the age of twenty-four, he began sitting in with musicians in Mexico City and on his trips back to Guanajuato, but he never participated in topadas. He chuckles, "Me invitaban, pero les decía que no, porque yo nunca había andado en eso [topadas]. Tenía ganas, pero me faltaba valor." (They would invite me, but I would tell them no, because I had never been in that [topadas]. I had the desire, but I lacked courage.). As time went on, Salinas played regularly in Guanajuato and Mexico City. He participated in his first topada in the mid-1980s, playing across from Guillermo Velázquez. The circulating lives of the Sierra Gorda migrant huapangueros whom Salinas would learn from assembled a trajectory of cultural transmission that circled out from Xichú to Mexico City and back, binding life in both places. Huapangueros labored both in factories and in performance, producing a type of cultural adjacency between places through music making. This was the means by which Salinas and others intimated the flows of migrant life.

Velázquez returned to Xichú in 1976 after working in Mexico City for three years—he'd had enough. Shortly after arriving, he was approached by local huapangueros who had noticed his musical talent and encouraged him to give it a try. He was familiar with huapango arribeño from his childhood in Xichú and had even dabbled briefly in songwriting while living in Mexico City, yet he had never imagined becoming a huapanguero. After some convincing, he picked up the guitarra quinta huapanguera and studied the décima, and his life as a troubadour was set in motion. Within a few short years, he would form part of the group Los Leones de la Sierra de Xichú alongside violinists Guillermo Guevara and Mario González—another violinist, Leonardo (León) Lara, stepped in and out of the group—and the vihuelero Pascual. Velázquez recalls:

A mí me tocó recibir la tradición como se acostumbraba siempre. Primeramente, acercándome por instinto, por un llamado poderoso a donde sucedía la música y la poesía sin entender qué era una décima, sin entender qué cosa era una topada, qué era un son, qué era un jarabe, pero estar ahí cerca en el calor de la fiesta. . . . Y luego a pegármele a los cantadores . . . por los caminos a las fiestas, a estar con ellos, a oírlos, a amanecerse. . . .

Fue delirante. . . . Abrí el corazón a la plática que ellos hacían. . . . Además de aprender los rudimentos—técnica, mánico, pisadas, los tonos, tonadas de la valona—yo me iba dando cuenta de la intimidad de la tradición.

———————————————

(I came to receive the tradition as had always been customary. First, I instinctively approached it, through a powerful calling that drew me to where music making and poesía were taking place without understanding what a décima was, without understanding what a topada was, what a son was, what a jarabe was, but I was there in the warmth of the fiesta. . . . Then I latched on to the singers . . . onto their travels to fiestas, being with them, hearing them, staying up through dawn with them. . . . It was ecstatic. . . . I opened my heart to the things they spoke of. . . . Apart from learning the rudimentary skills—technical know-how, strumming, chord positions, chords, the melodies of the valona—I was slowly becoming aware of the intimacy of the tradition.)

Velázquez's and Salinas's formations as huapangueros are inextricably linked to migrant life in Mexico City. In the case of Salinas, the shifting geographies of performance are clear. Velázquez, however, would soon voice the lived conditions of these very flows through the toilsome (lyrical) flow of performance itself.

VERSES AND FLOWS

Performers of traditions, Charles Briggs (1988) proposes, do not merely isolate and reproduce particular texts but rather assume responsibility for invoking shared patterns of form and meaning. Expressly, vernacular performance is an active, reflexive, and interpretive experience that involves both listening to the world in which audiences live and voicing the existential problems that fit their experiences. This requires practitioners to attend to the social location of the public they are in dialogue with. Velázquez contextualizes this idea in relation to the process of poetic composition:

El trovador es un condensador de la colectividad, es un antena que concentra en sí lo que en la comunidad es inquietud, es anhelo, es sueño, es memoria, es necesidad de expresión. En ese sentido, el trovador expresa los intereses de la comunidad y los suyos propios, que muchas veces pueden ir más adelante o más atrás de la comunidad. No por el hecho de que yo sepa hacer un verso quiere decir que ya soy capaz de expresar el interés de la comunidad—eso se logra a través de mucho tiempo, de mucha dedicación, de mucho deseo de llegar a traducir en los versos lo que la gente quiere decir. Eso tiene que ver con la responsabilidad que tiene el poeta, el trovador para estar permanente atento—"¿Qué sucede aquí, que sucede allá?"

(The troubadour is a conduit of the collectivity; he is an antenna that absorbs what is uncertainty, is desire, is dreamt, is memory, is in need of expression in the community. In that sense, the troubadour expresses the interests of the community as well as his own, which many times may be ahead of or lagging behind those of the community. Merely because I know how to craft a verse does not mean that expressing the interests of the community is a given—that is attained across a great span of time, of commitment, of the desire to translate through verse what the people want to say. That has much to do with the poet's burden of responsibility, for the troubadour must be permanently attentive—"What is happening here, what over there?")

Performance articulates a collective social location while at the same time bearing the capacity to imagine a world beyond it, a sensibility Jill Dolan refers to as the "utopian performative" (2001: 457). This imaginative territory maps the interstices of the present interactions of intersubjective understanding in momentary glimpses of possibly better conditions of existence—out to sweet home Chicago. My intent here is to take seriously the enactment of expressions of the possible, for if social location is relational, that is, positioned between personal experience and public meanings, then it stands to reason that poetic voicings trace and assemble themselves through the social topographies of the intersubjective everyday—the felt conditions that often demarcate a marginalized existence unfolding "here" or "over there." This having been established, huapango arribeño's narrative mappings of lived life during the 1970s and into the 1980s should be juxtaposed with the unstable field of institutionalized discourses that legitimized the political-economic order of things in Mexico at that time. Such discourses privileged their own *models of circulation* in the production of new social enclosures and exclusions, particularly in relation to the role of migrant labor in the neoliberal economy (Briggs 2007, 2012). Huapangueros, in contrast, reconstituted performance practice amid the shifting geographies of social life and voiced the existential conditions of migrancy in the most crucial of spaces—the flows of the topada.

When Velázquez first began participating in topadas in the late 1970s, veteran huapangueros would at times engage him with fundamento themes designed to test his poetic competence. One in particular was "Charlemagne and the Peerage of France." He recalls, "Era un tema que los viejos trovadores empleaban frente a un nuevo poeta para calar si de veras estaba involucrándose en lo qué era la obligación del trovador en relación a la poesía y a los temas" (This was a theme that veteran poets would employ when in front of a new poet to see whether he was truly committing himself to the responsibility of being a troubadour in relation to poesía and foundational themes). When engaged with this theme, Velázquez, in his riposte, would appropriate the paradigmatic treatment of war and conquest in order to poetically narrate contemporary instances of social unrest. He replied to these petitions with the following:[11]

Si más antes había la ignorancia
de los hechos de historia de atrás
Carlomagno, Roldán, Fierabrás
las Cruzadas, los pares de Francia
hoy en día dejemos constancia
de los hombres que con valentía
se sacuden la vil tiranía
con coraje y anhelo genuino
hoy hablemos del Che y del Sandino:
¿DE QUÉ PUEDE TROVAR HOY EN DÍA?

———

If before there was ignorance
about historic deeds of the past
Charlemagne, Roland, Fierabras
the Crusades, the peerage of France
today let us make note
of the men who with great bravery
shed themselves of vile tyranny
with anger and genuine desire
today let's speak of Che and Sandino:
TODAY, WHAT MAY BE RENDERED IN VERSE?

This dialogic shift in poetic content is embedded in the contiguous fabrics of social, economic, and political changes occurring throughout the hemisphere at that moment in time. Velázquez does much more than index these conditions (i.e., the spread of revolutionary fervor and U.S. interventionism), however; he assists in a larger process in which the genre of huapango arribeño begins to powerfully embody this new metaphysics—the experiences of migration among its nascent huapangueros, specifically. Not only do new huapangueros speak to the lived tensions of mobility, social and political transformation, and the tense back-and-forth of laboring, but they are themselves forged as practitioners through these shifting geographies and political circumstances. Velázquez lucidly explains this in relation to his poetic compositions at the time:

[Son] retratos de lo que yo veía en la fábrica y que traducía creativamente a la migración de la gente del noreste hacia el Distrito Federal. . . . Lo que hice fue incorporar en esas poesías toda una experiencia vivida en carne propia por mi padre y que yo veía en ese tiempo como un fenómeno tangible de la gente emigrada de la Sierra [Gorda] al Distrito Federal . . . del campesino temporalero. . . . Ahí está plasmado tanto lo que yo en lo personal viví, como lo que estaba viendo que pasaba en ese tiempo.

([They are] portraits of what I saw in the factory, which I then translated to creatively render the migration of people from northeastern Guanajuato to Mexico City. . . . In those poesías I incorporated the lived experience of my father and what I saw at that time, a tangible phenomenon experienced by the people who migrated from the Sierra [Gorda] to Mexico City . . . by the seasonal peasants. . . . Mirrored there is what I personally lived and what I saw that was occurring at that time.)

Huapango arribeño served as a space for voicing the realities of a hostile political climate, migrancy, and the multiple negotiations of economic livelihood that enfolded the intersubjective day-to-day between Xichú and Mexico City.[12] In his words, Velázquez became conscious of many things, not because of participation in a political movement, but rather out of necessity, born of an existence mired in the dizzying circulations of migration and the alienations of work and the city, life-changing experiences common among Sierra Gorda migrants. Huapango arribeño was itself a strategy of survival, an aural poetics that cradled the social imaginings of this community. He illustrates this with grueling detail in his poesía entitled "En Busca de Chamba" (In search of work). It chronicles the arduous search for employment in Mexico City, capturing the nervous flows of everyday work.

ESE LUNES MUY DE MAÑANITA
MADRUGAMOS EN BUSCA DE CHAMBA
AHÍ VI COMO ESTÁ DE CARAMBA
Y QUE TRATO LE DAN AL PAISITA[13]

Con los ojos cargados de sueño
prendí el radio donde dan la hora
"tres y cuarto," se oyó sin demora
"tres y cuarto," pensé con empeño
mi pariente me dijo risueño:
"Todavía es muy temprano compita,
nos echamos otra pestañita,
y cuando oigas que digan las cinco,
entonce' si nos paramos de un brinco":
ESE LUNES MUY DE MAÑANITA

A las cinco y minutos nos fuimos
a esperar que pasara el camión
y ahí mismo empezó la cuestión
porque apenas, apenas cupimos
a codazos y como pudimos
agarrando nuestra petaquita
nos hicimos hasta una esquinita
al pendiente de algún mala maña
porque aquí nunca falta cizaña:
ESE LUNES MUY DE MAÑANITA

Tlalnepantla me entró por los ojos
como un panorama tedioso
cielo pardo y ambiente brumoso
puestos, bardas, premura y enojo
entre prisas y semáforos rojos
iba mi alma como la abejita
que volando a su florecita
no hace caso a más inquietudes
empezaban la vicisitudes:
ESE LUNES MUY DE MAÑANITA

De las seis a las nueve, las diez
estuvimos la bola de gente

esperando que un tal gerente
revisaba sus listas del mes
salió el viejo con mucha altivez
muy peinado y de corbatita
a decir que en su fábrica ahorita
no habría chamba quién sabe hasta cuando
y nosotros oyendo y sudando:
ESE LUNES MUY DE MAÑANITA

De ahí fuimos a otras compañías
pero en todas siempre era lo mismo
la tristeza, el sudor, el bolismo
y "que vuelvan entre ocho días"
me sentí con las manos vacías
pobre, lejos, una basurita
una cosa que nadie acredita
que no tiene ningún valimiento
y de veras me entró sentimiento:
ESE LUNES MUY DE MAÑANITA

———

ON THAT EARLY MONDAY MORNING
WE WOKE AT DAWN IN SEARCH OF WORK
THERE I SAW HOW DIFFICULT IT WAS
AND HOW THEY TREAT THE COUNTRYMAN

With eyes heavy with sleep
I turned on the radio to hear the time
"quarter after three," it quickly replied
"quarter after three," I thought with great effort
my roommate said jovially:
"It's still too early, buddy,
let's get a little more shut-eye
and when they say it's five
surely then we'll be up in a flash":
ON THAT EARLY MONDAY MORNING

Minutes after five we were off
to wait for the bus to come
and right then the hustle began
as we barely, just barely, made it on

we elbowed our way as best we could
with our little satchel
we crammed into a corner
always wary of any trickster
for here malice is surely always present:
ON THAT EARLY MONDAY MORNING

I observed Tlalnepantla with my eyes
like a tiresome scene
a dark sky and hazy bustle
stalls, fences, urgency, and anger
amid hastiness and red stoplights
my soul traveled like the little bee
that flies to its flower
it pays no mind to misgivings
as the vicissitudes commenced:
ON THAT EARLY MONDAY MORNING

From six to nine, to ten in the morning
there we were, a swarm of people
waiting for some such boss
to look over his monthly lists
the old man appeared arrogantly
finely combed and with a necktie
to tell us that in his factory
there wouldn't be any work until who knows when
as we listened and sweated:
ON THAT EARLY MONDAY MORNING

From there we went to other companies
but it was the same at all of them
the sadness, the sweat, the humiliation
and "return next week," they would say
I felt empty-handed
poor, estranged, like trash
something that no one values
that has no worth whatsoever
and I truly felt great sorrow:
ON THAT EARLY MONDAY MORNING

Veteran poets—those who would bait Velázquez with Charlemagne—also echoed this emergent structure of feeling as their poetics likewise flowed through the rhythmic and processual tensions of lived experience at this historical juncture. For instance, my grandfather Mauro attended to the economic crisis of the early 1980s and subsequent migration to the United States in the following two poesías.[14]

QUE VAYA CON DIOS PORTILLO[15]
SE VA PARA OTRAS NACIONES
SE VA MUY AGRADECIDO
CON CANTIDAD DE MILLONES

El año mil nueve y cientos
en el año ochenta y uno
gobiernos uno por uno
desde los primeros tiempos
llevaban sus elementos
a lugares conocidos
sus palacios muy lucidos
sus casas muy relujosas
recordando de esas cosas:
QUE VAYA CON DIOS PORTILLO

Pues no hay celos, ni hay agravios
aunque andamos en desfortuna
de él no tuvimos ayuda
los pequeños propietarios
nomás los ejidatarios
de toditos los ejidos
¿quiénes son los más consentidos?
según por lo que estoy viendo
nada le fuimos debiendo:
QUE VAYA CON DIOS PORTILLO[16]

Ya va tener su salida
se va para otro lugar
con todo su familiar
de nuestra patria querida
y viene otro de Colima
siguiendo el mismo destino

esto digo en mi sentido
con mi corta inteligencia
ya lo declaró la prensa:
QUE VAYA CON DIOS PORTILLO

Ya no volvimos a verlo
pero lo que nos dejó implantado
en los pueblos todo caro
nomás nos dejó el recuerdo
luego que entró ese gobierno
todo bien encarecido
cervecerías y los vinos[17]
lo digo quedito y recio
lo levantó de precio:
QUE VAYA CON DIOS PORTILLO

———

MAY PORTILLO GO WITH GOD
HE'S OFF TO OTHER NATIONS
HE DEPARTS, INDEED GRATEFUL
WITH UNTOLD MILLIONS

The year nineteen hundred
in the eighty-first year
governments one by one
since the beginning of time
have taken their paladins
to familiar places
their lavish palaces
their luxurious homes
as I remember such things:
MAY PORTILLO GO WITH GOD

I am not jealous, nor resentful
although we are in misfortune
we had no help from him
the small property owners
only the *ejidatario* (shareholder of common land)
of all the ejidos
who are most favored?

as far as I can tell
we owe him nothing:
MAY PORTILLO GO WITH GOD

He is on his way out
he's off to another place
with all of his family
from our beloved country
and another from Colima is on his way[18]
to carry on the same legacy
I say this with all my senses
with my limited intelligence
the press has reported it:
MAY PORTILLO GO WITH GOD

We won't see him again
but he left us with some legacy
everything is expensive in the towns
we are left with his memory
as soon as that administration came to power
everything became overpriced
beer and even wine
I say it softly and loudly
everything went up in price:
MAY PORTILLO GO WITH GOD

SE ACABARON PRETENSIONES
POR EL MAÍZ ENCARECIDO
HASTA LOS MÁS COPETONES
A BUEN PRECIO LO HAN COMIDO

En fin, les voy a recordar
del año ochenta y tres
el año viene al revés
ya no hay ningún temporal
muchas tierras sin sembrar
por toditas las regiones
por ahí se oyen los clamores

de lo que ya origina
muchos le entran a la harina:
SE ACABARON PRETENSIONES

Las aguas se están secando
en todos los nacimientos
van a ser puros tormentos
por lo que se está mirando
las fechas se están llegando
de aquellos historiadores
dejaron implantaciones
de lo que va suceder
¿cómo le iremos a hacer?:
SE ACABARON PRETENSIONES

Muchos que se van al norte
piden prestado el pasaje
las mujeres al talache
y de allá les mandan reporte
"as la milpa y tumba el monte;
por allí les van los dólares"
y yo he visto que en ocasiones
ya no los quieren allá
los avientan para acá:
SE ACABARON PRETENSIONES

De toditos los estados
van al norte a trabajar
unos vienen y otros van
como grandes ciudadanos
de puritos mexicanos
son más de cinco millones
que han dejado sus regiones
y también a su familia
comiendo puritita harina:
SE ACABARON PRETENSIONES

———

PRETENSES HAVE COME TO AN END
TO EXPLAIN OVERPRICED CORN

EVEN THE MOST WELL-OFF
HAVE CONSUMED IT AT AN EXPENSE

In sum, I'm going to remind you
of the year eighty-three
it is all upside-down
there is no harvest
much land has not been cultivated
in all of the regions
the outcry can be heard
because of what has begun
many are now eating wheat flour:
PRETENSES HAVE COME TO AN END

The waters are drying up
in all of the wellsprings
we'll have to rely solely on rain
from what can be seen
the day is approaching
spoken of by historians
they left chronicles
of what is to occur
what are we to do?:
PRETENSES HAVE COME TO AN END

Many of those who go up north[19]
borrow money to fund their journey
and the women, now to the hoe
and from up there men delegate duties
"tend the cornfield, clear the weeds;
I'll be sending dollars"
I've seen that on occasion
they don't want them [migrants] over there
they throw [deport] them back this way:
PRETENSES HAVE COME TO AN END

From every state
they go up north to work
as some return, others leave
of our great citizens

a great quantity of Mexicans
more than five million
have left their regions
and also their families
eating nothing but wheat flour:
PRETENSES HAVE COME TO AN END

With sobering wit, Mauro comments critically on the devastating legacy of López Portillo's presidency: theft, corruption, an economy in ruins, inflation, and the precarious status of the ejido in the face of what would soon develop into full-blown neoliberal reform. During López Portillo's administration, land redistribution was primarily focused on improving the conditions of established ejidos (Lomnitz 1992: 163). Yet, after the discovery of Mexico's petroleum reserves, the Sistema Alimentario Mexicano (Mexican Food System) was created in 1980 with the express goal of encouraging farmer self-sufficiency and agricultural production through increased access to loans, among other incentives. The effectiveness of the Sistema Alimentario Mexicano, braced by a network of agencies tenuously subsidized by petrodollars, is debatable, although some believe it increased debt and bureaucratic dependence among ejidos (J. Fox 2007; Spalding 1985). Given this set of circumstances, Mauro asks, "De toditos los ejidos, ¿quiénes son los más consentidos?" (Of all the ejidos, who are the most favored?), as if anticipating the chaos that would befall the Sistema Alimentario Mexicano in 1983 and the political fallout in the wake of Mexico's debt crisis. Thus, he bids López Portillo farewell and in the second poesía poignantly elaborates on the hardships that led many to migrate to the United States.

Mauro's commentary in "Se Acabaron Pretensiones" must be considered within the broader perspective of U.S. agricultural trade policy and the banning of Mexican wheat imports in 1983. The embargo, it was explained, was enacted to prevent the introduction and spread of the Karnal bunt fungus, a pathogen found in a relatively small geographic area in Mexico. The consequences were manifold: (1) the United States proceeded to dump its own subsidized wheat onto the Mexican market to compensate for unmet domestic demand within Mexico resulting from the diseased crop; (2) Mexico began to phase out its own mismanaged protectionist agricultural policies (those policies that were partly blamed for the disease outbreak); (3) these dismantling efforts were extended to the subsidized corn industry, setting the stage for later disruptions by NAFTA (Goulet and Kim 1989); and (4) U.S. wheat flour quickly became cheaper than corn for making tortillas, particularly under the drought conditions the Sierra Gorda was experiencing. This safeguarding of U.S. markets from tainted Mexican agricultural imports was the means by which the United States would not only restrict future shipments of Mexican agriculture but also saturate the Mexican consumer market with its own subsidized products, in turn devastating local agricultural economies.[20] Mauro is lucidly aware of these transnational bureaucratic workings in his poetic linking of migration, local agriculture, and the U.S.-Mexico political economy. This compelling picture illustrates the multiple circulations of contesting cultural forms rooted in Mauro's intimate knowledge of everyday life in the Sierra Gorda during the early 1980s and it stands as an expressive archive that foreshadows the conditions of Mexican migrant life in the 1990s—policing and deportation.

Mauro's and Velázquez's poetic works have similarities that speak powerfully to how lived politics informed performance. It would have been interesting to see them debate and share tales, despite having become practitioners at two rather distant moments—1925 and 1976, respectively. Their experiences and knowledges of migrancy informed the axis of their fundamento and have been part of their survival. And just as their aesthetic voicings evince a highly contemporary iteration of huapango arribeño, performance is part of a larger expressive field that has continually poeticized disparities between social locations. Troubadours, as Sierra Gorda natives explain, occupied a particular role in provincial life throughout most of the twentieth century, for they recounted matters of local history, regional geography, and global significance through topada performance at a time when there was little access to radio, television, or public schools in the more remote parts of the region. The dialogic exchange between troubadours within topada performances necessarily exposed the complex circulations and relationships between knowledges emergent from the people of the region, huapangueros' representations, and official sources (i.e., history books, local governments, and media accounts). Given the dynamics of huapango arribeño, these interdiscursive circuits have necessarily shifted along with the performative resources huapangueros have brought to bear over time. Although there is always a capacity for the circulation of a sonic poesis, particular sentiments emerged for huapangueros in the 1970s and 1980s that were embedded more and more in the expectation of migratory flows between places.

XICHÚ'S FESTIVAL, A PALIMPSEST

Xichú's very first huapango arribeño festival took place on December 31, 1982, the date on which the town already hosted one of its two annual topadas. This is still the case, yet the festival now begins on December 29 and concludes on January 1. The yearly festival is an integral part of life's rhythms for Xichú's residents, something to look forward to. It rose in significance beginning in the wake of Mexico's debt crisis by way of circumstances that will soon become clear, as Guillermo Velázquez and his brother Eliazar developed two projects aimed at revitalizing the spaces of huapango arribeño. The idea was to facilitate the connection between veteran and younger practitioners. Through a chance meeting with Leonel Durán, the director of the Dirección General de Culturas Populares (General Directorate of Popular Cultures), the brothers garnered financial support for organizing huapango arribeño workshops throughout the Sierra Gorda of Guanajuato and a festival in Xichú to honor veteran huapangueros.[21] The workshops were centered on both transmitting the rudimentary musical skills and familiarizing students with poetic forms.[22] Sessions were held once or twice a month in the towns of Xichú, Victoria, and San Luis de la Paz. Lately, the workshops have, to varying degrees, been incorporated into the programming and outreach activities of municipal *casas de cultura* (cultural centers) throughout Guanajuato, Querétaro, and San Luis Potosí. In one sense, these workshops might be considered an "invented tradition," an idea famously introduced by Eric J. Hobsbawm and Terence O. Ranger in reference to the innovation of symbolic and ritual practices (1983: 2). While this idea typically references types of historical forgery in the service of nation building, the situated reenactment by nonhegemonic groups of practices concerned with dignifying cultural resources can also be a type of innovation that likewise seeks to establish a sense of contiguity between present-day expressions and their antecedents.

For a number of years, the festival was principally organized as an homage to veteran huapangueros, known as the Festival de Homenaje a los Viejos Maestros Huapangueros (Festival in Honor of Veteran Huapanguero Masters). Elder musicians were publicly recognized, given a modest token of appreciation, and invited to participate in a public forum to speak about their experiences and their art. In 1982, at the first festival, Pancho Berrones, Tranquilino Méndez, Antonio García, Antonio Escalante, Agapito Briones, Tomás Aguilar, Ceferino Juárez, Román Gómez, Pedro Carreón, and Lorenzo López were honored.[23] Now the festival is known as the Festival del Huapango Arribeño y de la Cultura de la Sierra Gorda (Festival of Huapango Arribeño and the Culture of the Sierra Gorda) and each year attends to a thematic focus; to this day, however, the apex of the festival remains the topada. Close to six thousand people ring in the New Year dancing in Xichú's central plaza to the oscillating performances of two huapango arribeño ensembles, an all-night topada that begins at midnight and lasts roughly ten to eleven hours. In addition, the organizing committee has been and continues to be composed of Xichú natives (musicians, campesinos, migrants, local residents, etc.), and the funding is primarily independent of official institutions and municipal monies. While in the beginning the local municipal government helped fund the festival, in the mid-1990s their support was withdrawn in the midst of a popular grassroots movement against local caciques who had exerted control over local politics for decades and were accused of election fraud. Some of those who spoke out against this corruption were also involved in organizing the festival, including Guillermo Velázquez and his family, all of whom subsequently faced an organized backlash; in particular, the municipal government attempted to appropriate the festival's public spaces by organizing a counter *semana cultural* (cultural week), which is now defunct, just before the start of the Festival del Huapango Arribeño y de la Cultura de la Sierra Gorda. The organizing committee now relies on grassroots fund-raisers and modest donations from Sierra Gorda natives. These funding sources are announced publicly on the night of December 31 every year. While the festival is rooted in Xichú and its history of topadas at the start of each New Year, it is by no means isolated from other places. The vectors that attach Xichú to Chicago and other sites in the United States also exist when organizing and fund-raising. These connections play out through personal relationships and necessary transnational flows of resources, much like what happens in the binational civic efforts organized by hometown associations (Bada 2010).[24] Esperanza, for instance, is friends with both Guillermo Velázquez and his wife, Maria Isabel "Chabe" Flores Solano. Because of their close relationship since childhood, Esperanza organizes fund-raisers in Chicago for the Xichú festival. She has lived there for twenty years and has been collecting funds for the festival for six.

The importance of women in the happening of huapango at events like this is vital. Their presence as practitioners remains marginal, yet there is a potential for shifting this overall dynamic within its practice. Lay folklorist Socorro Perea, for instance, began recording and performing on the radio with Los Cantores de la Sierra in the late 1970s.[25] However, because she interpreted the poetic works of troubadour Antonio Escalante rather than introducing her own poetry, she didn't fully assume the troubadour role. Maria Isabel "Chabe" Flores Solano, in turn, is perhaps the first woman to assert her presence within an ensemble as a full-time member and participant, having grown into the tradition in her childhood. She was born in the Xichú mine settlement and grew up alongside Guillermo Velázquez in Xichú proper. At the age of twelve, she joined the church choir, where she developed her powerful vocal style. Her love of music, she shares, is in part due to her father, Ruperto Flores, also a huapango arribeño troubadour. She recalls:

> Mi papá influyó mucho a mí y a una hermana que también canta. . . . Cuando éramos así niñas, mi casa en Xichú era un a posada para toda la gente que llegaba de las comunidades. . . . No había carreteras antes, entonces toda la gente que llegaba el fin de semana se tenía que quedar para hacer sus compras, para ir a misa el domingo, para arreglar algún asunto, entonces tenían que pedir permiso en las casas para dormir ahí. En mi casa llegaban alrededor de cincuenta a cien personas. . . . Todo lo que yo iba aprendiendo en la escuela lo hacíamos los fines de semana; hacíamos como un especie de teatro para la gente que llegaba. Igual, incorporábamos a las muchachas que llegaban de los ranchos; las poníamos a bailar, o a cantar, o a declamar, o a hacer juego. . . . Luego también empezamos a cantar algunas canciones. Entonces llegaba alguna gente y mi papa nos hablaba, "le van a cantar a esta señora." Desde muy niña nos puso él a cantar.

> (My dad very much influenced me and my sister who also sings. . . . When we were just girls, my house in Xichú was a lodging house for all the people who arrived from surrounding communities. . . . There were no roads at that time, so all the people who arrived on the weekend stayed to do their shopping, to go to mass on Sunday, to go about their business, so they had to ask permission to stay in the homes of the locals. Around fifty to a hundred people arrived at my house. . . . Everything I was learning in school we would perform on the weekends; we did a sort of theatre for the people who arrived. Likewise, we included many of the girls who came from the rural communities; we would have them dance, or sing, or recite, or play games. . . . So then we would also sing some songs. People would arrive, and my dad would say, "You are going to sing for this woman." He encouraged us to sing from an early age.)

The way Flores Solano describes it, she enjoyed her lively home and the way her father insisted that she cultivate her talents. Her familiarity with huapango arribeño came by way of observing and listening to him perform, in addition to encountering the music at topadas. By the time she was a teenager, however, she and her sister were more interested in dancing huapango, not just listening. Their mother forbade them to do so. Still, she smiles as she reminisces about how she wanted to be a part of it, sneaking off with her sister to dance when they managed to escape their mother's gaze while strolling around the plaza during topadas.

From 1973 to 1976 Flores Solano studied at a social work school in Celaya, Guanajuato, after which she returned to Xichú to work and came across Velázquez, much to her surprise, as he had previously been on the path toward becoming a priest. He explained why he had left his studies and told her about his time in Mexico City and his decision to pursue huapango arribeño. She remembers that she shared with her some of his poesías: "Fue una revelación. Empecé a tomar conciencia de que es lo que hacían los trovadores . . . y a valorar lo que hacía mi papa." (It was a revelation. I began to be conscious of what troubadours did . . . and to value what it was my father did.). These old childhood friends fell in love and married in 1979. After Los Leones de la Sierra de Xichú released their first studio recording in 1982, the group was invited to perform some of their material in Mexico City.[26] On this occasion, Velázquez invited both Don Benito Lara—a noted huapango dancer from Xichú—and Flores Solano to dance during the performance. From that point forward, both became members of Los Leones de la Sierra de Xichú. Flores Solano sang a few poesía planta melodies and songs written by Velázquez on the group's second and third studio recordings, *¡Viva el Huapango!* (1985) and *Me Voy pa'l Norte* (1986). She participated in a poetic controversia with Guillermo Velázquez in the form of a decimal on the latter album. There, they played the roles of transnational migrant and wife, engaging each other in a jocular exchange on the topics of migration, domestic life, and gender roles. I include it here:

Guillermo: ¿MUJER POR QUÉ ME AMENAZAS?
Chabe: ESO ES LO QUE TE HAS GRANJEADO
Guillermo: YO CREO QUE DE CRUEL TE PASAS
Chabe: Y TÚ DE DESOBLIGADO

Ch: (1) Te largas así nomás
G: por la carestía que azota

Ch: no es cierto se te alborota
G: viejita ya ponte en paz
Ch: yo acá ni estufa de gas
G: la leña hace buenas brazas
Ch: malejos en ti que trazas
G: ¿que más te puedo decir?
Ch: pero te has de arrepentir
G: ¿MUJER POR QUÉ ME AMENAZAS?

G: (2) No sé yo que me reprochas
Ch: ¿qué crees tú que pueda ser?
G: la verdad no sé mujer
Ch: pues que todo lo derrochas
G: ¿mejor, por qué no lo mochas?
Ch: porque no creas que he acabado
G: me tienes arrinconado
Ch: como chivo en el corral
G: ¿por qué me tratas tan mal?
Ch: ESO ES LO QUE TE HAS GRANJEADO

Ch: (3) Al norte has ido tres años
G: pero sin suerte ni modo
Ch: no es cierto te gastas todo
G: ya déjate de regaños
Ch: tampoco tú te des baños
G: aflójame tus tenazas
Ch: otros haciendo sus casas
G: yo no soy hombre de bienes
Ch: vergüenza es lo que no tienes
G: YO CREO QUE DE CRUEL TE PASAS

G: (4) Te lo juro por Diosito
Ch: yo creo ni tú te la crees
G: será la últimita vez
Ch: yo no te creo, ni el bendito
G: déjame darte un besito
Ch: no seas tan desvergonzado
G: dime que estoy perdonado

Ch: ni eso ni nada te digo
G: te pasas de cruel conmigo
Ch: Y TÚ DE DESOBLIGADO

———

Guillermo: WOMAN, WHY DO YOU THREATEN ME?
Chabe: THAT IS WHAT YOU HAVE EARNED
Guillermo: I THINK YOU ARE BEYOND CRUEL
Chabe: AND YOU HAVE BEEN NEGLIGENT

Ch: (1) You leave all of a sudden
G: because of scarcity and crisis
Ch: not true, you are just rowdy
G: old lady, calm down
Ch: I'm here without a stove or gas
G: firewood makes for good fuel
Ch: you are on a mischievous path
G: What else can I tell you?
Ch: but you should feel guilty
G: WOMAN, WHY DO YOU THREATEN ME?

G: (2) I don't know why you reproach me
Ch: what do you think is the reason?
G: woman, I don't know
Ch: well, you waste everything
G: why don't you give it a rest?
Ch: oh, I'm not close to finished
G: you have me cornered
Ch: like a goat in the corral
G: why do you treat me so bad?
Ch: THAT IS WHAT YOU HAVE EARNED

Ch: (3) You've been up north three years
G: but without any luck
Ch: not true, you spend all the money
G: oh, stop with the scolding
Ch: you too stop doing the same
G: loosen your grip on me
Ch: others are building their homes

G: I am not a man of means
Ch: what you are is embarrassing
G: I THINK YOU ARE BEYOND CRUEL

G: (4) I swear to God
Ch: you don't even believe it so
G: this will be the last time
Ch: I don't believe you, neither does God
G: let me give you a kiss
Ch: don't be so crass
G: tell me that I am forgiven
Ch: I won't tell you that or anything else
G: you are beyond cruel with me
Ch: AND YOU HAVE BEEN NEGLIGENT

This and other exchanges, according to Flores Solano, voice a critique of traditional gender roles and politics. Further, as a full member of Los Leones de la Sierra de Xichú she has exerted her voice, at once shifting the male tinge of the music itself.[27] Her only self-ascribed limit is performing at topadas because she does not hold herself to be a troubadour, meaning that although she writes décimas she does not improvise them. She has observed with admiration female *decimistas* (décima poets) from other poetic traditions who do so, such as those in Puerto Rico, Uruguay, Argentina, and Cuba, some of whom performed at the festival in 2012. Over the years she has been involved with various topadas and festivals nonetheless, always negotiating her path through the multiple roles she occupies—organizer, performer, mother—and her work on the Xichú festival and the workshops has been crucial in maintaining those spaces. On the whole, her presence has reoriented the tradition to be more inclusive of women because she stands out as a powerful voice and performer, both onstage and on recordings. Huapango has opened to this gender subjectivity as of late and embraced female practitioners who have joined in music making; although few, many of them are young and up-and-coming talents.

An aural poetics in this space begins with listening to what is unfolding in the present—people, stories, and the movements of both from Mexico to Chicago and back. Think of Xichú in this way: it is a time as much as a place. It is the everyday for many, and a once-a-year place for some—never so far away because once the festival topada concludes, it's already less than a year away . . . and for people in faraway places like Chicago, Xichú is always present, part of them, part of what builds the rhythm of who they are on the U.S. side of the border. To recognize huapango as it is—a living and breathing contingent voicing—is to follow its movements, its flows in and out of places, coming and going, arriving when called on by the people who listen to and participate in it. It is why they help fund the festival, and, for those who can, it is why they return . . . physically or in memory . . .

. . . The bus ride was bumpy, and the fog was thickening in the mountains, but the town is bright and clear, and I'm at the top of the hill. I head down to the dry stone streets, gazing over quiet backyards; a boy is washing the sidewalk in front of his mother's shop. She watches the work being done. Christmas decorations are still up. The *panadería* (bakery) opens and closes on its own time. Sometimes there is sweet bread in the morning; sometimes it isn't ready until later in the day. If you're hungry, you can always head down to the small pop-up restaurant on the corner of the plaza. I just sit on a white iron bench and drink some café de olla. I take my time. After a while, I take a walk with no clear destination in mind, but only to get a sense of the rhythm of things today, the goings-on, the conversations, and to see who's around. I once ran into Valentín, but not today. I don't see anyone in particular who is familiar to me, so I head back to the plaza. The man who builds the tablados has already begun construction, each in its place. People know him as Güero (fair-skinned) because of his light complexion. Teenagers are hanging streamers from the church to a house across the way. The people up top yell, "Higher! Lower! To the left!" Meanwhile, a young man helps Güero layer the top of the tablados with *rama de zapotillo*, big green fronds that protect the musicians from the weather.

The town is now filling up with people who will soon parade up and down the streets—a *caminata*, as they call it—announcing to all that the festival has officially begun. Children, men and women, and several towering *mojigangas* (giant puppets) will follow the musicians to the top of the hill at the entrance of the town, where décimas will be recited with a sense of beginning. I will walk down the hill again, this time with someone I know, reconnecting with each step.

Calls echo out, snaking through the plaza and the public areas of the town on this long night, now clamoring, having filled up and welled over with people, vendors, sounds, smells, performances, exchanges, glances, everything. . . . People, history, and transnational mappings—from active fundraising efforts to the everyday lives of the people who live here and are connected to others far away—occupy and flow through this space, mapping out connections that play out as the music rises and the air grows colder; the feelings of attachment to the town and its festival throw themselves together with each passing moment. This is Xichú's festival . . .

Artists and performers, invited or otherwise, understand the festival in terms of a necessary and unique cradle of creativity that carries with it a particular life-giving politics. Alexis Díaz Pimienta, a Cuban decimista who has participated in the Xichú festival as an invited artist on two separate occasions, comments on the social role of the decimista in Latin America as a voice of the people and social struggle.[28] The festival organizers, in turn, also emphasize that the festival exists each year as an autonomous space, a grassroots effort unencumbered by local politics because it does not rely on the municipality for support—it is a space of the people. At the twenty-sixth annual festival, the organizing committee proclaimed in a public statement:

> En esta hora tan difícil de México, está en manos de los ciudadanos libres que cultivamos la esperanza desde distintos oficios y actividades, el no permitir que la mediocridad y corrupción de los políticos, la voracidad de los grandes empresarios, los intereses de lucro y comercio, o el crimen organizado, coarten nuestro derecho a vivir con dignidad, con alegría, con libertad; así mismo, tampoco podemos permitir que nos impidan ejercer nuestro derecho a disfrutar lo mejor del arte y de la cultura, y preservar valores como el de la solidaridad y el sentido de pertenencia a una colectividad.

> (In this difficult hour in Mexico, it is in the hands of free citizens who cultivate hope, from distinct walks of life, to not allow mediocrity and political corruption, corporate greed, for-profit interests and commerce, or organized crime to restrict our right to live with dignity, with joy, with freedom; likewise, we cannot allow them to prevent us from exercising our right to enjoy the best of art and culture, and to preserve values like solidarity and the sense of belonging to a collective.)

Everyone, including those same artists and organizers, realizes the festival is also a space of conviviality and music making, *es fiesta*.

Within this palimpsest of meanings, we may locate the vitality that Xichú represents, as a locus of energy for huapango arribeño, as a transnational place where a topada happened, happens, and is expected to happen. Within this space created by performance, connections between people are forged through movement that is itself a calling out, a bridging across the borders of politics and economy, crossing beyond the chrono-tropic borderings of national culture (vitality beyond the trope of melancholia). The density of this layering is about lives, bodies, and stories that are themselves part of Xichú as a singular location, but equally about how huapango arribeño can aesthetically voice the ugliness and beauty, dread and desires, of life and mobility. This embodied aesthetic is produced, circulated, and received along sentient lines . . . you feel the music. You feel the poetry. You feel all manner of places—Xichú among them—and you present yourself to them and within them, and then carry them with you as you cross into other places . . . as Lidia's husband, José, does, who, although a native of Xichú, is now working in Florida, but was also once laboring away in Atlanta . . .

Lidia lives on the outskirts of Xichú, atop a hill overlooking both the cemetery and the abandoned mine that once sustained the town; nowadays, remittances from the United States play a major role in the town's economy. With a quick smile she approaches me while I'm waiting in the plaza and asks me what time it is. "Five o'clock," I say. She asks if I'm from Querétaro or San Luis Potosí. She doesn't recognize me and knows that people from the surrounding region are in town for the festival. I say, "No, I'm coming from Chicago." Her eyes light up. With a wider smile that speaks of her fondness for him, she says her husband is working in Florida, picking oranges. He was in Atlanta before that. The fact that both he and I live in the United States means, to her, in some distant way, that we have something in common. His name is José, and he's also a huapanguero, she tells me.

Later, during the topada, as the ensembles are playing in their tempestuous rhythm, I see Lidia again, at about midnight. She's stationed with her children near the same arch as my friends and I. We smile and greet each other, and she invites us for breakfast after the topada. We agree, and she eagerly makes arrangements. She wants to talk about the United States, her past experiences working there; she wants to make a connection with us. She misses José, who can only ever come home for a few weeks at a time. In between visits, she waits for his phone calls at the public telephone stall . . .

As the topada is ending that following morning, she guides us to her home. We ascend the streets leading up the mountain, passing others who, just like us, have been up all night, who are still in a haze, music and verses slowly fading from their ears. She apologizes in advance for the modesty of her dwelling. We stop for tostadas, other ingredients, and I buy us some soft drinks in case her children want a *refresco* too (but they are sleeping, tired from the night's festivities). As she cooks, I look out over the mountains. "There are caves out there," she comes over and points, "just a few miles away. They're worth seeing." Her view over Xichú provides all the decoration her home needs. It is minimal, made of cement, and contains only the barest of necessities. The kitchen is downstairs, but it's too hard to take food up and down the dark stairwell with its steep and uneven steps so she has a portable stove on the second floor where the view is. She goes out of sight behind a curtain for a moment, and I hear the beginnings of a huapango CD playing. She comes out smiling and plates up food.

Over eggs, beans, and tostadas we learn that she worked in three different states in the United States: packing poultry in Alabama, working as a domestic in Las Vegas while she was pregnant, and then picking tomatoes in California. She wants to go back to California to live someday. She asks whether we've been to those places. She tells us how José learned to play huapango with other huapangueros who were working in Mexico City. His presence in Florida now influences her way of living in Xichú, the rhythms of her days: waiting for phone calls, listening to huapango, and listening for people from far away to remind her of him in his absence, to remind her of the bodily traversal between places that feel at once near and far to her—nearer when she hears José's voice and farther when she's waiting for him to call. The topada reminds her of him too . . .

WAITING FOR DAWN

The sun has been down for hours; it is close to nine in the evening. Arid mountains surround this all but abandoned town, or so the darkness would lead one to believe. If you look closely, you can see the outlining shadows towering overhead, though looking up in the dim moonlight can be disorienting. I'm sure this place is vibrant on a warm afternoon, but I wouldn't know; I've never been here before, and it's freezing. It's Christmas night in Atarjea, Guanajuato. The temperature is unbearable outside, and the lines of pale stone houses look just as cold and empty. Inside the municipal auditorium, however, life seems to have gathered. It's not terribly warm, well, not if you're sitting, but it's another thing if you're dancing . . .

Graciano invited my family and me to come tonight—he's from around here but is living in central Texas now (you'll hear more of his story in the following chapter). He knew I was going to be in Querétaro through the holidays, not far from Atarjea. It's Christmas, and the celebratory events organized include pageants, plays, horse races, and tonight's topada, all a part of Atarjea's *fiestas navideñas* (Christmas festivities). They will continue through the New Year. Tonight, Mario González is accompanying Graciano, and across the way are Pablo Armendariz and Sebastián Salinas. Like Salinas, Pablo Armendariz is from neighboring Xichú. He's lived most of his life in the region, although he's migrated seasonally to the United States over the past decade for work—picking oranges in Florida, working construction in northern Mississippi and Atlanta. This is a familiar rhythm of life for many of the people in attendance tonight. They are visiting from those very places, spending the holidays with family for a stint, with jobs waiting for them back in the United States. In fact, some will be in Xichú on New Years just a few days from now, dancing away before heading back to labor across the border, many of them clandestinely—frigid river waters, desert walks, and unforgiving terrain wait for them too. So the rhythm of this town revolves around holiday occasions like this, from Christmas to patron-saint festivities and so on, as people who have migrated to distant places return at these times yearly to visit loved ones, to check in on things, to bring gifts. Indeed, this is Graciano's story too. And this evening bears witness to the intertextual connection between ritual discourse, musical expression, and social interaction—a moment of composition and creative exchange where melodies and décimas sound out to build a loud, felt, and circulating dialogue that tells the story of migration in its very enactment.

As the night wears on, both ensembles engage in the rhythmic and tensive building of the topada, its musical and poetic scaffolding—sounds, gestures, movements echoing out, reverberating in the auditorium filled with people. The competitive camaraderie gives rise to a dialogue between the two troubadours, a moment of composition that will extend beyond this night, beyond Atarjea. Indeed, it will be continued three years later when Graciano and Pablo Armendariz face each other in yet another topada, this time at the Festival del Huapango Arribeño y de la Cultura de la Sierra Gorda in Xichú, picking up where they left off, ringing in the New Year as thousands listen and dance. On that occasion in Xichú, the topada begins like any other. Graciano lleva la mano (has the hand). As expected, both troubadours begin with poesías to introduce themselves and their fellow musicians and to greet the audience. Graciano, in his second intervention, performs a poesía dealing with Christmas, the New Year, and the holiday season in general. It seems this is the initial poetic theme he wants to attend to. Pablo Armendariz, however, does not respond in kind, instead continuing with another introduction-type poesía. In his third intervention, Graciano again continues with the holiday theme, yet, to my surprise, he interrupts his own poesía with an improvised décima to the rhythm of the valona in which he petitions Armendariz to shift into the bravata portion. This is very unorthodox considering how early in the engagement it is and the fact that the temas de fundamento have not been fully attended to. Graciano then follows with a poesía de bravata, the only type he will perform for the remainder of the engagement—nearly nine hours. What follows is a play-by-play summary of the jousting between them as they maneuver within an emergent field of dialogic and interdiscursive exchanges, positioning themselves relative to one another with critical attention to (1) the conventions and structural rules governing performance (reglamento) and (2) the recurring grammar and rhetorical logics of composition (fundamento). I begin with Graciano's improvised décima petitioning the bravata:

> Uso mi frase sonora
> para poderme expresar
> miren quiero comenzar
> pues ya se llegó la hora
> en esta temprana hora
> a la música de en frente
> y también aquí a esta gente
> **este permiso les pido**
> porque para esto he venido
> **con permiso al presente**
>
> ———
>
> I use my sonorous phrase
> so that I may express myself
> understand that I'd like to commence
> for the time has come
> at this early hour
> to the musicians in front
> and also to the people who are here
> **I ask for your permission**
> for this is why I am here
> **with permission from those present**

Despite the fact that Graciano performs three poesías de bravata, Pablo does not respond in kind in his respective interventions, declining Graciano's invitation to commence the bravata portion. As mentioned above, Pablo has also chosen not to expand on the initial poetic theme established by Graciano. In fact, Pablo has instead performed poesías dealing with the art of huapango arribeño as a sort of tema de fundamento. This is an early attempt to transition la mano away from Graciano—a resonant strategy of establishing tension by not following your counterpart's lead and baiting them to instead follow you. However, in his fourth intervention, Pablo forgoes performing a poesía altogether and instead begins with a decimal that castigates Graciano for what he considers to be a breach in the performative rules of engagement, for he believes that Graciano has not appropriately petitioned him to enter the bravata portion in accordance with the reglamento.

(decimal)
¿CUÁNTO IGNORO TU SABER?
GRACIANO, TE ESTOY ESCUCHANDO
DI DE QUÉ ME ESTÁS TRATANDO
PA' PODERTE COMPLACER

(1) Estos años me han servido
¿no sé ni de qué se trata?
no te contesto bravata
porque no me la has pedido
sabe el público lucido
y aunque no lo quieras creer
no te vayas a ofender
yo te digo ante el presente
¿tú donde tienes la mente?
YO IGNORO TU CONOCER

(2) Tú vienes muy bravucón
a esta fiesta, a este rango
desprestigias el huapango
o' sea, a su tradición
en esto hay educación
¿sabes lo que estoy pensando?
un loco te estoy juzgando
ante el público lucido
¿qué quieres con tu alarido?
NOMÁS TE ESTOY ESCUCHANDO

(3) Al compás de los violines
entre gentes educadas
yo para esas marrulladas

no soy Cándido Martínez
dime ¿cuáles son tus fines?
mira vente declarando
¿qué es lo que vienes buscando?
bajo de este cielo de antemano
mira tú dime Graciano
¿QUÉ ES LO QUE VIENES BUSCANDO?

(4) Mis años tienen esmero
y en estos lugares bellos
para esos atropellos
pide permiso primero
y ante este público entero
todos lo podemos ver
cualquier ave comprender
que nada te has declarado
dime de qué me has tratado
PA' PODERTE COMPLACER

———

HOW CAN I IGNORE YOUR (IN)EXPERIENCE?
GRACANO, I'M LISTENING TO YOU
TELL ME WHAT YOU ARE ENGAGING IN
SO THAT I MAY OBLIGE

(1) These years have served me well
as if I wasn't aware of protocol?
I won't answer your bravata pleadings
because you haven't asked me properly
the lucid public knows
and even if you don't believe it
don't be offended
I tell you before those present
where has your mind gone?
I IGNORE YOUR KNOWLEDGE

(2) You've arrived rambunctious
at this fiesta, at this place
you disparage huapango
in other words, the tradition

there are manners involved in this
do you know what I am thinking?
I am accusing you of being crazy
before this lucid public
what do you expect with such howling?
I'M LISTENING, KEEP UP YOUR TALKING

(3) To the rhythm of the violins
amid well-mannered people
for such mischief
I am not Cándido Martínez
tell me what your intentions are
look, declare yourself
what is it that you are wanting?
beneath the sky and beforehand
look, you tell me, Graciano
WHAT DO YOU WANT FROM ME?

(4) I am careful owing to my years
and in these beautiful places
for such recklessness
ask permission first
and before this entire audience
we can all see it
any bird understands
that you have declared nothing
tell me what you are engaging in
SO THAT I MAY OBLIGE

Despite his protests, Pablo reluctantly follows Graciano's lead and engages him in poesías de bravata in his following intervention:

(poesía)
ADENTRO VÁMOSLE DANDO
HAY QUE DISCUTIR UN RATO
ESTÁ SERVIDO TU PLATO
YA NO TE ESTÉS MALPASANDO

Atención, mucha atención
Graciano en mis decimales

yo soy el Pablo Armendáriz
que critican bravucón
y si hoy vienes rezongón
las pruebas te voy ir dando
que yo no me ando dejando
de poetillas limosneros
y dile a tus vareros:
ADENTRO VÁMOSLE DANDO

———

COME ON, LET'S GET TO IT THEN
LET'S DEBATE A WHILE
I'VE SERVED YOU UP A GOOD HELPING
SO YOU WON'T GO ABOUT MALNOURISHED

Attention, pay much attention
Graciano, to my decimales
I am Pablo Armendáriz
the one criticized for being a braggart
and if you are ornery today
I'll be giving you proof
that I have no intention of giving in
to peddler poets
so go on now and tell your violinists:
COME ON, LET'S GET TO IT THEN

This is Pablo's first poesía de bravata. In effect, as has been mentioned, Graciano is still guiding the topada, as Pablo has now reluctantly followed him into the bravata portion. However, Pablo does something rather ingenious. During his decimal he petitions Graciano to move on to the key of A with a riddle. Up until this point both ensembles had been playing in the key of D. This is yet another attempt to make Graciano follow his lead.

(decimal)
GRACIANO SI BRAVATA QUIERES
SI ERES DE LOS TROVADORES
DE ESOS SIETE MAYORES
¿DIME, CUÁNTAS SON MUJERES?

(1) No hables nomás por hablar
dale brillo a tu alegato

hoy en Xichú Guanajuato
aquí te voy a calar
si me puedes contestar
con tus versitos me hieres
digo que hoy de mí tú esperes
por hay te va el aporreón
contéstame en la ocasión
SI ES QUE TÚ BRAVATA QUIERES

(2) Tanto me la estás buscando
y sin tener experiencia
y hoy en la concurrencia
de esto te estoy preguntando
fíjate y bien ve observando
entre señoras, señores
si es que eres de los mejores
sólo decirte me resta
de esto dame una respuesta
SI ERES DE LOS TROVADORES

(3) Graciano ya tanta alegata
te crees un poeta de claves
y ni tan siquiera sabes
como pedir la bravata
y ahora que de ti se trata
por estos alrededores
te dicen tus servidores
te pregunto en la ocasión
que cuántas mujeres son
DE ESOS SIETE MAYORES

(4) Pa' que te luzcas bonito
si sabes, nada te cuesta
quiero escuchar tu respuesta
ante el público todito
y no te pongas marchito
si bravata es lo que quieres
no andes con falsos quereres
te hablo sin vanidades

de siete tonalidades
¿DIME, CUÁLES SON MUJERES?

———

GRACIANO, IF BRAVATA IS WHAT YOU WANT
IF A TROUBADOUR IS WHAT YOU ARE
OF THE SEVEN MAJOR KEYS
TELL ME, WHICH ARE WOMEN?[29]

(1) Don't talk just to quack
let your claims shine
today in Xichú, Guanajuato
here I am going to test you
if you can answer me
with your little verses, you'll wound me
I say that today on me you should wait
for here comes the trouncing your way
answer me on this occasion
IF BRAVATA IS WHAT YOU WANT

(2) You're picking this fight
and without any experience
and today before those gathered
this I am asking you
listen and observe
amid ladies and gentlemen
if it's true that you are among the best
I have only this to tell you
so that you may give me a response
IF A TROUBADOUR IS WHAT YOU ARE

(3) Graciano, enough with your claims
you think yourself a great poet
yet you don't even know
how to ask for the bravata
and now that the matter concerns you
around these parts
your humble servants tell you
I ask you on this occasion

how many women form part
OF THE SEVEN MAJOR KEYS

(4) So that you may look good
if you know, then no skin off your back
I want to hear your answer
before this entire audience
and don't become withered
if bravata is what you want
don't go about with false desires then
I speak to you without fancy vanities
of those seven keys
TELL ME, WHICH ARE WOMEN?

Disregarding the suggestion to switch keys, Graciano continues playing in the key of D, as does Pablo. Further, Graciano's poesías are increasingly baiting Pablo to engage in a bit of heightened play. Pablo decides to take advantage of this, increasing the tension and beginning to portray Graciano's demeanor as out of touch, even *grosero* (coarse and rude), positioning himself as the more demure troubadour. This is all designed to incite an audience response.

(poesía)
MUCHO CUIDADO HAS DE IR TENIENDO
Y MÁS RESPETO A LA CONCURRENCIA
NO TE ARBORECES SI NO HAY PACIENCIA
¿PARA QUÉ TE ANDAS COMPROMETIENDO?

Una persona que es precavida
no cualquier tonto le avienta tierra
yo a mí me gusta que me den guerra
pero sí, todo con su medida
tú si no tienes otra salida
ya mejor bájate y vete yendo
porque con eso que estás haciendo
pierdes contienda con amistades
con todas esas vulgaridades:
MUCHO CUIDADO HAS DE IR TENIENDO

―――

YOU'LL HAVE TO BE MORE CAREFUL
AND PAY MORE RESPECT TO THOSE GATHERED
DON'T GET ANGRY, FOR IF YOU DO NOT HAVE PATIENCE
THEN WHY DO YOU COMMIT TO THESE ENGAGEMENTS?

A person who is cautious
is no fool fanning the earth
as for me, I like to engage in battle,
but everything in moderation
if you don't have another way out
you'd better descend and get going
because with what you're doing
you'll lose the contest with your friends
with all of these vulgarities:
YOU'LL HAVE TO BE MORE CAREFUL

Graciano counters with the following decimal. Recall that the apparent antagonism or fighting is, at most, a surface-level battle. The taunting tension within the encounter is more akin to the turbidity where two rivers meet, a necessary and desired tension through which terms, course, topic, and response unwind, bind, and clash. As tension builds, excitement grows. In part, Graciano is recontextualizing Pablo's earlier decimal "CUANTO IGNORO TU SABER," specifically recycling the theme of its second décima where he proclaims "en esto hay educación" (there are manners involved in this).

(decimal)
PABLO, YO EN LA EDUCACIÓN
VERÁS QUE ME IMPORTA UN BLEDO
PIENSO QUE TUVISTE MIEDO
O TE HICISTE ACATÓN

(1) No me preocupo tampoco
y aquí lo digo presente
de testigo está la gente
que siempre has estado loco
y que te patina el coco
lo sabe la población
y ahora me sales chillón

verás que en lo del arribeño
mira no espantas ni el sueño
PABLO, YO EN LA EDUCACIÓN

(2) Yo siempre he sido formal
y que la gente lo sepa
Pablo, tú como poeta
eres purito nagual
y no vales un tamal
y esto no lo digo quedo
y lo digo porque puedo
no sé que te habrá pasado
vienes todo atarugado
VERÁS QUE ME IMPORTA UN BLEDO

(3) Digo porque es menester
y lo quiero recalcar
le pregunto yo a Eliazar
andando en este quehacer
mejor fuera ahí Roger
y hoy que derivarlo puedo
verás que me importa un bledo
Pablo, no eres competente
y que lo sepa la gente
CREO QUE TUVISTE MIEDO

(4) No me salgas con jaladas
dices que estás educado
sabes bien que estás taimado
y hoy me vienes con habladas
son puritas marrulladas
y lo digo en la ocasión
Pablo, yo en la educación
verás que me importa un bledo
tal vez ya tuviste miedo
O TE HICISTE ACATÓN

————

PABLO, IN THE WAY OF MANNERS
YOU'LL SEE I DON'T CARE ONE BIT

I THINK YOU WERE AFRAID
OR YOU'VE BECOME A COWARD

(1) I don't worry either
and here I say this
for these people can bear witness
that you've always been crazy
and your noggin spins its wheels
the whole world knows it
and now you're being a crybaby
you see that in arribeño
you don't even frighten drowsiness
PABLO, IN THE WAY OF MANNERS

(2) I have always been well behaved
and so the people know it
Pablo, as a poet
you are just a trickster
and not worth even a *tamal*
and I do not say this softly
and I say this because I can
I don't know what has happened to you
it seems you've become loopy
YOU'LL SEE I DON'T CARE ONE BIT

(3) I say because it is necessary
and I want to emphasize
I ask Eliazar[30]
as I go about in this task
it would have been better to face Roger
and today when I can ponder it
you'll see I don't care one bit
Pablo, you're not competent
and so the people may know it
I BELIEVE YOU WERE AFRAID

(4) Don't confront me with falsehoods
you say that you're well-mannered
you know well that you're a crafty trickster

and today you come to me with false claims
they're nothing but lies
and I say this on the occasion
Pablo, in the way of manners
you'll see I don't care one bit
perhaps because you were afraid
OR YOU'VE BECOME A COWARD

Here, Graciano is expressing dissatisfaction with Pablo's refusal to engage him more deeply in bravata. Further, Graciano responds to the assertion that he has somehow crossed the line by dismissing the notion that he lacks manners. In effect, he is calling Pablo's bluff, suggesting that Pablo is not as demure as he claims, for indeed it is widely known that Pablo can be a bit heavy-handed in topadas—a point Pablo himself acknowledges in the first décima of his poesía de bravata, "ADENTRO VEÁMOSLE DANDO." As a counterpoint to Graciano's emergent position, Pablo now petitions Graciano to engage him in poesías de esdrújula. This now makes two petitions on Pablo's part thus far, the first being to shift to the key of A. In that regard, Graciano and his ensemble have in fact shifted to the key of A; however, Pablo has chosen not to follow Graciano's lead, remaining in the key of D!

In the following decimal, Graciano points out that he has la mano, suggesting that Pablo is in no position to petition him and argues that Pablo has in fact failed to engage him on two accounts: the initial theme of the holidays and the shift to the key of A. The competitive camaraderie is reaching a fever pitch.

(decimal)
SI CONOCES EL REGLAMENTO
¿PA' QUÉ ECHAS ESOS BRINQUETES?[31]
ERES DE LOS MÁS TRANZUDOS[32]
TE LO DIGO CON CIMIENTO

(1) Tu poesía de Año Nuevo
nunca la pude escuchar
y ahora quieres reclamar
y en el verso decir puedo
Pablo, de veras estás lelo
y hablas de conocimiento
no sigues el reglamento
y dices ser trovador

¿dónde está el LA mayor?
SI HABLAS DE CONOCIMIENTO

(2) Yo te lo digo de plano
usando mi entonación
mira en esta ocasión
siempre he llevado la mano
y tú pareces zutano
verás que mi voz no miente
y así te digo de frente
debes de seguir la cosa
ay Pablo, burra olorosa
AVIENTAS UNOS BRINQUETES

(3) Roger y Mario, te digo[33]
tal vez estén como tú
pues andan con tu inquietud
todo el rato te han seguido
y aunque para eso han venido
verás que en la planta mientes
y ante estas bellas gentes
tú dices ser trovador
pero eres puro hablador
ERES DE LOS MÁS TRANZUDOS

(4) Me pides la encadenada
y creo que hasta la esdrújula
mira que te falta brújula
pues en versos no vales nada
si en esto vas de bajada
y te lo digo a su tiempo
también te digo contento
no me vas apantallar
y me quieres recalcar
PABLO, TÚ DE REGLAMENTO

———

IF YOU ARE FAMILIAR WITH THE REGLAMENTO
THEN WHY ARE YOU THROWING SUCH A FIT?

YOU ARE ONE OF THE BIGGEST BACKSLIDERS
I SAY THIS FROM EXPERIENCE

(1) Your poesía about New Year's
I never heard it
and now you want to protest
and I can say this in verse
Pablo, you really are slow-witted
and you speak of being so wise
yet you don't even follow the rules
and you claim to be a poet
where is your A major?
IF YOU SPEAK OF BEING WISE

(2) I tell you plainly
using my intonation
look, on this occasion
I've always had la mano
you look just like any other
you'll see that my voice does not lie
and I tell you this face-to-face
you should follow the rules
Oh, Pablo, you smelly oaf
YOU ARE THROWING SUCH A FIT

(3) Roger and Mario, I tell you
perhaps they, just like you
are also getting anxious
they've followed you all along
and although they've come to perform
you'll see that in your base quatrain you lie
and before these beautiful people
you claim to be a troubadour
but you're nothing but a talker
YOU ARE ONE OF THE BIGGEST BACKSLIDERS

(4) You ask me for an encadenada
and even an esdrújula
look, you lack a compass

well, in verses you are worthless
you are in swift decline
and I say this just in time
and I also tell with glee that
me, you will not duress
your plan is just to fret and stress
PABLO, YOU KNOW NOTHING OF REGLAMENTO

Next, Pablo explains his refusal to follow Graciano in a decimal, which he precedes with a poesía de esdrújula to which Graciano does not respond. By this juncture in the topada, both troubadours are refusing to engage directly with the other's petitions. Yet their most prolific engagements are precisely those that constitute metalinguistic critiques of each other's performance that explain why they are refusing to engage with one another directly. In other words, they have resorted to indexical constructions of indirect speech regarding the flow of performance with particular attention to reglamento and fundamento, actively shaping the contours of each vernacular theory. This chain of music and poetics has grown dense and intentioned/in tension—the audience is listening with rapt attention.

(decimal)
HAY QUE SEGUIR ADELANTE
CONTESTA TU SERVIDOR
NO TE SIGO EN LA MAYOR
PORQUE ERES UN IGNORANTE

(1) Un poetilla como tú
así de desordenado
aquí no se había parado
en este Real de Xichú
solo te deseo salud
ya ante el público escuchante
te dice tu contrincante
pa' contestar porquerías
mira, yo no soy Isaías
Y AL PROSEGUIR ADELANTE

(2) Mira Graciano ni hablar
Isaías siendo un buen amigo
él se rebajó contigo

por allá por el Chilar
él se puso a contestar
a tu blasfema, tu error
y hoy el público honrador
eso lo sabe donde quiera
esa mugrosa tontera
CONTESTA TU SERVIDOR

(3) No se fije usted Cucito
le digo con prontitud
en mi pueblo de Xichú
a Graciano juzguen loquito
yo frente a él no me aguito
aunque sé que es un error
aunque él se crea en esplendor
contesto y no es por relajo
yo con él no me rebajo
PA' SEGUIRLO EN LA MAYOR

(4) No te voy a contestar
como ese poeta Isaías
contestar tus fechorías[34]
yo no me voy a igualar
ni me voy a rebajar
tu serás muy elegante
te sentirás el triunfante
ante gentes congregadas
no contesto marulladas
PORQUE ERES UN IGNORANTE

———

WE MUST CONTINUE ONWARD
ANSWERS YOUR HUMBLE SERVANT
I WON'T FOLLOW YOU IN A MAJOR
BECAUSE YOU'RE A FOOL

(1) A little poet like you
so disorganized
had never set foot here
in this Real de Xichú

I only wish you good health
and before the attentive audience
your opponent says to you
to answer rubbish
look, I am not Isaías[35]
NOW CONTINUING FORWARD

(2) Look, Graciano, why even mention
Isaías being a good friend
how he stooped to your level
over there by el Chilar[36]
he began engaging with you
in your blasphemy, your mistake
and today among the honorable public
it is well known all over
that you peddle filthy nonsense
ANSWERS YOUR HUMBLE SERVANT

(3) Don't worry, don Cucito[37]
I say to you promptly
if in my town of Xichú
they deem Graciano to be crazy
before him I am not worried
even though I know it's a mistake
even though he believes he is splendid
I answer, and it's not for bantering
I won't stoop to his level
I WON'T FOLLOW HIM IN A MAJOR

(4) I'm not going to answer you
like that poet Isaías
to answer your boasts
I'm not going to do as he did
nor will I lower myself
you may think yourself elegant
you may feel triumphant
before these people gathered
but I do not answer nonsense
BECAUSE YOU'RE A FOOL

By this point, Graciano and Pablo have taken distinct metalinguistic paths. Graciano is performing in the key of A and continues on with the bravata, while Pablo remains in the key of D and baits Graciano with poesías de esdrújula. In his third-to-last intervention, Graciano finally takes Pablo up on his offer and performs a poesía de esdrújula, ceding la mano momentarily. Pablo responds in kind, but by this point the sun has come up and both ensembles are growing a bit weary and have also shifted to the key of G, signaling that things are coming to an end.

(poesía)

PONTE MUY ÁGUILA SI ERES POÉTICO
PORQUE EN LA RÍTMICA NO TIENES PRÁCTICA
SE ME HACE EQUÍVOCO QUE EN TU DIALÉCTICA
TE SIENTAS CÉLEBRE Y ESTÁS HERMÉTICO

Ahora los técnicos en matemática
se ven urgidos por algo sólido
algún versito que fuera válido
casi no se usa en la aritmética
ahora la rima es más dinámica
más eficaz en lo aritmético
por eso pílfaro si eres poético
hecha tu cántica que sea romántica
para que el público mire tu réplica
PONTE MUY ÁGUILA SI ERES POÉTICO

———

BE VIGILANT IF YOU'RE POETIC
BECAUSE IN RHYTHM, YOU ARE NOT TRAINED
YOU DON'T IMPRESS ME WITH YOUR DIALECTIC
YOU FEEL FAMOUS AND AIRTIGHT

Now technicians of mathematics
they attend urgently to sound things
some simple logic once deemed valid
is seldom used in such arithmetic
now the rhyme scheme is more dynamic
more efficient in its design
so pilfer it if you're such a poet
if you want to make your song romantic

to make the public admire your reproduction
BE VIGILANT IF YOU'RE POETIC

—Graciano

(poesía)

TÚ NO ERES MÚSICO NI MENOS POÉTICO
TIENES ORÍGENES DE SER MAMÍFERO
PARECES TÍTERE POBRE MORTÍFERO
CONTÉSTAME ÚNICA ESDRÚJULA MÉTRICO

Como eres bárbaro con otros poéticos
así es que trátame, no te dé lástima
si no eres ídolo de la fantástica
sobre lo rítmico y versos métricos
siempre hay estímulo entre los sintéticos
si tus ventajas son como cosmético
derecho tírame menos diabético
tú te crees sabido y muy altísimo
pareces víbora pobre idiotísimo:
TÚ NO ERES MÚSICO NI MENOS POÉTICO

———

YOU ARE NEITHER A MUSICIAN NOR A POET
YOU HAVE MAMMAL ORIGINS
YOU'RE LIKE A LIFELESS PUPPET
ANSWER ME ONLY IN THE ESDRÚJULA METRIC

As a barbarian with other poets
that's how you treat me, shamelessly
yet you're not the fantastic idol
ruling rhythmic and metric verse
there's always praise between fakes
your advantage is cosmetic
be a straight shooter, less diabetic
you think you're well known and high up
but you're like a poor, idiotic snake:
YOU ARE NEITHER A MUSICIAN NOR A POET

—Pablo

Including their respective reconciliatory and farewell decimales—which also contained jibing commentary and were preceded by poesías de bravata—the ensembles shared thirty interventions total, fifteen each. The topada began around half past midnight and ended close to eleven o'clock in the morning— the atmosphere remaining charged the entire night. Afterward, the two ensembles had breakfast together. Pablo and Graciano chatted briefly but seemed to keep it to pleasantries. The euphoria had not yet lifted, and I'm sure their heads were still swimming in décimas. And those that rang out early that morning, just before dawn, were indeed part of a string of transnational saludados, or greetings (more on this in chapter 5). Both Graciano and Pablo called out to people in attendance and afar, making them felt in Xichú, enacting a series of connections that rippled through the audience, legible, sentient, disparate words and images coming together and leaving residues on everyone gathered. For someone like Lidia, the mention of Atlanta echoed through the flesh, José momentarily beside her as Pablo improvised a heartfelt decimal to a friend as the sun was coming up . . .

> Simón, lo vamos a creer
> esto que dice quien canta
> **de cuando estuve en Atlanta**
> yo tengo que agradecer
> y cumplo con mi deber
> ante este público honrado
> no sé si hayas escuchado
> esta humilde versería
> repito con alegría
> OYE, SIMÓN MI ESTIMADO
>
> ———
>
> Simón, can you believe
> what is said by this singer
> **of when I was in Atlanta**
> I am grateful to you
> and I fulfill my duty
> before this honorable public
> I don't know if you can hear
> these humble verses
> I say again with much happiness
> LISTEN, MY ESTEEMED SIMÓN

DE LA VALONA AL RAP, OR THE "LOST DECADE" BLUES

In 1982 the Mexican peso depreciated by 80 percent; capital flight increased to astronomical levels; Central Bank reserves were nearly depleted; foreign banks refused to continue lending; and Mexico's finance minister declared the country incapable of servicing its debt. President López Portillo famously shed tears during his State of the Union address as he announced the expropriation of the country's private banks.[38] In response, the International Monetary Fund and World Bank officiated Mexico's debt renegotiations and dismantled Keynesian growth once and for all. In its stead, they enacted a series of market-oriented reforms premised on financial deregulation. Mexico's debt crisis marks the beginning of a larger period of economic crisis in Latin America, ushering in what is often termed the "Lost Decade" (Lomnitz 2003). Fueled by a propagandistic critique of governmental paternalism and elaborate public relations campaigns extolling the virtues of collectivity, the Mexican government veiled contractions in social spending in the image of direct democracy with thousands of *comités de solidaridad* (solidarity committees). The more prominent corporatist social programs that provided aid for the poor, infrastructural public works projects, and basic health care and education services were the Instituto Mexicano del Seguro Social (Mexican Social Securtiy Institute)/Coordinación General del Plan Nacional de Zonas Deprimidas y Grupos Marginados (General Coordination of the National Plan for Depressed Areas and Marginalized Groups) under Presidents De la Madrid and López Portillo, in addition to the Programa Nacional de Solidaridad (National Solidarity Program) during the de Gortari administration. This transference of state responsibilities to civil society sought to placate social discontent associated with the devastating impacts of anticipated structural adjustment: increased poverty, greater inflation, and higher unemployment (Bohórquez Molina et al. 2003; Massey, Durand, and Malone 2002).

Guillermo Velázquez and Mauro's poetics distilled this new repressive politics of social reproduction, otherwise obfuscated by official neoliberal discourses of *solidaridad* (solidarity)—or what Mauro referred to as *pretensiones* (pretenses). Forged amid this transformative moment, their vernacular poetics disarticulated technocratic castings that masked the withdrawal of the nation state from its commitments to labor and society (Robinson 2003: 244). The neoliberal "extension of commodity relations into the public, family, and community spheres" (244) was accomplished under the ideological guise of faux communitarianism grounded in "a discourse of historical continuity . . . employed to legitimise a neoliberal economic reform agenda that in reality represented a significant break from the statist and economic nationalist development model that had been favoured by the PRI [Institutional Revolutionary Party] since at least the 1930s" (Sheppard 2011: 514). These social enclosures were part of broader spatializing practices that brace what James Ferguson and Akhil Gupta (2005) term the topographies of state vertical encompassment in their spatial analysis of neoliberal governmentality. The bureaucratic practices of solidaridad reached deep into the communities of the Sierra Gorda and were the means by which the Mexican state reproduced a renewed sociospatial scalar order that displaced many and catalyzed out-migration (Bohórquez Molina et al. 2003). Ultimately, huapango arrribeño troubadours voiced the consequences of institutionalizing corporate profitability rather than social sustainability in everyday life—to survive people had to settle for wheat-flour tortillas and also migrate to Mexico City and across the U.S.-Mexico border.

Huapango arribeño's space of vernacular poetics provided a countervailing understanding of these broader social transformations in which the collective imaginary of Sierra Gorda natives was brought to bear. This "history from below," to borrow from Robin Kelley, indeed demonstrates how cultural expressions are "diagnostic of power" (1994: 9) but, more important, reveals the scope of communicability of official narratives of neoliberalism and the breaches within them.[39] At the dawn of the 1980s, economic displacement and labor migration were the everyday iterations of an emergent neoliberal order, and in the face of these oscillations and flows, huapango arribeño expressively embodied a "socially constitutive self-activity" that offered utopian glimpses of life beyond the language spaces of austerity (Cleaver 1979: 18). To this point, on Los Leones de la Sierra de Xichú's first studio recording released in 1982, Guillermo Velázquez follows a version of "En Busca de Chamba" with this impassioned decimal:

EL ALMA DESFALLECIDA
SE RECOBRA, SE LEVANTA
Y ES UNA LUMBRE LA VIDA
QUE ABRASA Y QUE SE AGIGANTA

(1) Los bolísmos, los enojos
de algo me han ido sirviendo
no es lo mismo ir comprendiendo
que vivir cerrado de ojos

diario puertas con cerrojos
diario mascando la brida
"que vuelva, que no hay cabida"
y entre gritos y aventones
va encontrando las razones
EL ALMA DESFALLECIDA

(2) Metro, camión, ejes, viales
del diario vivir al trote
de chalán, cargando el bote
puras chambas eventuales
propinas y mecapales
este nudo en la garganta
y cuando ya no se aguanta
al espueleo de las penas
la sangre que hincha las venas
SE RECOBRA, SE LEVANTA

(3) El tiempo no es la derrota
ni lo que nos extravía
no es el sol ni la sequía
lo único que nos azota
cuando esta conciencia brota
y encuentra tierra llovida
cuando se enraíza y anida
entre cada recoveco
el alma es un leño seco
Y ES UNA LUMBRE LA VIDA

(4) Esto de andar asoleado
para arriba y para abajo
lo de no encontrar trabajo
lo de vivir arrimado
sentirse desenraizado
pesadumbre tanta y tanta
todo lo que nos quebranta
pensamiento con dolencia
al arder se hace en conciencia
QUE ABRASA Y QUE SE AGIGANTA

THE TATTERED SOUL
RECOVERS, PICKS ITSELF UP
AND LIFE IS A FIRE
THAT EMBRACES AND IS SET ABLAZE

(1) The humiliations, the anger
they have served me well
for it is not the same to go about understanding
as to live with your eyes shut
daily, with latched doors
chewing on the bridle
told "come back later, today there is no room"
and amid shoves and shouts
it finds the reasons
THE TATTERED SOUL

(2) Metro, bus, intersections, avenues
daily life on the move
a hawker peddling with a bucket
always haphazard jobs
workaday tasks for tips
this tight knot in my throat
when one can no longer tolerate
the goading of such punishment
the blood that swells in the veins
RECOVERS, PICKS ITSELF UP

(3) Time is not defeat
nor the only thing that alienates us
neither the sun nor drought
is the only thing that lashes at us
when consciousness springs forth
and it finds damp earth
when it anchors and nests itself
in every nook and cranny
the soul is a piece of dry wood
AND LIFE IS A FIRE

(4) To go about sun-drenched
up and down
unable to find work
to live on the fringe
to feel unrooted
so much, so much sadness
everything that breaks us
heavy, aching thoughts
as they sting become consciousness
THAT EMBRACES AND IS SET ABLAZE

Just as in the early 1980s, the United States continues to loom throughout Xichú's poetic imaginings as a "predominant external 'other'" (Sheppard 2011: 510); this sonic and poetic tethering—evidenced in the topada between Graciano and Pablo, for instance—brings us to where we began, to the echoes of Robert Johnson's utopian imaginings. His blues were ultimately about hope, about migration, and about home. This also brings us back to Chicago via hip-hop one final time, for there exists a certain resonance here, particularly as recently arrived Mexican migrants live out their lives amid the present era of heightened migrant restriction, straddling divides along the lines of class, race, and citizenship, much like their African-American antecedents. And a palimpsestual place like Xichú both acknowledges distances and bridges them, as "tattered (migrant) souls" "pick themselves up" with "knots in the back of the throat," amid the turmoil of neoliberal migration, making their festival happen every year. The space of huapango arribeño performance voices these material and imagined connections, in addition to many others, at the sonic level even a connection to hip-hop . . . perhaps a somewhat unconventional connection but relevant in the present discussion, as Velázquez voices in a recent set of recorded décimas he calls "De la Valona al Rap" that speak of social enclosures to be denied and cultural distances to be bridged:

Sin perder el corazón
voy de la valona al rap
y no hay "generation gap"
ni folclórica traición
es la certera intuición
de que no hay que segregar
ni hacer ghettos, ni arrestar
y a los hechos me remito

todo cabe en un jarrito
sabiéndolo acomodar

———

Without losing my way
I flow between the valona and rap
for there is no "generation gap"
nor betrayal to tradition
it is the absolute intuition
that there is no need to segregate
neither to create ghettos nor to isolate
and I refer to these truths
that everything fits in a little earthen pitcher
grace is doing and knowing how

In this recording he trades off décimas with his son, Vincent, a hip-hop MC, Guanajuato native, and active member of the Xichú festival's organizing committee. Vincent recently made the trip up to Chicago with his mother to participate in a fund-raiser for the festival—an event organized by Esperanza. As he introduced the artists participating that evening, he burst into an impromptu décima flow in full-throated MC swagger, his hip-hop cadence distinct from that of the troubadours he invoked:

En esta festividad
al decirlo soy puntual
por su solidaridad
y apoyo incondicional
es casi una realidad
el sueño del festival

Cuando los poetas serranos
recuperan nuestra historia
reavivan en la memoria
nuestros íntimos arcanos
se hacen música las manos
la dignidad se agiganta
cada verso en la garganta
brota pristino y rotundo
y es el México profundo
la Sierra Gorda que canta

I say this fittingly
in this festive gathering
because of your solidarity
and unconditional support
the dream of our festival
is nearly a reality

When mountain poets
invoke our history
our intimate mysteries
come alive in memory
hands become music
dignity grows large
full-throated verses
spring forth pristinely and resoundingly
the sonorous Sierra Gorda
is the deep-rooted Mexico

Months later, at the festival back in Xichú, Los Leones de la Sierra de Xichú performed for the thousands in attendance. Vincent joined them onstage. He has become part of the group as of late, lending his talents as a dancer and at times incorporating his stylized hip-hop décima poetics. Much as migrants in the present continue to push the boundaries of where home exists, Vincent and Los Leones push the boundaries of tradition as they made transcultural connections between the worlds of huapango and U.S.-American musics—from the valona to rap—recognizing the social import and shared synergy that both brands of vernacular poetics possess as oral traditions: "there is no generation gap." As the musicians strummed out a valona on that cold December night, Vincent shouted out the following in between vigorous violin remates, echoing his flow in Chicago, echoing his father's poesía three decades earlier, voicing both a critique of power and a message of hope:

Soy cantante y bailador
un sociólogo rapero
soy un mc huapanguero
saltimbanqui y trovador
en un indignado amor
mi canto a México estriba

y en esta hora decisiva
a pesar de los abrojos
con dulce llanto en los ojos:
yo sí le grito: ¡qué viva!

———

I am a singer and a dancer
a sociologist rapper
I'm a huapanguero MC
an acrobatic troubadour
my song for Mexico derives from
this an indignant love
and in this decisive hour
in spite of the thorn bushes
with sweet tears in my eyes:
I WILL RAISE MY VOICE AND CHEER, "MAY IT [MEXICO] LONG
LIVE!"

Vincent punctuated this hip-hop huapango mash-up with a resounding, "Desde la Sierra Gorda, estas décimas van para el Ejercito Zapatista de Liberación Nacional por veinte años de lucha!" (From the Sierra Gorda, these décimas are dedicated to the Zapatista National Liberation Army for twenty years of struggle!), a shout-out that resonates now more than ever as transnational Canadian mining interests have returned to Xichú and its surroundings. Although the area has been deemed a protected biosphere, this has not stopped lobbyists from influencing municipal politicians to scale back certain environmental protections. This conflict is just now beginning to play itself out, but it represents the type of neoliberal exploitation around the country that the Zapatista National Liberation Army has denounced.

The Zapatista National Liberation Army is a subtext to the entirety of this chapter. In the ruins of the debt crisis of 1982, six self-proclaimed Marxist revolutionaries arrived in the dense Lacandon jungle in Chiapas a year after the economic calamity. Seasoned organizers and activists emboldened by the political and economic instability in post-1968 Mexico, they escaped persecution in the remote jungle with dreams of launching a guerilla war against the Mexican government. The enigmatic Subcomandante Marcos arrived in 1984. A teacher (some say a university professor), he was entrusted with instructing the indigenous population in reading, writing, Mexican history, and Marxism, but it was he who became the student, finding lessons of hope in the jungle during the Lost Decade. In his writings he has often made mention of *el viejo* Antonio, an indigenous elder who became a teacher to him, giving legitimacy to the Zapatista National Liberation Army's presence in the indigenous communities before their official uprising on the morning of January 1, 1994—just as NAFTA took effect (Higgins 2000). I end with a portion of a story Marcos tells of el viejo Antonio, a story about a dream at the edge of dawn, about the unbinding that is central to intimacy and that brings us full circle to the connections between music and hope, between performance and politics, between poetics and material realities, between dreams and survival, between verses and flows that cross the borders of nations, of "cultures," of sounds, of genres—*de la valona al rap* or, in the case of Marcos, from huapango to . . . well, I won't spoil it for you:

> Me encontraba, pues, escuchando en la grabadorita una música y, en algún momento, no sé cuándo, me di cuenta de que a mis espaldas estaba el viejo Antonio. Y sin que viniera al caso, le bajé un poco al volumen porque sabía que iba a hablar él . . . y empezó a platicar esta historia de los sueños buenos y malos.
>
> . . . soñamos que somos mejores; mejores seres humanos, mejor hombre o mejor mujer, según cada quien o cada cual, y que en ese sueño uno sentía que no era perfecto pero que era mejor que el minuto anterior, que el día anterior, que el año anterior. Sentía que era más completo porque era grande su escucha para el otro, porque era buena la palabra que le regalaba al otro, porque sabía que no estaba solo y que había otro que luchaba por él, en lo mismo, en el mismo lugar, en esa tierra que estaba siendo soñada en el sueño, pero existía, como quiera, fuera de él. Y decía el viejo Antonio, que en ese sueño donde somos mejores era tan rico el color y la música que había, que a veces se hacía una música. Decía que el sueño en que somos mejores, cuando se escapaba de nuestras cabezas, de nuestro sueño, y pasaba la vigilia cuando estábamos despiertos, era una música. Y antes de irse me dijo, "el sueño de ser mejores es, en muchas veces, como la música que estabas escuchando." Y se fue.
>
> Quienes me entendieron lo que estoy diciendo, y lo están pensando, saben que lo que estaba escuchando era un son jarocho. El son y el huapango fueron las dos hojas de la ventana por la que me asomé primero a lo que era la música y los musiqueros. Después, se abrió una puerta—el rock.

(I was listening to music on a small radio, and at some point, I don't know when, I realized that el viejo Antonio was standing behind me. And without him asking me I lowered the volume because I knew he was going to speak . . . and he started telling this story about good and bad dreams . . .

. . . We dream that we are better; better human beings, better men or women, whatever the case may be, and in that dream you didn't feel perfect, but felt that you were better than the previous minute, than the previous day, the previous year. You felt more complete because you listened wholeheartedly to the other, because the word the other gave you was good, because you knew that you were not alone and that there was another fighting for you, in the same struggle, in the same place, in the land that was being dreamed in the dream, that existed nonetheless outside the dream. And el viejo Antonio would say that in the dream in which we are better, the colors and sounds were so rich that they became music. He would say that the dream in which we are better, when it escaped from our minds, from our sleep, and passed into our consciousness when we were awake, it came in the form of music. And before he left he said, "The dream of being better is many times like the music you were listening to." And he was gone.

Those who understand what I am saying and are considering it know that what I was listening to was a son jarocho. Son and huapango were the windows through which I first peered, opening my eyes to what music and musicians were. Then another door opened—rock and roll.)

FOUR

REGIONAL SOUNDS

Mexican Texas and the Semiotics of Citizenship

If we view a border not simply as a line on a map but, more fundamentally, as a sensitized area where two cultures or two political systems come face to face, then the first border between English-speaking people from the United States and people of Mexican culture was in the eastern part of what is now the state of Texas.

—AMÉRICO PAREDES, "THE PROBLEM OF IDENTITY IN A CHANGING CULTURE"

Soy de Guanajuato, San Luis Potosí, Austin, Garland, de aquí, todos lados! (I'm from Guanajuato, San Luis Potosí, Austin, Garland, from here, all places!)

—DANIEL, TEXAS

Why is a foreigner singing the national anthem. I realize it's in San Antonio, but that still ain't Mexico.

—@LEWIEGROH, TWITTER

The rhetoric of a postracial society often leaves little room to speak critically about race and how it forms the basis of many forms of inequality and injustice in the United States without being erroneously accused of being racist.[1] For some of my students, this notion usually dissipates once we begin exploring concrete examples of ongoing racial discrimination in the United States: the criminal justice system, housing segregation, racial profiling, and more. While I privilege discussion of institutionalized racism, I often begin by introducing high-profile examples of interpersonal bigotry, usually sourced from social media, as an entry point for our discussions. In the summer of 2013, one such incident became the focus of national controversy during the National Basketball Association finals between the Miami Heat and the San Antonio Spurs. The ensuing semester my students gasped as I displayed the following tweets in class:[2]

Ok what in the fuck is this beaner doing singing our national anthem?

—@LEBLANCIV

Why was the kid singing the national anthem wearing a mariachi band outfit? We ain't Mexican

—@THOMASDESTEFANO

This lil Mexican snuck in the country like 4 hours ago now he singing the anthem

—@A2DAO

Who let this illegal alien sing our national anthem

—@MCYRUS2

At the opening of game 3 of the series, eleven-year-old Sebastien De La Cruz stood in the packed AT&T Center in San Antonio, Texas, and delivered a stellar performance of "The Star-Spangled Banner." The young *Charro de Oro* (golden charro)—his show-business moniker—specializes in mariachi music and has gained national recognition, even appearing as a quarterfinalist on the popular television show *America's Got Talent*. A native son of San Antonio who is equally proud of his Mexican heritage, De La Cruz donned his mariachi regalia as he sang for the thousands in the arena and the millions watching on television. These distant observers objected to his performance and immediately took to social media to express their disapproval, unleashing a torrent of racist commentary before he was even done. Most of the disparaging remarks centered on his Mexican heritage, visibly indexed by his outfit. In their eyes, anything "Mexican" was fundamentally incongruent with being "American," which reveals the entrenched attitude that Mexicans and any semblance of Mexicanness exceed the boundaries of American identity.[3] This vitriol not only reinscribed a racially normative understanding of Americanness but also went a step further in defining De La Cruz's un-Americanness—or Mexicanness—in terms of citizenship (or lack thereof). Simply put, being Mexican disqualifies one from the entitlements of "our" full citizenship: "Who let this illegal alien sing our national anthem."

Coincidentally, De La Cruz's performance occurred in the shadow of one of the most important monuments in the story of U.S. westward expansion—a physical shrine, or memory-place as Richard Flores (1998) has written, that is operative in officializing narratives of American imperial prowess in the guise of bravery (against cowardice), progress (against superstition), and hard-fought liberty (against tyranny). The AT&T Center is located a mere three miles from the Alamo mission.[4] The master symbol of the Alamo, Flores (2002) argues, has inscribed a narrative of Mexican inferiority, which casts Mexicans' heritage as deficient and thus wholly opposed to American virtues (which the brave martyrs at the Alamo embodied). Focusing on the economic transformations of the late nineteenth century in Texas, Flores makes a case for how "remembering the Alamo" at that time mobilized a cultural memory that "socially incriminated" ethnic Mexicans and thus "[placed] the burden and responsibility of the socioeconomic displacement of Mexicans on Mexicans themselves and [posited] their 'uncivilized, inhuman, and socially threatening behavior' as the cause" (2002: 107). A full century later, the ire sparked by De La Cruz's performance is a continuation of this same semiotic work. Indeed, the echoes of Mexicanness as quintessentially un-American ring loudest in relation to a political-economic formation in which Mexicans' subjugation is naturalized. While today's context is no longer that of the late nineteenth-century rise of commercial agriculture and the race-based domination over Texas-Mexicans that made it possible, the everyday subjugation of transnational migrant labor nonetheless continues. In this way, the connection between nineteenth-century American expansionist ideologies and the current criminalization of Mexican migrants is not so distant. One could even say they are directly linked, for the Mexican-American War—in part catalyzed by the Texas independence movement—established the U.S.-Mexico border as we have come to know it.[5]

With this in mind, we regularly hear talk of the American dream, a framing that configures social membership in the space of the U.S. nation-state with adherence to an aspirational and forward-looking ethic conceived in terms of physical movement to a new locale where fresh opportunities are available. This ethic is supposedly grounded in civic duty, hard work, and a broadly conceived American creed of enterprise and self-reliance (the pursuit of happiness) that assures success for those who make the best of the limitless opportunities available to them. Often, the imagined primordial subject at the center of this narrative is the "immigrant." Indeed, the chant of a "nation of immigrants" is routinely mobilized to imagine, in an embodied way, this industrious essence of the nation-state. Linguistic representations of the American dream and a nation of immigrants, however, construct a racial formation that equates citizenship with whiteness, such that persons of color are forever assumed to lack the cultural capital that would afford them full membership in the nation-state. This exclusionary reality speaks to the gap between the theoretical universality of citizenship and its practical marginalizing effects, as Renato Rosaldo (1989) has commented. In other words, "full citizenship and cultural visibility appear to be inversely related. When one increases, the other decreases. Full citizens lack culture, and those most culturally endowed lack full citizenship" (198). When it comes to migrants in particular, their movement into the space of the U.S. nation-state requires a "cultural stripping away" so that they, their children, their grandchildren, and so on can eventually become part of "a national culture that erases their meaningful past autobiography, history, heritage, language, and all the rest of the so-called cultural baggage" (210–211). What else did De La Cruz's attire—not to mention his skin color—signify but culture? His stylized performance of "The Star-Spangled Banner" on the holiest of national stages—that of a major sporting event—was deemed fundamentally incongruent with what it means to be American.

After the rabid social media response, the San Antonio Spurs invited De La Cruz for an encore performance of the national anthem before game 4, at which he was introduced by then mayor Julian Castro. Defiantly, he again donned his mariachi outfit, this time consciously expressing a stylized control over his otherwise racialized body, an argument that both Catherine Sue Ramírez (2009) and Luis Alvarez (2008) have made in relation to Mexican-American zoot-suiters in the United States during World War II.

Now let's circle back to the context in which this all took place—Texas. As @LewieGroh so eloquently put it: "Why is a foreigner singing the national anthem. I realize it's in San Antonio, but that still ain't Mexico." This statement recognizes some overlap between nations while refusing to acknowledge ethnic Mexicans as members of the American polity. The realization that it's San Antonio is an admission of its history as a distinctly Mexican-American city. However, the immediate labeling of De La Cruz as a foreigner necessarily casts him and all of Mexican Texas outside the boundaries of American belonging, much as they have been excluded historically, often through violent means. According to this logic, no matter how much ethnic Mexicans assimilate, perceived racial difference is equated with an otherness that America has no room for—they will never be real (white) Americans. This example illustrates the relationship between race, geography, national culture, and aesthetics within the context of Texas. And certainly Texas is an ideal site on which to transpose the nationalist scriptings of the United States, for Anglo Texas, in particular, "has always been given to a sharp and mythological exceptionalism" rooted in notions of freedom, an independent spirit, bravery, and greatness (Limón 2011: 112)—everything is bigger in Texas. This distinctly ethnoregionalist nationalism impels Texas to imagine itself not as constituting part of an imperial project but rather as having freed itself from a foreign empire, Mexico. In this way, Texan exceptionalism operates as a microcosm of American exceptionalism; however, its uniqueness is also contingent on the perceived "difference from the racialized and stigmatized presence of people of Mexican origin in the state" (112).

With this context and the De La Cruz incident in mind, these pages explore what Josh Kun (2005) has elsewhere described in relation to African-American cultural poetics: that "others" can "too, sing América" (143). To further the argument that marginalized communities can form subjectivities beyond the essentialist borders of the American racial formation, I look to the presence of huapango arribeño in Texas in relation to its most immediate musical counterparts—Tejano and regional Mexican—to illustrate the contentious semiotics that surround ethnic-Mexican music making in Texas, particularly the contradictory ways in which regionalism, nation, and citizenship intersect. Ultimately, I show that claims to musical regionalism as a type of symbolic distancing from the spaces of both the Mexican and U.S. nation-states are paradoxically undergirded by nationalist aspirations. These contradictions shed light on the spatial politics of huapango arribeño performance as a transnational practice that exceeds the material and cultural boundaries of both Mexico and the United States.

FUEREÑOS

A tragic flaw, José E. Limón (1994) laments, is woven into Américo Paredes's work—a modern tragic sentiment that treats Mexicans from south of the border, or *fuereños*, to use Paredes's construction, rather ambivalently, if not with disapproval. Paredes, Limón argues, attributes the demise of Mexican society in South Texas between 1870 and 1930 to the presence of fuereños (and also gringos) and goes on to suggest that their offspring—best represented by the *pocho* (U.S.-born assimilated Mexican)—have little to offer in the vein of heroic expressive culture. The war of old has ended, the victory of the dominant is near complete, and the mexicano stands, or perhaps lies, socially and culturally defeated. It is here that Limón picks up the story, as he ethnographically renders the expressive culture he grew up with as an urban child of fuereños in South Texas, "[mumbling] 'damn-foolishness' into microphones and [dancing] to it" (1994: 93). His exploration of art and ritual as a political form is duly noted here. However, much as Limón departs from Paredes, I open up further possibilities regarding cultural poetics in Texas that both Paredes and

Limón might not have foreseen, for their mexicanos were native-born, not migrants. In the spirit of my predecessors, I too must pick up where they have left off. So here I extend my analysis beyond Limón's *postmodern mexicano*—a distinctly positioned cultural subject that, nevertheless, stands at a distance from the Mexican migrant and therefore from the immediate politics of the U.S.-Mexico border. This physical boundary looms in both his and Paredes's work as a distant historical formation such that the politics of the border—at the moment in which each is writing—shadow their respective works, ultimately remaining absent. The contemporary border politics at the time of this book's writing began to take shape most acutely with the signing of NAFTA in 1994, the year that marks the publication of Limón's *Dancing with the Devil: Society and Cultural Poetics in Mexican-American South Texas*. This year bore witness to an emerging set of cultural logics and economic processes that have deeply impacted Mexican migrants in Texas, namely, renewed structural adjustment in Mexico, which catalyzed migration into the United States across a highly militarized border. Still, much as Limón extends Fredric Jameson's (1991) discussion of postmodernity, Roger Rouse (1991) has done so as well but with attention to Mexican migrants, which is perhaps most applicable in the present discussion. While I choose not to dwell on a discussion of postmodernity (which has been exhausted by these and other works), opting instead for more recent theoretical formulations regarding the U.S.-Mexico border (De Genova 2005; Inda 2006; Lugo 2008; Rosas 2012; Zavella 2011), it must be noted that I nevertheless follow in the wake of Limón's and Rouse's interventions into Jameson's theorizing, for I too look beyond high art and literature and focus instead on "the lives of those 'ordinary' people who inscribe their transient texts in the minutiae of daily experience" (Rouse 1991: 18–19).

"Traes la jarana, Alex?" (Do you have your jarana, Alex?), Graciano asked. I gestured that it was in the car. Graciano was certain I had it with me, and maybe I was nervously anticipating this moment. Earlier that afternoon we had met at his home just outside of Austin to chat and listen to music. The beginnings of fieldwork. At this point we had known each other for about a month. Our friendship would blossom after this evening.

The afternoon meeting was cut short. He had a huapango engagement to get to and asked whether I wanted to tag along, on the condition that I would bring my jarana. I hadn't expected this, but I eagerly said yes with the hope of listening to some huapangos and enjoying the evening, drinking a beer or two, maybe even dancing. So he jumped in his truck and sped off, and I followed. As the sun set over the city, we merged onto I-35 toward downtown Austin, took the Cesar Chávez exit, snaked our way through East Austin, and continued on, way, way east of the highway, to a predominantly working-class African-American neighborhood. We pulled up to a convenience store—a predetermined location where two violinists would be waiting. I spotted them right away. Salomón was smoking a cigarette. Valentín was scratching a lotto ticket he had purchased inside. I stepped out of the car and greeted them. I had met them only once before.

We caravanned to the engagement. It was dark by the time we arrived. We all parked in a row across the street from the home I presumed was our destination, stepped out, and walked over to Graciano's tailgate. They took out their instruments, and Graciano asked, "Traes la jarana, Alex?" And there I was, standing outside a stranger's home in East Austin, tuning my instrument with the rest of them, not sure what was about to happen. But this scene was familiar to them. In fact, they were doing this every weekend, had been doing it for years, as were many other musicians—from Austin to Dallas, Houston to Mississippi . . .

Once the instruments sounded to Salomón's liking, Graciano signaled us to cross the street. We trekked through the front yard and toward the side of the house in question, ducked underneath a few untrimmed fruit trees, and stopped at the wooden gate leading to the brightly lit backyard. We paused for a moment. You could hear the people on the other side—laughter, a boom box playing, children screaming. You could smell the food—steamed corn tortillas and *barbacoa* (barbecued meat). People's movements shifted the light filtering through the cracks in the gate. I got goose bumps. Nerves or the temperature dropping? Graciano shushed us just before he unlatched the gate. Suddenly, we burst in singing "Las Mañanitas" with full huapango arribeño flair. I quickly realized it was someone's birthday party as I struggled to remember the words, stumbling my way through. The fifty or so people packed into the modest backyard met us with applause and quickly arranged chairs for us to sit and play as soon as the obligatory birthday serenade was over. These folks wanted sones, jarabes, and improvised verses. Before I knew it, I was furiously strumming away to a valona as Graciano greeted the family gathering with a decimal.

I played the entire engagement that evening—from eight in the evening to three in the morning—as people danced at arm's length from us, stomping on pieces of plywood placed on the ground just in front of where we were seated, a makeshift tarima that rang out alongside the sounds of police sirens, subwoofers from cars on the street, and the engines of jets preparing to land at the nearby airport. While I intuitively recognized the various elements of the music, I had never played huapango arribeño with an ensemble. There's a first time for everything . . . I kept saying to myself, "What happened to just dancing?" In between Newport cigarettes and swigs of tequila, Salomón assured me I was doing fine. I refused to believe it, feeling inexperienced and unprepared, but smiled along with him and laughed because we were enjoying ourselves, after all. The story of my involvement with these musicians and community begins here in the early 2000s, but they had already been doing this for about a decade.

In 1985 huapango arribeño crossed into the United States for the first time. A Houston-based hometown association (HTA) invited two huapango arribeño ensembles to perform at a topada benefit dance organized to raise funds for a church construction project back in Cerritos, San Luis Potosí. At that time, HTAs were not as commonplace as they are today.[6] Yet, even in the mid-1980s, these then-nascent migrant organizations helped provide disaster relief, fund charitable work, and finance infrastructure projects for their communities of origin (building roads, churches, clinics, sewage plants, schools), as well as support civic, cultural, and religious events and festivals (Vertovec 2004). On the occasion in question, the Houston-based HTA had successfully acquired short-term tourist visas for two ensembles. The first consisted of troubadour Cándido Martínez, accompanied by Guillermo Guevara (primera vara), Refugio "Cuco" Rodríguez (segunda vara), and José Martínez (vihuela). The second included troubadour don Lencho Olvera, accompanied by Eusebio "Chebo" Méndez (primera vara), Sebastián Salinas (segunda vara), and Osvaldo (vihuelero). The first ensemble crossed successfully, while the second was denied entrance at the border. Needless to say, the topada didn't happen. Cándido Martínez and company played the engagement alone. He vividly remembers, "Habían puros paisanos—hartos de Rioverde, Rayón, San Ciro de Acosta, Cárdenas, Cerritos, Matehuala, de todos lados. Eso no me lo esperaba." (There was nothing but countrymen—a whole bunch from Rioverde, Rayón, San Ciro de Acosta, Cárdenas, Cerritos, Matehuala, from all over. I wasn't expecting that.) Months later, don Lencho Olvera and his musicians tried their luck at crossing once again and this time they were granted entry.

They headed straight to Houston where they played another dance organized by the same HTA.

The first topada in the United States would come a few years later. According to Guillermo Velázquez, it occurred in Dallas, Texas at a similar-type HTA event in the early 1990s. Guillermo Velázquez and Los Leones de la Sierra de Xichú were first invited to the United States in 1988 where they performed at both a San Ciro de Acosta HTA benefit dance in San Diego, California and a Mexican music festival in Los Angeles. They subsequently began traveling to Dallas, Texas, regularly to perform at HTA fund-raisers, and it was at one such event in the mid-1990s where they had a topada with don Lencho Olvera and his huapangueros.[7] At around this same time there begins to emerge a robust community of huapangueros that is crucial to the story in this book. Through multiple circumstances (work, family, mutual friends, social networks), don Lencho Olvera, vihuelero Senovio, violinist Homero, troubadour Graciano, and violinist Salomón came to find one another in the Austin area in 1995 and began rehearsing and performing. Two years later, Sebastián Salinas joined them. I now briefly tell their stories, of how these musicians (Senovio, Homero, Graciano, and Salomón) came to find one another in Texas.

Senovio, Doña Rosa's husband, had arrived in Central Texas in 1990. He left Guanajuato and crossed clandestinely into the United States; after arriving, he notes, "Yo dejé de agarrar un instrumento por como unos cinco años, pues aquí no había nada" (I didn't play my instrument for about five years, well, there was nothing [no music] here). This all changed after he met Homero and Graciano in 1995. Homero, a violinist, came to the United States as a teenager in the late 1970s. He had cousins and uncles in Southern California who helped him find work picking oranges, lemons, and grapefruit. He remained in the United States for five years without returning to Mexico and then began traveling back and forth, staying for months at a time in both California and Guanajuato. In the early 1990s he came to the Austin area with friends to work in construction and has made it his home ever since. His career as a huapango arribeño violinist began there after he met the musicians mentioned above. However, he had already tried his luck as a troubadour in the late 1980s in Guanajuato where he performed mainly at velaciones. When he did participate in topadas he did so playing vihuela alongside the likes of don Lencho Olvera, Cándido Martínez, and others.

Graciano left northeastern Guanajuato for Central Texas in the mid-1980s. He initially held a series of odd jobs, working as everything from a ranch hand, truck driver, and busboy to a commercial construction worker. Years later he came to successfully run his own construction business. In light of this, he reminds me, "¡Yo nomás estudié hasta segundo de secundaria!" (I only went to school up until the eighth grade!). Graciano continues, "Yo me vine pa' acá, como todos, buscando un mejor porvenir, a mejorarse uno su vida económicamente" (I came over here, like everyone, searching for a better future, to better one's life chances economically). Though he grew up listening to huapango arribeño and, according to him, desired to become a practitioner at an early age, his life as a huapanguero began after arriving in the United States. Yet, before crossing the border, he first migrated to live in Mexico City at the age of seven. He reminisces about this with a smile and recalls the day his older brother, who also resided in Mexico City at the time, returned from a visit to Guanajuato. "En ese entonces apenas salían las grabadoras de cassette. Mi hermano se fue al rancho por unos días y resulta que hubo una tocada de huapango por allá y grabo algo de la música que tocaron." (At that time tape recorders were just coming out. My brother went home for a few days, and it turns out there was a huapango performance, and he recorded some of the music they performed.) Graciano's brother played the recording for him. He says, "Algo cambió dentro de mi ese día" (Something in me changed that day). Memories of his childhood stirred in him; when he and his family attended weddings and baptisms, huapangueros provided the music. Nearly a decade after arriving in Central Texas, Graciano befriended the famed troubadour don Lencho Olvera, in addition to Senovio and Homero. Inspired by his newfound friends, Graciano collected all the bootleg huapango arribeño recordings he could find, bought a guitarra quinta huapanguera from don Lencho Olvera, and began rehearsing with Senovio and Homero. Despite his initial struggles, some encouraged him, like the violinist Salomón, who arrived in Central Texas shortly thereafter.

Salomón's father, also a violinist, initiated him in the art of huapango arribeño at the age of ten. He first began by playing sacred music at funeral wakes. By his late teens, he was performing professionally at weddings, birthdays, and local dances, although a good portion of his adolescence (well into his twenties), he explains, was also spent working in the mines in the states of Coahuila and Jalisco. He migrated to Central Texas for the first time in the mid-1990s.

These individual musicians became the foundation of the huapango arribeño community in the United States, which now boasts ensembles in Austin, Dallas, Houston, northern Mississippi, and, most recently, northern California, Florida, and Tennessee. It is often the case that veteran musicians from Mexico arrive in the United States, work, perform, and take the time to instruct novice musicians, like Graciano, such that young huapangueros have now come of age on the U.S. side of the border, learning the musical trade by performing largely for migrant communities. I tell one such story in the following chapter, and this chapter opens with the words of Daniel, a young vihuelero from Guanajuato who has made Texas his home, feeling equally a part of both places. Much as the above scene indicates, these musicians play at family gatherings and celebrations—weddings, birthdays, and baptisms— and at topada dances organized for their own sake or for the benefit of HTAs. Still, in what is supposedly the live-music capital of the world, much of their artistic labor goes unnoticed. Indeed, Mexican migrants' contributions to the fabric of social and cultural life in the United States are largely ignored, save for the sake of consumption. U.S. Americans' desire for Mexican food, Mexican libations (or simply the appropriation of Spanish morphology—*rita*—to market tropical beverages), and celebrations of Mexican holidays (as an excuse to engage in debauchery) relies on a facile reification of Mexican culture that enables a type of aping rooted in notions of primitivism (Taussig 1993).[8]

With this in mind, let us return to where we began. *Mexican* is often equated with noncitizenship in the American racial imaginary, a perspective that enables native-born Texas-Mexicans to distinguish themselves from fuereños like don Lencho Olvera, Senovio, Homero, Graciano, and Salomón. This sentiment, Limón suggests, manifests itself in a Texan ethnonationalism among Mexican-Americans that is paradoxically "premised on a stigmatized Mexican-American historical identity . . . simultaneously keyed on being a modern Texan" (2011: 113). This is to say, the identity of a modern Texas-Mexican, or Tejano, is considered distinct from that of recently arrived Mexican migrants (113). Amid these tensions, Graciano tells how the sounds of huapango arribeño have crossed into the United States, carving out a place nonetheless:

UN SALUDO DOY DE CORAZÓN
AL ESTILO DE GUANAJUATO
AQUÍ EN TEJAS TOCAMOS LOS CUATRO
COMO SE HACE POR NUESTRA REGIÓN

Guanajuato nos dio la partida
sin problemas cruzamos la raya
a esta región llegamos sin falla
con deseos de un cambio de vida
entre razas y fe dividida

y sufriendo discriminación
empuñamos un día el diapasón
de la quinta, vihuela, o violín
y aunque no hemos llegado hasta el fin:
UN SALUDO DOY DE CORAZÓN

Navegamos para este lugar
con ayuda de Dios el señor
nos trajimos la planta y la flor
y acá en Tejas se pudo regar
hoy se empieza a ramificar
convertida en huapango y en son
y por eso nuestra tradición
hoy renace aquí en estos rincones
con las rimas, huapangos y sones:
UN SALUDO DOY DE CORAZÓN

———

I SEND OFF A HEARTFELT GREETING
IN THE STYLE OF GUANAJUATO
WE FOUR [MUSICIANS] PERFORM HERE IN TEXAS
JUST AS IT'S DONE IN OUR REGION

Guanajuato bid us farewell
we crossed the line without a fuss
we arrived successfully in this region
with the desire to better our lives
amid different races and contentious beliefs
and suffering discrimination
each day we wield the fingerboard
of the quinta, vihuela, or violin
and although we have not seen the end:
I SEND OFF A HEARTFELT GREETING

We made our way to this place
with the help of God, our savior
we brought the plant and flower
and here in Texas we nurtured it
today it begins to branch out
as huapango and son

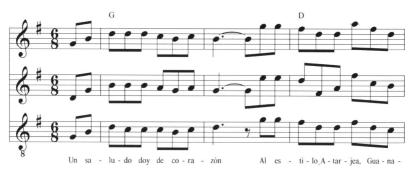

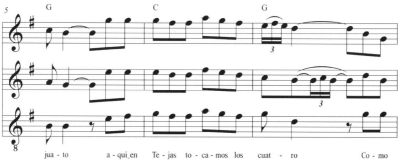

EXAMPLE 4.1 *Poesía planta* "Un saludo doy de corazón" by Graciano

and so our tradition
is reborn today here in these corners
with rhymes, huapangos, and sones:
I SEND OFF A HEARTFELT GREETING

In this poesía example we witness how migrants voice the workaday realities of border politics through music and verse, just as it's done in "our region," as Graciano says without hesitation, layering the cultural geography of the Sierra

PLATE 1 Guillermo Velázquez perched atop his *tablado* on New Year's Day (Xichú, Guanajuato)

PLATE 2 Foothills on the horizon (San Luís de la Paz, Guanajuato)

PLATE 3 *Huapangueros* wait out the mountain fog (La Florída, Querétaro)

PLATE 4 *Huapangueros* serenade an arriving *quinceañera* court (Central Texas)

PLATE 5 Central plaza *tablado* (La Zona Media, San Luis Potosí)

PLATE 6 *Jarabes* in the offing (San Luis de la Paz, Guanajuato)

PLATE 7 The all-female *huapango* group Las Palomitas Serranas (Xichú, Guanajuato)

PLATE 8 Sierra Gorda (Pinal de Amoles, Querétaro)

PLATE 9 Daybreak in the key of G (Xichú, Guanajuato)

PLATE 10 Backyard *tablado* (East Texas)

PLATE 11 María Isabel "Chabe" Flores Solano (center) leads musicians in *cantos a lo divino* (sacred songs) at a cemetery observance (Xichú, Guanajuato)

PLATE 12 Senovio minding his backyard garden (Central Texas)

PLATE 13 Lines across Xichú

PLATE 14 Midsummer dance-hall *topada* (Central Texas)

PLATE 15   In back of Zeferino's home (northern Mississippi)

PLATE 16 The morning after (Xichú, Guanajuato)

Gorda atop Texas. And another return is in order, for this migrant décima poetics in Texas provides a curious (re)connection to Paredes's work. While this is less known, Paredes's first scholarly passion was the vernacular décima poetry along the U.S.-Mexico border, not the corrido (Bauman 2012).[9] Given his ambivalence toward Mexican migrants, it might have disturbed Paredes's presumed cultural atlas to know that the décima—his first love—made a comeback of sorts, but not among the people in the southern Texas region his scholarship celebrated. Rather, the décima took hold among a vibrant community of fuereños in the 1990s, right in Paredes's backyard.

ETHNIC-MEXICAN MUSICAL REGIONALISM

Origins: Tejano

In *Dissonant Divas in Chicana Music: The Limits of La Onda* (2012), Deborah R. Vargas critiques the heteromasculinist historiography of Texas-Mexican music that has largely silenced the presence of women performers. Here I forgo a genealogy of Texas-Mexican music, which is available elsewhere (M. Peña 1985, 1999). Instead, cognizant of Vargas's critique, I follow her in offering a certain reorientation of Texas-Mexican music, specifically the corrido. In doing so, I problematize Tejano music's regionalist claims by situating the corrido, typically considered the primordial beginning of Texas-Mexican music, as an elusive transnational form with "no particular allegiance" (to Texas) (M. Peña 1985:160).[10] Indeed, the corrido can be heard across the United States and Mexico in multiple forms and forums: performed by *corridistas* (ballad singers) in the Mexican Costa Chica region and along the Arizona-Sonora border, coursing into homes over the airwaves of commercial radio, flowing out of corner-cantina jukeboxes, blasted by DJs for packed nightclubs in Chicago and Los Angeles, belted out among families at intimate backyard gatherings, and sung for thousands of adoring fans at arena concerts. Of course, within the context of Texas, the corrido's imagined offspring— the accordion-based *conjunto* and brass-based *orquesta*—combined, along with a sundry of other styles (rock, rap, jazz, country), to produce the more contemporary Tejano music proper (M. Peña 1985, 1999). While it has been correctly acknowledged that Texas-Mexican musics are indeed hybrid forms, the claim persists that they form essential markers of a unique Texas-Mexican identity. Within a transnational context, however, the primordial corrido can no longer boast of regional specificity. Thus, I briefly outline its history of movement and change to further disentangle essentialist assumptions embedded in the cultural ecology of Mexican music more broadly. In doing so, I set the stage for understanding how the transnational practice of huapango arribeño—or the multiple movements beyond its region of origin—should be taken on its own terms: much as for the corrido, huapango arribeño's listeners and practitioners carry their expressive archives with them, and these movements are legitimate and necessary.

The corrido is, conventionally speaking, a narrative story set to music, a balladic musical form that continues to resonate in the cultural imagination of the ethnic-Mexican community. It offers evocative artistic renderings of extraordinary events, historical incidents, and emotional stories that connect with listeners, eliciting powerful responses along the way. The storied aspects contained therein concern characters and their actions across specific settings. These emplotted events hold listeners' interest as they unfold in dramatic fashion, revealing details of encounters and epic undertakings, gradually driving toward a climactic moment of action before drawing to a close— at times offering the proverbial moral of the story. The Mexican corrido dates no further back than the nineteenth century, and its narrative roots owe much to the Spanish novelesque romance that preceded it, a ballad type that flourished in Renaissance Spain, following an expansive lineage of epic poetry that goes back to medieval European traditions. Spanish soldiers, colonial officials, and settlers subsequently introduced the romance to the New World colonies in the sixteenth century, where it was widely adopted as a style, including along New Spain's northern-frontier territories in what is today the southwestern United States. The *romance corrido*, or swiftly sung ballad, emerged as a popular variant that proved easily adaptable to local contexts, becoming Mexicanized and, consequently, forming the most influential precursor to the corrido. While some scholars locate the corrido's origins in the interior of Mexico by pointing to a corpus of ballads dealing with struggles against the dictatorship of Porfirio Díaz in the late nineteenth century, others, most notably Paredes, maintain that the Texas-Mexico border region was its birthplace. The corrido, he suggests, was forged through the transformations experienced by border Mexican society in the mid-nineteenth century, particularly the social and political fallout surrounding the Texas Revolution (1836), the annexation of Texas by the United States (1845), and the subsequent Mexican-American War (1846–1848), in which over half of Mexico's territory was ceded. The interethnic tensions between Anglos and Mexicans that resulted from these conflicts played a central role in shaping cultural life in this area. In turn, the corrido appeared along the U.S.-Mexico border as a specific generation of musicians fashioned this musico-poetic form to chronicle confrontations between Mexicans and figures of social and political authority.

The first-known corrido extolling the deeds of a border Mexican in this manner is that of Juan Nepomuceno Cortina, who in 1859 led an uprising of Texas-Mexicans in the Brownsville, Texas, area in response to the transgressions of Anglo newcomers. Only fragments of this corrido have survived, however; the oldest border corrido available in its entirety is "El Corrido de Kiansis," which speaks of the first Texas cattle drives north to the Kansas railheads. As the demand for beef increased in the eastern United States after the conclusion of the American Civil War, many Texas-Mexicans partnered with Anglo outfits to drive herds north in the 1860s, lending their superior *vaquero* (cowboy) expertise to their English-speaking counterparts. This contrast in aptitude for the cowboy trade is voiced in "El Corrido de Kiansis"—an articulation of intercultural conflict arising from vocational rivalry rather than outright violence. However, border heroics, violent encounters, and elusion of authority became commonplace material for the corrido during this formational era, producing ballads to commemorate Catarino Garza's (1891) revolt against Porfirio Díaz, Gregorio Cortez's (1901) brush with the Texas Rangers, the Texas-Mexican uprising led by Aniceto Pizaña (1915), and other incidents throughout the U.S. Southwest, like the social banditry of Joaquín Murrieta in California. This expressive urgency extended well into the time of the Mexican Revolution (1910–1920), during which bardic figures accompanied the insurgents, composing ballads about military exploits, monumental battles, and revolutionary figures.[11]

With the passing of the period of U.S.-Mexico border conflict and the drama of the Mexican Revolution, the corrido was propelled into the realm of popular culture, providing the narrative backdrop for a number of commercial films of the comedia ranchera variety produced during the golden age of Mexican cinema (1930s–1950s). Paredes (1993) has accused this brand of corrido of being thinned in its social content as a commercial variety, while María Herrera-Sobek (1990) has pointed to the highly gendered imagery embedded in its lyrical renderings, as notions of manliness usually intersect with understandings of Mexican identity that offer disparaging views of women and equally problematic visions of masculinity. Nevertheless, by the 1960s and 1970s, accordion-based Texas-Mexican conjunto and northern Mexican norteña groups, including Los Alegres de Terán and Los Tigres del Norte, began narrating the trend toward illegal drug smuggling, giving rise to the so-called *narcocorrido* (corrido about drug trafficking). Today, popular bands versed in the accordion-based norteña and brass banda styles have greatly popularized the narcocorrido genre across Mexico and the United States through chart-topping albums, arena concerts, and television performances, singing of the exploits of drug traffickers and extolling their lifestyles. Most recently, the content of these ballads seems to have acquired greater significance given the explosion in transnational narcotic-related violence in Mexico and along the U.S.-Mexico border as rival cartels battle for territory in the context of the Mexican government's all-out drug war since 2006. The international boundary between Mexico and the United States, however, has consistently been home to smuggling of one sort or another, from the early twentieth-century trafficking of textiles to the smuggling of hard liquor during Prohibition in the United States in the 1920s. The corrido has chronicled this with ballads like "Mariano Reséndez" and "Los Tequileros." By the 1960s and 1970s, the most famous renderings of smuggling in the corrido were no doubt those voiced by Los Tigres del Norte, who rose to fame with "Contrabando y Traición" (Contraband and betrayal). Although narcocorridos already existed, this was the first to achieve widespread commercial success. Presently, narcocorridos have shifted in their form, from narrative stories—based on events, real or fictitious—to more sensationalized renderings told from the point of view of the drug trafficker, often invoking well-known tropes typical of the smuggling underworld, including references to exaggerated violence. The success of this latest iteration of the corrido speaks strongly to the concomitant expansion in transnational markets for its production and consumption. In fact, the current center of the lucrative narco-music industry is Los Angeles, California. Boasting a unique melding of ranchero sensibility with American inner-city flair, this commercial corrido hybrid is now the centerpiece of a regional categorization far removed from—if not symbolically opposed to—its originary space in Texas.

Semiotics: Regional Mexican

In Thomas Turino's (2003) work on musical nationalism in Latin America, Mexico figures prominently as he sets up his theoretical ideas on the ways in which nationalist discourses necessitate processes of cultural homogenization. Turino details how unified sociocultural entities—on which subjective feelings of belonging based on national sentiment are inscribed—often utilize music as an important expressive vehicle for this semiotic work. Nationalist musical expressions nevertheless typically draw on and subsequently mainstream regional forms of music in order to reach a broader audience, that is, to construct a national public. This canon creation, if you will, indexically links regional identities to the nation by repeatedly enumerating them in conjunction with one another in officialized spaces and discourses so as to portray them as constitutive of the symbolic whole of the nation. In this way, "an abstract, 'nation,' is given flesh and blood, a perceivable form" through a mosaic of "our folklore" imbued with feeling (196).

Since the mid-1990s, however, a different set of Mexican musics have been marketed under the label regional Mexican, a moniker interchangeable with *onda grupera*. The most prominent are norteña and banda. The genesis of these marketing categories dates back to the 1980s and is deeply tied to the interests of a growing transnational music industry.[12] The contemporary regional Mexican category and its use in marketing select folk-derived Mexican musics, however, presents a curious return to what could be termed a set of prenationalist identities, or subjectivities tied to histories of specific regions that are home to particular variants of musical practices that, in this fervent regionalist imagining, exist in opposition to national musics (most obviously Mexican son, as discussed in chapter 2).[13] Indeed, norteña and banda fall outside of the national canon of son and have historically been viewed as marginal musics. Their journey from lowbrow regional musics to mainstream popularity is embedded in Mexico's shifting cultural landscape in the wake of intensified transnational migration after NAFTA, with the subsequent increased buying power of Mexican migrants from these regions in the United States. However, while the regional Mexican label has produced discourses around these musics as unique localized sounds sited in specific geographies, their histories reveal them to be hybrid forms whose performative elements and stylistic features result from a set of unique social, economic, and cultural exchanges that speak to deep transnational histories. Whether the introduction of the button accordion to northern Mexico after Germans migrated there to work on the railroads in the late nineteenth century, or banda public performances in the cosmopolitan port city of Mazatlán, these transnational histories undermine the notion that these musics are authentically regional and thus expose the "simulacrum-like nature of tradition" (Madrid 2008: 53). Furthermore, both musics actively incorporate other transnational genres within their repertoires—from Colombian *cumbia* to romantic ballads and so on.[14]

Nevertheless, the semiotics of style surrounding the regional authenticity of these musics rely on the previously discussed ranchero chrono-trope that claims attachment to a primordial Mexican time and space. Regional Mexican's claim to localized uniqueness paradoxically continues the work of imagining the nation along essentialist lines—placing Mexican cultural identity in the rancho time-space construct and thus inscribing a unified Mexico somewhere out there, allá, at the periphery of modernity.[15] Given the flattening aspects of regional Mexican's aesthetics, cultural outsiders are often unable to identify the stylistic differences between these musics—it all sounds like "circus music," as I've heard native-born Mexicans in Texas say time and again. The perceived musical indistinguishability facilitated by the regional Mexican category has become linked to migrants, similarly perceived as a uniform and homogeneous group.

Politics: TEX-mex ethnonationalism

A particular species of ethnonationalism, Limón (2011) observes, has taken hold among Mexican-Americans in Texas—or Texas-Mexicans, or Tejanos— and music has emerged as a primary vehicle for the formation of discourses that emphasize the Texas part of this assumed regional heritage. Indeed, there is a precedent for imagining Texas-Mexican social identity through music—Flores's (1992) work on the corrido "Los Sediciosos" comes to mind. However, while these earlier iterations were ideologically opposed to Anglo encroachment in Texas and therefore emphasized solidarity with the Mexican nation-state, recent ethnonationalist sentiments consider Tejano identity to be threatened by the presence of Mexican "immigrants." The forceful articulation of this fear of erosion may be linked to the dislocations experienced as a result of a globalized political economy and, relatedly, to intensified Mexican migration to Texas, which is directly tied to transnational relationships— NAFTA, for instance. As one might expect, this ethnonationalist regionalism is not without its own contradictions, for it "overlaps with that of Anglo-Texan [identity] in complicated ways—to think oneself a Tejano in a historically oppressive Texas is often an exercise in ambivalence and irony with a dash of muted affirmation" (Limón 2011: 113). To emphasize Texas and thus simultaneously underplay Mexicanness is to (1) silence the history of oppression of Mexicans at the hands of Anglos; (2) tacitly identify with the U.S. nation-state through the technologies of citizenship and thus ignore that such oppression occurred under its authority, whether through nineteenth-century westward expansion or twentieth-century practices of legal discrimination; and (3), in the present context, position oneself in allegiance with the underpinnings of a broader racial formation that looks on one's own ethnic (Mexican) identity with disdain.

This final contradiction, however, is resolved by deracializing illegality, that is, by ascribing to a supposedly juridically neutral notion of citizenship that considers it to be solely about national sovereignty and subsequently disassociates national belonging from racial hierarchies (Dick 2011b: 36): Tejanos take issue not with Mexicans but so-called illegal aliens. There's a difference. At the level of musical expression, to object to regional Mexican is to protect a truly homegrown American music, Tejano. Sebastien De La Cruz unwittingly found himself at the center of these contradictions among race, culture, citizenship, nation, and regionalism. Recall that instead of wearing distinctly Tejano regalia—a vaquero outfit, perhaps—he donned the most "Mexican" of costumes, a function of him performing mariachi, not Tejano music. As a native of San Antonio, Texas (and thus a U.S. citizen), he escaped the stigma of his ethnic identity among his Texas-Mexican supporters, who share his "foreign" heritage but believe that they, as privileged U.S. citizens, possess the freedom to appropriate its symbols: you can dress up like a Mexican, but in the end you believe yourself to be American. Such compartmentalization was not to be had among De La Cruz's critics, however. Again, for them, Mexican identity is equated with illegality—end of discussion. And we can count Texas governor Rick Perry among them. In July 2014 he testified at a special field hearing for the House Committee on Homeland Security in McAllen, Texas, regarding the ongoing child-refugee crisis of Central American children fleeing into the United States: "And what you have seen is a catalyst that has been growing year by year and people understanding that if you will get from wherever you are to the border of the United States, you can cross and the federal government is not going to impede you from coming into this country and staying here. And that is why Americans are upset."[16] The suggestion that the U.S. government does little to impede migrants crossing the U.S.-Mexico border grossly misrepresents the actual border politics, policies, and material realities faced by migrants who cross. Furthermore, while the posts that began this chapter expose the types of racialized thinking that undergird discourses of illegality, Perry's muted juxtaposition of a disembodied "catalyst" with "Americans" performs the official work of veiling that very racism. Specifically, the unnamed "catalyst" and "people" are in reality unaccompanied migrant children from Central America who are fleeing violence. Beyond framing these children as outside the nation-state—and the boundaries of citizenship—the semantic work of such discourse is also highly gendered, fueling a moral panic concerning migrant fertility. Leo R. Chavez comments, "During the most recent, post-1965 wave of immigration, Latina reproduction and fertility, especially of Mexican immigrant women, have been ground zero in a war of not just words but also public policies and laws" (2008: 71). Although social scientific evidence does not support these pejorative views, this imagined reproductive threat looms and has sparked serious discussion among U.S. lawmakers about repealing the birthright-citizenship clause of the Fourteenth Amendment. Most recently, Senators Mitch McConnell and Lindsey Graham have directed their attacks at the U.S.-born children of undocumented migrants. While they endlessly campaign on family values, when it comes to Latinas/os they denigrate expecting mothers; they label them "drop-and-leave culprits," and their offspring "anchor babies," generating an atmosphere of abjectivity for young migrants who are considered discardable (Gonzales and Chavez 2012: 258). Perry, however, clearly identifies "Americans" and suggests they are unified in their anger. While juridically neutral double-speak derides those "catalysts" and "people" for their lack of citizenship, these anonymous "others" are burdened by race (as are native Texas-Mexicans, irrespective of their own contradictory positioning). Or, as @ LeBlancIV put it, "Ok what in the fuck is this beaner doing singing our national anthem?" Despite ethnonationalist logics Texas-Mexicans might wield to imagine themselves as part of the U.S. nation-state, they will be considered "forever foreign" (Lipsitz 2006).[17] As a case in point, as I write these pages, San Antonio is boasting of its newly constructed family-friendly migrant-detention facility. An exercise in ambivalence indeed—"it's good business."

While the regionalist discourses that surround the regional Mexican and Tejano genres coat themselves with the patina of ranchero and Texan use values, respectively, they rely on nationalist imaginings to consolidate their publics. What is more, these abstracted publics are separated by the borders of culture and citizenship—concepts that are discursively reinscribed in relational opposition to one another: regional Mexican versus Tejano. Nevertheless, huapango arribeño has made its way amid this complicated terrain. Its practitioners negotiate the conditions of their bordered lives—or the very real material consequences of "too much culture" and a lack of citizenship—and in doing so rework the horizons of where their music exists, challenging nationalist fixings at the level of institutional politics and discourse in Mexico, as well as at the level of everyday stigmas and exclusions in the United States. Their embodied flows of performance necessarily expose the relationality between places. And this—despite his own ambivalence toward Mexican migrants—is something that Paredes understood quite well, that indeed the primary medium of being in place is the body, for the body bears on it the trauma, violence, and conflict that it has known and felt in its placial inhabitations. It is why Paredes spoke of the border as a "sensitized area" and why he argued that the importance of everyday poetics along the border came into relief only once one considered the viscerally lived and storied social world out of which they emerged. Narrative, place, and everyday life intersected in ways that made the corrido necessary and elusive, much like huapango arribeño. To suspend either music style in time and space is to deny how its verses and flows exist precisely because they capably transcend the boundaries of nation, region, and place.

WE MADE OUR WAY TO THIS PLACE

A bridge is a connection called up by desire—the desire to move, to greet, to reunite, to make a living. It's a desire to *go* so that a return can come into being—a crossing. It's a necessary trajectory. It's an impulse or a plan, a tactic of change. It's when your own body loosens and you feel a connection with another being, a place, a verse, a melody, and both of you are affected—the other next to you, embracing you. It's what the narrative space of performance calls into being—the story conveyed, the emotion elicited, the echoes of meaning that touch. These imaginings are simultaneous with memory and often become politicized in contexts of violence and injustice. It's why the corrido was so crucial in a social world where "literal death—flesh-ripping death—[abounded] . . . as a consequence of politics" (Limón 1992: 73). Connection and memory were necessary to living in the Texas-Mexican borderlands. For Mexican migrants, the politics of death and dying have not receded. Presently, discussions around self-deportation have led to heightened levels of violence throughout migrant communities. The suggestion is that conditions be made so unbearable that undocumented migrants will make the prudent and responsible personal decision to leave their homes in the United States. Fearing the worst under these circumstances is oftentimes justified—measures aimed at checking the immigration status of all reasonably suspicious individuals have been proposed in several states (those in Alabama, Arizona, Georgia, and most recently Texas have garnered the most national attention). Many of these initiatives are committed to an extension of the racializing logics of the U.S.-Mexico border into the continental United States—its thickening (Rosas 2012)—which lends migrant illegality a certain banality among the general public, particularly in the context of enhanced deportation tactics in the wake of the 2016 Presidential election. New fears, new stories, and new violence have generated waves of distrust. An increase in the number of migrant detention centers. The Islamic State of Iraq and Syria. Black Lives Matter. "Build the Wall!" Death. Desire. Problems. I anticipate hearing poesías and decimales that explore all of these things as well as personal stories from a migrant perspective, telling of the workaday, of both the elation and struggle of having arrived at a place where you feel unwanted but that is also your home.

"We made our way to this place," says Graciano. His poesía is "a vehicle for collective witness," chronicling how he and others arrived in Texas, how they've made it their home, and what kinds of meanings continue to mount up therein (Lipsitz 2007: xii). To make one's way is to reach out, to stake a claim, and it involves a particular set of interpretive practices that aid in mapping the social surroundings of that experience. In the present case, it requires a sensing aurality attuned to the realities of transnational living and the politics of criminalized mobility. However, I don't intend to naively romanticize huapango arribeño poetics as some pristine resistive thrust that somehow expresses the "semblance of ready-made dogmatic coherence," as Nicholas De Genova (2010) has suggested with respect to interpretations of the migrant mobilizations in 2006 (which I discuss in chapter 6). On this point, Limón (1983) has previously challenged such uncritical views of expressive performance as "scenes of communitas." To be sure, his ethnographic exploration of South Texas dance halls hinges on an understanding of how those spaces are shot through with the contradictions of late capitalism. But in his seminal work "Western Marxism and Folklore: A Critical Introduction" (1983), Limón makes a theoretical contribution to the analysis of folk performance that I, just like Flores (1995) before me, will apply here. Limón crafts an argument that shifts our analytical focus from the content to the form of performance, suggesting that the "oppositional quality in all folklore" may be found in the social relations it instantiates.[18] He restates this contention in a recent work with reference to the marketable products of popular culture:

> They are also fundamentally market commodities with exchange value. Put perhaps too simply, all such artfulness is marketable even as some of it might even speak paradoxically against such marketability, and as market commodities, they are, in classical Marxist terms, products of alienated or estranged labor and cannot help but reproduce some such alienation in their consumers. By contrast, all folklore, the poetics of everyday life—understood as democratically constructed and emergent, free-flowing performance either in language or in material craft or a combination of

both—largely escapes this alienating origin and consequence and indeed by its very existence argues against such alienation. (2012: 104–105)

In following this line of argument as it pertains to the context of undocumented Mexican migrant performance, I extend Limón's position by engaging yet another dimension of commoditization: the migrant body, which is systematically reduced to a disposable commodity within the context of U.S.-Mexico border enforcement. The form of migrant performance may thus be understood as a mode of creative and generative social exchange where unauthorized migrant bodies enact and lay claim to a life (*bios*) that is otherwise denied them (more on this in chapter 5).

Mexican migrants are not considered human beings north of the U.S.-Mexico border: they are laborers, criminals, or, most egregiously, "drop-and-leave culprits" and rapists. Their embodied presence is both in and against capital; it is the loudly voiced "¡Aquí estamos y no nos vamos!" As De Genova explains, "*Here we are, 'illegal' and without rights—but because you depend upon our labour, you are powerless to expel us; thus, we defy your power, and we're not going anywhere* . . . an enunciation of (transnational) labour as constitutive of (global) capital, inextricably within capital, but also against capital—rightless, 'illegal,' but insubordinate all the same" (2010: 120). The moment of huapango arribeño performance is a productive form in its enactment of a new social relation. But—emplaced within this context—its emergent content also begs attention. Décimas are a repository of mobility, of emplacement. They are immaterial knowledges, undocumentable aural poetics that elude the prevailing commoditization of the migrant body itself. They are what Diana Taylor in *The Archive and the Repertoire: Performing Cultural Memory in the Americas* refers to as embodied ways of knowing and transmitting memory that forge subjectivities—they are "that which disappears, or that which persists, transmitted through a nonarchival system of knowledge" (2003: xvii). Within this context, embodied migrant knowledges are integral in sustaining a transnational cultural formation, for they voice affiliations that affirm social structures that are otherwise dehumanized and denied. They make their way to places. In these moments of perceiving or listening to performance, the emplacement of the self—across borders—relies on the presence of the body in perceiving external qualities. However, the boundary of the body or of a place is not firm and is determined only through sensing; the flesh becomes flesh as it senses (Massumi 2002), at times in flesh-ripping contexts. In the work of Bataille, transgressive behavior allows a person to exceed the false boundedness of the self (the flesh) to encounter the other and return changed. These multiplicities are bound through what Maurice Merleau-Ponty (1968) calls reversibility, which is the mutually constitutive relationship between self and nonself, inside and outside—a dual orientation, inward and outward, in which all sensations reverberate back on an individuated self. Bodies touch, so minds touch; bodies are bound to others before being bound back to the self—a crossing.[19]

Significantly, crossing exceeds place, extends the body. It opens up an extension beyond a boundary. You step through a bridge and necessarily take a less "bounded-horizontal" gaze (R. Alvarez 2012: 541). You stand at the apogee of this bridge, far from the earth, and you remember and imagine. Here, you feel you can almost peer over either horizon in any direction. The bridge is outside of things, and it necessitates movement, a crossing, the realization of desire (it exists because of it), or at least the attempt. I continue to narrow in on this sense of crossing through the concept of place, which implies form but has a capricious tendency toward formlessness. Place as a concept has in recent years become important in discussions of political economics, representation, and new applications of phenomenology, particularly in the field of cultural geography. British geographer Tim Cresswell writes that place is "space invested with meaning in the context of power" (2004: 12). J. Nicholas Entrikin (1991: 6) and other phenomenologists understand place to be an "areal context of events, objects, and actions" in which narrative plays an important role as a means of mediating between the particular and universal visions of place as a concept that, I would add, is communicatively constituted through "intersubjective discursive practices and the circulation of discourse" (Bauman 2005: 145). I see place as neither a social construction nor a bounded formulation of local culture (the genius loci) that assumes a unique identity within space.[20] Like Edward S. Casey (2000), I see places as physical and metaphysical swarmings of meaning, economic relations, and shared experiences, but, rather than binding tightly the edges of place, I prefer to emphasize the relationships and tethers among places, the many bridges that shimmer in and out of existence.[21] We may think of this dynamic in terms of transnational histories and connections, those that were outlined earlier in relation to Mexican music and that are silenced by regional discourses.

And so we may begin thinking about all the possibilities that could be bridged across something like a border. What nonharmonious connections, turbulences, underbellies, and disruptions might these bridges entail? When is a bridge a closure, an entrance, an entire world? In terms of affect, this question relates less to the result of having crossed, the finality of it, than to the bridge itself, the moment of crossing with all of its intensities—the present-tenseness of it all, the collapsing of place through saturated imaginings that reach out and suddenly drag things into view, when adjacencies occur, and people and moments fold together—bands of elasticity stretching across an ever more vast expanse of space. Vectors are carefully woven into supple bridges hastily made from the bodies of people, from scraps of sentiment; these are bridges that carry intentions—a tree limb is carefully walked, a message is sent over a physical wire, an improvised verse carries over distances, over time, eventually reaching the person it was sung for.[22] Intimacy happens in between the cusps at each end of the bridge. What does its crossing sound like?

DEEP IN THE HEART OF TEXAS

Sweat is trickling down the side of your face, welling at the back of your neck; the heat and humidity are smothering. It's a typical sweltering July evening in Central Texas, close to ten o'clock. The incandescence of city lights in the distance washes over the starry night sky, an amber glow that crowns the ball-room outside of town where Mexican migrants have gathered. Some sit along concrete bleachers, others lean out across the flanking metal railing and peer leisurely toward the crowd of several hundred below. These soon-to-be dancers are nestled in between two stages acting as tablados, positioned at opposite ends of the dance floor. An indistinguishable murmur of laughter and conversation nervously crescendos every now and then, in anticipation of the topada everyone is awaiting.

I know the musicians set to perform well. A few drove in from northern Mississippi—just south of the Tennessee border—for the night; this is hard to imagine, considering that Hurricane Katrina pounded the Gulf Coast a mere two weeks ago. Earlier, I asked how they fared during the storm, as I can imagine the beating the small town must have endured, not to mention their mobile home. The hurricane, they tell me, had lost much of its force by the time it reached them. Fallen trees and downed power lines were the extent of the damage. Surely—they knowingly anticipate—they will be folded into the rapid-response labor force required to clean up and repair the region (Elliott and Pais 2006; Fussell 2009). They already work in construction, pave roads, and plant pine trees in those parts. A few years later, I'd find that most had moved to Tennessee: "En Mississippi ya no hay gente, se han ido a Memphis. . . . Se puso dura la ley." (There aren't that many people in Mississippi; they've all gone to Memphis. . . . The law [local authorities] got tough.)

Meanwhile, the multitude sways to and fro, wave after wave of shifting bodies stirring the dust beneath them into a cloud. This gathering of flesh, this uncontained breathing mass, is that which thrives, crisscrossing the U.S.-Mexico border in spite of the low-intensity violence mobilized against it, signaling the fragility of empire in the post-9/11 ruins of NAFTA (Hardt and Negri 2004; Rosas 2012). Four silhouettes appear on one stage, moving leisurely with their instruments—two violins, a vihuela, and a guitarra quinta huapanguera. They assume their positions, exchange glances, and confer quietly, subtly coaxing the music about to be played. They gaze over at the other stage, now similarly occupied by a matching ensemble, waiting patiently. A collective sigh rushes across the congregation, quieting the chatter, tilting bodies forward as everyone focuses on the shadows emerging before them. Suddenly, the strumming of instruments booms out through the sound system; elaborate fiddle melodies erupt, followed by the soaring voice of the troubadour. The pulsing 2/4 cadence echoes forcefully, measured, trembling through the body, ascending upward, embracing those present, as do the unraveling verses. Student and teacher face off tonight— Graciano and don Lencho Olvera. Graciano begins by improvising a decimal planta:

DÁNDOLES LAS BUENAS NOCHES
LES BRINDO LA BIENVENIDA
EN ESTA FIESTA FLORIDA
HOY QUE SE ABREN LOS BROCHES

———

BIDDING YOU ALL A GOOD EVENING
I OFFER YOU A WARM WELCOME
IN THIS FLORID FESTIVITY
NOW THAT THE SPACE HAS BEEN OPENED

Everyone is fully absorbed. Graciano scans the scene before him, his mind weaving in and out of the audience, shaping embryonic thoughts into *moving* verses, eliciting a chorus of gritos. Salomón is at his side, bowing away fiercely on his violin. And the moment opens up, as he suggests, growing wide and dense with spatiotemporal imaginings binding, stretching, reaching across the stark geographies of transnational life as he and the opposing troubadour, his old mentor don Lencho Olvera, skillfully layer the present-tense currency of this time and place with that of El Caracol, San Luis Potosí, Mexico. Don Lencho Olvera in his own improvised decimal:

Les honro con mi presencia
y antemano lo sostengo
por segunda vez que vengo
ya que Dios nos dio licencia
gracias a la omnipotencia
mi canto ya se quedó
en el verso se notó
tierra donde alumbra el sol
los de allá del caracol:
DE TODOS SOY SERVIDOR

———

I honor you with my presence
and in advance I make known to you
I've come here for the second time
by the grace of God
thanks be to the omnipotent one
my sonorous voice remains
it has been noted in the verse
land where the sun does shine
to all those from El Caracol:
YOUR WISH IS MY COMMAND

A transnational migrant, don Lencho Olvera has lived his life between the United States and his native San Luis Potosí since the 1980s. Once a miner in the central region of that state, he now labors in construction in the Dallas, Texas, area. He poeticizes his humble beginnings:

ES EL ZAPOTE LA TIERRA MÍA
TIERRA FLORIDA DONDE NACÍ
ES MEXICANA Y ES POTOSÍ
ALLÁ ES ENCANTO DE MI ALEGRÍA

En ese rancho yo fui nacido
esa memoria no se me pierde
porque en el pueblo allí de Rioverde
allí mi nombre fue escribido
ciertas personas fueron conmigo
a dar los datos de mi teoría
en el juzgado con fecha y día

quedó archivado mi nacimiento
bajo las leyes de un reglamento:
ES EL ZAPOTE LA TIERRA MÍA

Yo de Rioverde soy ciudadano
mis documentos me acreditaron
que en aquel templo me bautizaron
para que fuera yo un buen cristiano
el señor cura ahí con su mano
me persignaba y me bendecía
ahí rezaba y también decía
"mis bendiciones te harán feliz"
porque en el estado que es de San Luis:
ES EL ZAPOTE LA TIERRA MÍA

———

EL ZAPOTE IS MY NATIVE LAND
FLOWERY EARTH WHERE I WAS BORN
IT'S MEXICAN AND OF POTOSÍ
THERE LAY THE ENCHANTMENT OF MY HAPPINESS

In that rural hamlet I was born
that memory does not escape me
because in the town of Rioverde
there my name was written
certain people went with me
to attest to my existence
in court, the date and time
of my birth were archived
according to the rule of law:
EL ZAPOTE IS MY NATIVE LAND

I am a citizen of Rioverde
my documents confirm this
that I was baptized in that church
so that I may be a good Catholic
at the baptismal font the priest
with his hand did bless me,
there he prayed and also said
"God's blessings will make you happy"

because in the state that is San Luís:

EL ZAPOTE IS MY NATIVE LAND

And the debate commences . . . The topada began at close to ten in the evening and is scheduled to end around three in the morning. Graciano lleva la mano and begins; however, there is a problem, or so don Lencho Olvera insists. Recall that it is custom during topadas for ensembles to begin playing in the key of D, then move on to the key of A, and end in the key of G. Yet Graciano takes it on himself to begin in the key of A. It's a livelier key to play in and, considering the shortness of the topada and the time they are commencing, he thought it fitting. Why waste time in D? Don Lencho Olvera immediately makes an issue of this and begins to engage Graciano with a few clever digs. In the midst of this, Graciano turns to me, "Estos son puntos que dan guerra" (These are points that yield battle). Below are excerpts of their initial decimal exchanges:

(2) Ante todo espectador
ya que ahorita principiemos
la afinación que aquí te vemos
el diablo de "La mayor"
a mí me causa temor
desde luego presentí
en mi canto le advertí
al hacer mis verserías
buenas noches gentes mías
YA VINE Y ESTOY AQUÍ

————

(2) In full view of the spectators
now that we have commenced
the musical key that you have bestowed
oh, the bedeviled A major
it strikes fear in me
I suspected you might do such a thing
and in my sonorous voice I warned
still, in crafting my verses
I say good evening to my people
I HAVE ARRIVED AND I AM HERE

—don Lencho Olvera

(2) Aún no empieza la bravata
y decirlo lo primero
mil saludos al versero
hoy que de cantar se trata
si al principio me maltrata
yo le doy salutación
porque esa es mi convicción
y a él le mando mil laureles
rosas y también claveles:
PORQUE ASÍ ENCONTRÉ "LA" AFINACIÓN

———

(2) The bravata has yet to begin
so, first, I must send
a thousand greetings to the troubadour
today, when singing is the task at hand
for even if you begin by scolding me
I still send you a greeting
because it is my conviction
and so to him I send a thousand laurels
roses and also carnations
FOR THIS IS "A" MUSICAL KEY I HAVE CHOSEN

—Graciano

(3) Lo siento en este día
sé que me castiga el pecho
el pueblo quiere bien hecho
sobre todo la alegría
pero que la culpa no sea mía
por estos alrededores
por mis maestros "los trovadores"
Graciano saludarte quiero
primera vara y segundero
GRACIANO, GRACIAS POR TUS FLORES

(4) También a tu jaranero
quiero darle mi expresión
se merece un galardón

lo he dicho como versero
porque es un gran compañero
del destino y se entona
la verdad como una broma
hay Graciano qué bien me hiciste
esas flores que me diste:
HASTA AQUÍ LLEGÓ EL AROMA

———

(3) I regret today
that my lungs are troubling me
the people expect things to be done right
above all else to have a good time
but it shall not be my fault
out in these parts
it is in the hands of my teachers "los trovadores"
Graciano, I want to greet you
the first and second violin, too
GRACIANO, THANK YOU FOR THE FLOWERS

(4) Also your jaranero
I want to express to him
that he deserves an award
I've said this as a troubadour
because he is a great companion
of the calling and of great talent
but truly, I tease when I say
oh, Graciano, you have done well by me
with those flowers you gave me
I CAN SMELL THEIR AROMA FROM HERE

—don Lencho Olvera

The dancers bend long and pivot rapidly, their inertia extending out to different parts of the body only to tumble back to its core, giving off heat, exchanging energy, carefully patterning their individual movements, shadowing those of others, some heads bobbing up and down, others thrown back, arms swinging, swaying, bottoms rocking back and forth, huffing and puffing along. The steps grow louder, building a sonic wake that mirrors the music being vigorously bowed and strummed. Its tones sweep across the skin, and its utterances linger, caught in the air, fading but slowly as Graciano and don Lencho Olvera dynamically maneuver between the warmth of the gathering and distant places, crafting poetics that are close at hand, that drag things into view, tracing the assemblages and trajectories of transnational migrant life in Texas, where the embodied voicing of "Yo de Rioverde soy ciudadano, mis documentos me acreditaron" (I am a citizen of Rioverde, my documents confirm this) exposes the viscosity of illegality . . .

There is nothing so simple as a place and a nonplace, but there are places, and those places exist in dialogue with other places in the present, and they are layered on top of each other in the past and future so that the idea of time becomes messy . . . So imagine "Can you say hello to my friend?," an audience member at a topada asks a troubadour, without pause, without regard for distance, geography, the physicality of absence, or the materiality of how a voice echoes out, colliding with mountains, dissipating over deserts. The question is asked metaphysically, trusting that a physical greeting might or might not eventually arrive, and that the friend will be called forth momentarily. In the request, there is a matter-of-factness that a lyrical greeting is just as real as shaking a person's hand. It is just as poetically coded and coated with desire— it's desire itself; it exists wholly in that space of desire. It's an evocation of imaginings (in the future, beyond) that closes distances.[23] Without hesitation, the troubadour takes up the call to "send off a heartfelt greeting." There, in the heat of the topada, as music and poetics rise to a fevered pitch, the name of the person desired is called out, stirring butterflies in the stomach, a buzzing that burrows into the ears, calling the attention of all present. The bridge is enacted, performed, sung, called out, and the audience is walking across it.

The bridge between material and immaterial borders, just like that between bodies and places, relies on openings to intimacy, the "openness of Merleau-Ponty's chiasmic body to the insertion of the other into it, an openness that claims my self before my self can ever be articulated as my own" (Evans and Lawlor 2000: 243). The self, then, appears as a "unity of sense" but transgresses that unity to include new experiences, building a bridge between the self and others (Barbaras 2004: 27–28). In the theories of the self of Sherry Turkle (1995), Alphonso Lingis (1998), Georges Bataille (1991), and others, the unity is an illusion, but lived experience currently requires the unitary self to be the most basic reality because the normal requirements of everyday life pressure people to be unitary actors (Turkle 1995: 15). However, there is excitement in the transgression of these oppressive and materially enacted requirements because they must be transgressed in order for the self and the other to join over that imposed yet quite material divide. The border and its concomitant logics of illegality necessitate this transgressive type of intimacy too, for the border calls the bridge and crossing into existence.

The next chapter flows from Graciano and don Lencho Olvera in Texas to an adjacent moment of aural poetics in San Luis Potosí to launch a critical attending to the embodied practice of huapango arribeño performance in the making—when the sonorous atmosphere of performance becomes saturated with the desires of those present, building adjacencies, (re)configuring connections in time and space that fold geographies together through densely layered politics and senses of place that touch suddenly, interrupting the border.

FIVE

FROM POTOSÍ TO TENNESSEE

Clandestine Desires and the Poetic Border

This place, on its surface, seems to be a collage. In reality, in its depth
it is ubiquitous. A piling up of heterogeneous places.
—MICHEL DE CERTEAU, *THE PRACTICE OF EVERYDAY LIFE*

The word of poetry enables otherness to be vividly present . . .
—DON IHDE, *LISTENING AND VOICE*

lo digo porque es así
en estos versos floridos
por allá en Estados Unidos
mi saludo doy aquí . . .

I say it because it is so
in these flowery verses
out yonder to the United States
I grant my greeting here . . .
—FIDEL, SAN CIRO DE ACOSTA, SAN LUIS POTOSÍ

"All the way to Tennessee . . ." This lyrical phrase invites thinking about poetically distant places, for one because it turns up in a beautiful, wistful decimal
transcribed later in the chapter. It has a nice ring to it, as though it should be
in a country song (and it may well be in one or two). The meter isn't quite
typical but feels familiar. Its spirit turns up often because of the sentiment
expressed. "All the way" crosses a distance and ties that sense of distance to a
place. There is the feeling that distance can be ever so long or intimately tight
regardless of the actual miles. Tennessee holds remnants of meaning that can
be called up—perhaps Nashville, the city and its music, the job your friend
had there, or perhaps Nashville, a southern center of American culture right
at its heart. A study published in 2014 identified Nashville, Tennessee, as the

most American metro area in the country because its demographics are so precisely average.[1]

Without a study to verify this, I can attest that as a musician and a writer *Tennessee* is a lovely, wistful word to speak or to sing, similar to "California Dreamin'" or "Georgia on My Mind," each with its own connotations. When a place-name is sung, we listen to and imagine not just the place but also the distance and the journey taken or not taken. That beauty on the surface, however, also has an underbelly of implicit barriers, of inequity, of injustice, lost love, death. And death is the *place* where this chapter ends because it is a reality that migrants face. It is the implication—the stake and the urgency—of the U.S.-Mexico border, what rests behind the poetic longing in the verses that follow.

One might say that any distance becomes poetic when intimacy is disrupted because we are forced to imagine each other instead of touching. But poetic distance doesn't operate in the same way as geographic distance in terms of duration or proximity. Michel de Certeau (1984) is a dependable source through which to explore the relationship between place and everyday life, but when it comes to transnational places and people, the stories told herein move into new theoretical territory. Connections (or intimacies) across geographic distance are a starting point to make sense of spatiality as a kind of poetic distance, and this chapter relies on Gilles Deleuze and Félix Guattari's *A Thousand Plateaus: Capitalism and Schizophrenia* (1987) as a map alongside de Certeau. A case can be made for grounding such concepts in ethnography. I do so with specific attention to how Mexican migrant communities voice their movements across multiple scales of time and space and thus construct place(s) in palimpsestual ways that undermine the assumed linearity of migration.

This book treats both distance and its poetic, imaginative crossing beyond metaphor. For instance, when a greeting is called out across a distance, "all the way to Tennessee," there is a feeling of duration and extension to that greeting, a sense that it matters both affectively and materially. There is a bridging that happens (in this case across the border), that takes shape because the border interrupts intimacy in a very material way, but not without itself being overtaken by intimacy again, often with the sonic timbre of a voice and the residue of its singing that sticks onto a person and travels far away. Sound is as real and material as it is ubiquitously immaterial. The complex physical properties of its production—its speed, friction, elasticity, patterning, and decay (Klatzky, Pai, and Krotkov 2000)—are transformed and modulated by that which it passes over and within. Sound travels slowly through water, fast and long over empty distances, heavily through the earth, but always with energy. Sound and spatiality are phenomenologically linked, for sounds "are always in motion; they emanate, radiate, reflect, canalize, get blocked, leak out, and so on" (Eisenberg 2015: 193). Yet the threshold of sound's "stretching" and "openness" has "no clear sense of horizontal boundary such as that of the 'roundness' of the visual field" (Ihde 2007: 102) and thus stimulates an auditory imagining in which an aural poetics emerges as a sonic interpretive mode bridging the material and immaterial dimensions of experience. In this way, its resonance spreads also in ethereal forms—through memory (both individual and cultural), through trauma, through storytelling, through repetition; it moves through obstacles (like social divisions), transmits the vibrations of its message, pierces the artificial divisions between things.

Indeed, the materiality of sound has been theorized through the notion of soundscape, a geographically bounded formulation ill suited for thinking through the aural poetics considered here as a performative practice that circulates transnationally. Therefore, I turn to the body, specifically, the way socially positioned listeners' engagement with huapango arribeño is mediated by the visceral and politicized relationship among the body, the U.S.-Mexico border, and the spatiotemporal dimensions of transnational migration. This social nexus is what lends the poetics in question their unique duration, a notion that attends to the materiality of both aurality and location across time. In other words, the sense of time embodied in sound is contingent on the contextual auditory field across which it is broadcast, a field contoured by perceptual and social surrounds (senses of place). Phenomenologists have argued that place matters using the concepts of habitus and Dasein, which demonstrate how place is inextricable from the existence of human bodies, materially and immaterially, through experience, consciousness, perception, or identity, depending on who is writing. The self is both emplaced and embodied, and the two are bound through, again, Maurice Merleau-Ponty's (1968) notion of reversibility. In this way, the primary somatic medium of being in place is the body. But the body not only reaches places but also bears the traces of the places it has known—these residues are laid down and emplotted within the body, and this incorporation ultimately shapes both body and place, for places are themselves altered by our having been in them. At last, these embodied memories of place ring out, especially during commemorative and performative moments. Thus, places move physically, which is to say that they travel over distances (with the body), and they move emotionally, which is to say that they affect us deeply (think of the phrase *moved to tears*) so that we are bodily aware, changed, and reconfigured. In this way, the bodies that move back and forth across Mexico and the U.S.-Mexico border are physically altered—by the heat, the brush, the torrent—and these movements are subsequently voiced aesthetically, animating an associational resonance, an embodied archive of crossing. Correspondingly, the embodied sounding of huapango arribeño touches—both materially and emotively—those whom it surrounds in the moment, those who are listening; it calls to mind the journey, the feeling of it all. But it also reaches out, crosses, pulling in those far away (separated by borders), fulfilling desires for intimacy, harks back toward locations both presently occupied and similarly remembered and imagined far away, separated by border politics. Put simply, huapango arribeño poetics are an embodied voicing of entextualized embodied experiences—bodies enter into texts in a dual sense. This chapter explores the immateriality of this performative sounding through the huapango arribeño practice of the improvised greeting, or saludado, to illustrate how poetics invoke and cross over to distant places, grasping at the people in and across those places as echoes of desire that touch and at last bring people together into the present time and space. This is how places *move*, emplotted on whatever body or sonorous melody or poetics (or combination of these) that can serve as a vehicle through the emergent quality of performance—an aleatory throwing together that keeps the connection strong, keeps it *moving* . . .

POTOSÍ: A PALIMPSEST OF TIME AND SPACE

You approach the doorway, and the bodies in the room shift as they acknowledge your silhouette; you amble into the flow of daily talk, maneuver into the spaces between the things to be said. We carry memories of how to perform everyday tasks such as this, much like making our way back to a place, or driving home from work without noticing that we are doing so, or playing a song from memory on the piano, years after learning it. Our bodies watch and remember, and we react in ways almost too subtle to notice, but it's all there. And *there we were*, huddled in Doña Lupe's *lonchería* (luncheonette) in Rioverde, passing the time. As mentioned at the very beginning of this book and as is surely obvious by now, my account of huapango arribeño is not a synchronicity of incidents within a bounded music scene but rather a tracing of moments and social actors that are crisscrossing cultural and physical borders and giving voice and listening across them. The following are a series of stories told to me, nested in time; as you read, you will travel deeper into places and into multiple pasts.

Stationed at the edge of the parking lot of a now-defunct shopping center, this small wooden structure is no larger than ten by fifteen feet and stands adjacent to the *estanquillo* (food trailer) out of which Doña Lupe serves food and beverages. Inside the modest shack, patrons sit on white plastic chairs at metal tables. Our feet rest on the dirt floor; our ears note the crackling embers in the back-corner *fogón* (brick-lined fire pit), where a pot of beans simmers. Dust from passing cars and specks of sunlight filter in and out, as do people— to eat and drink, to escape the heat, to say hello. Women and men hardened by labor-intensive work build the rhythm of this daily gathering—first they toiled in the surrounding milpas (cornfields) in their youth, and now they are paving U.S. city streets, rearing American children, cleaning offices and restaurants, constructing subdivision homes during their stints *en el otro lado* (on the other side). A man around my age, hunched over a steaming plate of food, sopping up the last bits of *chicharrón en chile verde* (pork stewed in green chili), muses, "Vive uno jodido por allá, pero si te toca suerte si te alivianas con algunos dólares" (Life is a struggle over there, but if you're lucky you're able to make a little money). I know many of these sojourners, some better than others. They split their time among Texas, California, Georgia, Illinois, North Carolina, and, here, San Luis Potosí, a state that forms part of the region that Mexican migrants have typically come from historically.[2] All cross the border to labor, and some labor at performance.

Sandra is also here today. She works for Doña Lupe and loves it when huapangueros stop by, as do I. This is why I spend a lot of time here; you never know which musician you'll run into. When we do, she and I always ask when the next and nearest topada will be. On weekends, she cranks up the huapango program on the local radio station—it is nearly deafening, echoing across the barren parking lot. She won a huapango dance contest some months back, too. We've all become friends, so much so that on occasion she and Doña Lupe ask me for a ride to the market when they're pressed for time and I happen to be around. It's easier to give me a free meal than to pay for a local taxi. It seems like a fair trade to me. We enjoy each other's company.

Salomón walks in. He exhales, wipes the sweat from his brow, and tosses his body into the chair across from me. He has been working all day loading and unloading cargo on commercial trucks—construction materials, food-stuffs, machinery, you name it. His clothes are dusty, and his baseball cap is faded from the sun. No huapango for him today, or tonight, but maybe over the weekend. Most days he makes a living at this job; he's been doing it for a couple of years now, since coming back from Texas. I buy him a beer.

He starts in, "¿Oiga, no se acuerda cuando nos perdimos por Atarjea?" (Hey, do you remember when we got lost around Atarjea?)

"Ni hablar; ¡eso sí estuvo algo canijo!" (Of course; that was quite a predicament!), I laugh and reminisce . . .

. . . We had spent the afternoon in Atarjea, Guanajuato, before heading off to a nearby community where he, Graciano, and two other musicians were to perform later that evening. In the meantime, much like today, Salomón and I, along with Graciano, stopped to have a beer at a corner lonchería, a tiny ground-floor room that served as both the living area and a dining room of sorts; the proprietor's home was located upstairs. She served up *tacos de cabeza* (braised goat head tacos) as family and patrons rushed in and out. Lukewarm Victoria beer for us. Only a few people could fit in the musty cramped space, which contained a few chairs, a single table, and a gas stove where the food simmered. The scent of barbacoa stuck to my skin, coating my arms and face. Still, we rested easy, just like many a time in Texas in each other's company.

"Alex," Salomón said, "no sea por nada, pero yo y Graciano, en el destino, en el otro lado, tuvimos varias aventuras y desaventuras" (It's not for nothing, but Graciano and I, in the calling, in the United States, we had a number of adventures and misadventures). Graciano chuckled and patted him on the back. We drank our beers—a windstorm was brewing outside . . .

Their friendship has grown over the years from traveling and performing on both sides of the border. Salomón reflects:

Pero eso sí, el (Graciano) me echó la mano lo que no se imagina. Él me ayudó mucho. Cuando más lo necesitaba, él me echó la mano. Yo por eso cuando él me preguntaba de una cosa y yo me daba cuenta que podía ayudarle en algo en esto de la música, pues lo hacía con gusto.

(No doubt about it, he [Graciano] helped me out like you wouldn't believe. He helped me out a lot. When I most needed it, he gave me a hand. And that's why when he would ask me about something and I felt I could help him with respect to the music, well, it was my pleasure.)

Graciano laughs, "Salomón me decía, 'Échele ganas, le aseguro que vamos a estar en una topada usted y yo'" (Salomón would tell me, "Give it your all,

I assure you that you and I will be in a topada"). Today they are waiting together in Atarjea, just like many a time in Texas. They wait for dusk, for the gathering of bodies, for a long night of music and poetry ahead . . .

Early the next morning—around four o'clock—we found ourselves in the midst of our own *desaventura* (misadventure) after the performance near Atarjea, helplessly navigating the labyrinth of unpaved narrow back roads high up in the Sierra Gorda, trying to make our way from the Guanajuato side of these mountains to San Luis Potosí, jostling about in the truck, precariously teetering on the edges of hillsides, ever-conscious of the menacing chasms below. Salomón and the other musicians (Graciano had stayed behind) knew these dirt roads by heart, but it was dark and drizzling, and we were all tired. Long night. For three hours—which seemed to drag on forever—we were lost, not knowing where to turn, what road to take. As we navigated those winding paths, I thought of David, a nephew of Graciano's, also from Guanajuato. We had chatted earlier, during the performance. He had spent six years working in the United States in the mid-1990s when he was a teenager. After living in Austin and Dallas, he finally settled in North Carolina. He spoke to me of his own varied misadventures, mostly his encounters with the migra. "No hombre, en camino al trabajo, tempranillo, luego se nos acercaban las patrullas en los semáforos. De un carro a otro, allí estaban. Vaya, nos bajábamos de la camioneta y corríamos como pinches conejos!" (Listen, man, on our way to work, early, the border patrol trucks would get close to us at the traffic lights. They were just a car over. Heck, we'd get out of the truck and run like fucking rabbits!) Nightmarish images of Riverside County police officers savagely beating undocumented men and women in Rodney King–like fashion flashed in my mind. Kicking them, clubbing them, slamming their bodies against the pavement on a stretch of Los Angeles highway in 1996 . . .[3]

It was daybreak by the time we finally reached La Florída, Querétaro. Back on track. Closer to San Luis Potosí. Relief.

I briefly step out of this cloud of memories and look over at Salomón— he is patting the dust from his clothes. He's on his cell phone, speaking to a relative, from what I gather. Maybe his niece? They lived together for some time back in Texas. Her mother—his sister—died unexpectedly here in San Luis Potosí during that stint. Though that was tragic, perhaps more traumatizing was the thought (nearly an expectation?) of dying along the border if they traveled to Mexico to attend the funeral, then had to journey back clandestinely. Border security is brutal. Over five thousand migrants have died while crossing since 1994 (Jimenez 2009; D. Martínez 2016; D. Martínez et al. 2014). An emotional and glassy-eyed Salomón once told me the story of the night he arrived in Central Texas. It turns out that don Lencho Olvera, whom he knew from playing huapango arribeño in San Luis Potosí, put him in touch with Graciano:

> Pasé en Matamoros y nos llevaron hasta Houston y luego de ahí nos lleva-ron pa' Austin. Graciano me recogió ahí por la 35, en el centro.
>
> Cuando yo llegué a la casa de Graciano ya le tenía comunicado a ellos [Homero and Senovio] que ya iba ir por mí y pa' que cuando yo llegara a la casa de Graciano que les iba hablar para que se fueran para allá a echar parranda un rato.
>
> Vamos llegando como a las ocho de la noche. ¡No hombre, que les habla de volada, "Ya está aquí, vénganse!" . . . Llegaron. . . . "Bienvenido," me dijo el Senovio. . . . Homero también, pues compañero del destino, del rancho. Yo venía cansado del camino, todo nervioso, iba por primera vez. . . . Yo no hallaba ni pa' dónde hacerme, todo avergonzado, tenso. Dice Graciano, "Usted ya está aquí en la casa, no se ponga de otro modo, está en su casa ya. Nos vamos a echar una copa de vino pa' ponernos alegres y echarnos unos sones aquí."
>
> Sacamos los instrumentos, nos afinamos, y nos ponemos a tocar. La primerita noche. Nos dormimos hasta las tres de la mañana . . . Tocamos, platicamos. . . . Y al otro día a trabajar.

(I crossed the border in Matamoros, and they [the smugglers] took us all the way to Houston, and then from there they took us to Austin. Graciano picked me up there by I-35, downtown.

When I arrived at Graciano's house, he had already let them [Homero and Senovio] know that he was on his way to pick me up and that he would call them over to celebrate for a while when I arrived.

We arrived at around eight at night. Man, he calls them right up, "He's here, come over!" . . . They arrived. . . . "Welcome," Senovio told me. . . . Homero, too, a companion of the calling from back home. I was tired from the trip, nervous; it was my first time [crossing]. . . . I didn't know what to do with myself, shy, tense. Graciano says, "You are here at home, don't be shy about a thing, you are in your home. We're going to have a drink to cheer up and then we'll play a few sones here."

We brought out the instruments, tuned them, and we started to play. That very first night. We went to bed at three in the morning. . . . We played, talked. . . . And the next day, off to work.)

For a moment, as I listen to Salomón's story I imagine myself resting idly in a familiar Chicano dive east of the freeway in Austin, the air thick with the faint scent of marijuana, yeast and alcohol, stale cigarettes, with my eyes focused on the flickering light of a neon beer sign that seems to dance to the thumping polka sounding from the jukebox. I step outside. Dusk. The soft colors drape the labyrinth of downtown buildings. I peer in the sun's direction, squint toward the highway—west. In the distance, underneath the highway overpass, I make out the silhouette of a lone figure, pacing nervously, smoking a cigarette. He dons a cowboy hat, with an overstuffed duffel bag at his side. Salomón, waiting on Graciano?

My mind snaps back into the present moment and place. Rioverde, San Luis Potosí. It turns out that Salomón's phone call was to arrange the possibility of a topada the following weekend across from Flavio.

Flavio, a young and talented troubadour once told me, "Si no tengo mi guitarra no ando a gusto" (If I don't have my guitar, I'm not at ease). He arrived in northern Mississippi in the late 1990s, though he's also spent time in Texas and Kansas. Networks of friends and acquaintances from San Luis de la Paz, Guanajuato, brought him there. Luckily for him, he works alongside fellow musicians (Zeferino and his father, who are from the same area in Guanajuato). Around these parts of Mississippi, the scenery is lush, gospel and jazz fill the radio airwaves, Baptist churches and Piggly Wigglys are familiar landmarks, trailer homes are the norm, and life moves at a rural southern pace. I would never have imagined that a community of Mexicans would take root here of all places. They have. And local policy makers have taken notice. "Juan Crow" is what some are calling the draconian measures that have been enacted over the past fifteen years to isolate and control the surging population of undocumented migrants throughout the American South. As of 2006, Georgia law denies undocumented migrants driver's licenses and bars them from receiving state social services, such as medical care. In Mississippi the Employment Protection Act (S.B. 2988), signed into law by Governor Haley Barbour in 2008, requires employers to use the E-Verify system to confirm legal identities and eligibility for employment (Stuesse 2016).[4] Flavio, Zeferino, and his father have worked at a number of jobs, among them planting pine trees in the area, laboring in manufacturing plants, and doing construction work.

Zeferino and Flavio are roughly the same age, born in the mid-1970s. At sixteen, Flavio was already performing in topadas as a troubadour. Zeferino, on the other hand, began playing alongside his father as a vihuelero when he was eight years old. His father began his own career as a violinist in 1963. By the time Zeferino was ten, he was playing atop tablados in topadas accompanying troubadours don Lencho Olvera and Amador Arredondo, among others. He remembers:

> Como a los diez años fue mi primer topada. Me invitó Amador [Arredondo]; él era el que más me invitaba. . . . Llegamos y ya estaba la bolota ahí, ya estaban los otros [músicos] tocando. Luego vi los bancos [tablados] que se acostumbran. Me subí temblando ahí por la altura y con los nervios de tocar al frente. Me subí y la apoyadera de los pies no alcanzaba yo y para recargarme no podía. . . . Siempre las demás tocadas me ganaba el sueño. A veces me dormía a medio son a media poesía. ¡Y ese día no! Tanteaba que me caía si me quedaba dormido. Toda la noche estuve bien alerto.

(I was about ten years old when I was in my first topada. Amador [Arredondo] invited me; he was the one who invited me to play the most. . . . We arrived, and the party was in full swing; the other [musicians] were already playing too. Then I saw the tablados that are customary. I was shaking as I climbed up because of how high they were, and I was already nervous because I was going to face off with the other musicians. I climbed up and found that my feet didn't reach the footrest, and I couldn't lean back either. . . . In other engagements I would always get sleepy. Sometimes I would doze off in the middle of a son or poesía. Not that day! I had the sense that I was going to fall at any moment if I fell asleep. I was alert all night.)

Zeferino picked up the violin in the United States. In fact, Sebastián Salinas was his teacher and his first topada as a violinist occurred in Texas—Salomón sat across the way! Now Salomón sits across from me in this dusty space . . . My mind snaps back to this place again . . .

Slivers of sunlight guide memories to the surfaces of our minds as we sit. This rather ordinary gathering is sticky with the residues of the United States. The spatialized dimensions of life extending across the border lie upon us, seep into Doña Lupe's lonchería. The moment is dense with the stark architectures of coinciding extremes "of ambition and degradation"—the lived-in structures of feeling of migrancy are palpably felt on either side of the border (de Certeau 1984: 91). This haptic falling together of place, flesh, and everyday life is compositional and often the generating force out of which huapango arribeño's narrative circulations achieve a heightened level of virtuosic expression, entextualizing the geographies of the day-to-day, reworking sociospatial conjunctures of social relations that compose innumerable places marked by mobility, emplacement, encounters, and multiple arrivals beneath the arch of illegality.

CLANDESTINE CROSSINGS

Graciano first introduced me to Ricardo when he invited the two of us to play a few engagements alongside him in Central Texas, I on vihuela and Ricardo on violin.[5] Ricardo had come to play the instrument in the United States even though his father, also a violinist, tried to teach him back in Guanajuato. Ricardo confesses that he had no real interest in learning as a child, but nowadays, "Si no fuera por el violín, no conociera a nadie por acá" (If it weren't for the violin, I wouldn't know anyone over here). Huapango arribeño has helped him make connections with people from Guanajuato and survive the alienation of undocumented life. He resides in the Dallas, Texas, area and has traveled back and forth, often returning to a steady restaurant job in the area:

> Se me pegaron algunas palabras del inglés cuando menos pa' evitar esos gritotes que me echaba el patrón de primero. . . . Lo que me daba era coraje, me agüitaba porque yo no sabía ni que me decía . . . pero después qué ya sabía poquito, ya no me gritaba tanto.

> ───────────────

> (I learned a few words in English to at least avoid getting yelled at by the boss as he used to in the beginning. . . . I would get angry. I'd feel down because I had no idea what he was saying to me . . . but later, once I knew a little [English], he wouldn't yell at me as much.)

Our friendship has grown over the years. We've performed at each other's side and at times at opposite ends in topadas. We faced off in Houston on one occasion. I accompanied Graciano on the vihuela, and Ricardo accompanied the troubadour Xavi across the way, while the four hundred people in attendance from Guanajuato and San Luis Potosí danced, hooted, and hollered.

TODO EL PÚBLICO ILUSTRADO
AQUÍ ESTÁN SUS SERVIDORES
COMIENZAN NUESTRAS LABORES
LES ENTREGO UN SALUDADO

En este breve momento
voy hacer mi versería
viene de la mente mía
aunque me falta talento
saludaré al momento
a este conglomerado
el momento se ha llegado
de hacer esta competencia
hoy que Dios nos dio licencia:
TODO EL PÚBLICO ILUSTRADO

———

ATTENTION, ENLIGHTENED PUBLIC
HERE ARE YOUR HUMBLE SERVANTS
OUR LABORIOUS TASKS NOW COMMENCE
I GIFT YOU WITH A GREETING

In this brief moment
I am going to craft my verses
they come from my own mind
although I lack talent
I will improvise a greeting
to this gathering
the moment has arrived
to begin this competitive duel
with the grace of God:
ATTENTION, ENLIGHTENED PUBLIC

—Xavi

GRACIANO YO SOY SEÑORES
AQUÍ LES TRAIGO MI TROVACIÓN
HOY LES ENTREGO MI CORAZÓN
SOMOS EL GRUPO LOS TROVADORES

Hoy mi destino ya está marcado
seré yo el símbolo de alegrías
entre huapangos y poesías
en las pachangas y los tablados
aquí por Tejas y en todos lados
donde se ofrezca dar pormenores
entre jardines y bellas flores
iré yo dando así mis versiones
siempre alegrando los corazones:
GRACIANO YO SOY SEÑORES

———

GENTLEMEN, I AM GRACIANO
I BRING YOU MY IMPROVISED VERSES
TODAY I GIVE YOU MY HEART
WE ARE THE GROUP LOS TROVADORS

Today the calling has brought me here
so I shall be a symbol of happiness
amidst huapangos and poesías
in parties and atop tablados
here in Texas and all over
wherever the opportunity arises to perform
amidst gardens and beautiful flowers
I will go about voicing my perspective
always bringing happiness to your hearts:
GENTLEMEN, I AM GRACIANO

—Graciano

Ricardo's most recent trek through Houston unfolded under entirely different circumstances:

Esta última vez que me fui pague una buena lana según pa' no caminar— que también se batalla algo, no creas que es tan fácil . . . ¡Ya me andaba pa' llegar! Como a las cinco de la mañana, ahí cerca del río, el coyote nos echó a una troca y en un crucerillo por ahí estaba una patrulla y se nos pego y estos le echaron todo a la troca y al último la metieron pa'l monte y se atrancó . . . ¡Uno luego va pa' bajo corriendo!

No me agarraron, pero sí me pusieron una buena corrediza. Bien oscuro y uno a correr sin saber a dónde va caer . . . Nos corretearon como a las

4:30 de la mañana y pues a correr los que pudimos. Unos pues todavía ni se alcanzaron de bajar de la troca, ahí mismo los agarraron . . . Yo me eché a correr tratando de seguir los que iban por allá, pero los otros corrían mas rápido que yo. Me metí al monte y luego, luego al suelo arriba de los nopalillos—!me di una buena espinada!

Me levanté y corrí y yo sentía que iba alguien detrás de mi. ¿Quien sabe si era un mismo compañero o uno de la migración? El chiste es que corrí y al último corrí un rato yo solo. Ya que sentí que no iba nadie, me pare a oír. No, pues se oía mas adelante hasta dónde quebraban ramas, dónde iban corriendo. Lo que entonces quise hacer fue alcanzarlos porque si no me iba quedar solo yo.

Al último si alcance unos y con esos me anduve. Nos juntamos como unos cinco. Pero entonces echaron el helicóptero . . . A mi y otro no me agarro, pero a otros—porque nos separamos pa' no estar amontonados—a esos que quedaron retirados, a esos si los agarraron. Y no, pues se bajo [el helicóptero] muy bajito, hasta nos echaba mucho aire.

Nos tuvimos todo el día siguiente ahí sin salir de la rama. Luego en la noche nos salimos. Y dijimos, "pues ya que si nos agarraran." Salimos y íbamos caminando pa' dónde pensamos que había quedado la troca . . . De repente nos asustaron, que se oye una corredera de gente. Era otro coyote que llevaba gente. Nos pregunto [el coyote] de dónde éramos y como estaba la cosa y porque andábamos ahí. Le contamos como estuvo la historia y le dijimos que nos llevara. No quería, pero al último siempre dijo que sí. Nomás pregunto que si teníamos quien respondiera por nosotros allá. Y le dijimos que sí. Le preguntamos cuanto nos iba cobrar y nos dijo . . . El nos llevo hasta Houston y ahí nos estuvimos hasta que llegara alguien quien trajera la feria pa' soltarnos.

Nos entretuvieron casi ocho días fíjate, ahí sin comer, sin nada. Creo que en esos días nomás nos dieron dos sopa "marruchin" pa' comer . . . Había mucha gente en la casita de dos cuartitos y una salilla. Nos juntamos cuarenta personas ahí. ¡No, imagínate! Ahí todos sin comer, sin bañarnos, sin nada. Al último, pues si la libramos, si pasamos.

———————————

(This last time that I crossed, I paid a hefty amount of cash, supposedly so I wouldn't have to walk—although you still struggle some, don't think it's easier . . . I almost didn't make it! Like at around five in the morning, there close to the river, the smuggler threw us in a truck and at a crossroads a patrol car tailed us, and these guys [the smugglers] floored it and ended up getting stuck in the brush. . . . One of them [the smugglers] got off and ran!

They [border patrol] didn't catch me, but they did chase me. It's real dark, and you run without knowing where you're going to end up. . . . They chased us at around four thirty in the morning, and those of us who could run ran. Some didn't even get a chance to get off the truck; they caught them right there. . . . I hightailed it and tried to follow the others up ahead, but they ran faster than me. I went into the brush and then, then hit the deck right on top of the cacti—I got pricked somethin' good!

I got up and ran, and I could feel someone behind me. Who knows if it was another companion or a border patrol agent? The point is that I ran, and in the end I found myself alone. Once I felt no one was behind me, I stopped and listened. All you heard up ahead were branches breaking where people were running. What I wanted to do was catch up to them; if I didn't, I'd end up alone.

Finally, I caught up with some people, and I stuck with them. About five of us grouped together. But then they brought in the helicopter. . . . They weren't able to catch another person and me, but some of the others—because we separated so we wouldn't be in one bunch—those who strayed did get caught. And, well, it [the helicopter] hovered real low; we could feel the heavy gusts.

We spent the entire next day there in the brush. We came out at night and said, "Well, so what if they catch us now." We came out and walked toward where we thought the truck had been. . . . All of a sudden we were startled by the sound of people running. It was another smuggler with people in tow. He asked us where we were from and how it was that we came to be out here. We explained what had happened and asked him to take us with him. He didn't want to, but in the end he agreed. He asked only if we had someone who would come for us over there [United States]. We told him yes. We asked him how much he was going to charge us and he told us. . . . He took us all the way to Houston, and we stayed there until someone came for us with the cash so we could be set loose.

Wouldn't you know it, we were cooped up there for almost a week without food, with nothing. I think during those days they only gave us two Maruchan ramen noodles to eat. . . . There were a lot of people in the small two-bedroom house with a tiny living room. They fit forty of us in there. No way, imagine that! Everyone there without food, without having bathed, with nothing. But in the end, we made it, we crossed.)

These experiences are commonplace—bodies battling the elements, navigating unfamiliar topographies, negotiating with unsympathetic smugglers, enduring militarized violence, hoping against all odds to make it across . . . all part of the story here.

The militarized U.S.-Mexico border is the operative demarcation in a racialized logic of labor subjugation, criminalizing those who cross it clandestinely. Given the "continuing escalation and normalization of immigrant death" (Rosas 2007: 82), this assault on the humanity of unauthorized migrants does not constitute so much a position against migration—which in the end is needed to meet labor demands—as a position against migrants themselves. They are constantly faced with the reality that theirs is a devalued and disposable form of human life. Death along the U.S.-Mexico border is not some terrifying blind catastrophe so much as a systemic wielding of technologies of exception and border architectures designed to shock the transnational migrant into submission within a space of extreme structural and cultural violence.

Ricardo barely survived the brush and cacti, barely escaped the always present threat of being shot in the back by a trigger-happy agent in the helicopter hovering overhead. Ricardo learns a few words of English to survive everyday humiliations in his place of work. Ricardo looks over his shoulder, suspicious of any semblance of authority, when walking down the street, when picking up his children from school, when on his way to play huapango.

The post-9/11 security framework has intensified punitive approaches to managing the undocumented, contingent on an increase in mass incarceration that has expanded forms of control and nation-state performativity beyond the edges of its territory.[6] As a case in point, the Obama administration's Secure Communities and later Priority Enforcement Programs enlisted local law enforcement in implementing the federal mandate of identifying and removing all criminal aliens who pose a threat to public safety. In the interim, however, we have witnessed the highly profitable extralegal detention of undocumented migrants. Powerful elites with connections to the migrant carceral complex are working diligently to continue its expansion— fabricating a moral panic around undocumented migration, proposing legislation to deal with the supposed problem, and shelling out lucrative government contracts to accomplish policy objectives.[7]

Born and raised in and around the municipality of Xichú, Guanajuato, Pascual picked up the vihuela when he was just a boy. In the late 1970s, he joined

Los Leones de la Sierra de Xichú alongside Guillermo Velázquez and two decades later began playing the violin. In 2005 he was invited to a series of huapango engagements in the United States, but he didn't make it across. In fact, Ricardo played in his stead. Pascual and a fellow musician tried their luck at crossing the border in the Eagle Pass, Texas area. They were apprehended. He explains:

> Pues tanteábamos que pagándole a nuestro coyote, pues podíamos llegar allá a chambiar. Uno, pues, no hay otra. Hay que intentar pasar y a veces las tanteadas no le salen como uno quisiera y esa ves nos agarraron. Y luego nos dieron cuatro meses, ¡chingao! Cuando a uno lo llevan por allá ni le dicen exactamente. Nos tuvieron encarcelados como delincuentes. Está gacha esa experiencia. Es triste. Es muy desgastante estar ahí.

––––––––––––––––

> (Well, we figured that if we paid the smuggler, well, that we would be able to cross to work. For one, well, there's no other way. You have to try and get across, and sometimes things don't turn out the way you would like, and that time they caught us. And then they sentenced us to four months, fuck! When they detain you, they don't explain things to you. They had us jailed like criminals. It's a horrible experience. It's sad. It's exhausting being there.)

Both musicians were detained for fleeing from the border patrol and not disclosing the identity of their smuggler; at least that's what they were later told. First held in the Val Verde County Correctional Facility, they were eventually transported to another privately operated federal detention facility in West Texas also managed by the Florida-based Geo Group. They remained there for four months as part of the federal government's Operation Streamline (2005), a zero-tolerance border-enforcement program under which individuals who cross into the United States clandestinely are forced into the criminal justice system rather than being routed through civil deportation proceedings. This fast-track program involves a mass trial for anywhere from forty to eighty immigration offenders per hearing. A group lawyer is typically provided for defendants in groups; nevertheless, most of those ushered through have a limited understanding of the process and of what they are ultimately being subjected to. First-time entrants are prosecuted with misdemeanors punishable by up to six months in prison. In the end, all those convicted end up with a criminal record, based solely on the immigration offense, excluding them from legal residence in the future.

Pascual is hesitant to speak about it in detail, a humiliating experience for him, and it's hard for me to picture him confined in a cell for months. I imagine he was subject to the same conditions as the detainees who led a prison-wide revolt in the West Texas facility in February 2009. Complaints about overcrowding and poor medical attention went unheeded for months and finally led to a two-day uprising. Substandard conditions and widespread abuses in several facilities across the country are often to blame for deaths, the result of cutting corners financially. Pascual has not tried to cross clandestinely again. This cold reality gestures toward Foucauldian analyses of the U.S.-Mexico border premised on his unfinished formulations of biopower and biopolitics as forms of governmentality that target human life as the object to be regulated.[8] It's nothing new.

DISORDERED MATERIALISMS IN THE BORDERLANDS

Critical analyses of the U.S.-Mexico border region have understood it as a historical site of racialized violence wherein political technologies have enabled the hostile management, surveillance, and indiscriminate killing of ethnic Mexicans since the nineteenth century. The conquest and colonization of more than half of Mexico's national territory in 1848 ushered in a new race- and class-based hierarchy that to this day continues to marginalize ethnic Mexicans, whether native to the United States or not. In the U.S. Southwest, Martha Menchaca (2001) argues, racial science historically played a significant role in the legal management of the ethnic Mexican population, specifically, with the conclusion of the Mexican-American War, it was assumed the Treaty of Guadalupe Hidalgo would extend full legal protection to Mexicans in the newly ceded territories, regardless of ancestry. U.S. racial-caste laws, however, abolished the political privileges that the Spanish and Mexican governments had given the people of the Southwest, for, it was argued, Mexicans were descendants of "Aztec savages" and thus, like all Native Americans, were deemed noncitizens. Phenotypic difference buttressed this racial logic. Not surprisingly, after over a century and a half, the boundaries of full citizenship—which in reality are contoured by the racial markers of whiteness—have yet to expand to include ethnic Mexicans (Haney-López 1996), thus making possible the commonsensical conflation of illegal and Mexican that undergirds state laws that racially profile and thus assume all ethnic Mexicans to be "illegals."[9]

In March 2013 it was estimated that 11.3 million undocumented migrants were residing in the United States, of whom roughly half were of Mexican descent (Passel et al. 2014).[10] In an age of globalized labor markets and flexible accumulation, the present strategies of containment operative along the border and in the continental United States work to subjugate an entire population of vulnerable workers who use transnational mobility to negotiate their life chances. Jonathan Xavier Inda argues that these extreme efforts are anticitizenship technologies that deem so-called illegal immigrants imprudent subjects, casting them into "ethical territories of exclusion" (2006: 108)—a contention that echoes Giorgio Agamben's (1998) notion of *bare life* at the margins of politics, deprived of legal subjecthood. While Agamben relies on an obscure figure from archaic Roman law (*homo sacer*) as a theoretical apparatus to illustrate the application of politics in establishing rule and exception, Inda's Foucauldian understanding of biopolitics explores the role scientific knowledge production plays in the discursive terrain that constructs so-called illegal immigration as an intelligible object of government capable of being regulated through calculable means. The overt focus of such discourses has been the ethnic-Mexican community (De Genova 2005: 91).[11] This form of governance through criminalization, Inda (2006) recognizes, is highly contingent on a racialized life politics reliant on systemic knowledges concerned with reproducing socially valuable forms of inequality (Lemke 2011). Similarly, Gilberto Rosas (2006) turns his attention to the overriding logics of "making live" and "letting die" central to Foucault's biopower within the purview of the U.S.-Mexico border. In agreement with Foucault, Rosas observes how racial knowledges fuel the white-supremacist "construction of killable or at least disposable" migrant subjects (2007: 84). In this regard, he views biopower as governmental strategies aimed at regulating and intensively subjugating racialized migrant bodies, using the threat of death to ensure economic productivity. Those who do not acquiesce to such circumscribed geographies of illegality—from home to work and back—are increasingly terrorized by intensified policing efforts designed to make everyday life unbearable.

These ethnographic and theoretical works critically explore the issue of Mexican migrant illegality, particularly how the migrant body has been systematically reduced to a disposable biocommodity within the current context of U.S.-Mexico border enforcement and migrant policing at a time of exponentially increasing transnational economic integration between the two countries. Although many die in the act of crossing, "many, many, more struggle to live, work, and, as the recent demonstrations across the United States suggest, challenge contemporary political relations," as Rosas (2006: 412–413) observes. The demonstrations referenced occurred in response to the Border Protection, Anti-terrorism, and Illegal Immigration Control Act (H.R. 4437), proposed in Congress in 2005—which I examine in the following chapter. Nevertheless, in Rosas, we glimpse an inspired vision of biopolitics. In his analysis of the underground sewer system connecting Nogales, Sonora, and Nogales, Arizona, referred to as the *barrio libre* (free 'hood) by the marginalized cross-border youth who inhabit it, he speaks of the contingent nature of sovereignty in which "daily challenges and negotiations by immigrants and the people of the border region of the United States and Mexico expose the rickety scaffoldings of the state" (2007: 97). Given the rise in state necropolitical technologies aimed at undocumented migrants seeking to be laborers, I, like Rosas, consider bodily negotiations and productions as refusals of the first order. This is to say, biopolitical production is to be considered as the total integration of all human creative capacities central to a social production— the production of, yes, material life mediated by economic relations, but also the transformative production of new forms of social life, forms of living derived from the body. I argue in the remainder of this chapter that corporeal manifestations of productive power in the form of performance constitute the cornerstone of an alternative biopolitics where the body and voice exist as instruments of self-valorizing labor amid the material and political ecologies of the U.S.-Mexico border.

Indeed, the borderlands analytic poses a material challenge to modernity's master narrative of the separation of space-time, whereby crossing the threshold of bordered geographies entails passing from one temporality to another, an ideological act that essentializes difference at the distal edges of progress (Brady 2000). While we bear in mind this disjunct, huapango arribeño's narrative productions provide another story, one that empties the semiological systems and higher-order social indexicalities that fix the border in place, reinscribe difference, and criminalize those who cross these thresholds clandestinely. These poetics encounter the violent cultural signification that normalizes migrant death and produces illegal subjects. Albeit cloaked rhetorically in the semantics of citizenship and democracy, the most contemporary ways of speaking about undocumented migration undeniably ooze a racializing lexicon that undergirds the project of white supremacy, transforming the seemingly neutral juridical category of illegal alien into a covert racial indexical that performs this pragmatics of reification key to producing the border, border violence, and bordered subjects—or an exploitable Mexican other (Dick 2011a). And while dominant discourses that rely on the categories of the citizen, the alien, and illegality struggle to reduce migrants to less-than-human others, the multitude who are living out their lives beneath the arch of these strategies of containment are engaging in their own (dis)orderings, invoking their own aural cartographies of lived life. In this way, the social worlds of transnational Mexican migrants rely on the readability of cultural concepts, images, and experiences that constitute chronotopic (re)configurations of a clandestine life en route—a dynamic and disruptive semiotic display of space-time soundings to which listeners align themselves in articulating their existence across national boundaries, beyond allá.

These entextualizations are fleeting; they convene and disappear; they are "launched within a space of contingency" where audiences are enfolded in present-tense aesthetic negotiations of circumstances and experiences grounded in the social currency of a here and now that reaches across borders (Stewart 1996: 4). These emergent vitalities reach out, pull, and intimate, signaling toward the role language and performance occupy in shaping transnational personhood, that is, in mediating the absorption of illegality within the daily lives of undocumented Mexican migrants. Louis Althusser's (2006) philosophy around the materialism of the encounter is helpful in crafting this non-teleological perspective, which underscores the elements of the contingent and the improvisational, providing a window into the present discussion on how migrants rebuke the structures of illegality through performance. Attention to the adverbial and aleatory presencing of events in juxtaposition to the patterned, geometric data about "things" (migrants) is necessary in unraveling how illegality is not inevitable at the level of the vernacular. Whereas the illegal immigrant is a ready-defined subject mobilized in the American imagination to create fear, suspicion, and anxiety—emotions that in turn justify punitive approaches to dealing with the undocumented—the Mexican migrants spoken of here express narratives about their daily lives and identities through huapango arribeño that extend beyond the narrative space of illegality. These luminous productions rest in a space of interruption of the cultural assemblages that constitute "America," assemblages that freeze "it" into essentialized objects with fixed identities—borders, or prefabricated landscapes already filled in with an abstract lexicon of democracy, sovereignty, security, and exceptionalism that "puts an end to the story of 'America' before it begins" (Stewart 1996: 3). There are gaps in this order of things and huapango arribeño's narrative productions provide a vehicle for their translation; huapango arribeño's poetics maneuver in this space, telling of a transnational cultural real. And audiences have a hand in building this aural poetics that circulates and is made legible across geographies. To this end, the ecology we can attend to is that of the "killing deserts," in Rosas's (2006) words, or the "ecologies of fear" (M. Davis 1998), "of terror" (D. Peña 1997), of "cruelty" (Mbembe 2003), of criminality. This move rests largely on privileging the sentient and bodily dimensions of huapango arribeño performance wherein individuals use their human creative capacities to develop sites for alternative expressions of their otherwise dehumanized voices. Sites where individuals voice stories and recognize themselves and others in the details of those stories. Where individuals listen with the intent of making symbolic connections. Where this saturated sonorous present is, at last, impermanent.

HASTA TENNESSEE

When one is facing the realities of restricted mobility, calling out to Tennessee and the loved ones who reside there is at times the only thing one can do on a cold winter night when huapango arribeño is in the offing, well aware that the troubadours who've dug in are capable of bringing those called out to into the same space and time . . .

Historian Julie M. Weise challenges the view that Latin American migration to the American South is a new phenomenon and thus questions the premise of what some scholars have termed the *Nuevo South*—a play on Henry Grady's famous proclamation in 1886 that the South was "New" (H. Davis 1990). In the decades following the Civil War, he and other "New South boosters," Weise (2012: 42) comments, "sought to convince the nation that the region had accepted its defeat in the Civil War, agreed that slavery and racial radicalism were illegitimate, and was now more committed to economic progress." The South that emerged, however, did not so much break with the past as perpetuate the same racial prejudices under the new guise of legally sanctioned segregation amid the collapse of Reconstruction. In the early twentieth century—in the wake of the Mexican Revolution, specifically— Mexicans began migrating to the South (to Tennessee, Mississippi, Louisiana, and Arkansas, to name a few places) in substantial numbers as they followed labor contractors to sugar parishes and cotton plantations, mainly, encountering and at times successfully navigating Jim Crow. This migration continued through the era of the Bracero Program, the binational labor recruitment program between Mexico and the United States from 1942 to 1964. Thus, while meant to signify a new cosmopolitan home for Latin American migrants, the imagined Nuevo South elides the historical record Weise uncovers—for present-day migration to the South is not without precedent. Further, the notion of a Nuevo South obscures how contemporary racial-class structures in the South express an unruptured contiguity with the racial tensions that have existed in the region since Emancipation (Weise 2012: 42). Now, just as then, inequity along the lines of race is centrally about the entitlements of citizenship. Newly arrived Mexican migrants in the South encounter the likes of Alabama's H.B. 56, job discrimination in Kentucky, limited access to health care in South Carolina, deplorable working conditions in Mississippi (Stuesse 2016), and housing segregation in Georgia and Tennessee. These experiences echo out—loved ones back in Mexico know of such conditions, of the daily humiliation and alienation.

While people are separated by great distances, somehow the mere voicing of a loved one's name can be the most meaningful way of bridging and crossing that divide. The desire to be in each other's presence seems to travel infinitely and for a moment, however brief, distant people and places are copresent . . .

San Ciro, San Luis Potosí, mid-January. It's around one in the morning, the temperature is just above freezing, and the ground trembles as I snake my way through the crowd of several hundred on the street—a sea of dancers stomping and kicking up dirt, exposing the dry bones of the earth beneath our feet. I brush past couples and briefly lock eyes with them as I wade through a fog of panting breaths, jostled about by the pounding rhythm of their patterned steps. Vibrations shudder through our bodies—entering and leaving. The pulsing 6/8 huapango strumming gives rise to interlocking fiddle melodies—the syncopation, trilled notes, restatements upon restatements. The deep, subsonic turbulence rumbles in the pit of the stomach, beginning in the bowels, clamoring out through the chest.

For days now, the town has been giddy, in the midst of its spirited patron-saint festivities. There is something new every day. Musical performances, dances, pageants, parades, horse races, and topadas are all part of this carnival-like energy. Last week's topada was held on the muddy grounds of the rodeo arena. Musicians and dancers alike were cradled by the whitewashed concrete structure on that occasion. Tonight, the flickering lights of carnival booths and rides float like fireflies above the crowded fairgrounds and reach the topada congregation that has gathered on the outskirts of town. Tonight, a dirt road lined by dry-laid stone walls and wiry mesquite trees plays host to the topada. I walk along, tightly, in between others, soaking in the smells of simmering and frying food from merchant stalls, the boisterous cackles and laughter of teenagers, the shouts of vendors calling out to passersby, the gestures of people beginning to drink and dance. I'm slowly making my way over to speak with the musicians in one ensemble. They're perched atop the tablado, towering above the audience at the far end of the street. I edge closer. The smells of damp mesquite and tobacco drift by. The bitter scent of *aguardiente* (sugarcane liquor) from someone's breath fills my nostrils. I finally reach my destination. I wave to the musicians from below, and two of them step down. We greet each other and comment on the cold.

In the midst of this scene, a middle-aged gentleman walks up to the tablado, beckoning to get the attention of the troubadour, Fidel, asking, "Oiga, me trova un saludado a . . ." (Hey, can you improvise a greeting to . . .). He briefly imparts details about himself and the person he wants greeted, a common exchange between audience members and musicians. During the subsequent musical intervention, Fidel crafts the following improvised decimal; it hangs in the air, and I perk my ears up:

EN ESTA IMPROVISACIÓN
MI SALUDO DOY AQUÍ
QUE SE OIGA HASTA TENNESSEE
EL SALUDO PA' RAMÓN

(1) Poniendo mi entendimiento
quiero ver por dónde empiezo
y de parte de Tereso
va mi saludo que intento
y hasta allá el complacimiento
pero de buena intención
por eso en mi trovación
quiero mencionar aquí
que vaya hasta Tennessee
ESTA IMPROVISACIÓN

(2) La gente me estará oyendo
mientras mi verso campea
del rancho del Atarjea
hoy memoria estoy haciendo

y lo mismo complaciendo
con gusto y con frenesí
lo digo porque es así
en estos versos floridos
por allá en Estados Unidos
MI SALUDO DOY AQUÍ

(3) Quiero hablarte en esta glosa
y el saludo va trovado
a Refugio, tu cuñado
y a su muy querida esposa
en esta noche gozosa
menciono porque es así
yo pienso que no mentí
mientras trovo y versifico
el saludo que ahora ubico
QUE SE OIGA HASTA TENNESSEE

(4) Con toda estimación
a través del decimal
¿Tereso, qué tal?
¿cumplí con la petición?
y dando terminación
hoy que el gusto se encartuche
y hasta Tennessee se escuche
EL SALUDO PA' RAMÓN

———

IN THIS IMPROVISATION
I GRANT MY GREETING HERE
MAY IT BE HEARD ALL THE WAY TO TENNESSEE
THE GREETING IS FOR RAMÓN

(1) Mustering my senses
I'll discern where to begin
and on behalf of Tereso
goes my intended crafted verse
and the complaisance goes out yonder
but of good intention
this is why in my improvised verse

I want to mention here
may it travel to Tennessee
THIS IMPROVISATION

(2) The audience must surely hear me
as my verse roams freely
the community of Atarjea
today I'm remembering it so
and likewise honoring
with pleasure and passion
I say it because it is so
in these flowery verses
out yonder to the United States
I GRANT MY GREETING HERE

(3) I want to speak to you in this gloss
and the greeting is improvised
for Refugio, your brother-in-law
and to his beloved wife
on this joyous night
I mention it because it is so
I don't believe I've lied
as I improvise and versify
the greeting that I now situate
MAY IT BE HEARD ALL THE WAY TO TENNESSEE

(4) With much esteem
by way of the decimal
Tereso, what say you?
did I fulfill your request?
as I formally conclude
today, may the pleasure be parceled up
and be heard all the way to Tennessee
THE GREETING IS FOR RAMÓN

A saludado is an improvised greeting, a public and momentary weaving together of imaginings and emotional registers that yields a narrative opening that traces out biographical and geographical connections across time, location, and affecting elements. *Saludado* stems from the word *saludar* (to greet): the saludado aesthetically hails forth persons through the complex decimal. This burst of creative energy appears and vanishes suddenly; it impresses itself on listeners through its laborious and momentary enactment. It embodies "a struggle between textuality and performativity that is both rooted in and responsible to the domain of talk" (A. Fox 2004: 43). Take the above example. Tereso—the gentleman I witnessed speaking with Fidel as I stood next to the tablado that morning—requested a greeting for his friend Ramón (and Ramón's sister and brother-in-law, Refugio), all of whom live in Tennessee but are originally from Guanajuato. The expressive material that orients Fidel's verbal art was generated in this instance of dialogic social exchange. This moment of ordinary interpersonal talk is the generative site of the dialogically constituted discursive sign, or saludado, which in turn reveals both the politics of quotation and the process of (recon)textualization that undergird the voicing of multiple subjectivities in the saludado's emergent textuality. Put more simply, the audience members play a critical role in giving form to the troubadour's compositional effort; therefore, we might describe this effort as an act of transposition involving a dynamic shifting of the indexical elements rooted in the original exchange (between troubadour and audience member) to a context of reporting in the form of a decimal (between troubadour and topada audience). The improvised saludado may be interpreted as the reporting of indirect discourse wherein an original chain of utterances—with its selective and dense ties to context—is recycled in another context (Hanks 1996: 211). This particular objectification requires the appropriation of interpersonal dialogue (and its indexical references to people and place), to be transposed with the aid of complex linguistic resources (the decimal form) and subsequently put on display for a public audience "where the skillful storyteller creates a world and moves in and out of it over the course of the telling" (212–213).

Transpositional skill, to use William F. Hanks's formulation, involves deictic movement, particularly the orienting of an emergent textuality—or discourse deixis—to itself, to the speaker, to the addressee, and to the overhearer in the event of improvised discourse. Inherently a speaker-centered notion, deixis is a manner of relating to the spatiotemporality of utterances, which therefore begs attention to who is speaking and where and when the speaking is occurring as a means of locating the people and objects being referred to in relation to the participants in the speech event. With respect to the latter, the unfolding decimal maps out spatiality—identifying both proximal and distal locations relative to the poetics—and denotes temporality by distinguishing between the time of the talk that anticipated the saludado and the time of the saludado itself. We therefore witness the narrowing of relative social distance between the speaker (the troubadour Fidel), the addressees (Tereso and Ramón, Refugio, and Refugio's wife), and the overhearers (Tereso and the entire topada audience). These are the linguistic means by which Fidel skillfully bridges and crosses geographic distances between people and places— between Potosí and Tennessee.

(Planta. Lines 2 and 3)
MI SALUDO DOY **AQUÍ**
QUE SE OIGA **HASTA TENNESSEE**

(Décima 1)
(Line 5) y hasta **allá** el complacimiento
(Line 8) quiero mencionar **aquí**
(Line 9) que vaya **hasta Tennessee**

(Décima 2)
(Line 3) del rancho del **Atarjea**
(Line 9) por **allá en Estados Unidos**

(Décima 4)
(Line 7) y **hasta Tennessee** se escuche

———

(Planta. Lines 2 and 3)
I GRANT MY GREETING **HERE**
MAY IT BE HEARD **ALL THE WAY TO TENNESSEE**

(Décima 1)
(Line 5) and the complaisance goes **out yonder**
(Line 8) I want to mention **here**
(Line 9) may it travel **to Tennessee**

(Décima 2)
(Line 3) the community of **Atarjea**
(Line 9) **out to the United States**

(Décima 4)
(Line 7) and be heard all the way to **Tennessee**

Proximal Location	Acknowledged Distance	Distal Location
aquí	hasta (Tennessee)	Tennessee
Atarjea allá		Estados Unidos

I now turn my attention to the grammatical persons involved in the decimal utterance, or participant deictics referring to social entities, their identities, and the relationships between them, namely, the speaker, addressee, and overhearer, in addition to those mentioned in the utterance. Within the context of the decimal, the troubadour is the point of orienting reference—he is located in the Potosí present. Those in attendance, while also in Potosí, are not directly addressed and thus may be considered overhearers. Moreover, while Tereso is directly mentioned and for all intents and purposes directly involved, given that his dialogue with Fidel is now objectified indirect discourse reported in the unfolding decimal, he is also, in a sense, an overhearer, for the primary addressees are in effect Ramón, Refugio, and Refugio's wife. To make further sense of this layered enunciation, I draw on Erving Goffman's (1979) participation framework. Fidel is at once the author (the saludado is his creation) and animator (he produces the utterances themselves—literally giving voice), yet Tereso is the principal, for those referenced are social entities with whom he entertains social relationships and who are of importance to him. Along the way, Fidel encounters and represents Tereso, Ramón, Refugio and his wife, and the audience.

(Planta. Line 4)	EL SALUDO PA' **RAMÓN**
(Décima 1. Line 3)	y de parte de **Tereso**
(Décima 2. Line 1)	**La gente** me estará oyendo
(Décima 3. Line 1)	Quiero **hablarte** en esta glosa
(Décima 3. Line 3)	**a Refugio, tu cuñado**
(Décima 3. Line 4)	y a su muy **querida esposa**
(Décima 4. Line 3)	¿**Tereso**, que tal?

(Planta. Line 4)	THE GREETING IS FOR **RAMÓN**
(Décima 1. Line 3)	and on behalf of **Tereso**
(Décima 2. Line 1)	**The audience** must surely hear me
(Décima 3. Line 1)	I want to **speak to you** in this gloss
(Décima 3. Line 3)	for **Refugio, your brother-in-law**
(Décima 3. Line 4)	and to his **beloved wife**
(Décima 4. Line 3)	**Tereso**, what say you?

This interconnective enregisterment of distinct persons links intimate relationships that are playing themselves out amid a transnational political economy, a social context familiar to those listening to the present poetic flow. Fidel maneuvers among these multiple voices throughout his improvised composition by alternating between metalanguage (as he refers to the above-identified persons, including himself, and their speech, that is, the saludado request) and object language (the actual improvised verses that unfold [Farr 2006: 232–234; Silverstein and Urban 1996]) as a reflexive strategy to personalize the greeting, indexing distant people, places, and contexts so as to fold them affectively into the present time and space. The metapragmatic references to the saludado itself within its own performance heighten the sense that the composition is fleeting, existing only in the moment in which it is uttered—it is something special to behold and to be heard. Fidel thus recognizes both the importance of the public's aural reception of his words and his privileged position as a performer.

(Planta. Lines 1, 2, and 4)
EN **ESTA IMPROVISACIÓN**
MI SALUDO DOY AQUÍ
EL SALUDO PA' RAMÓN

(Décima 1)
(Line 1) Poniendo **mi entendimiento**
(Line 4) va **mi saludo** que intento
(Line 5) y hasta allá **el complacimiento**
(Line 7) por eso en **mi trovación**

(Décima 2)
(Line 2) mientras **mi verso** campea
(Line 4) hoy **memoria estoy haciendo**
(Line 5) y lo mismo **complaciendo**
(Line 7) **lo digo** porque es así
(Line 8) en **estos versos floridos**

(Décima 3)
(Line 1) Quiero hablarte en **esta glosa**
(Line 2) y **el saludo** va trovado
(Line 8) mientras **trovo y versifico**
(Line 9) **el saludo** que ahora ubico

(Décima 4)
(Line 2) a través del **decimal**
(Line 4) ¿cumplí con **la petición**?

———

(Planta. Lines 1, 2, and 4)

IN **THIS IMPROVISATION**
I GRANT **MY GREETING** HERE
THE GREETING IS FOR RAMÓN

(Décima 1)
(line 1) Mustering **my senses**
(line 4) goes my intended **crafted verse**
(line 5) and **the complaisance** goes out yonder
(line 7) this is why in **my improvised verse**

(Décima 2)
(line 2) as **my verse** roams freely
(line 4) today **I'm remembering** it so
(line 5) and likewise **honoring**
(line 7) **I say it** because it is so
(line 8) in **these flowery verses**

(Décima 3)
(line 1) I want to **speak** to you **in this gloss**
(line 2) and **the greeting** is improvised
(line 8) as I **improvise and versify**
(line 9) **the greeting** that I now situate

(Décima 4)
(line 2) by way of **the decimal**
(line 4) did I fulfill **your request**?

There is, I must admit, something bittersweet about the wistful extension of a greeting that may never arrive. We might assume that Ramón will never hear this saludado, for he is clearly not in attendance but in Tennessee. Yet the dancing public is receiving and hanging onto every word, they themselves are migrants or have loved ones living on the other side of the border. Fidel's decimal affectively indexes these accrued layers of transnational life, enfolding Potosí and Tennessee, an affective tethering of geographies, associations, relationships, and memories, accenting the connections among them while shaping new connections in the present with those listening. Tennessee is far, but it is dragged into view through the momentary request, a request spurred on by an intimacy that is desired and so often severed by distance and politics. Despite the cold realities of migration, there is hope for life on, across, and

after the border, and, in the end, this discursive act does not so much constitute a politics of representation—although the saludado is certainly representational. The saludado is a politics of being, where the embodied voicing of a
name or a place unbinds the singularity of self, allowing a connection with the
desired other, despite their absence.

THE POETIC BORDER

Everyday life is the space of being that phenomenologists are concerned with,
the space of interruption Marxists speak about, the space of meaning that
cultural geographers want to understand. De Certeau (1984) directs us toward
the distinction between "strategies" and "tactics," therein to explore the
ways in which moments of movement and encounter (or tactics) found in
everyday life are in dialogue with officialized webs of discipline and representation (or strategy). That is, places, cities, and borders are labeled, defined,
and constructed purposefully into social and spatial divisions, which are in a
constant interplay as the ordered place warps and bends around daily life. De
Certeau's distinction between tactics and strategies makes for a useful juxtaposition between the concept-city and the city-in-the-making, or *poetic city*.
This concept of the poetic city opens up a way of speaking about the border as
itself poetic—as much as, or more so than, it is bounded.

The concrescence of a city or the rupture of a border is only the visible
limit to a vast array of invisible and irrepressible stories and crossings that
can potentially interrupt the strategies that invent the border. Practices that
fall outside of theoretical constructions of place are understood, through
de Certeau, as tactics—"a calculus which cannot count on a 'proper' (a spatial or institutional localization), nor thus on a borderline distinguishing the
other as a visible totality" (de Certeau 1984: xix). Tactics are not defined or
identified according to place, although they occur at times in response to the
forces of placemaking or the constraints of place (29). As such, tactics are the
impetuses, the actualizations, and the aleatory events that make up the heterogeneous world of the other in the practice of everyday life. Ongoing tactics
can momentarily (or continually) silence strategy, producing areas of "free
play" (106). These cracks in the pavement or border wall allow for saturations
of meaning to well up, stories to gather, and memories to haunt the otherwise
regulated notion of place, of the border. This is how performance in everyday
life is revealed to be *poetic* in its subtlest moments of interaction, encounter,
and arrival—when the saludado reaches the ears of those listening and makes
present that which is desired. It is in these moments that we encounter the

space of potentiality, where culture is not simply made available as an objectified form or practice; where we are instead forced to track its engagements, shifts, and dispersals; where we see the bundles of relationships and entangled processes that merge. In such moments, huapango arribeño is a site of translation that does not so much articulate the everyday as carve out a path, carrying forth aspects of what exceeds the moment itself in expressing its connectivity to other moments, places, and people, from Potosí to Tennessee—attuned, attentive, attached, embodied, though momentary. Indeed, practitioners often point to huapango arribeño's contingency. Celso, a troubadour from San Ciro de Acosta, San Luis Potosí, theorizes this very point in relation to the saludado.

> Cada día hay cosas nuevas que aprender, aún hasta de improvisar. Esto nunca se lo acaba uno. . . . Hay trovas espontáneas que se hacen. . . . Quedan tan bien que se queda uno sorprendido. . . . Y luego de repente dice el patrón [de la tocada], "Cánteme de vuelta, pero así lo mismo lo que cantó porque qué bien le salió" . . . Pero así como salió, se fue. Uno hace versos muy buenos de repente y se van.

(Each day there are new things to learn, even about improvising. One never sees an end to this. . . . There are spontaneous verses that are crafted. . . . They turn out so well that one is left mystified. . . . And then all of a sudden the patron [of the engagement] says, "Sing to me again, but the same as you just did because it came out so well!" . . . But just as it came, it went. One crafts very good verses all of a sudden, and then they're gone.)

Here, I turn to Paolo Virno's account of virtuosity as "an activity which finds its own fulfillment (that is, its own purpose) in itself, without objectifying itself into an end product . . . into an object which would survive the performance" (2004: 52). What matters, both materially and affectively, is what Mikhail Bakhtin refers to as "the event of striving, the axiological tension, which actualises itself thanks to that without any impediment, and becomes consummated" (quoted in Guattari 1995: 307).

Situated in a transnational context, huapango arribeño's narrative productions—the saludado, specifically—are generative compositions that attend to the lives of people who negotiate border politics on a daily level, becoming politicized along the way. In the saludado, a vehicle for voicing solidarities otherwise severed emerges as huapangueros cast undocumented migrants as friends, mothers, fathers, daughters, sons, wives, and husbands. They elaborate affinities earnestly, humanly, with "good intention," with "pleasure and passion," with "esteem," on "joyous" nights by way of "flowery verses" for those who are "beloved," to use Fidel's constructions. These poetics draw on the familiar, on the world at hand, to paint scenes that overwhelm and dramatically sweep over those present. Listeners' pleasure in such a personalized greeting lies in its impermanence. For performers, this means exercising a level of virtuosity in the moment for all to see. One may succeed or fail creatively in the act of improvisation, for there is no safety valve to limit the commitment to the aesthetic belief that one will get from "here" to "there," from embryonic thought to emotive decimal, all of which involves both technique and feeling. In the midst of such entrancing composition, saludados wrap around the audience, demanding and summoning their appraisal. The audible force of the soaring music, words, and phrases literally moves the congregation—they are received with the body, inciting patterned steps. These moments of performance also *move* the imagination into an affective space of self-knowing, self-making, distilling the most basic desires of clandestine bodies also moving from "here" to "there" across the border to make connections—a touchstone for a reservoir of meaning and community binding. The residues of all this are what Kathleen Stewart refers to as our "unfinished world," as that which some wish to be unconditional (citizenship, the border) is made into something far more contingent and human.

This flow of sound, language, and expression is a testament to the power of the human voice; it not only draws our attention to the political economy of discursive texts but, more important, signals a political economy of forms of living, particularly the energy that vernacular entextualizations are imbued with. In this flow performance serves as a key site of social interaction and subjectivity where tangled poetics rework the border, where the lyrical greeting that may never be heard threads a wistful line of desire between Potosí and Tennessee, where the aesthetic moment powerfully betrays the supposed boundaries and politics of geography, where the aural poetics of transnational migrant life interrupt topographies of racialized management without fear and with sobering honesty.[12] In El Refugio, San Luis Potosí, the troubadour Pánfilo crafts a saludado for a friend about to embark on the clandestine journey across the border:

ME PONGO A IMPROVISAR
CON MI CARIÑO SINCERO

Y PARA MI AMIGO QUINTERO
UN SALUDO VOY A ENVIAR

(1) Se destierra, lo ven
según estoy informado
se va para el otro lado
deseo que le vaya bien
como lo hace cada quien
y lo vuelvo a rectificar
si es que me puede escuchar
sobre el arte que prosigo
Quintero, fino amigo
ME PERMITO EL SALUDAR

(2) Al son de mi huapanguera
y al compás de los violines
complacerlo son mis fines
como una amistad sincera
y al paso y no a la carrera
en un rato amiguero
si se va para el extranjero
le deseamos lo mejor
de parte de un servidor
PARA MI AMIGO QUINTERO

(3) Yo quiero enviarle el saludo
de parte de sus amistades
ahorita sin falsedades
de mi instrumento me ayudo
ya que su amistad yo acudo
y en este verso primero
con un cariño sincero
reciban el pormenor
miren soy su servidor
EN MI ARTE DE HUAPANGUERO

(4) Con mi guitarra en la mano
ya cumplí con mi deber
y el verso le pude hacer
en el suelo mexicano

le doy me brazo y mi mano
en este hermoso lugar
lo mejor quiero desear
y en este verso le reitero
óigame amigo Quintero
ME PERMITO EL SALUDAR

———

I SET MYSELF TO IMPROVISE
WITH MY SINCERE AFFECTION
AND TO MY FRIEND QUINTERO
I SEND OFF A GREETING

(1) You see him, he is leaving his country
or so I have been informed
he is off to the other side
I wish him all the best
just as anyone would
and I say it again
that is, if he can hear me
as I carry on through verse
Quintero, fine friend
ALLOW ME TO GREET YOU

(2) To the sound of my huapanguera
and the rhythm of the violins
to honor you is my goal
as a sincere friend
and with patience, not hurriedly
during this moment among friends
if you go abroad
we wish you all the best
on behalf of your humble servant
FOR MY FRIEND QUINTERO

(3) I want to send you a greeting
on behalf of your friends
at this moment with no spuriousness
I am aided by my instrument
as I attend your friendship

and in this standalone verse
with sincere affection
may you all receive this detail
you see, I am your humble servant
IN MY ARTISTRY AS A HUAPANGUERO

(4) With my guitar in my hand
I have fulfilled my duty
and I was able to craft you a verse
on Mexican soil
I reach out and give you my hand
in this beautiful place
I want to wish you all the best
and I reiterate it in this verse
hear me, Quintero, my friend
ALLOW ME TO GREET YOU

Saludados offer up narratives that scrape against the cognitive guide of the extreme racial and linguistic profiling of Mexican migrants under the discursive
guise of patriotism and national security in the post-9/11 era. Placed within
this field of structural and cultural violence—specifically those designed to
inaugurate unauthorized migrants into lives marked by the brutal imposition
of work—these vernacular entextualizations of life lived under these circumstances constitute an embodied act of self-imagining and affirmation that
extends beyond the language spaces of containment. The saludado therefore
enacts an everyday spatial politics, for its aural poetics transgress the space-
time of illegality in two significant ways. First, it is a semiotic display of personhood that negates the stereotypical view of the Mexican migrant as threat
and instead reinforces a sense of dignity. Second, this construction of personas participates in a compression of time and space that makes the other
"vividly present" (Ihde 2007: 176). Bringing Tennessee into Potosí animates a
set of indexical relations that link verbal forms to "the extralinguistic horizon
of social knowledge" (Hanks 1996: 148), a process that gives public voice to
the perceptual social surround, making it mutually available to speaker and
(imagined) listener in a relation of copresence in spite of the U.S.-Mexico border. (See appendix B for additional saludado examples.)

This aesthetic process offers an opportunity to meditate on the affective
space of experience. Indeed, the experience of migration exists outside of salu-

dado discourse; however, the saludado harnesses the set of social relationships central to that experience in order to construct a poetics that *moves*—literally and figuratively—within a universe of familiar meanings. To return to de Certeau, stories "traverse and organize places; they select and link them together; they make sentences and itineraries out of them. They are spatial trajectories" (1984: 115). An everyday tactic, the saludado is cast out to bridge a distance; it is a story of crossing, a spatial practice that, in the case of dehumanized migrants, may also be understood as a compositional effort capable of heralding the "arrival of new social relations" (Attali 1985: 20). For in moments of meaningful performance, illegality becomes meaningless. In moments of performance that may seem casual, when words are sung, that which is denied—movement and intimacy—is reclaimed through the aesthetic voicing of the beauty and dread associated with mobility, weaving bonds between individuals through emotive strands of music and verse whose capacity to connect relies on a shared referential field of associations, in this case, those of transnational living.

EMBODIED SOUND

Huapango arribeño moves about with the people who engage in (and with) its performance, transforming along routes, unfolding differently in different places. Yet, just as place can modify practice, the moving about of practices can allow certain places to fold together at certain times, producing adjacency, a reciprocity that allows them to touch—places exist because of the materiality of the body (the primary somatic medium of being in place is the body). Nevertheless, this points to a level of interdiscursivity, or the enactment and connectivity of speech events (moments of speaking) across social life, where performance maps, locates, and binds near and distant places, echoing, in this case, from San Luis Potosí to Tennessee.[13] Though derived from singular locations, senses of place can travel as people voice and carry place through performance. This production of adjacency is another way of suggesting a politicized practice of respatialization that produces counter-topographies (social, cultural, and geographic), for the very real movement of vulnerable bodies back and forth across Mexico and the U.S.-Mexico border necessarily gives rise to musico-poetic expressions of these movements.[14]

Like all language, huapango arribeño *takes place somewhere*, occurring in specific social and spatial contexts and, at the same time, carrying senses of place in the communication itself. In this way, huapango arribeño's poetics act as a vehicle of space-time translation precisely because they both trace and embody a tensive phenomenology of transnational intersubjective negotiations contoured by migration, state-sanctioned violence, and the capitalist enterprise. More important, this being-in-the-world calls *the bridge into existence*, connecting seemingly distant locations fluidly and intensely through memory and the desire for intimacy, both of which yearn for places presently occupied and remembered. Edward S. Casey reminds us in *Remembering: A Phenomenological Study* that there is no need to privilege the mind as the source or container of perceptions, representations, or recollections; instead, he directs us to "body memory, place memory, and commemorations" (2000: xi). In fact, these locations around memory necessarily often overlap, and the desires invoked are connections from past to present and to different places and people in the future. Through huapango arribeño, those listening move through moments and places while the immediacy of the present fades into memory, fleeting—we all become an embodied archive. And you can rest here, between the material and immaterial, between matter and memory, between experience and the body . . . and between places.[15] There's no reason not to.

Hanks, in his assessment of French philosopher Merleau-Ponty's *schema corporel*, understands the human body as the "vantage point of perception" that mediates our interactional access to those outside of us (1996: 137). In other words, one's posture and self-awareness in relation to the phenomenal are privileged to the extent that we may understand the body as an experiential field "distributed over physical, physiological, conceptual, affective," and aesthetic modes of engagement, in this case with the lived consequences of the U.S.-Mexico border (254).[16] In this sense, and within the purview of a critical biopolitics, the discursive acts in question constitute an embodied practice of knowledge production, circulation, and reception, the means by which this unauthorized community *authors* and *authorizes* itself through sound. As affective corporeal acts, these authoring and authorizing practices are lived moments where unauthorized migrant bodies rebuke in embodied ways the broader logics of "merciless disposability" (Rosas 2012: 105). Virno writes, "This life, this body, are what contains the faculty, the potential, the *dynamis*. The living body becomes an object to be governed not for its intrinsic value, but because it is the substratum of what really matters: labor-power as the aggregate of the most diverse human faculties" (2004: 82–83). The creative capacities analyzed here claim and embody rights that unauthorized migrants allegedly ought not possess—the right of the citizenry to freely express itself, a bodily concern above all else. Applying a critical biopolitics to embodied aesthetics within the U.S.-Mexico transnational context helps to situate the expressions of communities subject to heightened political-economic violence as assertions of human dignity or bios through which they form awareness of and countervail the political economies in which they are positioned. Thus, to the idea of capitalist valorization—or the labor theory of value, which makes transparent "the alienating reductionism of capitalist command" (Cleaver 1992: 116)—we may add self-valorization, as Antonio Negri (1991) describes the self-determining positive project of self-constitution and creative affirmation, which is often central to political struggle (Gomez 2016; P. Gonzalez 2011).[17]

Given the long-standing scholarship on the folklore of the U.S.-Mexico borderlands, and the overarching contention that intercultural conflict generates an entire range of expressive forms that resolve social conflict on a symbolic level (Flores 1995; Limón 1994; Paredes 1958; Paredes and Bauman 1972; M. Peña 1991), the present analysis edges toward a treatment of the materiality of performance as a form of social production juxtaposed to biopower, or a biopolitics of performance.[18] In other words, bios is the engine of all production, and biopolitics—as a countervailing force exterior to biopower—constitutes "the possibility of a new ontology that derives from the body and its forces" (Lemke 2011: 72).[19] This is to privilege the transformative production of new forms of social life at the interstices of empire, whose mode of production attempts to absorb the multitude's productive capacity in the service of capitalist valorization. Here, the self-construction of alternative subjectivities is found in the creative moment of living labor itself (Cleaver 1992).[20] At one level, this is a question of locating saludados as critical texts that liberate the experiences of undocumented migrants, so often cast in political discourse as a threat to the well-being of the nation (L. Chavez 2008; Santa Ana 2002). Still, on yet another, more significant level, saludados may be understood as embodied acts of self-valorization expressed by people who are subject to genocidal policies designed to kill them as they cross the border and to exploit them once they make it across. These moments refuse the temporal enclosures of the capitalist labor process with an ephemeral sense of time opened up through, and by, the creative labor of performance. These moments offer glimpses of meaning, and then they are gone. They well up with desire and then dissipate. The saludado is praxis—a figure of aesthetic discourse emergent in the performative event in which it is realized—and then it's gone, bearing witness to the life and death of a melody . . .

DANCING WITH DEATH

It's the threading of an idea, often ordinary, commonplace. Between musicians and audience, between musical interventions, between the bouncing and dipping bodies of dancers and violinists, in part as the instrument demands— spirited patterns, intensive bowing. In between shared cigarettes outside in the cold of night and the warmth inside the noisy ballroom—concrete walls and tile floors creating cavernous acoustics. In between shouts and glances from the crowd.

The idea nestles in between troubadour Xavi and his guitarra quinta set against his body. He raises it upright, embraces it, looks up with eyes closed as if in prayer, thinking and crafting a saludado for Ricardo. You see, it's Ricardo's wedding in Guanajuato. Xavi, accompanied by Salomón, is facing troubadour Flavio, accompanied by Pascual, in a topada. He improvises, threading away:

PARA RICARDO FALCÓN
EN COMPAÑÍA DE SU ESPOSA
VOY A TROVARLE MI PROSA
NUESTRA FELICITACIÓN

(1) Hoy hago me versería
con mi quinta huapanguera
y lo hago a mi manera
en esta noche que ya es día
con jubilo y alegría
con harta satisfacción
estando en este salón
voy a poner todo esfuerzo
para trovarle mi verso
PARA RICARDO FALCÓN

(2) Saludarlo me permito
lo digo porque así es
trovando con sencillez
hoy le entrego mi versito
cantando le felicito
hoy por él hago mi glosa

que mi verso sea una rosa
el verso le quiero brindar
me permito el saludar
EN COMPAÑÍA DE SU ESPOSA

(3) Voy hacerle mi valona
porque así debe de ser
es correcto proceder
elogiando a su persona
y lo que amigos entona
aquí en esta noche hermosa
y hoy que de dicha se goza
recibe las adulaciones
para entregarte salutaciones
VOY A TROVARLE MI GLOSA

(4) Con violines y vihuela
permíteme que le cante
para seguir adelante
voy a prender la vela
de su nombre se nivela
y hoy hago mi versión
ante toda la reunión
como dije me repito
voy a trovarle un versito
DÁNDOLE FELICITACIÓN

———

FOR RICARDO FALCÓN
IN THE COMPANY OF YOUR WIFE
I WILL IMPROVISE MY PROSE
OUR CONGRATULATIONS

(1) Today I craft my verses
with my quinta huapanguera
and I do so in my manner
on this night, now turned to morning
with jubilee and happiness
with great satisfaction
as I stand before you in this dancehall

I will muster all of my energy
to improvise a verse for him
FOR RICARDO FALCÓN

(2) I allow myself to greet him
I say it because it is so
improvising sincerely
today I give you my little verse
I congratulate you with song
I craft my gloss for him today
may my verse be a rose
I want to offer you this verse
I allow myself to greet you
IN THE COMPANY OF YOUR WIFE

(3) I will craft you my valona
because it should be so
it's thus fitting to proceed
to honor your person
and what friendship calls to mind
here on this beautiful night
and today when you are filled with happiness
receive the adulations
so that I may give you salutations
I WILL IMPROVISE MY GLOSS

(4) With violins and vihuela
allow me to sing to you
in order to continue
I'm going to set things ablaze
your name is the foundation
and today I craft my verses
amid this reunion
as I said before, I'll repeat it again
I am going to craft him a little verse
THAT SAYS CONGRATULATIONS

Ricardo and his wife, both back from Texas for the summer, are dancing—in a white gown, a white cowboy tuxedo, right in between their guests, who occasionally look over at them and smile, grab their shoulders, embrace them in the same sentiment as Xavi's verses. Ricardo walks up to the musicians from time to time, playing host, asking whether they need anything. On one such visit, in between interventions, Salomón hands Ricardo his violin and gestures for him to sit and play. Ricardo tips his hat and begins to tune the instrument. As soon as Xavi begins the poesía planta, Ricardo begins to play, eyes closed. Scattered shouts and whistles from the crowd slowly build to a rumbling and raucous wave of cheers. The subtle hint of a smile forms around the edges of Ricardo's mouth. His eyes are still closed. (See appendix A, examples 9 and 10, for a musical transcription of portions of an additional decimal improvised by Xavi in honor of Ricardo and his wife.)

The convergence of these musicians in a single moment and place is an intimate coming together of bodies and aesthetic labor that circulate and transform along cross-border routes and geographies. They've all performed alongside and across from one another on several occasions. Tonight, they're all here, but their minds and those of many in the audience are, in part, also en el otro lado—Pascual was detained once; Ricardo was fortunate to make it across; Salomón is hesitant to take the risk yet again. The topada begins in one place and ends up in another. The shared give-and-take of music and poetry enfolds the lifeworlds of those present, articulating cold realities, recalling memories of others, celebrating the moment. It's all here. The knowledge of loved ones laboring away, or of oneself soon having to embark on the journey back to do the same, is present, threaded throughout the performance, invoked explicitly and implicitly where "the coalescing of imaginations fired by the conditions of ultimately contested and fragile states" (Rosas 2007: 96) is an affront to the border logics of disposability and death that always surround you if you are undocumented. But combinations of words and their expression are themselves a living exchange—between minds and bodies, between bones and flesh that produce and receive the timbre of voices and thoughts in the mind. The experience of migrant bodies is just such, and the desire to create, to perform the meanings of words, is a clandestine desire to win, to cross the border of self, to cross the border of place, time, and politics, and, thereby, to thrive, sculpting a self-valorizing poetics out of a political-economic situation that at times seems to defy any attempt to find meaning in it. This is entirely and intimately rooted "in the everyday frustrations of all of us, the everyday struggles to maintain our dignity in the face of power, the everyday struggles to retain or regain control over our lives . . . in the relations that we form all the time, relations of love, friendship, comradeship, community, cooperation" (Holloway 2002: 158). José E. Limón (1994) tells us that the tactical cultural weapons of the subaltern are the means by which they "dance with the devil." Yet the devil—the lived contradiction of late capitalism—is, in my opinion, death personified. Death by territorial denial. Death by prevention through deterrence. Death. Yes, one may dance with death, but one is capable of much, much more. Guillermo Velázquez crafts this verse:

> Es muy profunda su huella
> pero yo piso más fuerte
> tráiganme ahorita la muerte
> que quiero bailar con ella
>
> ———
>
> Her footprint is deep
> but I tread much harder
> bring me death this instant
> for I want to dance with her

A dance, sure, yet he concludes:

> Cuando del gusto me ayudo
> la muerte a mí no me manda
> quisiera saber si aquí anda
> para trovarle un saludo
>
> ———
>
> When I partake in joy
> death holds no grip on me
> I'd like to know if she is here
> so I may improvise a greeting for her

This is to engage, encounter, and contest death, to interpolate it with the very life force it seeks to obliterate. For migrants, this is to have faith that a fleeting poetics cannot be contained by the border; indeed, while they are disqualified from political life in the United States, this very condition paradoxically marks their situated bodily expressions as the most political.

Without this analysis, the magic of the saludado is lost to the moment in which it was sung. In the social context I have described here, to request the greeting makes sense—yes, figuratively, it possesses a certain logic, but, more important, and more literally, it animates the sensorial. It is not so much about whether the intended recipient can hear the greeting, but rather about how they are brought forth through a poetic narrowing of distance that is felt with the body. It is a necessary aural poetic affirmation of social structure. My analysis uses theory as a way to legitimize this harkening magic, but perhaps it would be better to end with an ethnographic moment . . .

I was recently speaking with a friend of a well-known violinist. He loves to be around musicians, to hear them rehearse, and he has plenty of his own stories to tell. On this night, as some of the musicians were finishing their musings, he started requesting sones. In between, everyone started telling stories. We spoke of huapango, of topadas, and he participated on an equal level, telling of this or that memorable encounter between musicians—what they played, what they said. As he reminisced, it got deeper, and it got personal. He spoke of how it feels to be on the experiencing end of the music:

> Cuando era niño, me acuerdo de unos músicos que seguido tocaban un son que me gustaba, un pajarillo, y se me grabó. Ya después le pedí ese mismo son a otro trovador. ¿Porque? Pues quería oírlo, claro, pero yo admiraba mucho a ese señor. Le hubiera besado los pies. Me encantaba como tocaba. Me acuerdo del momento cuando lo tocaba, cuando le escuche los versos, quería subirme a las ramas de los mezquites donde estaban pa' tocar la música.

> (When I was a child, I remember musicians would play a son I liked, a *pajarillo*, and it stuck with me. Later, I requested the same one from a different troubadour. Why? Because I wanted to hear it, sure, but I really admired that man. I would have kissed his feet. I loved how he played. I remember in that moment when he was playing, when I heard his verses, I wanted to climb up the branches of the mesquite trees above their heads so I could touch the music.)

There's nothing easy about climbing a mesquite tree, much like crossing a border. The thorns, the brush, the pain—they're all real, but desires are just as bodily, just as material.

SIX

HUAPANGO SIN FRONTERAS

Mapping What Matters and Other Paths

Los gringos no se la creen
dicen, "¡What happen my God!"
no descifran el "Zip Code"
de lo que sus ojos ven
no son seven, eigth, nine, ten
son chingos de orilla a orilla
en bilingüe maravilla
y para alegría de la raza
Martín Luther King se abraza
con Zapata y Pancho Villa

———

The gringos can't believe it
they gasp, "What happen[ed], my God!"
they can't decipher the zip code
of what their eyes gaze upon
it's not seven, eight, nine, ten
but a shit-ton [of people] everywhere
in bilingual marvel
and to the [Latina/o] people's delight
Martin Luther King embraces
Zapata and Pancho Villa
—GUILLERMO VELÁZQUEZ

Race relations in North America involve a blend of assimilationist efforts, raw prejudice, and cultural containment that revolves around a concerted effort to keep each culture pure and in its place. Members of racial minority groups receive a peculiar message: either join the mainstream or stay in your ghettos, barrios, and reservations, but don't try to be both mobile and cultural.
—RENATO ROSALDO, *CULTURE AND TRUTH*

In December 2005 the Border Protection, Anti-terrorism, and Illegal Immigration Control Act (H.R. 4437), otherwise known as the Sensenbrenner Bill, was proposed in Congress—another in a long line of policy initiatives aimed at expanding restrictions on migrants. Its provisions sought to make unauthorized migration a felony, punish those who aided undocumented migrants, provide $2.2 billion for the construction of seven hundred miles of fencing along the U.S.-Mexico border, and require the federal government take custody of undocumented migrants detained by local authorities. This legislation came on the heels of the failed Secure America and Orderly Immigration Act of 2005 (S. 1033), which aimed to establish a guest-worker program. The more extreme version of the Sensenbrenner Bill was ratified by the House of Representatives but failed in the Senate, which in the end passed a more moderate bill that left out the felony provision. In response, millions of people marched, boycotted, and rallied across the United States. This movement culminated in nationwide mobilizations in hundreds of cities around the country in May 2006 that drew more than three million people. Seemingly spontaneous, these mobilizations were anything but. In reality, they were the result of decades of activism and advocacy in the Latina/o community; this activism extended back to the 1960s but had begun to address border militarization and immigration policy since the passage of the Immigration Reform and Control Act in 1986 (Bada et al. 2006). This highly dramatized groundswell of protest was met with anger by "Americans," including politicians and pundits who gazed on with astonishment as disenfranchised communities lifted their voices and took to the streets. The comments of Jack Cafferty—formerly of CNN's *Situation Room*—capture this sentiment:

> Once again, the streets of our country were taken over today by people who don't belong here. . . . Taxpayers who have surrendered highways, parks, sidewalks and a lot of television news time on all these cable news networks to mobs of illegal aliens are not happy about it. . . . America's illegal aliens are becoming ever bolder. March through our streets and demand your rights. Excuse me? You have no rights here, and that includes the right to tie up our towns and cities and block our streets. At some point this could all turn very violent as Americans become fed up with the failure

of their government to address the most pressing domestic issue of our time. (April 10, 2006)[1]

The "menacing potential" (Massumi 2010) of violence by police and frustrated citizens loomed as I lived out those days in Austin, Texas, in the company of organizers and huapangueros.

The largest rally in Austin, Texas, occurred in April on the steps of the State Capitol. Among the speakers and performers were Graciano, Valentín, Homero, and Daniel. I was there aiding the organizers to set up and transport sound equipment. It was a makeshift affair without any pretensions to amazing sound quality; I recall dragging speakers in and out of a friend's car hurriedly in the midafternoon heat. The growing crowd was energized, despite enduring the unforgiving midday sun as they waited for the speeches and music to commence. Workers, families, and students, native-born and migrants, young and old, were massed together, eager to be heard. Graciano arrived forty-five minutes before he was scheduled to perform. However, the other musicians were running behind. They had asked off from work so that they could attend—a rather bold request. As the time approached, they were nowhere to be found. Finally, minutes before the performance time, I spotted Homero and Valentín. Daniel was missing. Amid the frenzy, Graciano pulled me aside, handed me a vihuela, and asked, "Listo? (Ready?)." I hadn't been expecting to get onstage, and my heart thudded as I prepared to perform my politics. We frantically tuned; snaked our way through the signs, banners, and people gathered at the Capitol steps; situated ourselves in front of the microphones; and waited for our cue, which immediately came. With over eleven thousand in attendance, although some police estimates were as high as thirty-six thousand, Graciano dug into the following verses:

(poesía)
CRUZANDO SIERRAS VOY DE MOJADO
POR LA FRONTERA CON RUMBO AL NORTE
ES QUE NO TENGO MI PASAPORTE
PARA VIAJAR HACIA EL OTRO LADO

Allá en mi rancho muy de mañana
salgo muy triste, muy pensativo
dejo mi casa con un suspiro
cantaba un gallo en voz campirana
mas la tristeza que me acompaña

de ver la vida que ya he dejado
dejo la tierra, dejo el arado
para salir rumbo a la frontera
quiso el destino que pobre fuera:
CRUZANDO SIERRAS VOY DE MOJADO

De Guanajuato me despedí
pasé en San Luis con harta tristeza
allá en el rancho mi madre reza
rogando al cielo y pide por mí
desde el momento que yo salí
a la frontera, pa'l otro lado
llevo en mi mente muy bien grabado
que si al cruzar me falla la suerte
o en el camino encuentre la muerte:
CRUZANDO SIERRAS VOY DE MOJADO

Allá en la sierra cruzando ríos
voy caminando por los dreñales
entre desiertos y matorrales
sufriendo a veces calores, fríos
esos recuerdos, esos martirios
que en carne propia los he pasado
qué licenciado, ni qué abogado
saben lo triste de la pobreza
vamos los pobres con la certeza:
CRUZANDO SIERRAS VOY DE MOJADO

Días y días en el camino
y con el cuero todo encallado
de cara y manos bien arañado
llego cansado a mi destino
pero como ando de peregrino
en otra tierra, en otro condado
tal vez la suerte me ha develado
y hallando chamba me echen pa' fuera
y hoy voy de nuevo pa' la frontera:
CRUZANDO SIERRAS VOY DE MOJADO

Con la tristeza dentro de mi alma
y la esperanza desquebrantada
vuelvo a mi patria, a mi morada
a recobrar un poco la calma
pero no encuentro tranquila mi alma
mi corazón está destrozado
nomás pensando que en el otro lado
muchos disfrutan de aquel paraíso
qué mala suerte que no se me hizo:
CRUZANDO SIERRAS VOY DE MOJADO

―――

I CROSS MOUNTAINS AS A WETBACK
ACROSS THE BORDER, I TREAD NORTHWARD
FOR I DO NOT HAVE A PASSPORT
TO TRAVEL TO THE OTHER SIDE

From my ranch, early in the morning
I depart pensive and with much sadness
I sigh as I leave my home
a rooster crows its mountain voice
a deep sadness follows me
for the life I leave behind
I leave the land, I leave the plow
as I head toward the U.S. border
it was my fate to be poor:
I CROSS MOUNTAINS AS A WETBACK

I said good-bye to Guanajuato
I passed through San Luis with much sadness
back home my mother prays
she has begged the heavens on my behalf
from the moment that I departed
to the border, to the other side
for in my mind I know very well
that if luck fails me as I cross
death awaits me along the path:
I CROSS MOUNTAINS AS A WETBACK

Up in the mountains, I cross rivers
I walk through sewers
through deserts and thick brush
suffering the heat, the cold
those memories, those agonies
that I have experienced in the flesh
what college graduate, what lawyer
knows the plight of poverty?
we the poor go on with certainty:
I CROSS MOUNTAINS AS A WETBACK

Days upon days of travel
with calloused skin
my face and hands scraped raw
I arrive tired at my destination
but as I am merely a pilgrim
in another land, in another county
perhaps bad luck has come to find me
and upon finding work I'll be deported
and I'll soon enough be across the border
I CROSS MOUNTAINS AS A WETBACK

With sadness deep in my heart
and my hopes dashed
I return to my country, to my dwelling
to calmly gather myself
but my soul is not at peace
I am heartbroken
as I ponder that on the other side
many enjoy the fruits of paradise
what bad luck, it was not so for me:
I CROSS MOUNTAINS AS A WETBACK

(decimal)

SOMOS YA VARIOS MILLONES
DE HISPANOS ACÁ EN EL NORTE
ALGUNOS SIN PASAPORTE
Y DE DIFERENTES REGIONES

(1) Muchos huyen de la guerra
con el alma decididos
a los Estados Unidos
se van dejando su tierra
la esperanza se destierra
huyendo los corazones
de diferentes regiones
buscando un nuevo presente
y con la mira de frente:
SOMOS YA VARIOS MILLONES

(2) Aunque el Congreso no quiera
darnos la oportunidad
luchamos por igualdad
y nos tienen donde quieran
somos la lumbre y la hoguera
vamos agarrando corte
haciendo un grande reporte
en toditas las ciudades
formamos ya cantidades:
DE HISPANOS ACÁ EN EL NORTE

(3) De todas partes del mundo
en masas van emigrando
y ya entre todos formando
un estilo más profundo
yo lo veo cada segundo
en los estados del norte
y haciendo un grande reporte
desde África y Sur América
vienen de Asia y a Norte América:
ALGUNOS SIN PASAPORTE

(4) Tanta discriminación
y seguimos adelante
es que el hispano parlante
siempre lucha con razón
aunque sea de otra nación
pero tiene sus razones

y uniendo los corazones
seremos un desafío
que brota desde el avío
Y DE DIFERENTES REGIONES

———

WE ARE NOW SEVERAL MILLIONS
OF HISPANICS LIVING HERE UP NORTH
SOME WITHOUT A PASSPORT
AND FROM DIFFERENT REGIONS

(1) Many are fleeing war
with their souls committed
to coming to the United States
they leave their homelands
hope is set in motion
hearts fleeing
from different regions
in search of a new life
and with determination:
WE ARE NOW SEVERAL MILLIONS

(2) Although Congress does not want to
give us an opportunity
we fight for equality
and they have us anywhere they want us
we are both flame and fire
as we gain ground
we construct a grand testimony
in all of the cities
we form great quantities
OF HISPANICS LIVING HERE UP NORTH

(3) From all parts of the world
in masses they emigrate
and altogether forming
a profound statement
and I see it every second
in the northern states
as we make a grand statement

from Africa and South America
they come from Asia up to North America
SOME WITHOUT A PASSPORT

(4) So much discrimination
but we forge ahead
you see the Hispanic is vocal
and always struggles on the side of reason
even if they are from another nation
but they have their reasons
and uniting hearts
we shall issue a challenge
that springs forth from necessity
AND FROM DIFFERENT REGIONS

The aesthetic choices in any given text, Harris M. Berger comments, "both constitute and comment upon the social world" (2009: 46), a point that has been made time and again in these pages and that requires, then, equal attention to the politics that entextualized subjectivities and categories bring forth. Graciano makes reference to the juridical workings of the U.S. nation-state, restricted mobility, and the political economy of migrant labor, mentioning the lack of a passport, the border, struggles for equality, and the heterogeneity of migrants in the United States. This complex articulation is located in the aural poetics of migrant performance and may therefore be considered to voice what Alyshia Gálvez terms "vernacular citizenship," or a cultural conceptualization of citizenship removed from the "exclusive domain of the state and its arbitration of subjects" (2013: 723). While I agree with Gálvez that such (vernacular, social, cultural, and postnational) conceptualizations of citizenship run the risk of (1) reifying juridical citizenship as the discrete domain of the nation-state, (2) positioning citizenship primarily as a mechanism for inclusion rather than as a technology that reproduces inequality, and (3) "reinforc[ing] rather than critiqu[ing] neoliberal notions of flexibility and entrepreneurship" (721), I believe Graciano's voicing captured a critical sense of citizenship cognizant of the relationship between transnational labor and capital, and how they are bound up with the politics of migrant mobility. While the aforementioned legislative efforts are part of the context for understanding the mobilizations of 2006, they are but one aspect of a much broader history—as has already been discussed at length in the preceding chapters—of nationalist compulsions that have constructed the

Mexican (migrant or otherwise) as an unassimilable threat, a cultural logic that has braced the juridical technology of migrant illegality. Nevertheless, illegality itself provided the basis for what Nicholas De Genova refers to as a "negative space of relationality, in contradistinction with the positivity of identitarian positions and attachments," which made the mobilizations in 2006 possible (111).

Graciano's poesía and decimal entextualized his border-crossing journey, voicing sentiments and experiences that many in attendance, and many across the country for that matter, could relate to in the flesh, juxtaposing the paths of the unauthorized migrant who crosses, treads, and transgresses—the *mojado* (wetback)—with those of the individual who travels freely, whose movements are authorized, for whom crossing is not a question of life and death. In this emergent textuality, that which migrants have in common is their "negative relation to the machinery of the state, which reduced them all to rightless denizens and de facto 'suspects'" (110)—an identity with no positive essence but instead a derided positionality. The politics that Graciano brought forth in this time and public space through his intersubjective voicing of the embodied experience of crossing and of border violence disrupted the content of a much broader set of xenophobic discourses presently defining clandestine crossings as invasions and clandestine lives as criminal. Further, the sheer embodied voicing was itself an audacious assertion of the existence of the incompatible and unassimilable presence of those who, "from the standpoint of order, truly *do not exist*" (108–109). In full recognition of this negative social relation, Graciano, at last, challenges migrants to live beyond a bordered existence as racialized labor, projecting out the material and affective potential of an amorphous and insurgent solidarity among migrants that is not quite in view, even as he is in the midst of present mobilizations that are approaching that very horizon:

(Decimal. Décima 4. Lines 6–9)
pero tiene sus razones
y uniendo los corazones
seremos un desafío
que brota desde el avío

———

but they [migrants] have their reasons
and uniting hearts

we shall issue a challenge
that springs forth from necessity

These mobilizations were the dramatic articulation of a much larger mobilization, that is, transnational migration itself. Migrant mobility is a social movement, a political struggle and insubordination forged within particular nation-states but embedded in the economic relations of global capital beyond them.[2] The music, poetry, and challenge called out to a captive audience may be understood as expressing not so much a desire for official inclusion as an incorrigible logic demonstrating migrants' "own uncountability, their 'countless'-ness" (109). Imagine how, each time the music stopped, especially during the poesía, the recited décimas reverberated against the stone steps and the Capitol walls, echoing all the way down Congress Avenue. The audience—rapt and responsive—yelled, whooped, and hollered at the end of each décima just before the music rushed in again. And those who knew how to dance huapango did so amid the sea of U.S. and Mexican flags. The intentional massing of bodies on the Capitol steps in Austin held its own powerful larger message of a place to be won and claimed in the American polity—a vernacular space of legitimacy and recognition, an affective copresence amid the indignities of policing. Indeed, many undocumented migrants who leave their homelands, as Graciano describes, also consider the United States their home, and the desire to congregate and move freely (on whatever highway or sidewalk, in any park) is grounded in the deeper desire to live with dignity—to find intimacy ("uniendo los corazones") and meaning ("sus razones") in daily life.

This moment and others like it across the country in the spring of 2006 established a national platform for a transnational panethnic citizenship rights movement that continues to challenge the politics of immigration and defiantly argue for the right to stay (Pallares and Flores-González 2010: xxiii). Now, perhaps more than ever, recent organizing—around the DREAM Act, for instance—is taking on the ferocious anti-immigrant politics that dominates the daily lives of migrants, reminding them that they may exist within the borders of the nation-state only as subjugated labor and not in any other meaningful capacity. In what remains, I attend to this tensive interstitial crossroads, in between nationalist rationalities that juridically erase Mexican migrant personhood and the multiple and mobile placial attachments migrants cultivate in daily life on their own terms—the "indecipherable zip codes" defining what and where home is.

MATTERING MAPS AND INTERAFFECTIVE STATES

Affect is often considered a somewhat nebulous force, indecipherable even, but Megan Watkins (2010) provides a way into affect by way of other people, as she moves beyond the notions of affect as preliminal or ephemeral, insisting instead on its lasting and building in capacity as cumulative. She writes that it is through "this capacity of affect to be retained, to accumulate, to form dispositions and thus shape subjectivities" that "a sense of self is formed through engagement with the world and others and the affects this generates" (269–270). Her conceptualization of "accumulating affect" aligns well with the theory of Georges Bataille (1991), particularly in her explanation of "interaffectivity," the changing sense of self in relation to that which is perceived as external. From a more directly and philosophically Bataillean perspective, Alphonso Lingis (1998) describes the same internal-external interaction as intimacy with the alien amid coexistence.[3] This speaks to how the intersubjective desire for recognition is realized through interpersonal relationships and transactions of all kinds.[4]

These general states of interaffectivity, however, are always "articulated and contextualized" *in place*, or emplaced, as Gregory J. Seigworth (2010: 21) suggests. Seigworth turns to the cartographic thinking of Lawrence Grossberg—particularly his concept of the *mattering map*, "a socially determined structure of affect which defines the things that do and can matter to those living within the map" (Grossberg 1992: 398)—in making this claim that place matters for interaffectivity. While Grossberg focuses on the power of popular culture in his analysis—specifically the invested passion, energy, and emotional involvement that is so much a part of fandom—he makes a case for how these "affective alliance(s)" exist as "sites of investment" within the structuring of everyday life, atop which specific identities are constructed in the company of others, in the midst of shared moments and experiences (1992: 84–85).[5] This concern with spatiality is a result of his interrogation of the modernist logics that constitute the terrain of identity politics—difference, individuality, and temporality. Grossberg (1996) amends the final aspect of this theoretical foundation by turning to spatiality in his discussion of agency.[6] Mattering maps, in this regard, come into being as contexts of sociality that are part of a larger politics and poetics of place. Interestingly, he braces his discussion of identity built around people's mattering maps by drawing on Stuart Hall's (1989) conception of ethnicity as a "political agenda" congealed by "points of attachment which give the individual some sense of 'place' and position in the world"—thought of in terms of locality, culture, language, and so on (133). This intellectual linkage provides a basis for understanding modes of attunement that come together in everyday life and erupt in extraordinary moments of intensity as transcendent of social differences (ethnicity, nationality, citizenship, age, and color, much as in 2006). Such social differences exist as spaces of desire where the political act binds personal experiences of migration into larger public meanings of belonging that map out a future "not quite in view from the present, a future that scrambles any map in advance of its arrival, if indeed the moment (as a demand on the social) ever fully arrives" (Seigworth 2010: 21). At this stage, we can move beyond, again, the idea of place as genius loci into a view of places as gatherings of intensity, the coming together of lived paths, sometimes durational and sometimes rather ephemeral. A space of desire melds into a cumulative swarming of experience, layered on top of and preceding other moments in which placeness wells up, where sensing bodies respond to a mutually held cohesion of sentiment—a "sonorous expanse whose density surges and rolls" (Lingis 1998: 14). This state of potentiality bloomed in the spring of 2006, and its impacts continue on in the activism of DREAMers and young people across the United States who are defiantly coming out as undocumented.

These ideas of interaffectivity and mattering maps are significant to this study of huapango arribeño because they open up another way of imagining cultural geographies that do not rely on fixed or primordial notions of lo mexicano. Taken on their own terms, the communities in question, while objectively considered Mexican, exercise agency in subjectively configuring who they are. Much of their defined subjectivities and mattering maps have to do with real struggles in daily life, cultural memory, and relationships and intimacies amid the pressures and borders—both discursive and material—of transnational migration. Neither the Mexican nation-state and its jingoistic excess, nor the disparaging ranchero chrono-tropic figurations that condemn ethnic Mexicans to the "savage slot"—to invoke Michel-Rolph Trouillot (2003)—have a monopoly on who these communities are, for they actively engage in configuring their own Mexicanness, for lack of a better word, through the ways they go about living. In sum, the lives of the people in question are unavailable for metaphor: too much real, not enough symbolism. No systemic melancholia, no perpetual mourners here. These final stories are told to emphasize the connections among people that assist in developing a sense of belonging, of home, and feeling authorized to cross and communicate between places.

MATTERS OF LIFE . . . COSAS DE LA VIDA . . .

Huapango arribeño and its associated mattering maps not only escape segregationist ideologies that labor to fix the nation-state in place but also negate essentializing discourses concerning the Mexican character—sounds and sentiments succinctly expressed in the song "Camino de Guanajuato" (The path of Guanajuato), taken as representative of a certain Mexican archetype. Here I disarticulate the rather famous poetics of "Camino de Guanajuato" and its references to geography and cultural life in that state. Its most salient motif is arguably a brazen fatalism that echoes a long-standing and ongoing set of narratives in the realm of Mexican intellectual thought and popular culture. I turn to this narrative of mortality that exceeds vitality first, because by doing so the exceeding vitality of the poetics of huapango arribeño comes into surprising relief, particularly when expressed by and for those who leave Guanajuato for the United States to increase their life chances, always conscious of the dangers along the path. In the case of Guanajuato, its people and musicians mediate a set of transnational cultural connections to *another* Guanajuato, another *state* (of desire), where the paths and politics of performance challenge the cartographies of a nationalism and a musical ecology that reinscribe the myth of the fatalistic Mexican and his or her "nostalgia for death" (Bartra 1992: 21).

A geographic crossroads, the state of Guanajuato is home to an array of vernacular music traditions. The most widely recognizable is the canción ranchera (country song)—long deemed the ideal-typical expression of Mexican music culture (Mendoza 1961)—and its most noted twentieth-century proponent is perhaps José Alfredo Jiménez. The ranchera's history as a distinctive musical form, however, extends back to the nineteenth century. Arguably, it emerged out of the unique syncretism of the *cancionero* (minstrel) tradition, European salon musical styles, and the performance practice that was part of agricultural fairs in central Mexico, in addition to the lyrical stylings of both the Spanish romance and, later, the corrido (Gradante 1982). Both Vicente T. Mendoza (1961) and Ruben M. Campos (1928) trace the ranchera prototype—in terms of musical and thematic content—to the nineteenth-century composer and musician Antonio Zuñiga. "Camino de Guanajuato" owes much to this genealogy of influence, as does Jiménez, its composer.

Jiménez was born in Dolores Hidalgo, Guanajuato, in 1926, and his "Camino de Guanajuato," so the story goes, is a heartfelt tribute to an older brother who died in Salamanca, Guanajuato. One verse points toward this memory:

> Camino de Guanajuato
> Que pasas por tanto pueblo
> No pases por Salamanca
> Que ahí me hiere el recuerdo
> Vete rodeando veredas
> No pases porque me muero
>
> ———
>
> The path of Guanajuato
> That passes through so many towns
> Don't go by Salamanca
> For there the memory pains me so
> Travel on through surrounding paths
> Don't pass through there because I'll die

The remaining strophes take the listener on a journey through the state, evoking cities, towns, and events, which one can assume held some significance for Jiménez—from the Christ statue atop the Cerro del Cubilete, the mountain-hill in the municipality of Silao (perhaps an off-handed reference to the *Cristero* Catholic militant rebellion of the 1920s); to the town of Santa Rosa in the mountains just east of the state capital, where just beyond rests Dolores Hidalgo, the cradle of Mexican independence; and, finally, of course, to the festive carnival fairs in the city of León, where life is hastily gambled in sport, as Jiménez tells us:

> Bonito León Guanajuato
> Su feria con su jugada
> Ahí se apuesta la vida
> Y se respeta al que gana
> Allá en mi León Guanajuato
> La vida no vale nada
>
> ———
>
> Beautiful León, Guanajuato
> Its carnival fair with its games of chance
> There life is gambled
> And winners are respected
> There in my León, Guanajuato
> Life is worthless

However, the emotional core of Jiménez's composition, to borrow a concept from ballad scholarship, is perhaps expressed in the ranchera's first verse, its opening couplet to be exact:

No vale nada la vida
La vida no vale nada
Comienza siempre llorando
Y así llorando se acaba
Por eso es que en este mundo
La vida no vale nada

———

Worthless is life
Life is worthless
It begins with a cry
And with a cry it surely ends
That's why in this world
Life is worthless

While this candid pronouncement—"worthless is life, life is worthless"—is unique to this ranchera, the emotive import is not, as Olga Nájera-Ramírez (2007) argues. In her work she draws on performance studies to make a case for the ranchera as a type of melodrama, "a discursive space characterized by the intensity of emotion" (456). It is this emotional weightedness that transforms the ranchera into a "culturally sanctioned [site] in which the ideas and values of a community are not merely displayed but, more important, transmitted, produced, reproduced, and contested" (460).[7] Her critical take represents an intervention into essentializing discourses that have taken the ranchera to be an authentic expression of the true Mexican national character, particularly as it pertains to working-class fatalism. With the work of William Gradante (1982) in mind, she writes, "In addition to assuming that indulgence in passion is uniquely Mexican, such readings assume that the ranchera, like the people to whom it speaks, is simple, unsophisticated, and therefore transparent in meaning" (458). She braces her position by drawing on Américo Paredes's seminal "On Ethnographic Work among Minority Groups: A Folklorist's Perspective" (1993), where he outlines how researchers have failed to recognize the aesthetic dimensions of ethnic-Mexican ways of speaking, instead proceeding "as if language had only one level of meaning or as if informants were incapable of any kind of language use but that of minimum communication," resulting in major communicative breakdowns that have led to the misinterpretation of various forms of speech and performance as straight factual verbal reporting (82). This proclivity for interpretive shallowness is also endemic to the work of Octavio Paz (1961), a figure taken to task by both Paredes (1993) and José E. Limón (1994). In the present discussion concerning Guanajuato, I cannot help but do the same, for Paz's claims regarding the existential Mexican condition edge perilously toward a type of cultural ecology, where the essence of the Mexican character is seen as a product of its environment: the geography of Guanajuato, for our purposes, is destined to produce melancholic beings. Similar intellectual claims, as Stanley H. Brandes (2006) observes, have in large part also promoted the caricature of the morbid Mexican who is irreverent toward and yet obsessed with death. And expressive culture, it is believed (as Paz indicates), is the wellspring of this sentiment; put another way and given our present textual analysis, it is through their authentic poetry that the people claim "la vida no vale nada," particularly in Guanajuato one would assume.[8]

While the melancholic voicing of "Camino de Guanajuato" offers up an imagining of place, nostalgically coated with a certain pastoral air, its opening lines have nonetheless come to represent a particular mattering map operative in the workings of a territorializing machine that "maps how much room there is to move and where and how movement is possible" (Grossberg 1996: 102)—where metaphor and poetics become literal, transparent iterations of what it means to be Mexican. Place, character, nation, and nationalism are indistinguishably inscribed onto this imagined cultural geography and the myth of the melancholic being (Bartra 1992). The critical scholarship of Paredes and his students has done much to discredit this myth, yet it continues to circulate. For instance, in her recent work on Mexican norteña, Cathy Ragland (2009) resurrects Paz to brace her analysis of the thematic treatment of death in corridos authored by the late Chalino Sánchez. She writes, "The Mexican poet and essayist Octavio Paz explains that, unlike his North American or European counterpart, the 'Mexican' does not fear or avoid death, but rather 'looks at it face to face, with impatience, distain or irony.' Paz writes, 'Our songs, proverbs, fiestas and popular beliefs show very clearly that the reason death cannot frighten us is that life has cured us of fear. It is natural, even desirable, to die and the sooner the better' (1985, 58). It is understandable, then, that after his death, Sánchez's popularity soared throughout California and Sinaloa" (Ragland 2009: 162). If Ragland had instead mentioned that Sánchez's artistic work was contiguous with the corrido of border conflict, particularly given that death and dying often find themselves emplotted in the narrative story (in dramatic fashion, no less), then perhaps her claim would be less concerning. But if we follow her cultural logic, braced by the essentialist pseudo-psychology of Paz, not only does Sánchez sing about death, but he longs for it, and—given his posthumous popularity—so do his adoring Mexican fans. Although she attempts to inject her analysis into the present-day political economy of U.S.-Mexico migration by claiming that "from the Mexican immigrant perspective, the narcotraficante represents mexicanidad, particularly in the way he deflects U.S. authority and rejects assimilation and acculturation" (197), she does so with the aid of the essentialist trappings of Mexican cultural nationalism. Further, her claims to represent the "immigrant perspective" largely draw on musical texts, those of Los Tigres del Norte, to be precise. Their songs, according to her, "provide unity and power through a shared imagination of a Mexican identity and immigrant nation that exists through sheer determination, hard work, and pride" (182). While this listing of virtues leans toward an empathetic perspective, I am disinclined to accept claims to "know" Mexican identity politics given the logic outlined above. Indeed, one senses a bit of irony in her claims to be writing against U.S. journalists' understandings of the narcocorrido, which often amount to an "'orientalized' interpretation of the Mexican people and their culture . . . where Mexicans are portrayed as eccentric, backward, passive, sensual, and distant"; for she unwittingly reinscribes those same interpretations by virtue of her reliance on notions of "mexicanidad" as they pertain to death (196). Claudio Lomnitz's (2005) recent work on the genealogy of death as a Mexican totem helps explain how it has been woven into nationalist discourse, processes of state formation, and both commercial and public spheres from the colonial period through the post-Revolutionary era, including its contemporary transnational pilgrimage into the space of the U.S. nation-state. However, these ideas are not exclusive to popular culture and political discourse but also circulate in scholarly accounts; thus, Ragland's interpretation, as Lomnitz suggests, is unfortunately "ill intentioned, because it . . . claims that [Mexicans] are indifferent to the core value of an allegedly universal humanism: the sanctity of life" (57).

Ragland's work fits into the larger cultural studies framework that focuses on the interplay between mass culture and the postmodern social field of interaction, where critical politics and commodity production overlap, that is, in telling the complex story of identity making and the marketing forces entangled within it. Largely missing in this approach is a critical discussion of the U.S.-Mexico border but, more important, direct communication with the people who cross it. This lack of engagement is problematic when one is assigning attributes (such as morbidity) to their character, desires, and identities. To continue with the norteña theme, I am reminded of the example often invoked by those who write about borderlands music and its thematic treatment of migration—the song "La Jaula de Oro" (The gilded cage), popularized by Los Tigres del Norte in the mid-1980s (J. Saldívar 1997). Los Tigres are credited with staggering record and concert ticket sales, have received various awards from the music industry and accolades for their philanthropy, have starred in feature films, and have achieved a level of visibility previously unknown among groups performing Mexican folk-derived popular musics. It is such stardom that leads journalists like Elijah Wald to refer to Los Tigres as "the most eloquent musical chroniclers of immigrant America" (2001: 151), and "La Jaula de Oro" is often used to support this opinion. Written by Enrique Franco, the song tells the story of a Mexican migrant who has been settled in the United States for ten years, yet who is haunted by memories of not only his native Mexico but also his vexed existence in the United States: his children deny their heritage and don't speak Spanish, his life has been reduced to incessant work, and he is constantly policed—ultimately, the great nation of America is like a prison.

In his analysis of "La Jaula de Oro," José David Saldívar draws on George Lipsitz's (1994) concept of "dangerous crossroads" in exploring the space of cultural practice where critical politics and commodity production overlap, or a "space of survival and self respect" in the realm of mass culture "in light of the government's doctrine of low-intensity conflict" (1997: 1). I ask: Do the politics of migrants' expressive cultural production merely hint at or insinuate critiques of power? What of their interaffective attunements? Although he attempts to render the political possibilities between commerce and expressive culture, Saldívar does not ground cultural forms within everyday lives. Such interpretive approaches perform a particular mattering map, where indeed everyday life is worth less (that is, occupies a subordinate role in analysis), in spite of Saldívar-inspired claims that "Chicana/o cultural studies actively launches a protracted struggle for alternative culture, representation, social justice, and equality" (Chabram-Dernersesian 2006: 3).[9] What is at stake to be lost within cultural studies projects that privilege the metaphorical borderlands at the expense of the material conditions of bordered lives and the border itself? We "[empty] the border of its political significance" (Rosas 2012: 150) and thereby lose the impact of multivoiced entries into imagining other experiences than our own in order to envision the problem at hand, or the everyday impacts of oppression (political, material, or ideological). For it is within and in between the current political lexicon of neoliberal governance, war, and virulent racism that we can and ought to locate the conjunctures that allow us to see how exactly it is that communities in transition defiantly build themselves and, in the process, map what matters.

HOME

Places, feelings, people thrown together are what become moments. These cultural productions fade and linger, always retaining an active tethering to adjacent and unfolding moments, a palimpsest dense with meanings—inseparable, ongoing, past and present. The same is true for spaces that also serve as bridges, vessels for connecting the experiences of people who are traveling on long paths, to and from. Doña Rosa's home is one such bridge. You can almost tell from the smells alone . . . simmering cow stomach, pungent onion, cleaning chemicals, traces of perfume, candle wax, dirt from outside, sweat on bodies . . . a comingling of sensory traces that explain how people come in and out of this place, full of desire and memories, bringing with them the places they've been and imaginings of where they're going.

"Tengan muchachos, me acaba de llegar este quesito de Rioverde." (Here you go boys, this cheese just came in from Rioverde.) Doña Rosa hands us a plate of bean-and-cheese tacos, the cheese courtesy of a family friend who recently returned from Rioverde, San Luis Potosí. Senovio, Graciano, Valentín, Homero, Xavi, and I are all gathered at her home. We eat, chat, and serenade her at her behest. Doña Rosa is the unrivaled matriarch of her home, which she works out of as a *cocinera* (cook). Every day she labors at preparing large meals for clients' celebrations and gatherings (quinceañeras, weddings, birthday parties, baptisms). She makes mole, rice, beans, *asado de Puerco* (pork in red chile), *ensaladas* (salads), and more, and on the weekends folks stop in to buy freshly made menudo straight out of her kitchen. Adelaida R. Del Castillo suggests that women like Doña Rosa and their transnational homes "assist in the creation of community through the use and maintenance of sociocultural patterns of interaction based on the social networks of the sending community" (2007: 99). I couldn't agree more. In part, Doña Rosa's occupation affords her a degree of economic independence, which elevates her status within the home and reinforces her role as a mediator between distant communities and the social lives of those who travel between them. Her home serves as a haven for border crossers (many of whom happen to be musicians) traversing the I-35 corridor—not an easy task. Her home is a crucial place for those who need somewhere to stay, rest, eat, and acquire information about jobs or the whereabouts of friends and family.

Originally from San Luis Potosí, Doña Rosa was mainly raised in the municipality of Victoria, Guanajuato, not too far from Xichú. The small mountain community where she grew up, she boasts, hosted big fiestas navideñas that drew everyone from the surrounding rural area.

> Ahí en la punta del cerro haz de cuenta que hay una explanada grandota y ahí se hace la fiesta. Hay música y todo. Bien bonito que se pone cada año. . . . Hay comida para toda la gente que vaya. Ahí la comida la hacen mis tías. Toda la gente que va de la familia, porque somos mucha familia, entre todas cocinan, para atender a toda la gente que vaya. Ahí no importa te conozcan o no te conozcan, ahí se le da de comer a toda la gente.

> (There on the top of the hill imagine a big plateau, and that's where they have the fiesta. There is music and everything. It's very nice every year. . . . There is food for all the people who go. My aunts make the food. Everyone from the family who goes, because we are a large family, they all cook in order to feed all the people who go. It doesn't matter if people know you or if they don't, everyone is fed.)

She carries this generosity and conviviality with her; they are intimately present in her Central Texas home, which people, friends, and strangers travel in and out of. She arrived in the United States in the mid-1990s and immediately began laboring as a domestic worker—cleaning houses, cleaning and caring for children, mainly. That same year she and Senovio met and fell in love at a performance by Guillermo Velázquez and Los Leones de la Sierra de Xichú in downtown Austin, no less. Los Leones had been invited to play a fund-raiser for a San Luis Potosí HTA:

> Yo lo conocí [Senovio] en un baile de Guillermo Velázquez y ese mismo día que lo conocí, ese día nos juntamos. Era una presentación de don Guillermo por la "Congress." Yo me vine del trabajo. Pues yo trabajaba en una casa, limpiaba una casa, cuidaba los niños y ahí me quedaba. Pedí permiso para venir y me vine al baile y lo conocí [Senovio] y ya no volví ni al trabajo, ni a la casa, ni nada. Ya tenemos desde ese entonces.

(I met him [Senovio] at a Guillermo Velázquez dance, and we got together the same day I met him. It was at a performance by don Guillermo on Congress Avenue. I came from work. Well, I was a housekeeper; I cleaned the house, I took care of the children, and I lived there. I asked permission to go to the dance, and I met him [Senovio], and I never went back to work, not to the house, nothing. We've been together since.)

As she explains, Senovio, who's sitting nearby, has a giant smile across his face. While Doña Rosa's husband and family are now firmly settled in the United States, her journey was difficult. She tells of how she left home against her mother's wishes. By that time they were no longer living in Victoria, having moved to San Ciro de Acosta, San Luis Potosí, for work:

Yo era la que siempre le hacía de cenar—le llevaba de cenar a la cama en su cuarto donde estaba viendo su novela. Le hice de cenar . . . pero yo ya sabía que yo me iba venir de escondidas. Me bañé, me puse dos pantalones escondí la chamarra . . . en unas matas de limón grandotas. . . . Le llevé de cenar a mi mamá y le dije, "mami, no hay pan; voy a ir a comprar pan, ahorita regreso." "Sí," me dice, "nomás no te tardes porque luego te pones a platicar con tus amigas y no llegas." Pero yo ya sabía que era para venirme. Y sí, me vine rapidito porque ya el autobús estaba ahí, el que venía a Rioverde. . . . Agarré el autobús a Rioverde y de Rioverde me vine. Pero antes le dejé una carta a ella diciéndole que me iba venir, que no se preocupara. . . . Se la dejé con una amiga, pero que no se la entregara ese día hasta el otro día que yo ya viniera para acá.

Yo camine dos días y dos noches. . . . Veníamos diez y ocho personas—dos mujeres y puros hombres. Ya cuando cruzamos ahí se quedó la otra muchacha. Ya de ahí para acá ya nomás era yo de mujer. . . . Llegamos llenos de garrapatas. Encontramos víboras, de esos puerco jabalinas. . . . Yo me acuerdo bien clarito que venía un muchachito de catorce años—él ya no podía. Él ya decía que lo dejaran en el monte. Ya bien ampollado él ya no podía caminar. Y yo le decía, "No te vas a quedar, nos vamos a ir todos." Yo me venía mero atrás con el. Todos caminando y yo mero atrás con él muchachito. . . . Gracias a Dios sí llegamos todos. Nos levantaron en una Suburban a todos y nos llevaron a Houston. Llegamos a unos apartamentos—nos metieron a todos en un cuarto y yo era la única mujer, puros hombres. Y si ya te digo, yo me aventuré bien a venirme caminando. Es bien difícil venirse uno así caminando. Mucha gente ya vez cuántos no se mueren en el camino—ve uno muchas cosas.

(I was the one who always made supper for my mother—I would bring her dinner to her bedroom where she was watching her soap opera. [That night] I made her dinner . . . but I knew that I was going to sneak off. I showered, put on two pairs of pants; I hid my jacket in the big lemon trees out front. . . . I took her dinner and I told her, "Mommy, we don't have any bread; I'm going to buy bread, I'll be back shortly." "Okay," she said, "just don't be too long because I know how you get to chatting with your friends." But I knew I was going to come [to the United States]. And yeah, I left quickly because the bus was there, the one headed to Rioverde. . . . I caught the bus to Rioverde, and from Rioverde I came. But before I left, I left her a letter telling her that I was coming to the United States and for her not to worry. . . . I left it with a friend but told her not to deliver it that day, but the day after, once I was well on my way.

I walked two days and two nights. . . . There were eighteen people—two women and the rest were men. As soon as we crossed, the other girl stayed behind at the border. From that point on I was the only woman. . . . We got full of ticks. We found snakes and those javelina pigs. . . . I remember very clearly that there was a fourteen-year-old boy in the group—he wasn't going to make it. He was telling us to leave him in the brush. His feet were blistered and he couldn't walk. And I said, "You're not staying, we're all going to make it." I walked with him at the back of the group. . . . Thank God we made it. We were picked up by a Suburban and they took us to Houston. We arrived at some apartments—they put us all in a room, and I was the only woman in a room full of men. And yeah, I tell ya, I took my chances crossing. It's very difficult crossing the border walking. A lot of people, you know, a lot of people die—you see a lot of things.)

The things she doesn't say are palpable. Without assuming what her silences entail, we know her story is one of trauma and a great deal of fear. "You see a lot of things" is ambiguous, referring to the things that are either unspoken or forgotten, a refusal to label moments like surviving the brush, walking on difficult terrain, saving someone's life, being the only woman among strangers, experiencing the feelings associated with leaving her mother. Her story is hers—to tell or not, to feel or not. She was twenty-two. She desired economic and social independence, and migration was the answer, despite the dangers involved. At the time of this telling, sixteen years had passed, and her family and home were of her own making in Central Texas. She works, sends her children to school, pays her bills, and goes about daily life without hesitation, but she is not naive about the dangers that still loom.

In Patricia Zavella's chapter "The Divided Home" (in her book published in 2011), she argues that ethnographic research is uniquely poised to show that "economic, political, or social dislocation often disrupt[s] family life, especially for the poor" (157). Here family is the key ideological construct within which social control, surveillance, and struggles take place, but it is simultaneously a refuge from externally imposed tensions. Stories like Doña Rosa's help illustrate these tensions. Doña Rosa shares the story as her husband, Senovio, sits by her side. They hold hands. The trauma of those crossings is something they carry together, but there is also hope here. After all, she and Senovio met in the United States, they have their family here, and their home is always open to those who need it. Thus, the residues of recent crossings are often present on those who travel through their home, a welcoming space amid the uncertainty or a refuge after a tragic journey. There is no way to boil down the complexity of their stories and their lives into a single running thread of an emotion, melancholy, or any other pathos.

On this occasion, we've gathered at her home for an early evening *travesiada* (informal jam session). Graciano, Senovio, and Homero just got off from work. Xavi is passing through and staying the night (recently arrived from Mexico). And I received the call to head over just as I was leaving the university. I arrived and joined the group gathered outside under her carport. A few minutes later, Valentín drives up and makes his way over, visibly limping. Xavi asks, "Pues que le paso?" (What happened to you?). Valentín launches into an elaborate and entrancing story: "No creé, andaba en el jale y que me dejé caer de donde estaba descargando piedra pa' echarme a correr. Nomás de repente vi que corrían los demás y los seguí! Yo ni cuenta porque corrían pero ahí iba yo." (You won't believe it. I was at work and I leapt from where I was unloading stone so that I could run. I just saw everyone else run and I followed. I had no idea why they were running, but there I was.) I ask, "Y eso?" (And that?). He shrugs, "Según gritaron que era la migra. Y yo que me dejo caer y que me voy lastimando la pierna. Mire nomás!" (Supposedly it was ICE. I leapt down and hurt my leg. Would you look at that!). In this moment there was an odd connection between information elicited (in the course of an interview, for instance) and the way things play out in everyday life. These moments erupt in seemingly banal passages of conversation that are densely occupied with the politics of belonging. In this moment I'm everything but an ethnographer, and I remember the fears and violence experienced by my own family members—entering places of work nervously, ducking down in the back seat of a car, making sure to speak in your best English when approached by strangers. Despite the contingencies of living in response to the migra, these migrants continue as they are, doing what they do.

Many of these musicians travel back and forth between Mexico and the United States in varying capacities; some reside primarily in the United States and periodically visit Mexico, others vice versa. For many who scrape by working low-wage jobs in the United States, playing music helps supplement their income, while others in Mexico make their living primarily through playing music. Yet, no matter the capacity in which they engage in either music or work, these *common* acts of everyday social life play out in spaces like Doña Rosa's home, a mattering map in and of itself with wildly extensive clusters of vectors bridging all the places of the people who come through. This evening she directs the musicians, asking for this song, that huapango, a valona. Her eyes laughing, she reminds me, "Me gusta la música a mi de corazón. Mi viejo lo sabe. Si se la pasaran tocando aquí día y noche, yo anduviera bailando." (I love this music. My husband knows it. If you all played here day and night, I'd be dancing just the same.) She's emplaced—huapango around her, calling out to her. This is home. She directs, and Valentín massages his painful leg from time to time. "Por el temor que uno les tiene [la migra]" (All because one fears them [ICE]). He shakes his head, tips his sombrero back, and begins to sound the next huapango on his violin. Doña Rosa feigns a dance step as she stands up, circles the musicians, and walks out into the dusty yard. Another car just pulled up. She waves and invites them in.

HUAPANGO WITHOUT BORDERS

Es el primer festival
en los Estados Unidos
en Austin, la capital
nos encontramos reunidos
y a todos hay que llevar
por éste sean bienvenidos

———

It's the first [huapango] festival
in the United States
in Austin, the [state] capital
we find ourselves gathered

and we must bring along everyone
this one [musician] welcomes you

—Zeferino, Austin, Texas

The sizable community of people and musicians from Guanajuato, San Luis Potosí, and Querétaro located in Central Texas and Mississippi has been practicing huapango arribeño at a grassroots level since the 1990s, and they recently organized an all-day festival. The event hosted dozens of huapango arribeño and huasteco musicians, and over a thousand people attended—Zeferino's improvised verse above sets the stage for this unprecedented gathering. From two in the afternoon until two in the morning, ensembles took turns performing short huapango sets while the audience packed the dance floor. The event was held at a ballroom on the outskirts of town, a relatively isolated spot that is well known as a destination for entertainment. The day of the festival, street food vendors set up tents and fryers in the afternoon heat, children overwhelmed the bounce houses, and families occupied the tables inside, covered with rented white linens. As the sun set, the ballroom filled up as huapangos and poetry steadily rang out. Despite the trapped heat inside, people danced, their bodies drenched with sweat, all awaiting the moment when a mini-topada would occur between Flavio and Xavi.

In the final stages of their efforts, I was asked to join the organizing committee, symbolically more than anything else, but a request I was humbled by, nonetheless. As part of my participation, I was also asked to perform with my huapango huasteco counterparts from the Midwest. We played two brief sets and waited for the topada, which finally came—the entire gathering headed out onto the dance floor, hollering at the verses and saludados, exhausted from the heat but still taking spin after spin on the dance floor. It's a lot like in Guanajuato or San Luis Potosí or Querétaro, but here people dance in a circle, a slow-moving herd, Texas-Mexican style. This way of dancing is typically adopted by migrants in many musical contexts. I recall this being the case in my childhood; at quinceañeras and weddings, migrants danced counterclockwise à la Tejano, but with no Tejanos in sight. You can see all the dancers pass by once, twice, three times. Anyone not dancing is watching them go around. Stomping, moving, stomping, spinning—zapateado meets *taquachito*.[10]

The weight of this gathering comes into relief if we consider the atmosphere within which it is taking place, indeed the border politics experienced by Doña Rosa and the experiences she discloses—a story that regularly finds itself told through huapango arribeño poetics. But in this moment nothing matters but the moment itself, a story in itself. Flavio digs into a decimal.

QUE SE ESCUCHE EL DECIMAL
AHORITA INMEDIATAMENTE
SALUDOS PARA ESTA GENTE
INICIANDO EL FESTIVAL

(1) Hablando con frenesí
y cada quien habla lo suyo
a mí por cierto es orgullo
el haber llegado aquí
de mi parte digo así
y hago este memorial
contemplándolo legal
no existe ningún pretexto
el público está dispuesto
QUE SE ESCUCHE EL DECIMAL

(2) El tiempo lo amerita
es cierto, ¿quien dijo no?
pos Graciano nos invitó
a esta fiesta tan bonita
gracias a la fe bendita
de mi parte muy consciente
con cariño evidente
de mi parte el palabrear
en el viento ha de quedar
AHORITA INMEDIATAMENTE

(3) Con gusto placentero
mis versos son bendecidos
y a todos mis amigos
los saluda este versero
felicitarlos es lo que quiero
organizadores igualmente
yo lo digo atentamente
buscando los acomodos
y saludándolos a todos
SALUDOS PARA ESTA GENTE

(4) Nuestros compañeros
siempre, siempre complaciendo

y la gente lo está viendo
ahorita en estos senderos
porque somos huapangueros
de grupo musical
es un día especial
les dedico mis versitos
saludos a todititos
INICIANDO EL FESTIVAL

———

MAY THE DECIMAL BE HEARD
IMMEDIATELY, IN THIS MOMENT
GREETINGS TO THESE PEOPLE
AS THE FESTIVAL BEGINS

(1) I speak passionately
and everyone speaks as they will
as for me, I am proud
to have arrived here
I say this on my behalf
and I craft this memorial
contemplating it legally
there is no excuse
for the public is willing
MAY THE DECIMAL BE HEARD

(2) Time has warranted it [the festival]
it is true, who said no?
Graciano invited us
to this beautiful festivity
thanks to our blessed faith
and consciously on my behalf
I say this carefully
as I search for the right words
and greetings to all of you
IMMEDIATELY, IN THIS MOMENT

(3) With a pleasurable joy
my verses are blessed
and to all my friends

this verse maker greets you
I want to congratulate you
likewise I cheer the organizers
with obvious affection
the words on my behalf
will be left to the wind
GREETINGS TO THESE PEOPLE

(4) Our compañeros are
always, always at your disposal
and the people are seeing this
right now on these paths
because we are huapangueros
of a musical group
it is a special day
I dedicate to you my little verses
greetings to everyone
AS THE FESTIVAL BEGINS

Flavio's decimal nods to the people, relationships, and histories that have made the festival possible. Though the occasion is the festival, there is also a subcommentary on the very existence of huapango arribeño in the United States, its lack of borders, its transnational unfolding, the ways it has convened communities across geographies for years. Because this festival is a pinnacle of the genre's existence in that part of Texas, indeed throughout the South, as it has drawn groups from Tennessee, Mississippi, and other states, there is a sense of urgency. There is an importance to the textualization of the moment as an immediate and fleeting memorial, ready to be imprinted and retold.

Again, Grossberg (1996) introduces spatiality as a corrective to the time-based modernist construction of identity that has been considered in these pages. I have considered spatiality ethnographically with attention to what I term *aural poetics*, a relational process of sonic enactment and reception that makes the other present, that builds intimacy, that travels, that crosses. In doing so, I have employed the tools of linguistic analysis, particularly the work of Mikhail Bakhtin (1981). And Bakhtin too is perhaps another point of departure, certainly for Félix Guattari's own theorizing around subjectivity. While Grossberg's spatial envelope—the mattering map—is useful, Guattari's engagement with Bakhtin takes us even further in imagining the living social exchange in the construction of subjectivity. In other words, Guattari understands subjectivity as a coming together of a set of heterogeneous, plural, and polyphonic registers in productive relation. This understanding requires an analytical move beyond traditional binary interpretive structures and toward an ethico-aesthetic paradigm—"either we objectify, reify, 'scientifise' subjectivity, or, on the contrary, we try to grasp it in the dimension of its processual creativity," which involves attention to intersubjective linguistic relations, as well as the "incorporeal Universes of reference such as those relative to music" (Guattari 1995: 13, 9). With this in mind, huapango arribeño embodies a tensive mediation as an indispensible meeting ground for the aesthetic and highly public elaboration of experience. Its performance is contingent on a dynamic and polyphonic exchange between public and individual lives. It is made legible and connective in this way, for only through the space of a shifting social imaginary does it become seductive, confessional, arresting, evocative, inspiring, vulnerable, nervous, sobering, wistful, and euphoric. In these ways, performance takes hold as a transformative force, as an element that contributes to the shared stories of migrant lives, with those stories then taking on a life of their own in the moment of their aesthetic voicing, touching those present, washing over their dancing bodies. Stories—now a bundle of music and poetics—tremble beneath the skin as layers of tone and timbre build and fold in on themselves, pulling back tightly, spreading out, only to build and release again, like so many waves, stirring a sense of elation.

Caught within this dramatic dispersal are the people themselves, those who simultaneously produce and receive this "narrated world" (Stewart 1996: 181)—both practitioner and audience—their lives now transformed through a living (musical and discursive) poetics that places everyone inside the story itself: a vertigo of narrative, encounter, and embodiment. Embryonic thoughts become artistic form—elements centrally emergent from experience, which is itself constituted by overlapping forms of sociality. And here we arrive at the resonance of music and poetics, at that which makes performance *moving*—the density of lived life.[11] It is the shared and aesthetically voiced experience of clandestine border crossings, the intimate conviviality after a hard day's work, the unthinkable shock of a loved one's death, the grueling journey from the rural Sierra Gorda to Mexico City for work and then the journey back again. It's battling cancer, picking up the pieces after Hurricane Katrina, getting drunk and dancing alone for no particular reason, waiting for the weekly phone call from a loved one or relative en el otro lado. It's lives dedicated to the musical and poetic craft of huapango arribeño as a calling—el destino. These shared experiences are commonplace among huapangueros and the audiences for whom they perform. The work of huapangueros is that of translating this polyphonic connectivity, transforming it into a story, generating a new shared experience (through performance) in which everyone present is bound up together in the same interpretational space of living in that moment (of performance)—a cultural dialogics of self-authorization that emplaces lives in relation to others no matter where they are, irrespective of borders, refusing nationalist rationalities that reduce personhood, that dictate where home is, that tell "others" that they don't belong aquí (here).

Flavio's decimal reveals precisely this; it reveals how he felt in that moment, the need to both stay true to the genre and offer a testimonial suitable for the evening, something meaningful. So there's a weight to the line "contemplating it legally" that expresses a sentiment of precision, abiding by the tradition set forth by those who have come before and attending to the needs of huapango itself. He's saying he's going to do it by the book. At the same time, he offers a slight gesture toward the reality of migration as part of the daily lives of all in the room when he says "right now on these paths." While subtle, the nod signifies that all who are present are on paths that have led them to this moment, and they have arrived here and now. It's a similar sentiment to a line by Graciano in chapter 4: that we who are present have "made our way to this place." This type of announcement of everyone being present is a way of extending el destino to the audience, who are part of the calling during the performance. Further, huapango has arrived, crossed the border and made its way to this place. There's a complete embrace of that moment and place that invites all participants to make it their own, an embrace that must be heard . . .

HOMECOMING

I recently visited the home of my grandfather, Mauro, for the first time in many years, where I sat and drank pulque with my uncle Adrian. I searched for Mauro, though he's long been gone, visiting different homes perched along the fertile mountainsides, finally arriving at his old place. Adrian has taken up residence there. He plays and sings too, and his guitar hangs alongside dozens of pairs of huaraches, which he makes and sells. There are piles of bundled papers withering from the humidity like beds of *hojarasca* (fallen leaves), as well as dusty stacks of vinyl records, seemingly undisturbed for decades; there is no sign of a record player. I came to ask him about Mauro's journals, which passed into my possession. Mauro was unlettered, though an immeasurably talented lyricist, and he had his children write down his poetry for him in different styles of handwritten scrawl. I thought that by learning who scribed for him I could envision how he composed and how he translated happenings, events, and people into décimas, crafting stories that transcended place as they were told and retold during topadas and performances throughout the Sierra Gorda.

I hold Mauro's journals in my hands, bound in red leather, with items tucked in here and there. I carefully wrap them in cloth. I pass from place to place. And I think of my Aunt Susanna, who wrote down many of the lyrics her father, Mauro, dreamed up . . .

DE ESOS TIEMPOS YO ME HE DE ACORDAR
DE LOS AÑOS QUE TANTO HE SUFRIDO
YA ME CANSO DE TANTO CANTAR
POR LA FUERZA, SERÍA MI DESTINO

Recuerdo del año once
la fecha en que yo nací
todavía existo por aquí
recordando desde entonces
cuando el peso era de bronce
no es mentira, ni es hablar
cuando se ganaba un real
no traíamos ni sombrero
nada más los ricos tenían dinero:
DE ESOS TIEMPOS YO ME HE DE ACORDAR

No traíamos ni calzones
nada más con un braguerito
sin huaraches, descalcitos
¡ah, que tristes situaciones!
yo he visto que en ocasiones
que esos tiempos tal vez volverán
de eso me pongo a pensar
y del año dieciocho para acá
una cruel calamidad:
DE ESOS TIEMPOS YO ME HE DE ACORDAR

Recuerdo de aquellos días
la fecha se me ha grabado
cuando mi padre tomó armas y fue soldado
tiempos de Porfirio Díaz

fue un gobierno de energía
los mandaba encarcelar
con leyes de fusilar
fue un hombre asesino y cruel
treinta años duró en el poder:
DE ESOS TIEMPOS YO ME HE DE ACORDAR

———

THOSE TIMES I SHALL REMEMBER THEM SO
OF THE YEARS THAT I SUFFERED SO MUCH
I'VE NOW GROWN TIRED OF SO MUCH SINGING
BUT THIS STRENGTH, IT WOULD BE MY CALLING

I remember the year 1911
the date on which I was born
I'm still around to this day
remembering since then
when the peso was made of bronze
it's no lie, it's not hearsay
it was so when you earned a wage
but we didn't even have a sombrero
only the rich had money:
THOSE TIMES I SHALL REMEMBER THEM SO

We didn't have underwear
only a little truss
without huaraches, barefooted
oh, what unfortunate situations
I've felt on certain occasions
that such times will perhaps return
I begin to think about that
and of 1918 onward
what a cruel calamity
THOSE TIMES I SHALL REMEMBER THEM SO

I remember those days
the date ingrained in my memory
when my father took up arms and became a soldier
the times of Porfirio Díaz
his was a powerful government

he would incarcerate at will
with the mandate of execution
he was a murderer, a cruel man
for thirty years he was in power:
THOSE TIMES I SHALL REMEMBER THEM SO

Mauro remembers the tumultuous years of his childhood—the legacy of the Porfiriato, the chaos of the Revolution, extreme poverty and violence—those most powerful experiences that shaped him. I can almost hear the verses he wrote in my head, and I can hear how he might have performed them. Susanna told me that I play guitarra quinta like him; my strumming style is a mirror of his. His timbre lives on as a story in her, as a style in me, so she tells me. To this day, she herself performs sacred songs at funeral wakes and velaciones for patron saints, and perhaps her voice rings out like his—the same songs, different throats, a palimpsest of meanings, timbres, recollections that evoke, shift, connect. And along the way, the places connected are configured by and through experiences inscribed onto the body—she is a child of the Querétaro mountains, once a site of ruthless Revolutionary violence. The unfulfilled legacy of the Revolution is still felt given the widespread poverty in that rural area, as in many across Mexico, the reason her own son tried crossing the border a few years back and drowned in the Rio Grande. "He had a scar on his lip," she tells me; it was the only way she knew with certainty that the bloated body sent back to Querétaro was indeed her son's. I never met him. In fact, it's only been in recent years that I've grown close to this side of my family. Nevertheless, these stories have come to live viscerally in me.

The body is an archive of memories and provides a forum for the critical production of countergeographies; as argued in the previous chapter, language always *takes place somewhere*, occurring in specific social and spatial contexts and likewise carrying senses of place in the communication itself, for the stories that rise up from this place or any place don't necessarily refer to a description of some nostalgic landscape, yet the place permeates the stories that pass through it by necessity, traveling across distances, the same distances people both live and die across. Necessity comes from the acts of living and the ways people are bound to each other, the necessity also of saying what needs to be said. Thus, it seems that a surmounting or crossing of some kind is always taking place (and it should now be clear that I mean *taking place* in the most literal sense). Indeed, the crux of my argument regarding the politics of huapango arribeño lies in the interruption and resumption of intimacy, abruptly, poetically, in place, and as sung in the verses shared throughout. How dehumanizing logics attempt to sever intimacy and how it is often regained by those reduced to a faceless mass, by people who actively voice, reinforce, and call out for that intimacy, recuperating and reinscribing it into their own life paths—building bridges. In the United States, for instance, at its core, the underprivileging of people of color has to do with the idea that they (we) do not deserve intimacy, or that they (we) can serve the state better, be better laborers, without it. Think about everything regulated for or against people of color, migrants in particular—communicating, occupying public space, and more, all those channels through which we enact senses of intimacy—meaning that the viscosity of race and politics (Saldanha 2007) severs intimacy at the political level and denies the formation of meaningful communities. We are drops of water falling apart (a connection with others denied by the border, or by the policing of subjects to such an extent that people can only be at home or at work, for fear of being captured), but at the embodied level of race, the stories that are told bind people together into a torrent, a river, a pool . . .

While writing this book, I learned that Senovio, the huapanguero and husband of Doña Rosa, had passed on suddenly from cancer. Graciano wrote a poesía to honor him:

NUNCA VAMOS A OLVIDAR
LA VIDA DE JUAN SENOVIO
VOY HACER UN TESTIMONIO
QUE DEBEMOS RECORDAR

Dios le otorgaría sus dones,
músico y trabajador
en la fiesta, en la labor
guerrero de mil acciones
en la chamba, en tradiciones
no se le pudo tachar
y como queriendo jugar
con la guitarra y martillo
fue un hombre que tuvo brillo:
NUNCA VAMOS A OLVIDAR

Atento con el Creador
siendo su fe poderosa

se casó, tuvo su esposa
sus hijos, su gran amor
su vida era un resplandor
¿quién se podía imaginar?
que un torbellino al pasar
dejaría estragos y más
y ahora descansa en paz:
NUNCA VAMOS A OLVIDAR

———

WE WILL NEVER FORGET
THE LIFE OF JUAN SENOVIO
I AM GOING TO TESTIFY
SO THAT WE MAY REMEMBER

God would give him his talents
as a musician and a hard worker
in festive gatherings, on the job
a warrior of a thousand talents
laboring away, and in huapango
there was no fault in him
and as if he were playing a game
with guitar and hammer in hand
he was a radiant man:
WE WILL NEVER FORGET

Attentive to the Creator
with a powerful faith
he was married, he had a wife
his children were his great love
his life was resplendent
who could imagine
that a maelstrom on having passed
would wreak such havoc and more
and now he rests in peace:
WE WILL NEVER FORGET

Graciano attests to the multiple callings of life, work, and art that defined Senovio. Graciano's poesía is a voicing, a calling out, a declaration, a chronicling, a desire to connect, to invoke, to remember, to not forget, to liberate—a

scream.[12] This is intimacy. It's accepting that a person is gone, yet still desperately needing them with you. It's when upon that realization a sudden swell of warmth and bone-chilling cold wash over you at once—the knot in the back of the throat, dropping down through the bowels when you try to speak, instead gasping aloud in a sound between weeping and laughter. It's what Doña Rosa's tears and voice conveyed when at the festival in Austin the organizers gave her an award of appreciation for everything she and Senovio have done for this community. Without them, this massing of people and musicians in many ways would not have been possible: the years of hospitality, the meals, the friendship, a home. As she hesitantly walked across the stage, she wept in front of the hundreds of onlookers, finally taking the microphone to convey a few words of gratitude through her tears, Senovio's absence palpable.

As I write, I have presented stories imbued with history, culture, and politics in order to put on display the contortions and distortions of a coloniality that has historically denied the agency and subjectivity of "others" as active participants in the making of the world in which they live. True, this book is about Mexicans, about U.S.-Mexico migration, about the border, yet it extends beyond these things into matters of intimacy, sovereignty, and the aesthetic dimensions of contemporary lived politics. For that reason, it is my hope that this book makes points that many can grab onto for their own purposes or can use to initiate practices in the spirit of an alternative politics of an inessential commonality (Agamben 1993). For ethnographers, this requires resisting the ritual of privileging anthropology's own "intellectual" context, which typically devalues the words of others while simultaneously admitting to being educated by their insights. So when an ethnographer asks "Where is your family?" or "Where is your home?," should they not also be asking—and thus understanding—how multiple places matter, how they connect, how home can exist in a person or despite the feeling of being unwanted there.[13]

The desire for home, as a place embedded with family and friends, is part of transnational personhood, and the problematic regulating of where homes and families can be denies the humanity of those who carry a desire, a celebratory sense of being in *common*, and a vital need for the connections that the state and capital work to sever. The poetic echoes of this are—in these final verses—wrapped inside the polyphonic excesses of the tempestuous layerings of jarabes in the offing, coaxed dynamically, linked together, reclaiming home and all it entails, much like the people spoken of, as Graciano claims in Texas:

Yo lo digo sin tristezas
porque lo miro y lo creo
para eso del huapangeo
¡nomás aquí en Dallas, Tejas!

———

I say it without sadness
because I see it and I believe it
in questions of huapango merrymaking
Dallas, Texas, is the place!

And Guillermo Velázquez answers back in Guanajuato . . .

En Tejas hay mucha raza
mexicanos a Dios dar
aquí es casi como andar
en el patio de tu casa

———

There's a lot of *raza* [Mexican folk] in Texas
a bounty of Mexicans
here, it's just like being
on your house patio

A mirror, a bridge, a crossing, a calling . . . These verses create a back-and-forth space of knowing, a map of multiple places that matter in which people and experience flow over both material and cultural borders, interrupting them, moving beyond essentialist assumptions about Mexico and the Mexican, ascribing meanings to movement, suturing subjectivities that are simultaneously en route and emplaced, reflecting both politics and ways of living, affirming social bonds and structures otherwise denied.[14] The simultaneous "here" of both Texas and Mexico relies on the everyday, intimate, and textured presencing of your patio, your house, your home; of companions called out to, and the ubiquitous desire to know them, so that you may know yourself.

THEY DREAMED OF BRIDGES

El huapango arribeño sirve como un encuentro con el terruño. . . .
Es un puente frente a la incertidumbre de la migración . . .
(Huapango arribeño serves as an encounter with home. . . .
It is a bridge amid the uncertainty of migration . . .)
—ISAÍAS, VICTORIA, GUANAJUATO

It is about intimacy, a desire for life between all of us . . .
—CHERRÍE L. MORAGA, *I HAVE DREAMED OF A BRIDGE*

On his visit to Latin America in late spring in 2013, President Barack Obama gave a highly optimistic—and highly criticized—speech in Mexico, praising its economic prosperity and the strength of its democracy. Addressing a crowd of largely high school and college students, he spoke of the promise of newly elected Mexican president Enrique Peña Nieto's reformist political agenda and the need for continued transnational economic cooperation with the United States. He emphasized the possibility of achieving these goals by lauding the enduring strength of Mexico's inherited traditions—a long-standing poetics of culture:

> In modern times, Mexico's blend of cultures and traditions found its expression in the murals of Rivera and the paintings of Frida, and the poetry of Sor Juana and the essays of Octavio Paz. And Paz once spoke words that capture the spirit of our gathering here today—in this place that celebrates your past, but which this morning is filled with so many young people who will shape Mexico's future. Octavio Paz said, "Modernity is not outside us, it is within us. It is today and the most ancient antiquity; it is tomorrow and the beginning of the world; it is a thousand years old and yet newborn." . . . You live at the intersection of history that Octavio Paz was referring to.[1]

The place to which President Obama was referring was the iconic courtyard of the Museo Nacional de Antropología, where he delivered his remarks—an appropriate setting that illustrates the nexus of political economy, poetics, and ethnography that undergirds the entirety of this book. Indeed, and perhaps fittingly in the shadows of the custodial institution of Mexican culture, such appeals to the virtues of history and heritage are to be expected as typical public relations protocol in matters of international diplomacy. However, to draw on Paz in articulating a vision for Mexico's future is peculiar, particularly given Paz's treatise on Mexican fatalism. This reliance on a dated cultural narrative, nevertheless, signals the ways in which continued calls for modernity are enabled by primitivist notions of Mexico as stubbornly unmodern.

LISTENING

In a U.S.-Mexico transnational setting, the border between the two countries is axial in a modernist reification in which, according to an evolutionary fantasy, "crossing the border entails crossing from one temporality to another" (Brady 2000: 178). In his work on Nor-tec dance and music among transnational Mexican youth, Alejandro L. Madrid (2008) speaks to this "desire for modernity," as he terms it, where Mexico (as localized or assumed heritage) and the United States (as global and cosmopolitan) are placed in binary opposition—the latter constructed as progressive, and the former as a signifier of cultural stagnation. Similarly, Hillary Parsons Dick explains how political economies of Mexican migrant discourse often establish opposing images of Mexico and the United States, casting the United States as a forward-looking place of opportunity while locating Mexico in "a backward present-past" that is simultaneously home to "positively valued tradition" (2010: 280). While these homegrown perspectives are vernacular in scope, they reflect a broader ideological construction. At a time when 49 percent of the Mexican population is living in poverty, precarious free trade with the United States continues to destabilize the livelihoods of countless Mexicans, and drug cartel violence deeply steeped in a transnational economy is palpably felt, to invoke picturesque cultural images—from murals to tradition—as comforting sources of strength trivializes and conceals how this reality is indeed embedded in the broader project of modernity, now more appropriately an "asymmetrically organized neoliberal globalization" (Rosas 2012: 14).

Appeals to an iconicity of mexicanidad occur regularly and loudly in public forums. And Obama's usage of this aged symbol complex proliferates a "politics of culture" (Briggs 2012) where the referential—ensconced in emblems of tradition assumed to hold a heightened level of meaning—substitutes for the everyday "cultural real" (Stewart 1996). That is, rather than speak about people directly or allow them to speak for themselves, Obama substituted and so reinscribed a patronizing image of ethnic Mexicans as being helplessly entrenched in the past or, rather, at being at the distal edges of empire—an ideological construction central to the material project of global industrial capitalism in this hemisphere (Lugo 2008). Such discursive work veils the contemporary day-to-day of a sluggish transnational economy, the explosion of violence across Mexico, deaths along the border, and the criminalizing of migrant communities in the United States with talk of unfettered free-market prosperity, democracy, and enfranchisement, delivered in the friendly tone of multiculturalism. The "intersection of history" in which Mexicans find themselves, then, is not so much a platitude of progress as an often cold and brutal place. In fact, one student listening in the audience remarked afterward, "What Mexico was [Obama] talking about?"

A related question has loomed throughout this book, particularly in the wake of the presidential election of 2016. At a juncture when the United States is making decisions about immigration reform, when politicians in both countries are rethinking their economic relationship, and when competing public discourses about Mexico are reinforcing divisions along the lines of race, class, gender, and citizenship across the border and back, I too have asked, "What Mexico are people talking about?" In exploring this question, I have turned to the voices of Mexican migrants (however they chose to define their transnational and ethnic-Mexican selves and the places those subjectivities are tethered to).

THE VOICE

Recall the etymology . . . atop the wood. *Huapango* is a designation of place irrespective of geography. It is standing your ground. Making noise. Making sound. Asserting your presence with your body. Huapango is dance music, and it is meant to be listened to and affirmed with the body . . . And in this very definitional sensing of huapango, as danced and heard, rests the reflexivity of performance—as destino, fundamento, reglamento, and otherwise—for huapango's meaning emanates from the perspective of those listening and subsequently dancing. In theorizing around intense moments that magnify these intersubjective dimensions, I have displayed how music is tied to emotion and embodiment, viscerally felt. Once more, situating this multisensual expressivity in everyday life pushed me into moments of encounter—a tensive material connection with others that opened a door for moving beyond the authorial voice, turning instead to an argument for how ethnography is filled up with dialogues that lend themselves as experiences crucial to political evaluation in theory and in practice (Grosz 1994: 94). This ethnographic tracing of embodied modulations from the inside out has enabled a vision of how experience onto and through the body impels personhood beyond dominant logics—beyond those of race and illegality in this case. As I am a child of migrants, the journey presented in these pages has been dauntingly personal. Keith Berry notes, "Exploring the roots of our ethnographic stories means directly and shamelessly studying our personalized relationship to ethnographic research as cultural phenomenon" (2011: 167). For those of us deemed "native anthropologists," this highly personalized dimension of ethnographic immersion is highly political within a postcolonial critical context as we find ourselves engaged in the larger project of decolonizing anthropology—its commonly held and taken-for-granted representations of otherness so endowed with institutional authority (Rosaldo 1989). These circulating forms of often disparaging, damaging, and, more specifically, prejudiced forms of knowledge retain a deep legacy that extends well beyond the academy, which we labor to disarticulate through our scholarship. Thus, in a space of "radical democracy" (Berry 2011), ethnography may grow and branch into new possibilities so that, like huapango arribeño, it may be a calling out, calling forth, calling back, calling to and from. A calling where, like performance, ethnography may take hold as a transformative force, as an element that stories lives: a vertigo of narrative, embodiment, place, and *encounter* (as Isaías voices above) that is always moving, dialogic, intersubjective, and thus attentive to the shifting politics that surround us and the ways we in turn shape them as well.

Indeed, this is how I have come to understand huapango arribeño as ethnography in and of itself, and huapangueros as ethnographers. The experiential/narrative space of huapango is shaped by a methodological and theoretical approach in which the huapangueros I have transcribed are ethnographers, and poesía is ethnography. Of course, this approach requires a rethinking of ethnography as it exists beyond the walls of the academic institution, as something performed in everyday life. There is theoretical support for this everyday approach, particularly in related conceptualizations around the body, place, and time that come from feminist theory (such as Grosz 1994), but these have yet to inform practices of ethnography (deeply enough) across the spectrum of anthropology and related disciplines. While I don't claim to provide new theorizations of some of these themes of performance and social theory (Schutz 1967; Fabian 1983), which have been explained to the point of being obvious (though less commonly practiced), I do claim to be making an attempt at performing the ethnography I argue for, even as I am arguing for it—a bridge between a preset series of themes and problems.[2]

BRIDGING THEORY AND PRACTICE WITH THE BODY

There is a precedent for imagining such connections between theory and practice. In Cherríe Moraga and Gloria Anzaldúa's influential feminist anthology, *This Bridge Called My Back: Writings by Radical Women of Color* (1981), we encounter a poetics of the racialized body.[3] Both describe the unfair and violent (physical and psychic) position that exists as a gap and is filled with bodies intentionally placed in the midst of unresolvable issues like racial, gender, and political inequality. However, Moraga offers her body (her back) as a bridge for the women who are part of the book, saying, "I will lay my body down for that vision" (xix). The passage they create to get past these inequalities, particularly within the white feminism of the day, is not over, by, or around but *through*—accomplished by filling up silences with expressions of cultural feminism, fusing alliances, overcoming differences, and connecting struggles—crossing. The urge to write is as strong for Anzaldúa as the urge for survival—"there is no separation between life and writing"—and so she has the sense that she is writing with her blood, with her body (170). The artistic labor of those who populate these pages, whose bodies cross the threshold of the U.S.-Mexico border, they too dream of and build bridges; the gap is consciously filled by the desiring body calling out to exceed its racialized, gendered, and unauthorized status and thus return to a humanizing sense of self, enacting connections. Isaías's words, which I open with, convey as much: "Huapango arribeño serves as an encounter with home. . . . It's a bridge amid the uncertainty of migration." It claims a place because it connects with others, it crosses. The sentiment of performing as flesh and discerning the matter of living itself is evoked by Moraga and Anzaldúa, and huapangueros do much the same because they choose to bridge and cross the tensive social location they share with the communities for which they perform—the uncertainties, the violence, the intimacy desired. Indeed, subaltern identities exist between competing authenticated identities—they inhabit a third space, in the words of Homi K. Bhabha. Though much has been made of the space of liminality that borderlands theory identifies, its most significant contribution is how bridging collapses third spaces—which might otherwise convey the sense of dwelling—by crossing into generative sites that escape oppositional frames: others *live on* (the border). To dwell on the in-betweenness is to edge close to a sort of essentialism. So we might do better by imagining, instead of a condition, a becoming, or, in other words, the constant mobility of crossing, much as time itself is always a movement. Amalia Pallares writes of recent migrant activists, "Through tangling, intersecting, and *crossing* as they embody and perform the family, undocumented immigrant activists are both relying on existing forms of worthiness and creating new ones. In doing this, they are engaging in *a politics of motion* that enables the creation of a new space where there was not one, in their ever-present quest for *voice* and agency" (2014: 139; emphasis added).

LIFE BETWEEN ALL OF US

Guillermo Velázquez, who has appeared regularly throughout this book, has become like a bridge between places. He feels a calling to extend the practice and music to new audiences, which perhaps most embodies the idea of ethnography as also a kind of translation, retelling and using narrative as a way to move between times and places. He wants people everywhere to know about the happenings of the present and past in Mexico, the struggles of workers and migrants, and the tradition of huapango arribeño itself.[4] In that way, huapango arribeño is both the form and the subject of his ethnographic trade—décimas, both written and improvised, that he records and crosses to perform. Velázquez explains, "La tradición no es una reliquia del pasado, es un expresión del pasado en el presente que imagina el futuro" (Tradition is not a relic of the past; it is an expression rooted in the past in the present that imagines the future).

In this spirit, young Latinas/os throughout the United States, largely ethnic Mexicans, have taken to son jarocho, for instance, as a way of connecting, of voicing their politics through performance. Since 2007 the Fandango Fronterizo has been a way of bridging communities and responding to current immigration policy. At the Tijuana–San Diego crossing, next to the Pacific Ocean, musicians have gathered to play son jarocho while listeners on both sides of the iron bars marking the edges of these nations hold hands and dance as a "demonstration of support and kinship with the people on either side."[5] Simultaneously, in Austin, Texas, musicians have performed in front of the Travis County jail, a place that symbolizes the start of the border because it's the first step for thousands of undocumented migrants in a path of detention and deportation. Music, in these instances, is used as a form of protest to overtly reclaim a sense of humanity, to build connections across walls, and to dream of freedom (Kelley 2003). These protests come in the face of disturbing trends in U.S. immigration policy, including the Republican Party's embrace of Arizona's immigration policies, which some call the Arizonification of America; attacks on ethnic studies in academia, particularly Latina/o studies; the ongoing militarization of the border; the watered-down and expensive temporary citizenship offered to undocumented youth; the imposition of deportation programs as a way of further criminalizing and removing migrants en masse; and the offer of nothing more than second-class citizenship for migrants who manage to receive documentation.

Under the weight of these most challenging moments, Mexican migrants wield what Anzaldúa calls *la facultad*, a survival technique that bridges irreconcilable identities and realms. Therefore, this book examines less those negotiations of complex identities—Mexican or American, documented or undocumented—instead chronicling how migrants acknowledge all of that so that they too may get on with living because they have to. And in those moments of acknowledgement, embodied aesthetic acts animate an unassimilable presence that refuses to negotiate—"¡Aquí estamos y no nos vamos!" This is standing one's ground, asserting presence for its own sake, for one's own sake. Crossing. I echo once more that the undocumented are disqualified from political life in the United States, which paradoxically marks their everyday lives and expressions as the most political. Huapango arribeño *flows* in these moments as a way of giving voice to the connections (with others) that matter most: the "life between all of us," as Moraga claims, irrespective of where people are, where they go, or which people they return to.

To return to the spirit of verses and flows one final time: Guillermo Velázquez improvised the following decimal at a small press conference organized by Graciano leading up to the second annual huapango festival in Austin. During those days heavy rainstorms hit much of Central Texas, flooding surrounding towns and portions of the city of Austin. Velázquez took the opportunity to speak of flooding of another kind. He appropriated this metaphorical language—which when applied to Mexican migration typically bears an alarmist tone—and subverted the ideological constraints of nativist discourse by instead sounding a narrative flow of irrevocable presence, speaking of the rising tide of huapango music, the rivers of poetry, and the flood of people set to congregate in the city for the festival that weekend. Their presence and these sounds, he declared (in a state of emergency), were a force to be reckoned with:

HABRÁ EMERGENCIA MAÑANA
HAY ALERTA EN EL CONDADO
YA AUSTIN SE ENCUENTRA INUNDADO
DE MÚSICA MEXICANA

(1) Si aquí la atmósfera empuña
tormentas que nunca vimos
de donde nosotros venimos
excepto en Ciudad Acuña
ningún desastre rasguña
nuestra patria mexicana
y en cambio en tierra tejana
según datos nada chuecos
de alegres sones huastecos
HABRÁ EMERGENCIA MAÑANA

(2) Y el pronóstico del día
confirmadísimo está
mañana nos lloverá
convivencia y armonía
se verán ríos de poesía
como nunca se han mirado
y entre tablado y tablado
sombreros, botas vaqueras
por huapango sin fronteras
HAY ALERTA EN EL CONDADO

(3) Como algo digno de ver
huracán se avecina
pero no de llanto y ruina
sino de dicha y placer
la gente empieza correr
hacia ese alegre tornado
y ya la alarma ha sonado
y ya está en los noticieros

de músicos huapangueros
YA AUSTIN SE ENCUENTRA INUNDADO

(4) ¿Por qué un fenómeno tal
produce una dicha inmensa?
hay conferencia de prensa
y hay emergencia estatal
porque este hecho cultural
mucho, mucho nos ufana
en este fin de semana
caerá sobre Austin tal cual
un diluvio tal cual
DE MÚSICA MEXICANA

———

THERE WILL BE A STATE OF EMERGENCY TOMORROW
THE COUNTY IS ON HIGH ALERT
FOR AUSTIN FINDS ITSELF FLOODED
WITH MEXICAN MUSIC

(1) If, here, the atmosphere wields
storms the likes of which we've never seen
from where we come from
except perhaps in Ciudad Acuña
no such disaster comes close
to Mexican lands
however, on Texan soil
according to straight-ahead facts
conveyed through sones huastecos
THERE WILL BE A STATE OF EMERGENCY TOMORROW

(2) According to the day's forecast
it is confirmed without a doubt
that tomorrow there will be showers
of conviviality and harmony
rivers of poetry shall be seen
like never before
and in between the tablados
gathered will be cowboy hats and cowboy boots

for huapango without borders

(3) Oh, what a sight to see
a hurricane is looming
but it will not cause tears or ruin
but rather pleasure and joy
and so the people are rushing toward
the cheerful tornado
for the alarm has sounded
and it's all over the news
that scores of huapanguero musicians
ARE FLOODING AUSTIN

(4) Why does such a phenomenon
produce immense joy?
there is a press conference
and there is a statewide emergency
because this cultural event
makes us very, very proud
so on this weekend
a cultural flood will descend
upon Austin
OF MEXICAN MUSIC

There are many ways to view the flows and oscillations central to the border-lands. In this book the border is thought through ideas of place and presencing. If a geographic boundary or border is where a place (and likely multiple places) begins its presencing, then there can be touching between places that aren't adjacent or that don't overlap geographically so much as culturally or poetically. Practices move about with the people who engage in them, transforming along routes, details expressed referentially, pragmatically, in the minutiae of it all, which ultimately are the things that touch, the sounds, verses, and melodies latched on to. Through huapango arribeño this crossing over is made possible via the embodied experience of being in its presence, listening to the lyrical explosion of everyday life. These dense moments, palpably felt on either side, are discursive and aural cartographies, mattering maps, entextualized geographies, and narrative circulations that speak through people and play out through sound. Huapango arribeño is played, voiced, called out. You listen, you listen with your whole body. You latch on. You are present, here and there. The sounds of crossing are your voice and the voices of your family. They are the stories you've heard and told, the improvised poesía sung out that made you cry out. Your longings, your attempts at survival. You claim those sounds, claim some space, and walk across the bridge of your choosing. You bring the places you've called home with you. You've taken the border with you, sometimes on your back; sometimes you heave it around, and sometimes you just dance with it.

In November 2014 a series of seemingly unrelated events played out like a movie . . .

November 20:

On the eve of state-sponsored celebrations of the Mexican Revolution, protests erupt in Mexico in response to the mass kidnapping of male students from the Ayotzinapa Rural Teachers' College, who went missing in Iguala, Guerrero, two months earlier.

The Latin Grammy broadcast in the United States is interrupted by Barack Obama's official announcement of his executive order to prioritize the deportation of felons, not families.

November 24–25:

Nationwide protests break out in the United States in the wake of the announcement that the St. Louis grand jury did not indict police officer Darren Wilson for the fatal shooting of unarmed African-American teenager Michael Brown.

November 28:

A white middle-aged man, apparently motivated by anti-immigrant sentiment, opened fire on a federal courthouse and the Mexican consulate in Austin, Texas.

The soundtrack to this swirl of protest, politics, and violence, for me, took the unexpected form of a familiar song performed live on November 11 as part of the HBO-sponsored Veterans Day "Concert for Valor" on the National Mall. Against the backdrop of the United States' military involvement in the Middle East, this celebrity-infused spectacle was, among many other things, a highly public celebration of a neocolonial military-industrial complex. And perhaps this was why my hackles rose as Bruce Springsteen—the blue-collar leftist rocker—took to the stage with a twelve-string steel acoustic guitar in hand for a solo performance. After the deafening sounds of the rock bands that preceded him, Springsteen began plucking out a whining, jagged melody with a glass slide. It wavered atop a droning minor blues chord strummed out once every bar or so. His playing sounded like a dirge to me, and so I listened, not knowing where it was all going.

> Born down in a dead man's town
> The first kick I took was when I hit the ground
> You end up like a dog that's been beat too much
> Till you spend half your life just covering up

The violence of the opening lines drew me in. Images of Michael Brown's lifeless body and the forty-three students in Mexico flashed in my mind. I could almost see them (lying) there . . . But it was the chorus that shook me, as Springsteen's gravelly voice whispered a familiar refrain: "I was born in the U.S.A." Bearing no resemblance to the original, this dissonant version tugged at a corner in my mind. I recall hearing this song a thousand times as a child of the 1980s, but for the first time in my life, I listened . . .

Released in 1984 at the height of the Reagan era, "Born in the U.S.A." was intended as a social commentary on the hardships working-class Vietnam War veterans faced on their return from that conflict. Vietnam, Jefferson R. Cowie and Lauren Boehm (2006) suggest, served as a gloss for the social and economic siege of American blue-collar communities at the dawn of the 1980s. Although Springsteen intended this as a song of protest, there is a sonic irony here, for the haunting realism of his verses was regrettably silenced by the thunderous jingoism of "born in the U.S.A." Given its pop sensibility, the anthemic chorus always struck me as a facile sonic nationalism of the lowest common (musical) denominator, akin to Neil Diamond's "America" (released four years earlier). Springsteen's fist pumping embodied a certain white nationalism that I could not relate to as a U.S.-born child of Mexican migrants, nor did I want to. You see, I always mistook it for a full-throated patriotism, which aroused no such emotion in me.

It took me thirty years to listen past Springsteen's raucous refrain. And in light of the events of that November, I concluded that the song's deafness to race, in favor of a precarious working-class identity, was perhaps why I never heard the words of protest that anticipate the refrain's arrival each and every time. I suspect those in attendance in D.C. also came to this realization. They too listened to this sparse rendition amid the politics of the day. They took in the underlying message and critique. They booed in response. They'd been duped, it seems. Critical politics had no place amid the celebration of empire.

The force of this new verse melody, which now overpowered the whimper of a chorus, snagged at my ears in those tumultuous days. I listened intently to the story and the places spoken of through the sonic envelope of race and state violence, something Springsteen had accomplished on his release *The Ghost of Tom Joad* (1995) with specific reference to Mexican immigration, no less. All the same, the poetics of "a dead man's town," "a foreign land," and "the U.S.A." were radically amplified, and I heard it speak of the rampant extralegal killing of black and brown bodies like "dogs"; the ideological entrenchment of Latina/o "foreignness" amid legalized racial profiling in the wake of anti-immigrant legislation, including the Justice Department's guidance on racial profiling, which excludes the hundred-mile strip just north of the U.S.-Mexico border; and, finally, the fraught promise of the "U.S.A.," whose segregationist border politics police Mexican bodies, even as the expanding transnational economic integration with Mexico fuels the drug war's violence implicated in the events in Iguala.

Listening to the underlying *politics of life* in the United States requires "constant interrogation, . . . confrontation with the brutality of my county," Ta-Nehisi Coates (2015: 12) suggests, and this is indeed where this book began, with M. Jacqui Alexander's (2005) belief in the ongoing enterprise of making the world intelligible to ourselves—crossing, always. In my writing, this crossing has required that I transcend the supposedly closed boundaries of the discipline of anthropology, its discourses, its epistemic Western versus non-Western construction. Or, as many of my contemporary anthropologists of color argue, it has required that I engage in the political project of decolonizing anthropology, which necessitates that we recognize the forcible movement of bodies—as slaves, colonial subjects, and laborers—central to the colonial project but also that we too be *moved* by postcolonial struggles for liberation (Allen and Jobson 2016). Both senses are crucial in asserting a double-voicedness necessary to "[exposing] an anthropology that masquerades as objective science while employing [anthropology's] methods of study and analysis toward an ever more robust consideration of our social world" (132).

Beyond telling the story of suffering in a country that outstrips (Robbins 2013), however, decolonizing efforts are equally about loudly voicing stories of intimacy, of struggle, of refusal in the face of the tone-deafness of hate and disembodiment that is born and reborn again and again in the United States. A critical aurality, then, is necessary—an always urgent listening to the whole of America and voicing its story amid the deafening swell of a lethal white supremacy now relegitimized in the wake of the presidential election of 2016: the banning of Muslims, the construction of a "great wall," and the subjection of black lives to the sanctioned violence of "law and order." We listen past the chorus of "U.S.A." and the harmony it presumes—which is braced by a chauvinistic exceptionalism that has no room for *others*—and lend an ear to the multitude of voices whose experiences rest at the tensive center of the verses of the American story, or *versería*, as the huapangueros in this book would say. The struggles and voices of *others* are vital. For in the midst of anxieties, threats, and failures, these loud poetic imaginings, these sounds of crossing *take place* out of necessity, always.

MUSICAL TRANSCRIPTIONS

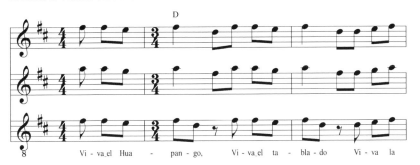

APPENDIX A, EXAMPLE 1 *Poesía planta* "Viva el huapango" by Guillermo Velázquez, from chapter 2

APPENDIX A, EXAMPLE 1 CONTINUED

APPENDIX A, EXAMPLE 2 *Valona* violin *remate*, key of G, from chapter 2

APPENDIX A, EXAMPLE 2 CONTINUED

APPENDIX A, EXAMPLE 3 *Valona* violin *remate,* key of A, from chapter 2

APPENDIX A, EXAMPLE 3 CONTINUED

APPENDIX A, EXAMPLE 4 *Son* "La Rosita Arribeña," key of D, from chapter 2

APPENDIX A, EXAMPLE 4 CONTINUED

APPENDIX A, EXAMPLE 4 CONTINUED

APPENDIX A, EXAMPLE 5 *Jarabe remates,* key of D, from chapter 2

APPENDIX A, EXAMPLE 5 CONTINUED

APPENDIX A, EXAMPLE 6 *Jarabe remates,* key of G with modulation to D, from chapter 2

APPENDIX A, EXAMPLE 6 CONTINUED

APPENDIX A, EXAMPLE 7 *Jarabe remates*, single violin, key of D with modulation to A, from chapter 2

APPENDIX A, EXAMPLE 8 *Jarabe remates,* single violin, key of D with modulation to E, from chapter 2

APPENDIX A, EXAMPLE 9 *Decimal planta* "Es muy poco lo que soy" by Xavi, from chapter 5

APPENDIX A, EXAMPLE 10 Glossed *décima* "Es muy poco lo que soy" by Xavi, from chapter 5

IMPROVISED SALUDADOS

Northern Mississippi

DON LENCHITO, MI ESTIMADO
OLVERA SU APELATIVO
ESTE VERSO LE SUBSCRIBO
DESEO QUE SEA DE SU AGRADO

(1) Hoy en este día del mes
espero que bien la pase
y por medio de mi frase
se lo digo con sencillez
porque la verdad así es
sobre el destino salado
y usted como apreciado
quiero tributarle honor
por medio de mi labor
DON LENCHITO, MI ESTIMADO

(2) Hoy aquí en este país
con cariño le diré
hoy le saludo a usted
que viene de San Luis
espero se halle feliz
mil poemas yo le digo
recordando como amigo

anocheciendo el día de hoy
estos saludes le doy
OLVERA SU APELATIVO

(3) A usted le estrecho mi mano
como amigo muy sincero
gracias a Dios verdadero
lo que le digo de plano
sobre este verso profano
perdón si no fue lucido
en mi verso le pido
tocando mi guitarrita
y como le dije ahorita
ESTE VERSO LE SUBSCRIBO

(4) Hoy ante la gente toda
como observador
le canta su servidor
yo veo que ustedes ahora
tomen cerveza o soda
o lo que ustedes han deseado
como le había recalcado
usted como gran amigo
y este verso le subscribo
DESEANDO QUE SEA DE SU AGRADO

Northern Mississippi
MY ESTEEMED DON LENCHITO
OLVERA, YOUR APPELLATIVE
I DEDICATE THIS VERSE TO YOU
I HOPE IT IS TO YOUR LIKING

(1) Today, on this day of the month
I hope you are enjoying yourself
and by way of my phrase
I say this quite simply
for the truth, it is so
about this rough calling

and you, who are held in high regard
I want to pay tribute to you
through my laborious efforts
MY ESTEEMED DON LENCHITO

(2) Today, here in this country
I will tell you with affection
that I greet you in improvised verse
as you come from San Luis
I hope you find yourself in good spirits
I tell you a thousand poems
recalling you as a friend
as the day turns into night
I give you these improvised greetings
OLVERA, YOUR APPELLATIVE

(3) I stretch my hand out to you
as a very sincere friend
thanks to the true God
what I say to you plainly
in this secular verse
forgive me if it was not lucid
in my verse I ask of you
as I strum my little guitar
and as I told you just now
I DEDICATE THIS VERSE TO YOU

(4) Today before all of these people
as an observer
your humble servant sings to you
I see all of you now
partaking in beer or soda
or whatever you desire
as I have stressed
you, as a great friend
and this verse I dedicate to you
I HOPE IT IS TO YOUR LIKING

—Flavio

Ríoverde, San Luis Potosí

COMO POETA TROVADOR
MI VERSO LOS GLORIFICA
FAMILIA SALVADOR
QUE EN CALIFORNIA RADICA

(1) Magdalena y Juan Manuel
su gran amor se destila
y los niños hacen fila
quieren morder el pastel
la boda es una miel
que belleza y que esplendor
les doy gracias al creador
con mi décima y mi glosa
en esta boda preciosa
COMO POETA Y TROVADOR

(2) Solo cariño trasudo
como poeta y verseador
familia Salvador
para ustedes va el saludo
ni tantitito lo dudo
yo sé lo que en mí radica
y mi corazón se aplica
y hoy que en el gusto navegan
desde California llegan
MI VERSO LOS GLORIFICA

(3) Hoy cada verso enlazado
es la ternura infinita
los novios me solicitan
que les cante un saludado
y yo estoy emocionado
creo que hasta siento rubor
pero todo es esplendor
y con íntimo decoro
escribo con letras de oro
FAMILIA SALVADOR

(4) Según me pude informar
la verdad me reconcilia
la suya es una familia
que ha tenido que emigrar
y viven de trabajar
según el novio me explica
y el mismo lo testifica
les brindo un verso en flor
familia Salvador
QUE EN CALIFORNIA RADICA

Ríoverde, San Luis Potosí
AS A TROUBADOUR POET
MY VERSE HONORS YOU
SALVADOR FAMILY
THAT RESIDES IN CALIFORNIA

(1) Magdalena and Juan Manuel
your great love is now proven
and the children line up
they want to bite the cake
the wedding is like sweet honey
oh what beauty and splendor
I thank the creator
with my décima and my gloss
at this lovely wedding
AS A TROUBADOUR POET

(2) Only with sweet affection
as a poet and verse composer
Salvador family
for you goes the greeting
I do not doubt it one bit
for I know what lies within me
and my heart is committed
and today that you are surrounded by joy
from California you have arrived
MY VERSE HONORS YOU

(3) Today each braided verse
is infinite tenderness
the wedded couple asks me
that I greet you
and I'm excited
I think I'm even blushing
but everything is a great splendor
and with intimate decor
I write in golden letters
SALVADOR FAMILY

(4) And so I was informed
the truth puts me at ease
that yours is a family
that has had to emigrate
and you live from your labor
this, according to what the groom tells me
and he testifies to this
I give you a verse in bloom
Salvador family
THAT RESIDES IN CALIFORNIA

—Guillermo Velázquez

Central Texas

OBSERVANDO EL INFINITO
YO CON ESTE SALUDADO
PONCHO DE DÓNDE ESTOY SENTADO
HOY TE BRINDO OTRO VERSITO

(1) Hoy que miro el universo
de veras la lejanía
te damos esta poesía
improvisando otro verso
y para ti lo disperso
con un cariño exquisito
lo digo recio y quedito
en la presente ocasión
Poncho va mi trovación
OBSERVANDO EL INFINTO

(2) Hoy con Valentín el varero
y también Homero en sus sillas
recibe estas poesías
y con Alex el vihuelero
saludarte lo primero
y el verso que he improvisado
para ti va dedicado
junto con tus familiares
recibe versos cordiales
DESDE DÓNDE ESTOY SENTADO

(3) Como humilde trovador
en esta noche bonita
saludo a tu mamacita
también a Poncho el señor
aunque no soy trovador
pero hoy que ando en este lado
el verso te he improvisado
yo lo digo ahorita, ahorita
en esta noche bonita
RECIBE ESTE SALUDADO

(4) Hoy que estamos en estancia
yo te lo digo Ponchito
esto se pone bonito
y el aire con su fragancia
nos brinda su abundancia
improvisando este verso
observo yo el universo
y brindo este saludado
desde dónde estoy sentado
PONCHO PA TI LO DISPERSO

Central Texas
AS I OBSERVE THE COSMOS
I WITH THIS GREETING
PONCHO FROM WHERE I AM SITTING
TODAY I GIFT YOU ANOTHER VERSE

(1) Today as I look up at the universe
indeed such a great distance
we gift you this poetry
improvising another verse
and for you I broadcast it
with an exquisite affection
I say it loudly and softly
on this present occasion
my improvisation is for you Poncho
AS I OBSERVE THE COSMOS

(2) Today with the violinist Valentín
and also Homero, both in their chairs
receive these poesías
and with Alex, the vihuelero
greeting you comes first
and this verse that I have improvised
is dedicated to you
along with your family members
receive these cordial verses
PONCHO FROM WHERE I AM SITTING

(3) As a humble troubadour
on this oh so pretty night
I greet your mother
and also your father
although I am not a troubadour
but today that I am out this way
I have improvised a verse for you
I say it now at this very instant
on this beautiful night
RECEIVE THIS GREETING

(4) Today as we are here
I tell you Ponchito
this is shaping up nicely
and the air with its fragrance
it offers us its abundance
improvising this verse

I observe the universe
and I offer this greeting
from where I'm sitting
PONCHO, FOR YOU I BROADCAST IT

—Graciano

El Refugio, San Luis Potosí
JUNIOR, TE CANTO
AL NORTE DE CAROLINA
CON MARTA, TU ESPOSA FINA
CON TU MAMÁ, LA DEL SANTO

(1) Pues, Alex no es por demás
de acuerdo a la invitación
ante toda esta reunión
continuando este compás
decirlo no es por demás
y aunque mi voz agiganto
con gusto y aprecio tanto
y sin dar un paso atrás
aquí estoy con tus papás
JUNIOR, TE CANTO

(2) Quiero escuches esta prosa
con estímulos muy grandes
formas familia Hernández
y con Sánchez y tu esposa
con atención cariñosa
un verso se te coordina
si, la trova se refina
al compás de los violines
dice Cándido Martínez
AL NORTE DE CAROLINA

(3) Junior te condecoro
a través de mis versitos
mándate unos verdecitos
que en México valen oro
tu mamá es un tesoro

dónde la amistad se inclina
y bajo esta estancia fina
aquí ante los invitados
vayan mis trovados
CON MARTA, TU ESPOSA FINA

(4) Continuando este debate
aunque no soy en mentor
pero soy tu servidor
Cándido el del Aguacate
discúlpame algún disparate
aunque mi voz agiganto
mas con estimulo cuanto
con todo este personal
ahí te mando un decimal
CON TU MAMÁ, LA DEL SANTO

El Refugio, San Luis Potosí

JUNIOR, I SING TO YOU
OUT TO NORTH CAROLINA
WITH YOUR FINE WIFE, MARTA
ALONGSIDES YOUR MOTHER, WHOSE BIRTHDAY WE CELEBRATE

(1) Well, Alex, it is in good measure
in accordance with the invitation
before this gathering
continuing on with this rhythm
saying it as such is in good measure
and although I raise my voice
with pleasure and much appreciation
and without taking a step back
I am here with your parents
JUNIOR, I SING TO YOU

(2) I want you to hear this prose
with great caring emotions
you form part of the Hernández family
and with Sánchez and with your wife
with loving attention
a verse is crafted for you

yes, the improvisation emerges
to the rhythm of the violins
Cándido Martínez says so
OUT TO NORTH CAROLINA

(3) Junior I commend you
by way of my little verses
send back some greenbacks [dollars]
for they are worth gold in Mexico
your mother is a treasure
upon which friendship relies
and amid this fine gathering
here in the presence of these guests
I send off my improvised verses
WITH YOUR FINE WIFE, MARTA

(4) Resuming this debate
although I am no mentor
but I am your humble servant
Cándido from el Aguacate
forgive me for any mistakes
although I raise my voice
what is more, with much affection
alongside these people
there you have it, I send you this decimal
ALONGSIDE YOUR MOTHER, WHOSE BIRTHDAY WE CELEBRATE

—Cándido Martínez

INTRODUCTION

1. For a discussion of how stereotypical group cues concerning Latina/os trigger anxiety among whites, see Brader, Valentino, and Suhay (2008).

2. These legislative efforts include H.B. 56 in Alabama, S.B. 1070 in Arizona, H.B. 87 in Georgia, S.B. 590 in Indiana, S.B. 20 in South Carolina, and H.B. 497 in Utah.

3. Michael Maly, Heather Dalmage, and Nancy Michaels (2013) suggest that nostalgia works as a tool to construct contemporary forms of whiteness in response to perceived place attachment.

4. The huasteca is an ecological region that spans several states, including Hidalgo, Puebla, Querétaro, San Luis Potosí, Tamaulipas, and Veracruz. It is home to several indigenous groups, including the Téenek (or Huastec), from whom the region derives its name.

5. Novak and Sakakeeny have elsewhere described this as a "feedback loop of materiality and metaphor" (2015: 1).

6. This recent preoccupation with sound and listening is best represented by Erlmann 2004; Feld and Brenneis 2004; Finnegan 2002; Kruth and Stobart 2000; and Nancy 2007.

7. This book augments other works on music and migration, including Thomas Turino's (1993) work on Peru, David B. Coplan's (1987) discussions of Lesotho migrants, Veit Erlmann (1996), Adelaida Reyes' (1999) work on Southeast Asian forced migration and music, and Tina K. Ramnarine's (2001) focus on Indo-Caribbean music.

8. In this way Ochoa Gautier subsequently also lends historical and cultural specificity to Arjun Appadurai's (1990) related and opaque language of "scapes."

9. The first scholarly conceptualization of the borderlands as a culturally contested geographic area between New Spain and the United States may be attributed to historian Herbert Eugene Bolton (1921), though much work has been done since with respect to the history of the borderlands (De León 1983; Montejano 1987).

10. Zavella draws on queer and feminist theory to further apprehend the cultural logics and "gendered formations of family and sexuality" (2011: 7) that play out

in the struggles of everyday life and exacerbate the inequalities associated with transnationalism.

11. This language is a purposeful nod to Anzaldúa's now-famous description of the border as "*una herida abierta*" (an open wound) (1987: 25).

12. *Doña* and *Don* are common honorifics used in deferential Mexican Spanish; they are part of local speech conventions used to convey respect.

13. The Spanish expression *da' las* (to give 'em)—short for *dar las nalgas* (to give your buttocks; a reference to getting screwed, comparable to the English colloquial expression *to give it up* in reference to a sexual offering)—is invoked as a phonetic equivalent of *Dallas*, the name of the city in Texas, which activates a linguistic pun frame that is typical of a kind of humorous verbal play commonly referred to as *albur*. See Chávez 2015.

14. References to the "migrant experience" throughout this book should not be understood as invoking a generalizable category of experience or a reification that "[erases] all substantive distinctions among historically specific migrations" and, in turn, propagates a certain "immigrant essentialism" (De Genova 2005: 71). Rather, these references attend specifically to the lives embedded within the transnational political economy of Mexican migration in the late twentieth and early twenty-first centuries.

15. My approach dialogues with work in phenomenology that explores the poetic relationship between the body and place (Appadurai 1988; Casey 2000, 1993; Feld and Basso 1996; Gupta and Ferguson 1992; Hirsch and O'Hanlon 1995; Rodman 1992; Stewart 1996; Stokes 1994).

16. Inspired by Rouse's (1991) notion of bifocality in reference to how Mexican migrants imagine their lives in Mexico and the United States simultaneously, Zavella (2011) makes the case for what she terms "peripheral vision." She writes, "As a form of transnational subjectivity, peripheral vision reflects the experience of feeling at home in more than one geographic location where identity construction takes place in the context of shifting ethno-racial boundaries and gendered transitions in a global society" (8–9).

17. De Genova's ethnographic work is particularly relevant in its description of the spatial production of what he terms a "Mexican Chicago" as a "reinvention of Latin America" owing to spaces in the city that "conjoin with multiple sites in Mexico" (1998: 89–90).

18. In her work on indigenous Oaxacan migrants, Lynn Stephen (2007) draws on Peggy Levitt and Nina Glick Schiller's (2004) concept of the social field to make a similar claim about how the everyday activities and relationships that shape experiences (of work, family life, and encounters with gender and racial prejudice, for instance) are in fact the lived connections through which transborder community emerges.

19. My use of *assemblage* going forward follows in the Marxist tradition of Deleuze and Guattari (1987), who in their work offer a corrective to vulgar (economistic) Marxist theories that previously proposed a deterministic correlation between the mode of production of material life and social relations. Deleuze and Guattari turn

away from this causality and consider instead a dialectical reading with respect to the connection between the social production of everyday life and economic material forces. While it could be argued that this more fluid perspective regarding the relationship between capital's constant search for socially necessary labor and the constant resistance on the part of those whose surplus labor is being appropriated is what Marx always intended, I find the poetics of Deleuze and Guattari's theorizing useful in the present ethnographic context.

20. Huapango huasteco is another form of vernacular music that is closely related to huapango arribeño; it is practiced along Mexico's central Gulf coast in the huasteca regions of Hidalgo, Puebla, Querétaro, San Luis Potosí, and Veracruz. It will make several appearances throughout this book.

21. In 2006 Reyes received the Mexican government's Premio Nacional de Ciencias y Artes (National Prize for Arts and Sciences) in the category Artes y Tradiciones Populares (Popular Arts and Traditions).

22. A *poesía* is a poetic composition made up of a set of décimas anchored by a base quatrain.

23. Throughout the book I represent base quatrains, or plantas, orthographically with all capitalization to indicate their function as syntagmatic and paradigmatic anchors of corresponding décimas that follow either the *pie forzado* or glossed styles.

24. Renee Stepler and Anna Brown, *Statistical Portrait of Hispanics in the United States*, Pew Research Center, Hispanic Trends, April 19, 2016, http://www.pewhispanic .org/2016/04/19/statistical-portrait-of-hispanics-in-the-united-states/.

25. Jens Manuel Krogstad, Jeffrey S. Passel, and D'vera Cohn, *5 Facts about Illegal Immigration in the U.S.*, Pew Research Center, April 27, 2017, http://www.pewresearch .org/fact-tank/2017/04/27/5-facts-about-illegal-immigration-in-the-u-s/.

26. While adjacent to the listed municipalities, Armadillo de los Infante is not officially considered part of the Zona Media.

CHAPTER 1: AURALITY AND THE LONG AMERICAN CENTURY

1. Presently, *fandango* and *huapango* refer to dance as a social gathering or event in the central and southern Gulf coast regions of Mexico, particularly where jarocho and huasteco musics are performed. After the struggle for independence from Spain (1810), sones, fandangos, and dance were accepted as legitimate cultural expressions of Mexican heritage—most of the insurgent militia elements that fought in the struggle were from the pueblo and identified with these forms of music and dance. By the mid- to late nineteenth century, Mexican elites would turn a deaf ear to such expressions in favor of European high culture: Italian opera, French salon dance styles, and so on. Still, vernacular forms continued to be practiced in their communities of origin during and after Porfirio Díaz's rule (1876–1911).

2. The second huapango featured in this scene is "La Presumida," which Barcelata claims to have authored. This particular huapango, however, forms part of the vernacular repertoire of huapango huasteco, and thus a more accurate claim would be that the specific arrangement featured in the film is his. Nevertheless, this practice of registering traditional huapangos with music publishers as original

compositions was commonplace at the time. For instance, Elpidio Ramírez of the emblematic Los Trovadores Chinacos—a huasteco trio that also included Nicandro Castillo—published "La Rosa," "El Gallo," "La Malagueña," "La Petenera," "El Toro," "El Caimán," "La Leva," "El Gusto," "La Huasanga," and "El Fandanguito" as his own in 1936 (Rivas Paniagua 2003).

3. Estoy como el gallo giro del palenque de la feria
   Pidiéndole a los galleros que me suelten a cualquiera
   Pidiéndole a los galleros que me suelten a cualquiera
   Y a ver si hago una ensalada con todita la gallera.

   Saca tu taburete Lucha María siéntate aquí
   Que te quiero ver sentada toda la feria cerca de mí
   Saca tu taburete Lucha María siéntate aquí
   Que te quiero ver sentada toda la feria cerca de mí

   Lucha María, mi linda sirena
   Cómo se pinta tu cuerpo en la arena
   Allá en la playa revientan las olas
   Como te ves en medio de todas.

   Lucha María, serrana linda del alma mía.

4. Pajarillo manzanero, llévame a cortar manzanas
   Pajarillo manzanero, llévame a cortar manzanas

   ¿Como quieres que las corte, si no me bajas la rama?
   ¿Cómo quieres que las corte, si no me bajas la rama?

   Presumida, presumida, deja ya de estar dormida,
   Presumida, presumida, deja ya de estar dormida,

   Ya me voy bien de mi vida y por ti llorando estoy
   Y por ti llorando estoy, adiós, vida de mi vida

   Pajarillo manzanero, llévame a cortar manzanas
   Pajarillo manzanero, llévame a cortar manzanas

   ¿Como quieres que las corte, si no me bajas la rama?
   ¿Cómo quieres que las corte, si no me bajas la rama?

   En el campo la sandia con la lluvia reverdece
   Con la lluvia reverdece en el campo la sandia.

   Se fué un amor que tenia
   Muy poco dolor es ese
   Me encontré otro el mismo día
   Que no espero se parece.

   Pajarillo manzanero . . .

5. Américo Paredes elaborates, "The characteristic traits of *machismo* are quite well known: the outrageous boast, a distinct phallic symbolism, the identification of the man with the male animal, and the ambivalence toward women—varying from an abject and tearful posture to brutal disdain" (1993: 215).

6. (JF) Soy charro de Rancho Grande
   y hasta el amor bebo en jarro;
   Y no hay potranca matrera
   Que me tumbe si me agarro
   Ay qué mi Dios tan pantera
   Cuando se viste de charro

   (M) Yo en Rancho Grande nací
   y nunca lo ando diciendo;
   Hay quienes no son de aquí
   y no más van presumiendo
   como uno que conocí
   y que sigo conociendo

   (JF) Yo no nací en Rancho Grande

   pero quiero este lugar;
   Hay muchos que por costumbre
   hablan no más por hablar
   hay muchos que prenden lumbres
   no las saben apagar

   (M) Las lumbres que yo he prendido

   no las apaga cualquiera;
   No todos somos iguales
   andando en la quemadera
   yo conozco caporales
   que se queman en la hoguera

   (JF) Hay uno que en el cantar

   da su envidia a conocer;
   Porque no fue caporal
   ni lo quiso una mujer
   corrió al palomo tan mal
   que al patrón hizo perder

7. Rather than dismissing the scholarship in question as simply racist, Paredes instead attributes the ethnocentrism in its rendering to ethnographers' gross inability to identify and understand emic language use. The ethnographer, he argues, ought to possess the competence necessary to recognize communicative frames and linguistic markers of performance, such that various forms of speech are not mistaken for

straight factual verbal reporting, for, as we know, language does not possess only one level of meaning.

8. Note that there is an argument to be made here about distancing an analysis of huapango from popular media treatments of the genre in favor of everyday and real-world encounters during ethnographic fieldwork.

9. The origins of this rural modernity can be traced back to the decades just before the Revolution and after the Reform War in late nineteenth-century Mexico, a time when the progressive and liberal versions of modernity began to reconcile with each other and to articulate an "official construction of tradition [that] necessarily visited certain features of Mexico's rural and artisan life, not only the pre-Columbian past" (Lomnitz 2001: 33).

10. The same can be said for *charrería*, as horsemanship skills were disseminated through similar means and transformed into a popular spectacle for the rural masses now located in urban settings.

11. When I speak of the conservative response to progressive policies, I am referring specifically to romantic representations of the hacienda system, symbolically opposed to agrarian reform, *ejido* (communal land) redistribution, and the nationalization of the oil industry (Hershfield 1996).

12. In their glossary to Bakhtin's *The Dialogic Imagination: Four Essays* (1981), Caryl Emerson and Michael Holquist clarify this further and suggest that the chronotope is "a unit of analysis for studying texts according to the ratio and nature of the temporal and spatial categories represented. The distinctiveness of this concept as opposed to most other uses of time and space in literary analysis lies in the fact that neither category is privileged; they are utterly interdependent. The chronotope is an optic for reading texts as x-rays of the forces at work in the culture system from which they spring" (1981: 425–426).

13. While film historians have argued that the heroic image of the charro sought to counter Hollywood representations that vilified Mexicans, Mexican cinema subsequently leaves us with the brazen macho, forever assigned to the pastoral realm.

14. Or, as Quijano and Wallerstein have elsewhere suggested, "the Américas were not incorporated into an already existing capitalist world-economy. There would not have been a capitalist world-economy without the Américas" (1992: 549). Implicit in these statements is the centrality of race in the project of modernity, particularly as Eurocentric epistemologies have historically justified the exploitative relationships so much a part of the ugly underbelly of modernity (Hogue 1996).

15. On this point, Henry C. Schmidt (1978) traces this sociology of national culture through Antonio Caso, Daniel Cosio Villegas, and Alfonso Reyes, and up through Samuel Ramos, wherein what begins as a tradition of pseudo-anthropology in the early twentieth century gives way to pseudo-psychoanalysis by the mid-twentieth century.

16. At this time he wrote what is perhaps his most famous work, *Notes on Mexico, Made in the Autumn of 1822.*

17. Nick Wing, "That Awkward Moment When the Tea Party Rally Gets Overtly Racist," *HuffingtonPost*, July 19, 2013, http://www.huffingtonpost.com/2013/07/18/gop-anti-immigration_n_3618392.html.

18. Poinsett's thoughts anticipate, furthermore, Gregory Bourke's (1894) ethnological musings concerning the inert Mexican presence in South Texas, an intellectual discourse taken to task by José E. Limón (1994).

19. While rancho iconography certainly circulates at the vernacular level, more work needs to be done that critically addresses the ways in which it is resignified—Madrid's (2008) work on nor-tec's uses of clichéd authenticity and Nájera-Ramírez's (2007) explorations of women's participation in the ranchera notwithstanding.

20. As a self-reflexive signifier deeply contoured by the inner logics of "objective science, universal morality and law, and autonomous art," modernity, as Jürgen Habermas (1983: 9) proposes, indexically mediates the transition between antiquity and an emergent Enlightenment moment of which it was the result. In the Mexican case, Madrid notes, "The cult of modernity . . . was not a consequence of the Mexican revolution; it was already the governmental ideal of Porfirio Díaz and could effortlessly be traced back to the liberal policies of President Benito Juárez" (2009: 8). Such currents—particularly Enlightenment liberalism—intensely shaped Mexico's independence movement and extended well beyond the nineteenth century, influencing nation-building practices during the 1920s.

21. In "Identity and Cultural Studies: Is That All There Is?," Grossberg critiques the logics that undergird the modernist concept of identity, and therefore the contemporary project of cultural studies—difference, individuality, and temporality. He in turn suggests a focus on "three corresponding alternatives: a logic of otherness; a logic of productivity; and a logic of spatiality" (1996: 89). With this in mind, Paul Gilroy (1993) makes a case similar to Hogue with regards to the utopian impulse within a transnational black modernity.

22. In the edited volume *Performing the US Latina and Latino Borderlands* (Aldama, Sandoval, and García 2012), one set of essays is grouped under "Ethnographies of Performance"; however, the chapters dealing with music lack an ethnographic impulse. There, authors provide textual analysis of songs by artists ranging from Lila Downs, Tijuana NO!, Los Tigres del Norte, and Molotov, among others. Although conducted with impressive theoretical acumen, the approach leaves much to be desired, particularly the essay "*No Somos Criminales*: Crossing Borders in Contemporary Latina and Latino Music," which bears the name of the academic panel "*No Somos* Criminales" that inspired the volume's publication. In this essay Aldama concludes that musical tracks

> can offer cultural and music scholars rich and complex opportunities to engage directly with what was a landmark essay of postcolonial studies by Gayatri Chakravorty Spivak titled "Can the Subaltern Speak?" (1988). If we take time to listen, we can hear how borderlands musics can and do create radical, hybridized, anti-racist, twenty-first century performative sites of social justice. In their defense of dignity and respect, these performances straddle the psychic politics of melancholy and

outrage. These song texts challenge the symbolic logic that drives racial, nativist acts of entitlement and the racial privilege of subjects who criminalize and rally against immigrants. (197)

While Aldama's claims relate to the analytical underpinnings of my work, I do not rely on the same line of argument, instead favoring an ethnographic approach, for there are hidden pitfalls in leaving out some analysis of how texts and media are received.

23. All references to *personhood* in this work relate to transnationalism and juridical categories around undocumented migration, illegality, and cultural violence aimed at migrants from Latin America. The term as I use it does not relate to the controversy around reproductive rights in the United States.

24. Limón elaborates the point in extended form:

But consider also folk music in Texas, as well as Mississippi, as Chávez (2010) has shown. He tells us of the autonomous, widespread, and dynamic presence of the folk musical form, the *huapango arribeño*, among Mexican immigrants from Querétaro and San Luis Potosí now mostly residing in Texas, where such music flourishes in transnational, interactive, communal, dueling encounters called *topadas*. But it may well be counter-proposed that these are, after all, recent immigrants, perhaps from rural sectors of Mexico, and that later than sooner, these expressive performances—one "emergent," one "residual"—will also give way in the urban, mass media life of Los Angeles, but also in increasingly urban Texas or, in the case of *huapango*, incorporated into mass media musical culture as "the latest sound," perhaps beginning with participation in Austin's South by Southwest followed by bookings and so on. Perhaps, but there is no evidence of such attenuation, and more than enough at least anecdotal evidence of other kindred performances in other genres in immigrant life. We could speak of *tamaladas and posadas*, but consider the now ubiquitous *taquerías* and taco trucks in Los Angeles and other places—the food, yes—but perhaps more significantly as sites of expressive conversation akin to Michael Bell's Brown's Lounge. But immigrants aside, the counter-argument might continue, what of third and later generation Mexican Americans—U.S. citizens? To the degree that they fashion their ethnicity through expressive forms, have they not become wholly the children of El Vez, George Lopez, Los Lobos, gang films, the occasional phrase in Spanish, occasional Mexican cuisine, lowrider shows and fashion, and Chicano art and literature? Perhaps, again, although I would say that the matter remains to be determined empirically before we reach such a conclusion, and I see little effort to do so, at least within the California cultural studies sphere that I have critiqued. (2013: 133–134)

25. Although Zavella acknowledges that "not all migrants experience melancholia," she describes it as "pervasive" (2011: 188) and emphasizes it in her chapter titled "The Divided Home." She differentiates mainly between "different configurations of melancholia" based on the factors that are most relevant to the construction of identity for her interviewees (159).

26. The incorporation of certain musical forms and the exclusion of others in the Mexican case is central to the processes of defining the borders of Mexican musical nationalism. Yet this institutionalized scripting (emergent from the academy, intellectual discourses, and popular culture), while hegemonic in scope, is easily "disturbed," as Vazquez (2013) argues in reference to Cuban music, for the idiosyncrasies—the difference articulated, embedded, and voiced through music making and performance in everyday life—provide a counterstory, a counternarrative to the cultural politics of authenticity.

27. There exist the *paya* in Chile, *punto* in Cuba, and *seis* in Puerto Rico, for instance.

28. The early twentieth-century border corridos "El Mosco Americano" and "Los Ambiciosos Patones" serve as examples.

29. Here I diverge not only from Madrid (2008) but also from the folklore of my most immediate intellectual precursors, a scholarly trajectory that has typically portrayed ethnic Mexican vernacular aesthetics as redressive symbolic activity that is key to alleviating hegemonic social stresses (Flores 1995; Limón 1994). This ethnographic writing emphasizes what vernacular expressions accomplish rather than what their structured motifs mean.

30. There are some works that offer an embodied critique of the expressive nature of transnationalism through daily experiential moments (Rosas 2012; E. Peña 2011; Farr 2006; Cintron 1997; Chavez 1992). Zavella's (2011) ethnography of migrant experiences, for instance, gives insight into the daily lives of working migrants. She dovetails her ethnography of migration with interviews of performers like Los Tigres del Norte, Quetzal, and Lila Downs who are engaged in the creation of transnational cultural memory as a form of activism.

CHAPTER 2: COMPANIONS OF THE CALLING

1. By the mid-2000s, ICE held about 23,000 people in detention on any given day and about 200,000 overall each year in over nine hundred facilities across the country (Akers Chacón and Davis 2006: 223).

2. The budget for ICE operations for the fiscal year 2009 alone was $5.93 billion. The fantasy of border control, as Douglas S. Massey, Jorge Durand, and Nolan J. Malone (2002) label it, wastes at least $3 billion in taxpayer money every year.

3. For instance, I made my share of communicative blunders when first embarking on this research, particularly with respect to my assumptions about huapangueros' approach to the topada. Given that practitioners tend to be exclusively male, I assumed the topada encounter was antagonistic in nature. Thus, I reduced its complex aesthetic enactments to acts of shrewd competition between men. My assumptions about masculinity in that space, however, were overturned. I became privy to the layered and dialogic parameters of performance, of the topada as a mirrored exchange where openings provided opportunity for conversation, debate, and engagement coated with a coresponsibility and accountability. These resonant intersubjective interactions during the topada became integral to my research, particularly where nonverbal communication, feelings, and gestures in the heat of this competitive camaraderie became points of tactile and sensorial

intensity, contact, attention, and realization of how huapango arribeño material-
izes intimately.

4. These questions of transformation and transmission have been explored at the
localized level of Veracruz, particularly with regard to how African, European, and
indigenous groups came together at the dawn of the colonial period to produce
this hybrid sound (Díaz Sanchez and Hernández 2013; Madrid 2013; Sheehy 1979).

5. In the case of Nor-tec, Madrid proposes, the very myths of Mexican national identity are collapsed—sacred pastoral images of tradition are rearticulated through a
kitschy modernist lens that provides a new perspective on "clichéd discourses of
authenticity" (2008: 23).

6. The exception here is Maximiano Trapero's volumes, *El libro de la décima: La poesía
improvisada en el mundo hispánico* (1996) and *La décima: Su historia, su geografía,
sus manifestaciones* (2001). While not exclusively focused on huapango arribeño,
these works attend to its formal poetics and place its practice within the cultural
landscape of Latin American décima traditions.

7. According to Stanford (1972), the *Diccionario de autoridades* (1726–1739) defines
son as "ruido concentrado que percibimos con el sentido del oído, especialmente
el que se hace con arte, o música" (focused sound we perceive audibly, especially
that with an artistic or musical quality). César Hernández Azuara (2003) indicates
that Gaspar Sanz makes use of the son idiom when alluding to various musical
pieces in his seventeenth-century instructional guide for the *Guitarra Española*.
Furthermore, Spanish Inquisition documents identify loud and obscene secular
music and dance styles banned by the Catholic Church in eighteenth-century
New Spain as types of son (G. Saldívar 1934).

8. With respect to musical expression, these efforts mirror those of late nineteenth-
century comparative musicology, primarily the interest in documenting disappearing primitive musics, driven by the quest for authenticity within the broader
project of colonial modernity (Bohlman 2002: 70).

9. Similar trends also occurred in neighboring countries: *afrocubanismo* in Cuba,
Brazilian *modernismo*, and Andean *indigenismo* (Behague 1991).

10. Roger Bartra considers this canonizing of Mexicanness necessary to the logics of what
he terms "official culture," an institutional production that has "legitimized underdevel-
opment and authoritarianism" through a jingoistic "surplus of symbolism" (2002: 63, 13).

11. Sheehy provides an attenuated definition of *son* that I find useful:

In Mexico, *son* may refer to a regional style of mestizo music or to certain melodies
of Indian cultural groups. In both cases, most *sones* have a rhythmic drive appropriate for dancing. Regional *mestizo son* traditions may be distinguished by instrumentation, instrumental technique, singing style, repertoire, and other traits. These
sones most often are structured around *versos* (sung poetic stanzas) alternating
with instrumental interludes. In contrast, Indian *sones* tend to consist of one or two
short melodic phrases, performed instrumentally and repeated at length. *Son* also
may be used generally to mean simply "tune" or "sound," reflecting its principal
usage in pre-nineteenth-century Mexican colonial times. (2006: 98)

12. Alfredo Guerrero Tarquín (1988) maintains that both the Sierra Gorda and the Zona Media were home to a convergence of myriad travel and commerce routes connecting the Gulf of Mexico and the Pacific coast, ostensibly traversed by countless *arrieros* (merchants, traders, carriers). One such route began in San Luís de la Paz, made its way up to Xichú (both in Guanajuato), passed through San Ciro de Acosta and Río Verde in San Luís Potosí, and finally reached Tampico, Tamaulipas on the Gulf. Another similar path also began in San Luís de la Paz/Xichú, however it then made its way to Arroyo Seco and Jalpan in Querétaro, reached Ciudad Valles, San Luís Potosí and ended, likewise, in Tampico, Tamaulipas. In the other direction, routes began in the Sierra Gorda of Guanajuato, made their way to Guadalajara, and finally reached the Pacific via the state of Guerrero. It is probable that among usual commerce and trade, musical instruments and stylings also traveled along these routes. For instance, the vihuela is vital to the music in Guanajuato's neighboring state of Jalisco. The incorporation of two accompanying violins is likewise found in the son de la tierra caliente of Michoacán, which borders both Guanajuato and Querétaro. The guitarra quinta and jarana huasteca are both instruments native to the adjacent huasteca region.

13. Ceferino Juárez was born in 1902, and his father, Severiano Juárez, was, according to collective memory, one of the more popular violinists of the late nineteenth and early twentieth centuries. His grandfather was also a practicing troubadour. Together they represent three generations of musicians stretching back to the midnineteenth century.

14. The individuals listed here are but a few among the vast number of musicians practicing huapango arribeño; I have chosen to include those whom I specifically encountered during the course of my research, be it in person or in memory.

15. The folklore of Carlos Vega (and his students Maria Ester Grebe and Isabel Aretz) and its preoccupation with the formal properties of music structure, with minimal focus on the social dimensions of musical production, comes to mind. This conceptual mode, Gerard Behague (1991) bluntly suggests in a critique of such work, seems to find justification across Latin America with the argument, we are studying our own country/people and we understand it/them best. This attitude persisted at the time Behague was writing, despite the theoretical advances in ethnomusicology offered by scholars like Alan Merriam, Bruno Nettl, and John Blacking, in addition to those of Steven Feld by the 1980s, which draw heavily on the "ethnography of speaking" and the communicative and social interactive dimensions of performance in the making.

16. The work of Parra Muñoz and others has carved out a certain level of discursive hegemony in mapping the proper place of huapango arribeño and its practitioners—a type of "intellectual colonialism" that still expresses the "influence of the Mexican post-revolutionary nationalist project" (Corona and Madrid 2008: 7, 6).

17. Paredes's (1958) seminal study of the corrido of intercultural conflict linked its emergence as a popular form and medium for social protest in the late nineteenth century to the transformation of Texas-Mexican society. Accordingly, the corrido derives its cultural agency from the conflict that attends Anglo-Mexican relations

along the U.S.-Mexico border and the emergence of a new racial-class structure (Paredes and Bauman 1972). The antagonistic social climate that grew out of the Anglo invasion of the Southwest, accordingly, was conducive to engendering countercultural responses by border Mexicans.

18. In *Sounds of the Modern Nation: Music, Culture, and Ideas in Post-Revolutionary Mexico* (2009), Madrid gives a historical account of the interplay among a diversity of musical aesthetics and cultural manifestations in post-Revolutionary Mexico, honing in on the intellectual currents of Mexican modernist and avant-gardist traditions that have been altogether obfuscated, excluded, or appropriated by the institutionalized narrative field of Mexican nationalism. The aesthetic reevaluations and negotiations therein, Madrid illustrates, represent a breach in the rigid teleology of nationalism developed by the state amid the social, political, and economic fallout of the Revolution.

19. The date was September 16—Mexican Independence Day.

20. This is a reference to a violinist who often plays alongside Gabino.

21. In a similar critique of the "mechanical materialism descended from the eighteenth-century Enlightenment," Fredric Jameson notes, "The problem with the body as a positive slogan is that the body itself, as a unified entity, is an Imaginary concept (in Lacan's sense); it is what Deleuze calls a 'body without organs,' an empty totality that organizes the world without participating in it. We experience the body through our experience of the world and of other people, so that it is per-haps a misnomer to speak of the body at all as a substantive with a definite article, unless we have in mind the bodies of others, rather than our own phenomenological referent" (2003: 713).

22. The décima also forms part of musico-poetic traditions in Argentina, Chile, Colombia, Cuba, Ecuador, Panama, Peru, Puerto Rico, the southwestern United States, Uruguay, and Venezuela.

23. Son here refers to a musical component, not the genre.

24. "Rigid" and "face-up" are an evocative reference to rigor mortis.

25. Mendoza (1947) defines the valona as the act of glossing a base quatrain with four corresponding décimas. For him, this is the most perfect incarnation of the gloss, though other less perfect forms exist, whereby a base quatrain is glossed by only two or three décimas, a practice he observed in the Tierra Caliente music of Mi-choacán. He claims that valonas also exist in the states of Guerrero and Veracruz. Both Gabriel Saldívar (1934) and Socorro Perea (1989) suggest the name *valona* comes from the Spanish word *valedor* (comrade), thus referencing this portion's possible laudatory role. Practitioners may utilize the gloss to showcase their impro-visatory skills, greeting and lauding the audience to this end. Mendoza, in contrast, claims that the term initially emerged as a referent for soldiers who arrived in New Spain from the Valona region of Belgium (a southern French-speaking area), who practiced the glossing of décimas. The evidence to support this is rather thin. Whatever the term's origins, the valona as poetic practice seems to have enjoyed great popularity in the first half of the eighteenth century throughout New Spain; however, at the time of Mendoza's research in the first half of the twentieth century,

he located its practice only in the states of Jalisco, Michoacán, Guerrero, and Veracruz. He makes no mention of its presence in the Zona Media or Sierra Gorda. In Jalisco and Michoacán, the valona usually takes on humoristic themes, and its musical structure is similar to that found within the huapango arribeño. However, for huapango arribeño the term *valona* is most often used to refer to the music that accompanies the gloss, specifically the violin interludes played in between each décima. The actual glossing of a base quatrain with corresponding décimas (what Mendoza calls *valona*) is referred to as the *decimal* by most arribeño musicians.

26. In their work on the sung décima along the Texas-Mexico border, Américo Paredes and George Foss (1966) similarly take notice of the interdependence of voice and music with regard to the harmonic structure of the sung décima. Specifically, they account for the "matching of individual lines of text to musical phrases and a pronounced tendency toward a parlando-rubato style" in conjunction with musical interludes: "there is no extended meter, the text lines or groups of lines being treated as short musical motifs. The only musical factors indicating an internal unity are the repeated 'vamp' figures in the instrumental line between phrases and the use of almost identical melodic material" (95, 97). Maximiano Trapero (2001) suggests that the melodies used in certain Latin American sung traditions—including the *milonga* in Argentina and Uruguay, the *cueca* in Chile, the *fulía* in Venezuela, and the *mejorana* in Panama—may have their origins in Spanish *soleas, fandangos,* and *villancicos.*

27. Tablados are at times also referred to as *tarangos* or *tapancos.*

28. Before high-tech audio systems were commonplace in the region, the sheer height of the tablados facilitated the acoustic range of the music.

29. Variants of "Presumidas," "Cuervos," "Conchitas," and "Rositas Arribeñas" are also played in the *huapango huasteco.*

30. Saldívar (1937) claims that the jarabe, a popular dance form in Mexico, has its origins in Spain. Its precursors include *danzas zapateadas* dating back to the sixteenth century, rooted in the *seguidilla* and fandango traditions. By the late eighteenth century, the jarabe had become a national phenomenon in Spain and subsequently made its way to Mexico. The name *jarabe*, Saldívar suggests, emerged in Spain in reference to the *jarabe Gitano*, a "degenerate" seguidilla form in both music and dance. Although denounced by the Catholic Church during the Inquisition in both Mexico and Spain, the jarabe—among other musical forms—emerged as a national cultural symbol after the Mexican War of Independence in 1810–1821. In the twentieth century, the jarabe has mostly been associated with the state of Jalisco and its vernacular string musics, most notably the mariachi.

31. Huapango arribeño practitioners in and around Jalpan de Serra, Querétaro, do not play sones, only jarabes, after the valona portion.

32. Scholars suggest this son derives from a sixteenth-century Spanish *zarabanda* dance, some argue that it has Sephardic Jewish origins, while yet others maintain that it is named after a women singer from Paterna de Rivera in the province of Cádiz—that "La Paternera," over time, has become "La Petenera" (Echevarría Román 2000).

33. Religious occasions where huapango arribeño is played include *velorios* (funeral wakes) and *velaciones* (vigils for Catholic holy figures). Aside from topadas, secular musical engagements are not of the *talón*/piecework variety (as when the mariachi plays a restaurant or bar for tips) but rather are family affairs where only one ensemble is asked to perform. Generally, ensembles don't stray from folk-derived styles.

34. As of the writing of this book, some of the more customary topadas in the region include the following:

- January 31 in San Ciro de Acosta, San Luís Potosí
- Mid-March in Pinal de Amoles, Querétaro
- March 31 in Miguel Hidalgo, Rio Verde, San Luís Potosí
- July 31 in Cerritos, San Luís Potosí
- September 15 in Victoria, Guanajuato
- September 16 in Xichú, Guanajuato
- November 12 in La Palma, Lagunillas, San Luis Potosí
- November 13 in San Diego, Rioverde, San Luis Potosí
- November 24 in Santa Catarina, Guanajuato
- November 25 in Rioverde, San Luís Potosí
- December 6 in Purísima de Arista, Querétaro
- December 12 in Ahuacatlán de Guadalupe, Querétaro
- December 31 in Xichú, Guanajuato

35. For a related discussion of the topada's structure, see Molina 2010.

36. On occasion, the end of a son may be treated like that of a jarabe, allowing the troubadour to also sing and improvise a quatrain.

37. Mario and Gabino are his accompanying musicians.

38. "Guillermo" refers to Guillermo Velázquez.

39. "Your compatriot" is a mocking reference to violinist Guillermo Guevara.

40. He is calling attention to a previous "romantic" poesía performed by Celso. In that poesía Celso narrates his pursuit of a young love interest, whom he refers to as a mermaid, and their fictitious trip to the ocean. Though that poesía, in some sense, dealt with the theme of the evening, Pablo believes both practitioners ought to be lauding women of the region through their verses, not romancing them. Hence, "y te fuiste hasta el mar" (you've gone all the way out to sea).

41. A reference to Eliazar "Chalo" Velázquez, a member of the committee that organized the topada, who, among other things, informed both practitioners that the thematic focus of the festival was la mujer serrana.

42. By "municipality" (*cabecera*) he means the town of Xichú, the head (*cabeza*) of the township of Xichú—its *cabecera municipal*.

43. William F. Hanks has this to say: "Verse and aesthetically worked discourse involve a twofold engagement of the metalinguistic dimension. In the first instance, the production and reception of such discourse relies upon speakers' ability to work with the details of expression—to align, play with, juxtapose formal elements in a concerted way. The special responsibility that a verbal artist assumes in 'perfor-

mance' is similarly a metalinguistic phenomenon, insofar as it amounts to recasting the relation between the expression itself and the participants in its production (the performer and the audience)" (1996: 194).

CHAPTER 3: VERSES AND FLOWS AT THE DAWN OF NEOLIBERAL MEXICO

1. Deborah R. Vargas's (2012) and Marco Cervantes's (2013) important work on the intersectionality between Texas-Mexican music and black diasporic traditions anticipates my discussion.

2. Nina Simone, "Mississippi Goddam," *Nina Simone in Concert* (Philips Records, 1964).

3. The recent works of Gaye Theresa Johnson (2013) and Anthony F. Macias (2008) offer in-depth accounts of the transcultural musical exchanges occurring between ethnic-Mexican and African-American communities in urban Los Angeles since the mid-twentieth century.

4. Although the proposition passed, it was struck down as unconstitutional years later by the federal courts, as it violated the Supreme Court rulings in *Graham v. Richardson* (403 U.S. 365 [1971]), which prohibits states from denying public assistance to noncitizens, and *Plyler v. Doe* (457 U.S. 202 [1982]), which determined that states must provide free public education to migrant children (Cornelius 2005: 778).

5. Public Citizen, "NAFTA's Legacy for Mexico: Economic Displacement, Lower Wages for Most, Increased Migration," January 6, 2015, https://www.citizen.org /sites/default/files/naftas-mexico-legacy.pdf.

6. These budding labor flows and their new social enclosures gesture toward what Michael Hardt and Antonio Negri (2000) term *empire*, or the contemporary network of hierarchical sovereign power that functions through always emergent global mechanisms of control, division, and conflict wielded by nation-states, supranational institutions, and transnational capitalist corporations.

7. The primary minerals found in the aforementioned Sierra Gorda mines include fluorite, gold, lead, mercury, silver, and zinc.

8. Harry Cleaver describes these extreme tensions: "Racial discrimination, academic regimentation, alienation, exploitation, imperialism, dehumanization, sexual repression, consumerism, environmental destruction—one after another these evils of modern society were exposed in a confusing array of conflicts that seems to threaten the very disintegration of that society" (1979: 24–25).

9. "Guerrilla" warfare is a reference to the armed guerrilla movement that took hold in the mountains of Guerrero in the 1960s and 1970s, whose central leaders included Genaro Vázquez Rojas and Lucio Cabañas.

10. Sebastián Salinas is referring to the urban outgrowth of Mexico City that technically transcends the federal district and is located in the surrounding state of Mexico.

11. There exists a rich corpus of musico-poetic traditions that have lauded the deeds of Charlemagne (Charles the Great, 742–814), the king of the Franks, including the French epic chansons de geste (the twelfth-century Song of Roland, for instance), Spanish *romances* (romantic-themed epic songs), and various décima practices across Latin America (Trapero 2001).

12. For a focused discussion of the décima's use to narrate the workaday problems of everyday life in South Texas, see Paredes's (1966) "The Decima on the Texas-Mexican Border: Folksong as an Adjunct to Legend."

13. *Paisita* is a truncated version of *paisano* (countryman). Thus, the final line of the base quatrain "Y QUE TRATO LE DAN AL PAISITA" lends itself to an alternate translation, "FOR THE COUNTRYMAN TO GET A JOB."

14. The economic crisis immediately preceded the Mexican debt crisis of 1982.

15. The Mexican president José López Portillo held office from 1976 to 1982.

16. Lines 2–7 of this décima are difficult to discern from the original handwritten poesía materials in my possession. The rendering here is a reconstruction based on conversations with Mauro's children, who would transcribe his compositions as he dictated them; he himself was unlettered.

17. The word *cervecería* literally means "brewhouse," but this is most likely an allusion to beer (*cerveza*) in tandem with *vino* (wine). While *cervecería* has the desired semantic effect, it also maintains the octosyllabic cadence of the lines of this décima, which may explain Mauro's decision to use the term.

18. "Another from Colima" refers to the then incoming Mexican president, Miguel de la Madrid (1982–1988), originally from Colima, Colima.

19. "Up north" refers to the United States.

20. After the implementation of NAFTA in 1994, shipments of U.S. corn to Mexico rose dramatically, from 288,681 metric tons in 1993 to 5.1 million metric tons in 2000 (Skinner 2002).

21. After completing their first studio recording in 1982, Guillermo Velázquez and Los Leones de la Sierra de Xichú were given the opportunity to formally present the material in the Museo de Culturas Populares (Museum of Popular Cultures) in Mexico City, where they subsequently met Durán and began to develop the workshop and festival projects. Furthermore, chance encounters also thrust Los Leones de la Sierra de Xichú into the world of Latin American protest song in the 1980s; some of the more emblematic artists include Victor Jara of Chile; Mercedes Sosa and Atahualpa Yupanqui of Argentina; Silvio Rodríguez and Pablo Milanés of Cuba; and Amparo Ochoa and Oscar Chávez of Mexico. As a consequence, Los Leones de la Sierra de Xichú have traveled to Europe and Japan, and throughout Latin America, introducing huapango arribeño as an expression of Xichú, Guanajuato, to people and artists all over the world.

22. Among the first musicians invited to give lessons were Lorenzo López, Agapito Briones, Lorenzo Camacho, Simitrio Aguilar, Asención Aguilar, and Miguel González, in addition to Velázquez himself. Valentín was invited to facilitate sessions in the 1990s. Also, Graciano actually attended sessions a decade earlier, just before migrating to the United States.

23. Mauro was among those honored in 1986.

24. Xochitl Bada's (2010) work is based in Chicago, although focused on the connections between that city and Michoacán, Mexico.

25. Los Cantores de la Sierra featured Román Gómez (primera vara), Ismael Martínez (segunda vara), Faustino Ojeda (jarana), and Antonio Escalante (guitarra quinta).

26. Very few musicians recorded before the 1970s, at which time Socorro Perea made three commercial recordings of huapango arribeño with Los Cantores de la Sierra. Ceferino Juárez (1902–1986), a violinist from Villa Juárez, San Luis Potosí, recalls a phonograph recording made in 1917. In 1985 Discos Corasón released *Antología del Son de México* produced by Eduardo Llerenas, Enrique Ramírez de Arellano, and Baruj Lieberman, which featured Toño Escalante y Los Gorriones de la Sierra (the same musicians as on Perea's recordings) and *El Conjunto de Pedro Sauceda* (featuring Eusebio Méndez, primera vara; Francisco Rivera, segunda vara; and Bruno Oviedo, vihuela). It wasn't until the early 1980s that Ángel González y Los Campesinos de la Sierra stepped into the recording studio, followed by Guillermo Velázquez and Los Leones de la Sierra de Xichú. The project was sponsored and funded in part by the Fondo Nacional para el Desarrollo de la Danza, produced by Naldo Labrín (Argentine musician and director of the group Sanampay), and recorded in conjunction with the Ediciones Pentagrama label, which had recently been launched.

27. Another woman who has played a similar role within huapango arribeño and deserves mention is Leonila González, the wife of troubadour Ángel González and a member of Los Campesinos de la Sierra. The huasteco tradition, in contrast, has seen a far greater presence of women performers: Esperanza Zumaya of Veracruz, Paty Chávez of Tamaulipas, and Reina Chávez from Querétaro, to name some of the more prominent contemporary practitioners. Also, in recent years, the abundance of son huasteco workshops throughout the huasteca regions has produced a large number of young practitioners, many of them women: the all-female huasteco ensemble Las Perlitas Queretanas comes to mind. Not to be left behind, the huapango arribeño workshops have also produced a few women violinists and troubadours.

28. Alexis has been invited to the festival alongside other décima artists, including his sister Adriana, Yeray Rodriguez (Canary Islands), José Curbelo (Uruguay), Martha Swint (Argentina), Luis Ortúzar (Chile), and Roberto Silva (Puerto Rico).

29. The answer is the key of A, or "LA" in Spanish, which is also the singular feminine definite article.

30. Here he is referring to Eliazar "Chalo" Velázquez, in the audience.

31. *Brinquetes* is derived from *brincos* (jumps).

32. *Tranzudos* derives from *transar* (literally, transaction), yet *tranza* or *tranzudo* is often used to refer to sneaky dealing or backsliding, in this case with regard to the performative rules of engagement. Although this word makes sense thematically, it breaks with the planta's parallelism. Graciano, it seems, could have used the more offensive *ojete(s)*, a nasty term used to refer to someone who is ungrateful and coarse (an asshole). However, such language would be considered a serious breach of etiquette. Graciano uses *tranzudo* in its stead, and, in preceding it with *brinquetes*, he conjures the word *ojetes* in the listening audience's imagination without having to actually utter the term.

33. Roger, vihuela, and Mario González, primera vara, are accompanying Pablo on this occasion.

34. *Fechorías* (boasts) is related to *facha* (appearance) and *fachoso* (ostentatious). *Fechoría(s)* suggests a vain boastfulness.

35. This is a reference to another troubadour, Isaías.

36. El Chilar is a reference to the rural hamlet, or rancho, El Chilarito.

37. "Don Cucito" refers to Refugio "Cuco" Rodríguez of Los Cucos, who are accompanying Graciano.

38. Roger Bartra comments,

> The problem was not only that [President López Portillo] set a reactionary, monetarist, and antipopular economic policy but that he carried it out with great ineffectiveness and much wavering. . . . The economic policies of the López Portillo administration promoted the expansion and autonomy of a financial sector that attracted enormous volumes of capital fleeing productive areas. It generated intense stock market activity based on stocks and bonds whose price had nothing to do with the process by which industrial capital was valued. This set off a speculative and rent-seeking euphoria that invented all kinds of businesses without any real productive base. (2002: 79)

39. While Kelley's analysis of the politics and poetics of black working-class daily lives as spaces of resistance is instructive, his reliance on James C. Scott's (1990) concept of infrapolitics is a theoretical disposition that relegates "unofficial" politics to the realm of the hidden (transcript). In contradistinction, although huapango arribeño may stem from a marginalized community (or silenced community, to recall Lomnitz), it is nevertheless public music and poetry that puts on display a community's aesthetics in highly visible spaces of performance.

CHAPTER 4: REGIONAL SOUNDS

1. For an extended discussion see Eduardo Bonilla-Silva's *Racism without Racists: Color-Blind Racism and the Persistence of Racial Inequality in America* (2014).

2. Gathered from the Public Shaming Tumblr (http://publicshaming.tumblr.com).

3. María Elena Cepeda (2010) makes a similar point in her discussion of the nativist backlash against the Spanish-language rendition of "The Star-Spangled Banner" performed by Latina/o recording artists in the wake of the immigrants' rights marches in 2006.

4. All one has to do is head west on Houston Street, a central corridor that runs through the downtown area and bears the name of Sam Houston, a major general in the Texas army who led the Texans to victory over the Mexican army at the Battle of San Jacinto in April 1836, just a month after the infamous battle in San Antonio.

5. De La Cruz, however, was not only Mexican-American but also a child. Perhaps this aspect of his identity speaks to the most egregious dimension of the politics of the U.S.-Mexico border. As I write, defenseless unaccompanied migrant children fleeing poverty, crime, and violence in Central American countries are attempting to cross into the United States. They suddenly find themselves at the center of a national debate in which bigoted U.S. citizens and politicians have recklessly

labeled them terrorists and drug smugglers, not to mention carriers of disease amid the present Ebola scare.

6. In Chicago, for instance, "the number of 'Mexican clubs' funneling money to specific localities in Mexico to build schools, roads and churches jumped from 35 in 1995 to 181 in 2002" (Vertovec 2004: 987).

7. Tourist visas acquired with the help of HTAs have facilitated their travels. Guillermo Velázquez recalls, "Cuando nos invitaron . . . los emigrados de Xichú y de la sierra qué se daban cuenta, llegaron a esas tocadas y era realmente emocionante para ellos y para nosotros encontrarnos allá en esos conciertos." (When they invited us . . . the migrants from Xichú and from the Sierra [Gorda] that found out, they came out to those engagements, and it was really emotional for them and for us to run into one another over there in those concerts.)

8. On the use of Spanish morphology, see Jane H. Hill's *The Everyday Language of White Racism* (2008).

9. While the décima was certainly not as widespread as the corrido, Paredes managed to write a significant amount around these poetics in South Texas, which once corresponded to Nuevo Santander, the Spanish colonial province established by José de Escandón in 1749. Six years earlier, as history would have it, Escandón also played a pivotal role in founding the now-famous missions in the present-day Sierra Gorda region of Querétaro. The purpose of his colonial administrative presence in both places was to pacify the local "hostile" indigenous populations, some of whom took refuge in the coastal jungle in southern Texas or the mountains of Querétaro. The two regions' shared history of conflict and conquest, particularly with regard to Escandón's role, seems a bit serendipitous, if only because of the emblematic expressive practices that took hold in the historical wake of these conflicts: the corrido and huapango.

10. Like Paredes, Peña displays a muted disapproval toward Mexican migrants, suggesting they pose a "substantial threat" to Texas-Mexican music given their lack of a meaningful association with the accordion-based conjunto style.

11. The corrido's spread also owes much to commercial printing presses and new recording technologies. In the late nineteenth century corridos were collected and published in broadsides and songbooks that were circulated en masse and were incorporated into the living oral tradition by the early twentieth century. Shortly thereafter, in the 1920s, recording companies like Victor, Okeh, Vocalion, and Decca began traveling to cities in the U.S. Southwest, such as San Antonio and Los Angeles, to set up mobile recording studios and record the repertoires of local artists, including corridistas. The resulting 78-rpm vinyl records circulated in commercial markets as "race records" and were broadcast over the new medium of radio, reaching an attentive transnational Mexican audience.

12. Alejandro L. Madrid notes:

The arrival of *Onda Grupera* into the Mexican entertainment industry coincided with the solidification of a new category in the U.S. Latino music industry, the so-called Regional Mexican music. In the 1980s, the increasingly large Latino population of the United States forced its music industry to recognize the importance of a previously fragmented Latino music market. Los Angeles, New York, San Antonio, and Miami had been the headquarters of the Mexican American, Puerto Rican, Tejano, and Cuban American music industries. . . . They created three music categories for this new all-embracing "Latino market": Afro-Caribbean (including Cuban, Puerto Rican, and Dominican genres like salsa, *merengue*, and *bachata*); Latino rock and pop; and Regional Mexican, an umbrella term encompassing all musics with roots in rural Mexico, including mariachi, *ranchera*, *norteña*, *banda*, and even Tejano music. (2013: 75)

13. A consolidated Mexican national identity, historians argue, emerges only after the Reform Wars of the late 1850s and certainly in a more institutionalized manner after the Mexican Revolution of 1910–1920.

14. Practices of sonic recontextualization are neither new nor exceptional; however, the contemporary intensification of these processes globally is "mediated simultaneously by the contradictory practices of epistemologies of purification—which seek to provincialize sounds in order to ascribe them a place in the modern ecumene and epistemologies of transculturation—which either enact or disrupt such practices of purification" (Ochoa Gautier 2006: 804). Arjun Appadurai describes the muted contradiction in such discourses as the contemporary "tension between cultural homogenization and cultural heterogenization" (1990: 5). While I am not interested in Appadurai's language of scapes, I do find his contention regarding the operational logic of the "new global cultural economy" useful, in other words, his view that it must be "understood as a complex, overlapping, disjunctive order, which cannot any longer be understood in terms of pre-existing center-periphery models" (6). If we accept Appadurai's argument, the intended symbolic weight of Mexican regional marketing comes into sharp relief in its expressed desire for the periphery amid global disjuncture. The aesthetics of this "fetishization of geography" (Corona and Madrid 2008: 18) are best represented by the previously discussed ranchero chrono-trope.

15. In the U.S. context, regional aesthetics, George Lipsitz (2007) has argued, take on a distinct politics, for they represent an "aggressive festivity" of a "recombinant Mexican identity" in the face of nativism.

16. "Field Hearing: Crisis on the Texas-Mexican Border: Surge of Unaccompanied Minors," July 3, 2014, https://homeland.house.gov/hearing/field-hearing-crisis -texas-border-surge-unaccompanied-minors/.

17. Mae M. Ngai (2004) employs the similar concept of "alien citizen."

18. This is, in part, an extension of an idea previously introduced by Herbert Marcuse (1977).

19. I am aware of the poststructuralist counterargument to this position, which rejects humanist and biological determinism and in turn argues that the authentic subject simply does not exist beneath the varied layers of culture and ideology; rather, the subject is merely a construction of those very discourses—human agency, if such a thing exists, bears little influence on self-making. Much of third-wave feminism,

while utilizing the insights of poststructuralism to reject biological determinist explanations for sex and gender, has also waged its own critique against poststructuralism, suggesting that it fundamentally obfuscates the ground for a feminist politics, for the poststructuralist position is premised on the idea that the "female" subject is incapable of participating in the construction of its own identity. Judith Butler's (1990) work on gender performativity and Linda Alcoff's (1994) feminist theorizing represent a direct challenge to this notion. For them, to transcend the category of woman is, yes, to deconstruct and de-essentialize this male-created concept, but this is merely the first step in actively building a useful and productive feminist identity politics. This is achieved through an exploration of the experience of subjectivity itself, in order to avoid both essentialism and poststructuralist nominalism.

20. "Place, in whatever guise is, like space and time, a social construct. This is the baseline proposition from which I start. The only interesting question that can then be asked is: by what social process(es) is place constructed?" (David Harvey, quoted in Cresswell 2004: 29).

21. In Casey's *Getting Back into Place: Toward a Renewed Understanding of the Place-World*, he aimed to "articulate an exact and engaged analysis of place more fully, and to trace out its philosophical consequences more completely, than has been done by other students of the subject" (1993: xv). To regain some recognition of the power of place, Casey first outlined a four-part history of Western philosophy's encounters with the concept. First, he refers to creation myths and the primordiality of place as something important to "avoiding the void," soon followed by Plato and Aristotle's detailed accounting for place in physics (Casey 1997: 3). The Middle Ages and Renaissance saw the assimilation of place into the universal extension of space, and later both place and space were subjected to universal time by modernist thinkers. At this time, place gave way to space, in what was perhaps the most significant moment for geographers' conception of place until late modern and postmodern times. Alfred North Whitehead, Edmund Husserl, Maurice Merleau-Ponty, Martin Heidegger, Gaston Bachelard, Michel Foucault, Gilles Deleuze, Félix Guattari, Jacques Derrida, and Luce Irigaray, to name a few, were all part of the reemergence of concern for place, not subordinate to space and time.

22. Cherríe Moraga writes in the preface to *This Bridge Called My Back: Writings by Radical Women of Color*, "How can we—this time—not use our bodies to be thrown over a river of tormented history to bridge a gap?" (1981: xv).

23. This is distinct from the constant retellings that saturate the social lives of people in Appalachia, chronicled by Kathleen Stewart (1996).

CHAPTER 5: FROM POTOSÍ TO TENNESSEE

1. Richie Bernardo. "2016's Metro Areas That Most and Least Resemble the U.S." www.wallethub.com. June 15, 2016. http://wallethub.com/edu/metro-areas-that-most-and-least-resemble-the-us/6109/.

2. This region still accounted for 45 percent of Mexican migrants in 2006, down from 60–70 percent during the 1970s (Rosenblum and Brick 2011).

3. Kenneth B. Noble, "Videotape of Beating by Authorities Jolts Los Angeles," *New York Times*, April 3, 1996, http://www.nytimes.com/1996/04/03/us/videotape-of -beating-by-authorities-jolts-los-angeles.html.

4. Other states that have enacted similar measures include Colorado, Georgia, Minnesota, Missouri, North Carolina, Oklahoma, South Carolina, and Utah. In 2008, the House of Representatives passed the Employee Verification Amendment Act (H.R. 6633), which requires federal contractors to use E-Verify for the next ten years to gauge its effectiveness. The measure failed in the senate. A similar bill was introduced in the Senate in January 2017.

5. Jason De Leon's (2015) recent work utilizes a four-field anthropological approach to studying migrant death and crossing along the Arizona-Sonora border. There, he offers similar ethnographic accounts to those contained in this chapter. Nevertheless, his analytical preoccupation with death at the expense of migrant vitality leaves the project at a theoretical impasse: in order to fully apprehend how prevention through deterrence is complicit in migrants' deaths—how it makes the Arizona desert a killing field, for instance—an analysis of how criminality is at the center of a racialized logic of labor subjugation is necessary. This is partly missing from this work, as is engagement with the theoretical contributions of Gilberto Rosas (2012) and Alejandro Lugo (2008).

6. Similarly, Achille Mbembe, in his formulation of necropolitics, attends to the sovereign's capacity to determine "who is disposable and who is not" (2003: 27).

7. For an extended discussion of how the private prison lobby was directly involved in crafting Arizona's S.B. 1070, see Martínez and Slack (2013).

8. The "murderous functions of the state," Mbembe writes, create "new and unique forms of social existence in which vast populations are subjected to conditions of life conferring upon them the status of living dead" (2003: 17, 40).

9. Similar measures have also been introduced in California, Colorado, Florida, Georgia, Indiana, Kentucky, Maine, Maryland, Mississippi, Nebraska, Oregon, South Carolina, Texas, Utah, and Virginia. See Alex Johnson and Vanessa Hauc, "States Seek to Copy Arizona Immigration Law," NBC *News*, February 3, 2011, http://www .nbcnews.com/id/41182588/ns/us_news-immigration_a_nation_divided/t/states -seek-copy-arizona-immigration-law/.

10. Jeffrey S. Passel et al., "As Growth Stalls, Unauthorized Immigrant Population Becomes More Settled," Pew Research Center, Hispanic Trends, September 3, 2014, http://www.pewhispanic.org/2014/09/03/as-growth-stalls-unauthorized -immigrant-population-becomes-more-settled/.

11. Luis F. B. Plascencia (2009) has examined the historical formation of the terms *illegal* and *undocumented* and their role in framing the debate over immigration, suggesting that both have contributed to the production of illegality. This debate over language rages on in mass-mediated forums, for instance, recent objections to the *New York Times*'s position regarding the term *illegal* as both neutral and appropriate has drawn criticism. Christine Haughney, "The Times Shifts on 'Illegal Immigrant, but Doesn't Ban the Use," *New York Times*, April 23, 2013, http://www.nytimes.com

/2013/04/24/business/media/the-times-shifts-on-illegal-immigrant-but-doesnt
-ban-the-use.html.

12. Here I partially reference the popular concept from Deleuze and Guattari (1987) known as "lines of flight," best understood as both immaterial and spatially material, which Keith Woodward and John Paul Jones III examine as "a phrase that signals an escape from an institutionalized apparatus of capture. The term has been invoked as an experimental resistance to the 'order words' of linguistic systems that limit alternative conceptualizations—just the sort of spatialization that might hover over material borderlands. For us, however, Deleuze and Guattari's conceptual spaces—and their political leverage—are anchored in a resolutely materialist understanding of spatiality" (2005: 237).

13. A comparison can be made to what Marcia Farr (2006) labels "Chicagoacán," which implies community across distance, or a transnational connection that is Mexican in scope. This connectivity she speaks of is—at its most fundamental— that between places irrespective of geography, where what binds is shared communicative practice and expressive culture, all of which relies on the realm of situated knowledge and memory, evincing, again, a generic intertextuality in which the poetic form entextualizes everyday life, thus relating to "some other discourse, or feature of discourse, to which the current discursive event indexically points" (Agha 2005: 2).

14. While the concept of reterritorialization, proposed by Deleuze and Guattari (1972), is useful here in imagining the desire for social equity, the saludado does not so much resignify the cultural meanings of inhabited spaces, substituting one for another, as actively enable a bridging between places such that it fashions a third space—to invoke Homi K. Bhabha (1994)—of free signification where communities can freely imagine one another.

15. Recently, Sydney Hutchinson (2011) has proposed the Foucauldian-inspired notion of kinetopia; however, the concept does not yield a dynamic idea of place, instead offering a stagnantly conceived sense of location based in a singular area of movement.

16. In her work on linguistic practices among Latina gang members, Norma Mendoza-Denton (2008) also explores how representational practices are differentially embodied via distinct modes of communicative media—ways of speaking, poetry notebooks, makeup, clothing, tattoos—that signal the relationality among language, the body, and materiality in crafting an intelligible semiotic system.

17. Negri (1991) appropriates the concept of self-valorization and applies it to processes that are beyond the reproduction of capital and that move toward the self-development of the working class through positive self-activity that bears the capacity for reinvention. This position steps beyond orthodox Marxism's focus on reactive struggles against capitalist domination by instead suggesting that the narrative of revolutionary subjectivity begins with humanity itself.

18. José E. Limón's (1982) earliest work on ethnic-Mexican joking places it within a repertoire of redressive symbolic action that emerges within the structural field

of what Victor Turner (1974) terms the "social drama." Likewise, Manuel H. Peña (1991), in his work on "treacherous-woman folklore" among Mexican men, and Rafaela Castro (1982), in her explorations of in-group humor among Mexican women, advance a view of jocular poetics as the iterations of displaced anxiety—a perspective reminiscent of the folklore of William R. Bascom (1954) and Mary Douglas (1966).

19. This contention—the polarity reversal between labor and capital, whereby all regimentation is understood as capital's response to labor insubordination—represents a critical deviation from the folklore studies of my intellectual precursors. Most notably, Limón (1994) relies on Fredric Jameson's (1981) *political unconscious* to bring Texas-Mexican folklore into relief. If we carefully consider Jameson's (1991) position—footnoted in his debate with Mike Davis (1985)—his intervention within the compelling dilemma of historicism is clear in its fidelity to a philosophical Marxism. That is, capitalist development for Jameson is driven ultimately by capital alone, and humanity is a hapless victim caught within its internal laws of motion. If this is so, then there is no realm of human self-valorization that exists outside capitalist domination.

20. The autonomist concept of *class composition* is key here in establishing how class power is associated not only with capitalist domination but also with workers' power to decompose capitalist social relations (Cleaver 1992). Conceptually, this stands as an expansion of Karl Marx's concept of the "composition" of capital, which details the organization of the production process with an emphasis on the aggregate domination of variable capital (human labor) by constant capital (machinery, tools, raw materials). In the autonomist formulation, the positive content of class struggle—in its broadest terms—is understood as going "beyond mere resistance to capitalism toward the self-construction of alternative ways of being," and this dynamism is the heart of the capitalist social relation and "a fundamental source of antagonism" against capital (Cleaver 1992: 106, 126). John Holloway writes, "Our existence, then, is not simply an existence within fetishised forms of social relations. We do not exist simply as the objectified victims of capitalism. . . . Rather, as the starting-point of this discussion—the scream—suggests, we exist against-and-in capital" (2002: 90).

CHAPTER 6: HUAPANGO SIN FRONTERAS

1. "Coast-to-Coast Marches for Immigrant Rights; Report: Administration Considering Nuclear Strikes in Iran," The Situation Room, *CNN*, [transcript], April 10, 2006, http://www.cnn.com/TRANSCRIPTS/0604/10/sitroom.03.html.

2. De Genova writes that the "transnational mobility of labour—like all labour under capitalism—necessarily has a double character, as (effectively subordinated) labour-*for*-capital while always also potentially labour-*against*-capital, which is never pre-determined and remains ever unpredictable and volatile" (2010: 112).

3. Lingis also writes, "The other's body is not first a material mass stationed before us and exposed to our inspection. . . . From the first, we find ourselves accompa-

nied, in our movements down to the levels of the field, by other sensibilities, other sentient bodies" (1998: 37).

4. Watkins (2010) focuses specifically on the pedagogical relation between teacher and student in building her argument around the ways in which acknowledgment plays into notions of self-worth.

5. Josh Kun (2005) also considers a certain spatiality with his concept of audiotopia in relation to popular music. Inspired by Michel Foucault's *heterotopia* as "a kind of effectively enacted utopia," Kun defines *audiotopia* as "the space within and produced by a musical element that offers the listener and/or the musician new maps for re-imagining the present social world" (23).

6. "Agency is the product of diagrams of mobility and placement which define or map the possibilities of where and how specific vectors of influence can stop and be placed. . . . Such places are temporary points of belonging and identification, of orientation and installation, creating sites of strategic historical possibilities and activities, and as such they are always contextually defined. They define the forms of empowerment or agency which are available to particular groups as ways of going on and of going out. Around such places, maps of subjectivity and identity, meaning and pleasure, desire and force, can be articulated." (Grossberg 1996: 102)

7. With this perspective, Nájera-Ramírez is particularly interested in the ranchera as a site through which women performers "may make feminist interventions" (2007: 457).

8. Elsewhere, Claudio Lomnitz similarly suggests that for Jiménez to claim that "life is worthless" is no better "than to legitimate an oppressive state that has done its best to dehumanize the people of Mexico" (2005: 55).

9. For quite some time mestizaje has been the most prevalent model utilized to write about the refigurations of ethnic-Mexican racial identity (Pérez-Torres 2006). The central axis on which the politics of mutability are rendered is that of hybridity and its role in shaping ethnic-Mexican culture and cultural production. Hybrid cultures have been understood to be the result of complicated exchanges between tradition and modernity, and also of the production of locality as an oppositional force embedded in its own dislocation (García Canclini 1995). Another notion of hybridity comes to us from Homi K. Bhabha (1994), who suggests that hybrid identities exist against the Euro-center's cultural fixity. Whatever the case may be, the master narratives of capitalist or Euro ontology, it is argued, are symbolically undermined by the presence of ambivalence. Still, no matter how ambivalent some might consider the borderlands of culture to be, borders do not cease to exist as sites of conflict (Rosaldo 1989).

10. *Taquachito* literally means "possum style"; it is a reference to the gliding movement typical to Texas-Mexican conjunto dancing.

11. Elsewhere, Ignacio Corona and Alejandro L. Madrid have critiqued the efforts of noninterdisciplinary ethnomusicological and musicological work that tries to "isolate music structures and texts from their social and cultural context in an

attempt to understand an ideal 'incorruptible' aesthetic meaning. As if the very analytical tools chosen to describe the musical phenomenon would not determine the aesthetic value to be found in the musical structures, as if the aesthetic values themselves were not politically and culturally informed, or as if the sounds had a fixed meaning independent from their social, historical, and cultural context, not to mention its reception and consumption" (2008: 6).

12. See John Holloway's *Change the World without Taking Power* (2002).

13. After interviewing 1,113 migrants who had just been deported, Slack et al. (2013) noted that "28% stated that their current home is located in the United States" (11).

14. Recognizing that music is always en route, Kun has written, "Music can be of a nation, but it is never exclusively national; it always overflows, spills out, sneaks through, reaches an ear on the other side of the border line, on the other side of the sea" (2005: 20).

CONCLUSION

1. "Remarks by the President to the People of Mexico," Office of the Press Secretary, White House, May 3, 2013; available at https://obamawhitehouse.archives.gov/the -press-office/2013/05/03/remarks-president-people-mexico.

2. My practice-based approach has been akin to non-representational thinking from the field of human geography.

3. Robert R. Alvarez Jr. (2012) presents a model for "bridging" that draws from Moraga and Anzaldúa's multilayered, critical approach. In critiquing U.S. state-centric scholarship that has "reinscribed the nation-state on the border" (539) and thus neglected how the border-security framework extends into the "interior range of the state" (552), Alvarez suggests using bridging to emphasize connections and contrasts that might inform new approaches to border studies, including ethnography. While calling for an understanding of bridges as "connectors . . . of the history and meanings of people and places" (552), Alvarez's critique still leaves much to be desired in terms of an ethnographic understanding of how such meaningful adjacencies between peoples and places are actually configured, for the claim that "the nation state is not tied to its borders" (552) evinces a continued state-centric approach, although his approval of "studies of musical genres" (542) and call for more ethnographic depth is encouraging. The door to what he calls a "refreshing cartography" (545) of borders and bridges for border studies is ultimately left open, the thought half-finished (in part, intentionally).

4. See the recently released album on compact disc *Serrano de Corazón* by *Guillermo Velázquez y Los Leones de la Sierra de Xichú* on Smithsonian Folkways Recordings (2016).

5. "Fandango Fronterizo Austin Solidarity Event," Austin Beloved Community, May 24, 2014, http://www.austinbelovedcommunity.org/event/fandango -fronterizo-austin-solidarity-event/.

Agamben, Giorgio. 1993. *The Coming Community*. Minneapolis: University of Minnesota Press.

Agamben, Giorgio. 1998. *Homo Sacer: Sovereign Power and Bare Life*. Stanford, CA: Stanford University Press.

Agha, Asif. 2005. "Introduction: Semiosis across Encounters." *Journal of Linguistic Anthropology* 15 (1): 1–5.

Ainslie, Ricardo. 1998. "Cultural Mourning, Immigration, and Engagements: Vignettes from the Mexican Experience." In *Crossings: Mexican Immigration in Interdisciplinary Perspectives*, edited by Marcelo M. Suárez-Orozco, 285–300. Cambridge, MA: Harvard University Press, David Rockefeller Center for Latin American Studies.

Akers Chacón, Justin, and Mike Davis. 2006. *No One Is Illegal: Fighting Violence and State Repression on the U.S.-Mexico Border*. Chicago: Haymarket.

Alcoff, Linda. 1994. "Cultural Feminism versus Post-structuralism: The Identity Crisis in Feminist Theory." In *Culture/Power/History: A Reader in Contemporary Social Theory*, edited by Nicholas B. Dirks, Geoff Eley, and Sherry B. Ortner, 96–122. Princeton, NJ: Princeton University Press.

Aldama, Arturo J. 2012. "No Somos Criminales: Crossing Borders in Contemporary Latina and Latino Music." In *Performing the US Latina and Latino Borderlands*, edited by Aldama, Arturo J., Chela Sandoval, and Peter J. García, 365–381. Bloomington: Indiana University Press.

Aldama, Arturo J., Chela Sandoval, and Peter J. García, eds. 2012. *Performing the US Latina and Latino Borderlands*. Bloomington: Indiana University Press.

Alexander, Bryant Keith. 2011. "Standing in the Wake: A Critical Auto/Ethnographic Exercise on Reflexivity in Three Movements." *Cultural Studies Critical Methodologies* 11 (2): 98–107.

Alexander, M. Jacqui. 2005. *Pedagogies of Crossing: Meditations on Feminism, Sexual Politics, Memory, and the Sacred*. Durham, NC: Duke University Press.

Allen, Jafari Sinclaire, and Ryan Cecil Jobson. 2016. "The Decolonizing Generation: (Race and) Theory in Anthropology since the Eighties." *Current Anthropology* 57 (2): 129–148.

Alonso Bolaños, Marina. 2008. *La "invención" de la música indígena de México: Antrop-ología e historia de las políticas culturales del siglo XX*. Buenos Aires: SB Ediciones.

Althusser, Louis. 2006. *Philosophy of the Encounter: Later Writings, 1978–87*, edited by Francois Matheron and Oliver Corpet. London: Verso

Alvarez, Luis. 2008. *The Power of the Zoot: Youth Culture and Resistance during World War II*. Berkeley: University of California Press.

Alvarez, Robert R., Jr. 1984. "The Border as Social System: The California Case." *New Scholar* 9 (1–2): 119–134.

Alvarez, Robert R., Jr. 1995. "The Mexican-US Border: The Making of an Anthropology of Borderlands." *Annual Review of Anthropology* 24 (1): 447–470.

Alvarez, Robert R., Jr. 2012. "Reconceptualizing the Space of the Mexico–US Border-line." In *A Companion to Border Studies*, edited by Thomas M. Wilson and Hastings Donnan, 538–556. Oxford: Wiley-Blackwell.

Anderson, Benedict. 1991. *Imagined Communities: Reflections on the Origin and Spread of Nationalism*. London: Verso.

Anzaldúa, Gloria. 1987. *Borderlands/La Frontera: The New Mestiza*. San Francisco: Aunt Lute Books.

Aparicio, Frances R., and Cándida F. Jáquez, eds. 2003. *Musical Migrations: Transna-tionalism and Cultural Hybridity in Latin/o America*. New York: Palgrave Macmillan.

Appadurai, Arjun. 1988. *The Social Life of Things: Commodities in Cultural Perspective*. Cambridge: Cambridge University Press.

Appadurai, Arjun. 1990. "Disjuncture and Difference in the Global Cultural Economy." *Public Culture* 2 (2): 1–24.

Appadurai, Arjun. 1996a. *Critical Dialogues in Cultural Studies*. London: Routledge.

Appadurai, Arjun. 1996b. *Modernity at Large: Cultural Dimensions of Globalization*. Minneapolis: University of Minnesota Press.

Attali, Jacques. 1985. *Noise: The Political Economy of Music*. Minneapolis: University of Minnesota Press.

Austin, John Langshaw. 1962. *How to Do Things with Words*. Cambridge, MA: Harvard University Press.

Azuara, César Hernández. 2003. *Huapango: El son huasteco y sus instrumentos en los siglos XIX y XX*. Mexico City: Centro de Investigaciones y Estudios Superiores en Antropología Social.

Bada, Xóchitl. 2010. "Mexican Hometown Associations in Chicago: The Newest Agents of Civic Participation." In *Marcha! Latino Chicago and the Immigrant Rights Movement*, edited by Amalia Pallares and Nilda Flores-González, 146–162. Chicago: University of Illinois Press.

Bada, Xóchitl, Jonathan Fox, Andrew D. Selee, and Mauricio Sánchez Álvarez. 2006. *Invisible No More: Mexican Migrant Civic Participation in the United States*. Washing-ton, DC: Mexico Institute.

Bakhtin, Mikhail. 1981. *The Dialogic Imagination: Four Essays*. Edited by Michael Holquist and translated by Caryl Emerson and Michael Holquist. Austin: University of Texas Press.

Barbaras, Renaud. 2004. *The Being of the Phenomenon: Merleau-Ponty's Ontology.* Bloomington: Indiana University Press.

Bartra, Roger. 1992. *The Cage of Melancholy: Identity and Metamorphosis in the Mexican Character.* New Brunswick, NJ: Rutgers University Press.

Bartra, Roger. 2002. *Blood, Ink, and Culture: Miseries and Splendors of the Post-Mexican Condition.* Durham, NC: Duke University Press.

Bascom, William R. 1954. "Four Functions of Folklore." *Journal of American Folklore* 67 (266): 333–349.

Bataille, Georges. 1991. *The Accursed Share, Volume 1: Consumption.* New York: Zone.

Batalla, Guillermo Bonfil. 1996. *México Profundo: Reclaiming a Civilization.* Translated by Philip Adams Dennis. Austin: University of Texas Press.

Bauman, Richard. 1972. "Differential Identity and the Social Base of Folklore." In *Toward New Perspectives in Folklore,* edited by Américo Paredes and Richard Bauman, 31–41. Austin: University of Texas Press.

Bauman, Richard. 2004. *A World of Others' Words: Cross-Cultural Perspectives on Intertextuality.* Malden, MA: Blackwell.

Bauman, Richard. 2005. "Commentary: Indirect Indexicality, Identity, Performance." *Journal of Linguistic Anthropology* 15 (1): 145–150.

Bauman, Richard. 2012. " 'First Verses I Ever Knew': Américo Paredes and the Border Décima." *Journal of American Folklore* 125 (495): 5–22.

Bauman, Richard, and Charles L. Briggs. 1990. "Poetics and Performances as Critical Perspectives on Language and Social Life." *Annual Review of Anthropology* 19 (1): 59–88.

Bauman, Richard, and Charles L. Briggs. 2003. *Voices of Modernity: Language Ideologies and the Politics of Inequality.* Cambridge: Cambridge University Press.

Bearns Esteva, Stuyvesant. 2011. "A la trova más bonita de etsos nobles cantadores: The Social and Spatiotemporal Changes of Son Jarocho Music and the Fandango Jarocho." PhD diss., University of California, Santa Cruz.

Behague, Gerard. 1991. "Reflections on the Ideological History of Latin American Ethnomusicology." In *Comparative Musicology and the Anthropology of Music,* edited by Bruno Nettl and Phillip Bohlman, 56–68. Chicago: University of Chicago Press.

Berger, Harris M. 2009. *Stance: Ideas about Emotion, Style, and Meaning for the Study of Expressive Culture.* Middletown, CT: Wesleyan University Press.

Berry, Keith. 2011. "The Ethnographic Choice: Why Ethnographers Do Ethnography." *Cultural Studies—Critical Methodologies* 11 (2): 165–177.

Bhabha, Homi K. 1994. *The Location of Culture.* London: Routledge.

Biehl, Joao. 2013. "Ethnography in the Way of Theory." *Cultural Anthropology* 28 (4): 573–597.

Blommaert, Jan. 2015. "Chronotopes, Scales, and Complexity in the Study of Language in Society." *Annual Review of Anthropology* 44 (1): 105–116.

Bohlman, Philip V. 1988. *The Study of Folk Music in the Modern World.* Bloomington: Indiana University Press.

Bohlman, Philip V. 2002. *World Music: A Very Short Introduction.* Oxford: Oxford University Press.

Bohórquez Molina, Jose Gerardo, Albero García Espejel, Diego Prieto Hernández, and Marco Antonio Rodríguez Espinosa. 2003. *Los pobres del campo queretano.* Mexico City: Instituto Nacional de Antropología e Historia.

Bourke, John Gregory. 1894. "The American Congo." *Scribner's Magazine* 15 (5): 590–661.

Bolton, Herbert Eugene. 1921. *The Spanish Borderlands: A Chronicle of Old Florida and the Southwest.* New Haven, CT: Yale University Press.

Bonilla-Silva, Eduardo. 2014. *Racism without Racists: Color-Blind Racism and the Persistence of Racial Inequality in America.* Lanham, MD: Rowman and Littlefield.

Brader, Ted, Nicholas A. Valentino, and Elizabeth Suhay. 2008. "What Triggers Public Opposition to Immigration? Anxiety, Group Cues, and Immigration Threat." *American Journal of Political Science* 52 (4): 959–978.

Brady, Mary Pat. 2000. "The Fungibility of Borders." *Nepantla: Views from the South* 1 (1): 171–190.

Brandes, Stanley H. 2006. *Skulls to the Living, Bread to the Dead: The Day of the Dead in Mexico and Beyond.* Malden, MA: Blackwell.

Briggs, Charles L. 1986. *Learning How to Ask: A Sociolinguistic Appraisal of the Role of the Interview in Social Science Research.* Cambridge: Cambridge University Press.

Briggs, Charles L. 1988. *Competence in Performance: The Creativity of Tradition in Mexicano Verbal Art.* Philadelphia: University of Pennsylvania Press.

Briggs, Charles L. 2007. "Anthropology, Interviewing, and Communicability in Contemporary Society." *Current Anthropology* 48 (4): 551–580.

Briggs, Charles L. 2012. "What We Should Have Learned from Américo Paredes: The Politics of Communicability and the Making of Folkloristics." *Journal of American Folklore* 125 (495): 91–110.

Briggs, Charles L., and Richard Bauman. 1992. "Genre, Intertextuality, and Social Power." *Journal of Linguistic Anthropology* 2 (2): 131–172.

Broyles-González, Yolanda. 2006. "Ranchera Music(s) and the Legendary Lydia Mendoza: Performing Social Location and Relations." In *The Chicana/o Cultural Studies Reader,* edited by Angie Chabram-Dernersesian, 352–360. New York: Routledge.

Buffie, Edward F., and Allen Sangines Krause. 1989. "Mexico 1958–86: From Stabilizing Development to the Debt Crisis." In *Developing Country Debt and the World Economy,* edited by Jeffrey D. Sachs, 141–168. Chicago, IL: University of Chicago Press.

Bustamante, Jorge. 1983. "Maquiladoras: A New Face of International Capitalism on Mexico's Northern Frontier." In *Women, Men and the International Division of Labor,* edited by June C. Nash and María Patricia Fernández-Kelly, 224–256. Albany: State University of New York Press.

Bustamante, Jorge. 1992. "Preface: A Conceptual and Operative Vision of the Political Problems on the Border." In *Demographic Dynamics of the US-Mexico Border,* edited by John Robert Weeks and Roberto Ham-Chande, v–viii. El Paso: Texas Western Press.

Bustamante, Jorge, Clark Winton Reynolds, and Raúl Andrés Hinojosa Ojeda. 1992. *U.S.-Mexico Relations: Labor Market Interdependence.* Stanford, CA: Stanford University Press.

Butler, Judith. 1990. *Gender Trouble: Feminism and the Subversion of Identity.* New York: Routledge.

Byrd, Samuel K. 2015. *The Sounds of Latinidad: Immigrants Making Music and Creating Culture in a Southern City.* New York: New York University Press.

Campos, Ruben M. 1928. *El folklor y la música mexicana: Investigación acerca de la cultura musical en México (1525–1925).* Mexico City: Talleres Gráficos de la Nación.

Cardona, Bertha A. 2007. *La música de México: La esencia de una nación.* Mexico City: Convergencia.

Cardoso, Eliana A., and Ann Helwege. 1992. *Latin America's Economy: Diversity, Trends, and Conflicts.* Cambridge, MA: MIT Press.

Carracedo Navarro, David. 2000. *Del Huapango Arribeño Te Cuento Risueño.* Querétaro, México: Unidad Regional de Culturas Populares de Querétaro.

Carracedo Navarro, David. 2003. *Vamos Haciendo El Ruidito.* Querétaro, México: Unidad Regional de Culturas Populares de Querétaro.

Carter Muñoz, Kim Anne. 2013. "Huapangueros Reclaiming Son Huasteco in Translocal Festivals: Youth, Women and Nahua Musicians." PhD diss., University of Washington.

Casey, Edward S. 1993. *Getting Back into Place: Toward a Renewed Understanding of the Place-World.* Bloomington: Indiana University Press.

Casey, Edward S. 1997. *The Fate of Place: A Philosophical History.* Berkeley: University of California Press.

Casey, Edward S. 2000. *Remembering: A Phenomenological Study.* Bloomington: Indiana University Press.

Casillas, Dolores. 2011. "Sounds of Surveillance: U.S. Spanish-Language Radio Patrols la Migra." *American Quarterly* 63 (3): 807–829.

Castro, Rafaela. 1982. "Mexican Women's Sexual Jokes." *Aztlan* 13: 273–294.

Cepeda, María Elena. 2010. "Singing the 'Star-Spanglish Banner': The Politics and Pathologization of Bilingualism in U.S. Popular Media." In *Beyond el Barrio: Everyday Life in Latina/o America,* edited by Gina M. Pérez, Frank A. Guridy, and Adrian Burgos Jr., 27–43. New York: New York University Press.

Certeau, Michel de. 1984. *The Practice of Everyday Life.* Berkeley: University of California Press.

Cervantes, Marco. 2013. "Squeezebox Poetics: Locating Afromestizaje in Esteban Jordan's Texas Conjunto Performance." *American Quarterly* 65 (4): 853–876.

Chabram-Dernersesian, Angie, ed. 2006. *The Chicana/o Cultural Studies Reader.* New York: Routledge.

Chakravorty Spivak, Gayatri. 1988. "Can the Subaltern Speak?" In *Marxism and the Interpretation of Culture,* edited by Cary Nelson and Lawrence Grossberg, 271–313. Urbana: University of Illinois Press.

Chamorro, Arturo E. J. 2000. *Mariachi antiguo, jarabe y son: Símbolos compartidos y tradición musical en las identidades jaliscienses.* Zapopan, Mexico: El Colegio de Jalisco.

Chávez, Alex. 2010. "Compañeros del Destino: Transborder Social Lives and Huapango Arribeño at the Interstices of Postmodernity." PhD diss., University of Texas at Austin.

Chávez, Alex. 2015. "So ¿Te Fuiste a Dallas? (So You Went to Dallas?/So You Got Screwed?): Language, Migration, and the Poetics of Transgression." *Journal of Linguistic Anthropology* 25(2): 15–72.

Chavez, Leo R. 1992. *Shadowed Lives: Undocumented Immigrants in American Society.* Fort Worth, TX: Harcourt Brace Jovanovich.

Chavez, Leo R. 2008. *The Latino Threat: Constructing Immigrants, Citizens, and the Nation.* Stanford, CA: Stanford University Press.

Cintron, Ralph. 1997. *Angels' Town: Chero Ways, Gang Life, and Rhetorics of the Everyday.* Boston: Beacon.

Cleaver, Harry. 1979. *Reading Capital Politically.* Austin: University of Texas Press.

Cleaver, Harry. 1992. "The Inversion of Class Perspectives in Marxian Theory: From Valorization to Self-Valorization." In *Open Marxism, Volume 2: Theory and Practice*, edited by Werner Bonefeld, Richard Gunn, and Kosmas Psychopedis, 2:106–144. London: Pluto.

Clifford, James. 1988. *The Predicament of Culture: Twentieth-Century Ethnography, Literature, and Art.* Cambridge, MA: Harvard University Press.

Clifford, James. 1997. *Routes: Travel and Translation in the Late Twentieth Century.* Cambridge, MA: Harvard University Press.

Clifford, James, and George E. Marcus, eds. 1986. *Writing Culture: The Poetics and Politics of Ethnography. A School of American Research Advanced Seminar.* Berkeley: University of California Press.

Coates, Ta-Nehisi. 2015. *Between the World and Me.* New York: Spiegel and Grau.

Coplan, David B. 1987. "Eloquent Knowledge: Lesotho Migrants' Songs and the Anthropology of Experience." *American Ethnologist* 14 (3): 413–433.

Cornelius, Wayne A. 2005. "Controlling 'Unwanted' Immigration: Lessons from the United States, 1993–2004." *Journal of Ethnic and Migration Studies* 31 (4): 775–794.

Corona, Ignacio, and Alejandro L. Madrid. 2008. *Postnational Musical Identities: Cultural Production, Distribution, and Consumption in a Globalized Scenario.* Lanham, MD: Lexington Books.

Cowie, Jefferson R., and Lauren Boehm. 2006. "Dead Man's Town: 'Born in the U.S.A.,' Social History, and Working-Class Identity." *American Quarterly* 58 (2): 353–378.

Cresswell, Tim. 2004. *Place: A Short Introduction.* Malden, MA: Blackwell.

Crozier, Michel J., Samuel P. Huntington, and Joji Watanuki. 1975. *The Crisis of Democracy: Report on the Governability of Democracies to the Trilateral Commission.* New York: New York University Press.

Davidson, Miriam. 2000. *Lives on the Line: Dispatches from the U.S.-Mexico Border.* Tucson: University of Arizona Press.

Dávila, Arlene M. 2004. *Barrio Dreams: Puerto Ricans, Latinos, and the Neoliberal City.* Berkeley: University of California Press.

Davis, Harold E. 1990. *Henry Grady's New South: Atlanta, a Brave Beautiful City.* Tuscaloosa: University of Alabama Press.

Davis, Mike. 1985. "Urban Renaissance and the Spirit of Postmodernism." *New Left Review* 1 (151): 106–113.

Davis, Mike. 1998. *Ecology of Fear: Los Angeles and the Imagination of Disaster*. New York: Metropolitan Books.

De Genova, Nicholas. 1998. "Race, Space, and the Reinvention of Latin America in Mexican Chicago." *Latin American Perspectives* 25 (5): 87–116.

De Genova, Nicholas. 2002. "Migrant 'Illegality' and Deportability in Everyday Life." *Annual Review of Anthropology* 31: 419–447.

De Genova, Nicholas. 2005. *Working the Boundaries: Race, Space, and "Illegality" in Mexican Chicago*. Durham, NC: Duke University Press.

De Genova, Nicholas. 2009. "Conflicts of Mobility, and the Mobility of Conflict: Rightlessness, Presence, Subjectivity, Freedom." *Subjectivity* 29 (S1): 445–466.

De Genova, Nicholas. 2010. "The Queer Politics of Migration: Reflections on 'Illegality' and Incorrigibility." *Studies in Social Justice* 4 (2): 101–126.

De Genova, Nicholas. 2012. "Border, Scene and Obscene." In *A Companion to Border Studies*, edited by Thomas M. Wilson and Hasting Donnan, 492–504. Oxford: Wiley-Blackwell.

De León, Arnoldo. 1983. *They Called Them Greasers: Anglo Attitudes toward Mexicans in Texas, 1821–1900*. Austin: University of Texas Press.

De León, Jason. 2015. *The Land of Open Graves: Living and Dying on the Migrant Trail*. Oakland: University of California Press.

Del Castillo, Adelaida R. 2007. "Illegal Status and Social Citizenship: Thoughts on Mexican Immigrants in a Postnational World." In *Women and Migration in the U.S.-Mexico Borderlands: A Reader*, edited by Denise A. Segura and Patricia Zavella, 92–103. Durham, NC: Duke University Press.

Deleuze, Gilles, and Félix Guattari. 1972. *Anti-Oedipus: Capitalism and Schizophrenia*. Minneapolis: University of Minnesota Press.

Deleuze, Gilles, and Félix Guattari. 1987. *A Thousand Plateaus: Capitalism and Schizophrenia*. Minneapolis: University of Minnesota Press.

Dent, Alexander Sebastian. 2009. *River of Tears: Country Music, Memory, and Modernity in Brazil*. Durham, NC: Duke University Press.

Díaz-Sánchez, Micaela. 2009. "(In)Between Nation and Diaspora: Performing Indigenous and African Legacies in Chicana/o and Mexican Cultural Production." PhD diss., Stanford University.

Díaz Sanchez, Micaela, and Alexandro D. Hernández. 2013. "The Son Jarocho as Afro-Mexican Resistance Music." *Journal of Pan African Studies* 6 (1): 187–209.

Dick, Hilary Parsons. 2010. "Imagined Lives and Modernist Chronotopes in Mexican Nonmigrant Discourse." *American Ethnologist* 37 (2): 275–290.

Dick, Hilary Parsons. 2011a. "Language and Migration to the United States." *Annual Review of Anthropology* 40: 227–240.

Dick, Hilary Parsons. 2011b. "Making Immigrants Illegal in Small-Town USA." *Journal of Linguistic Anthropology* 21 (S1): E35–E55.

Dolan, Jill. 2001. "Performance, Utopia, and the 'Utopian Performative.'" *Theatre Journal* 53 (3): 455–479.

Dorsey, Margaret, and Miguel Díaz-Barriga. 2011. "Patriotic Citizenship, the Border Wall and the 'El Veterano' Conjunto Festival." In *Transnational Encounters: Music and Performance at the U.S.-Mexico Border*, edited by Alejandro L. Madrid, 207–228. New York: Oxford University Press.

Douglas, Mary. 1966. *Purity and Danger: An Analysis of Concepts of Pollution and Taboo.* New York: Praeger.

Dunn, Timothy J. 1996. *The Militarization of the U.S.-Mexico Border, 1978–1992: Low-Intensity Conflict Doctrine Comes Home.* Austin: Center for Mexican American Studies, University of Texas at Austin.

Echevarría Román, Jesús Antonio. 2000. *La petenera: Son huasteco.* Mexico City: Programa de Desarrollo Cultural de la Huasteca.

Edberg, Mark Cameron. 2004. *El Narcotraficante: Narcocorridos and the Construction of a Cultural Persona on the U.S.-Mexico Border.* Austin: University of Texas Press.

Eisenberg, Andrew J. 2015. "Space." In *Keywords in Sound*, edited by David Novak and Matt Sakakeeny, 193–207. Durham, NC: Duke University Press.

Elenes, C. Alejandra. 2011. *Transforming Borders: Chicana/o Popular Culture and Pedagogy.* Lanham, MD: Lexington Books.

Elie, Serge D. 2013. "From Ethnography to Mesography: A Praxis of Inquiry for a Postexotic Anthropology." *Qualitative Inquiry* 19 (3): 219–231.

Elliott, James R., and Jeremy Pais. 2006. "Race, Class, and Hurricane Katrina: Social Differences in Human Responses to Disaster." *Social Science Research* 35 (2): 295–321.

Entrikin, J. Nicholas. 1991. *The Betweenness of Place: Towards a Geography of Modernity.* Baltimore: Johns Hopkins University Press.

Erlmann, Veit. 1996. *Nightsong: Performance, Power, and Practice in South Africa.* Chicago: University of Chicago Press.

Erlmann, Veit. 2004. "But What of the Ethnographic Ear? Anthropology, Sound, and the Senses." In *Hearing Cultures: Essays on Sound, Listening and Modernity*, edited by Veit Erlmann, 1–20. Oxford: Berg.

Evans, Fred, and Leonard Lawlor. 2000. *Chiasms: Merleau-Ponty's Notion of Flesh.* Albany, NY: State University of New York Press.

Fabian, Johannes. 1983. *Time and the Other: How Anthropology Makes Its Object.* New York: Columbia University Press.

Farr, Marcia. 2006. *Rancheros in Chicagoacán: Language and Identity in a Transnational Community.* Austin: University of Texas Press.

Faudree, Paja. 2013. *Singing for the Dead: The Politics of Indigenous Revival in Mexico.* Durham, NC: Duke University Press.

Feld, Steven. 1984. "Sound Structure as Social Structure." *Ethnomusicology* 28 (3): 383–409.

Feld, Steven, and Keith H. Basso. 1996. *Senses of Place.* Santa Fe, NM: School of American Research.

Feld, Steven, and Donald Brenneis. 2004. "Doing Anthropology in Sound." *American Ethnologist* 31 (4): 461–474.

Ferguson, James, and Akhil Gupta. 2005. "Spatializing States: Toward an Ethnography of Neoliberal Governmentality." In *Anthropologies of Modernity: Foucault, Governmentality, and Life Politics*, edited by Jonathan Xavier Inda, 105–131. Malden, MA: Blackwell.

Fernandez, James W. 1991. *Beyond Metaphor: The Theory of Tropes in Anthropology.* Stanford, CA: Stanford University Press.

Fernández-Kelly, Maria Patricia. 1983. "Mexican Border Industrialization, Female Labor Force Participation, and Migration. In *Women, Men and the International Division of Labor,* edited by June C. Nash and María Patricia Fernández-Kelly, 205–223. Albany: State University of New York Press.

Finnegan, Ruth H. 2002. *Communicating: The Multiple Modes of Human Interconnection.* London: Routledge.

Flores, Richard R. 1992. "The Corrido and the Emergence of Texas-Mexican Social Identity." *Journal of American Folklore* 105 (416): 166–182.

Flores, Richard R. 1994. " 'Los Pastores' and the Gifting of Performance." *American Ethnologist* 21 (2): 270–285.

Flores, Richard R. 1995. *Los Pastores: History and Performance in the Mexican Shepherds' Play of South Texas.* Washington, DC: Smithsonian Institution Press.

Flores, Richard R. 1998. "Memory-Place, Meaning, and the Alamo." *American Literary History* 10 (3): 428–445.

Flores, Richard R. 2002. *Remembering the Alamo: Memory, Modernity, and the Master Symbol.* Austin: University of Texas Press.

Fox, Aaron A. 2004. *Real Country: Music and Language in Working-Class Culture.* Durham, NC: Duke University Press.

Fox, Jonathan A. 2007. *Accountability Politics: Power and Voice in Rural Mexico.* Oxford: Oxford University Press.

Fussell, Elizabeth. 2009. "Post-Katrina New Orleans as a New Migrant Destination." *Organization and Environment* 22 (4): 458–469.

Gálvez, Alyshia. 2013. "Immigrant Citizenship: Neoliberalism, Immobility and the Vernacular Meanings of Citizenship." *Identities* 20 (6): 720–737.

García Canclini, Néstor. 1990. *Culturas híbridas: Estrategias para entrar y salir de la modernidad.* Mexico City: Grijalbo.

García Canclini, Néstor. 1995. *Hybrid Cultures: Strategies for Entering and Leaving Modernity.* Minneapolis: University of Minnesota Press.

García Canclini, Néstor. 2001. *Consumers and Citizens: Globalization and Multicultural Conflicts.* Minneapolis: University of Minnesota Press.

Garza Villarreal, Amy. 2014. "Places of Sanctuary: Religious Revivalism and the Politics of Immigration in New Mexico." PhD diss., University of California, Santa Cruz.

Giddens, Anthony. 1991. *Modernity and Self-Identity: Self and Society in the Late Modern Age.* Stanford, CA: Stanford University Press.

Gilroy, Paul. 1993. *The Black Atlantic: Modernity and Double-Consciousness.* Cambridge, MA: Harvard University Press.

Goffman, Erving. 1979. "Footing." *Semiotica* 25: 1–29.

Gomez, Alan Eladio. 2016. *The Revolutionary Imaginations of Greater Mexico: Chicana/o Radicalism, Solidarity Politics, and Latin American Social Movements.* Austin: University of Texas Press.

Gómez-Ullate García de León, Martín. 2011. "Desafíos poéticos y versadores populares." *Tejuelo: Didáctica de la Lengua y Literatura* 11 (1): 158–174.

Gonzales, Roberto G., and Leo R. Chavez. 2012. " 'Awakening to a Nightmare': Abjectivity and Illegality in the Lives of Undocumented 1.5-Generation Latino Immigrants in the United States." *Current Anthropology* 53 (3): 255–281.

González, Anita. 2010. *Afro-Mexico: Dancing between Myth and Reality*. Austin: University of Texas Press.

González, Martha. 2009. "*Zapateado* Afro-Chicana Fandango Style: Self-Reflexive Moments in Zapateado." In *Dancing Across Borders: Bailes y Danzas Mexicanos*, edited by Olga Nájera-Ramírez, Norma E. Cantú, and Brenda M. Romero, 359–378 Urbana: University of Illinois Press.

Gonzalez, Pablo. 2011. "Autonomy Road: The Cultural Politics of Chicana/o Autonomous Organizing in Los Angeles, California." PhD diss., University of Texas at Austin.

González-Paraíso, Raquel. 2014. "Re-contextualizing Traditions: The Performance of Identity in Festivals of Huasteco, Jarocho, and Terracalenteño Sones in Mexico." PhD diss., University of Wisconsin-Madison.

Gradante, William. 1982. " 'El Hijo del Pueblo': Jose Alfredo Jimenez and the Mexican 'Cancion Ranchera.' " *Latin American Music Review/Revista de Música Latinoamericana* 3 (1): 36–59.

Grossberg, Lawrence. 1992. *We Gotta Get Out of This Place: Popular Conservatism and Postmodern Culture*. New York: Routledge.

Grossberg, Lawrence. 1996. "Identity and Cultural Studies: Is That All There Is?" In *Questions of Cultural Identity*, edited by Stuart Hall and Paul Du Gay, 80–107. London: Sage.

Grosz, Elizabeth. 1994. *Volatile Bodies: Toward a Corporeal Feminism*. Indianapolis: Indiana University Press.

Guattari, Félix. 1995. *Chaosmosis: An Ethico-aesthetic Paradigm*. Bloomington: Indiana University Press.

Guerra, Santiago Ivan. 2011. "From Vaqueros to Mafiosos: A Community History of Drug Trafficking in Rural South Texas." PhD diss., University of Texas at Austin.

Guerrero Tarquín, Alfredo. 1988. *Reminiscencias de un viaje a través de la Sierra Gorda por Xichú y Atarjea*. Mexico City: Instituto Nacional de Antropología e Historia.

Gupta, Akhil, and James Ferguson. 1992. "Beyond 'Culture': Space, Identity, and the Politics of Difference." *Cultural Anthropology* 7 (1): 6–23.

Gupta, Akhil, and James Ferguson. 1997. *Culture, Power, Place: Explorations in Critical Anthropology*. Durham, NC: Duke University Press.

Habell-Pallán, Michelle. 2005. *Loca Motion: The Travels of Chicana and Latina Popular Culture*. New York: New York University Press.

Habermas, Jürgen. 1983. "Modernity—an Incomplete Project." In *The Anti-aesthetic: Essays on Postmodern Culture*, edited by Hal Foster, 3–15. Seattle, WA: Bay.

Habermas, Jürgen, and Frederick Lawrence. 1984. "The French Path to Postmodernity: Bataille between Eroticism and General Economics." *New German Critique* 33: 79–102.

Hall, Stuart. 1973. *Encoding and Decoding in the Television Discourse*. Birmingham, AL: Centre for Cultural Studies, University of Birmingham.

Hall, Stuart. 1989. "The Meaning of New Times." In *New Times: The Changing Face of Politics in the 1990s*, edited by Stuart Hall and Martin Jacques, 116–134. London: Lawrence and Wishart.

Haney-López, Ian. 1996. *White by Law: The Legal Construction of Race.* New York: New York University Press.

Hanks, William F. 1996. *Language and Communicative Practices.* Boulder, CO: Westview.

Hardt, Michael, and Antonio Negri. 2000. *Empire.* Cambridge, MA: Harvard University Press.

Hardt, Michael, and Antonio Negri. 2004. *Multitude: War and Democracy in the Age of Empire.* New York: Penguin.

Harvey, David. 1990. *The Condition of Postmodernity: An Enquiry into the Origins of Cultural Change.* Oxford: Blackwell.

Herrera-Sobek, María. 1990. *The Mexican Corrido: A Feminist Analysis.* Bloomington: Indiana University Press.

Hershfield, Joanne Leslie. 1996. *Mexican Cinema/Mexican Woman, 1940–1950.* Tucson: University of Arizona Press.

Heyman, Josiah McC. 1994. "The Mexico-United States Border in Anthropology: A Critique and Reformulation." *Journal of Political Ecology* 1 (1): 43–66.

Higgins, Nicholas. 2000. "The Zapatista Uprising and the Poetics of Cultural Resistance." *Alternatives: Global, Local, Political* 25 (3): 359–374.

Hill, Jane H. 2008. *The Everyday Language of White Racism.* Chichester, UK: Wiley-Blackwell.

Hing, Bill Ong. 2004. *Defining America through Immigration Policy.* Philadelphia: Temple University Press.

Hirsch, Eric, and Michael O'Hanlon. 1995. *The Anthropology of Landscape: Perspectives on Place and Space.* Oxford: Clarendon.

Hobsbawm, Eric J. 1962. *The Age of Revolution, 1789–1848.* Cleveland, OH: World.

Hobsbawm, Eric J. 1975. *The Age of Capital, 1848–1875.* New York: Scribner.

Hobsbawm, Eric J. 1987. *The Age of Empire, 1875–1914.* New York: Pantheon.

Hobsbawm, Eric J. 1994. *The Age of Extremes: The Short Twentieth Century, 1914–1991.* London: Michael Joseph.

Hobsbawm, Eric J., and Terence O. Ranger. 1983. *The Invention of Tradition.* Cambridge: Cambridge University Press.

Hogue, W. Lawrence. 1996. *Race, Modernity, Postmodernity: A Look at the History and the Literatures of People of Color since the 1960s.* Albany: State University of New York Press.

Holloway, John. 2002. *Change the World without Taking Power: The Meaning of Revolution Today.* London: Pluto.

Holquist, Michael. 1981. "Glossary." In *The Dialogic Imagination: Four Essays.* By M. M. Bakhtin. Edited by Michael Holquist and translated by Caryl Emerson and Michael Holquist, 423–434. Austin: University of Texas Press.

Hutchinson, Sydney. 2007. *From Quebradita to Duranguense: Dance in Mexican American Youth Culture.* Tucson: University of Arizona Press.

Hutchinson, Sydney. 2011. "Breaking Borders/*Quebrando fronteras*: Dancing in the Borderscape." In *Transnational Encounters: Music and Performance at the U.S.-Mexico Border*, edited by Alejandro L. Madrid, 41–66. New York: Oxford University Press.

Ibarra, María de la Luz. 2007. "Mexican Immigrant Women and the New Domestic Labor." In *Women and Migration in the U.S.-Mexico Borderlands: A Reader*, edited by Denise A. Segura and Patricia Zavella, 286–305. Durham, NC: Duke University Press.

Ihde, Don. 2007. *Listening and Voice: Phenomenologies of Sound*. Albany: State University of New York Press.

Inda, Jonathan Xavier. 2006. *Targeting Immigrants: Government, Technology, and Ethics*. Malden, MA: Blackwell.

Jakobson, Román. 1960. "Linguistics and Poetics." In *Style in Language*, edited by Thomas Albert Sebeok, 350–377. Cambridge, MA: MIT Press.

Jameson, Fredric. 1981. *The Political Unconscious: Narrative as a Socially Symbolic Act*. Ithaca, NY: Cornell University Press.

Jameson, Fredric. 1991. *Postmodernism, or, The Cultural Logic of Late Capitalism*. Durham, NC: Duke University Press.

Jameson, Fredric. 2003. "The End of Temporality." *Critical Inquiry* 29 (4): 695–718.

Jáuregui, Jesús. 2007. *El mariachi: Símbolo musical de México*. Mexico City: Instituto Nacional de Antropología e Historia.

Jimenez, Maria. 2009. *Humanitarian Crisis: Migrant Deaths at the U.S.-Mexico Border*. American Civil Liberties Union.

Jiménez de Báez, Yvette. 2008. "La fiesta de la 'Topada' y la migración al norte (una tradición de la Sierra Gorda mexicana y de áreas circunvecinas)." *Revista de Literaturas Populares* 8 (2): 347–375.

Johnson, Gaye Theresa. 2013. *Spaces of Conflict, Sounds of Solidarity: Music, Race, and Spatial Entitlement in Los Angeles*. Berkeley: University of California Press.

Johnson, Jean B. 1942. "The Huapango: A Mexican Song Contest." *California Folklore Quarterly* 1 (3): 233–244.

Keating, AnaLouise. 2005. *Entre Mundos/among Worlds: New Perspectives on Gloria E. Anzaldúa*. New York: Palgrave Macmillan.

Kelley, Robin D. G. 1994. *Race Rebels: Culture, Politics, and the Black Working Class*. New York: Free Press.

Kelley, Robin D. G. 2003. *Freedom Dreams: The Black Radical Imagination*. Boston: Beacon.

Goulet, Denis, and Kwan S. Kim. 1989. *Estrategias de Desarollo para el Futuro de México*. Guadalajara, Mexico: Instituto Tecnológico y de Estudios Superiores de Occidente.

Klatzky, Roberta L., Dinesh K. Pai, and Eric P. Krotkov. 2000. "Perception of Material from Contact Sounds." *Presence: Teleoperators Virtual Environments* 9 (4): 399–410.

Kruth, Patricia, and Henry Stobart. 2000. *Sound*. Cambridge: Cambridge University Press.

Kun, Josh. 2005. *Audiotopia: Music, Race, and America*. Berkeley: University of California Press.

Lang, John S., and Jeannye Thornton. 1985. "The Disappearing Border." *U.S. News & World Report*, August 19: 30.

Lemke, Thomas. 2011. *Biopolitics: An Advanced Introduction.* New York: New York University Press.

Levitt, Peggy, and Nina Glick Schiller. 2004. "Conceptualizing Simultaneity: A Transnational Social Field Perspective on Society." *International Migration Review* 38 (3): 1002–1039.

Limón, José E. 1982. "History, Chicano Joking, and the Varieties of Higher Education: Tradition and Performance as Critical Symbolic Action." *Journal of the Folklore Institute* 19 (2): 141–166.

Limón, José E. 1983. "Western Marxism and Folklore: A Critical Introduction." *Journal of American Folklore* 96 (379): 34–52.

Limón, José E. 1992. *Mexican Ballads, Chicano Poems: History and Influence in Mexican-American Social Poetry.* Berkeley: University of California Press.

Limón, José E. 1994. *Dancing with the Devil: Society and Cultural Poetics in Mexican-American South Texas.* Madison: University of Wisconsin Press.

Limón, José E. 1998. *American Encounters: Greater Mexico, the United States, and the Erotics of Culture.* Boston: Beacon.

Limón, José E. 2011. "This Is Our *Música*, Guy! Tejanos and Ethno/Regional Musical Nationalism." In *Transnational Encounters: Music and Performance at the U.S.-Mexico Border*, edited by Alejandro L. Madrid, 111–128. New York: Oxford University Press.

Limón, José E. 2012. *Américo Paredes: Culture and Critique.* Austin: University of Texas Press.

Lingis, Alphonso. 1998. *The Imperative.* Bloomington: Indiana University Press.

Lipietz, Alain. 1997. "The Post-Fordist World: Labour Relations, International Industry Hierarchy, and Global Ecology." *Review of International Political Economy* 4 (1): 1–41.

Lipsitz, George. 1994. *Dangerous Crossroads: Popular Music, Postmodernism and the Poetics of Place.* New York: Verso.

Lipsitz, George. 2006. *The Possessive Investment in Whiteness: How White People Profit from Identity Politics.* Philadelphia: Temple University Press.

Lipsitz, George. 2007. *Footsteps in the Dark: The Hidden Histories of Popular Music.* Minneapolis: University of Minnesota Press.

Loa, Angélica Natalia. 2005. "Performing Cultural Resistance: Chicano Public Art Practices toward Community Cultural Development." M.A. thesis, University of Southern California.

Lomnitz, Claudio. 1992. *Exits from the Labyrinth: Culture and Ideology in the Mexican National Space.* Berkeley: University of California Press.

Lomnitz, Claudio. 2001. *Deep Mexico, Silent Mexico: An Anthropology of Nationalism.* Minneapolis: University of Minnesota Press.

Lomnitz, Claudio. 2003. "The Depreciation of Life during Mexico City's Transition into the Crisis." In *Wounded Cities: Destruction and Reconstruction in a Globalized World*, edited by J. Schneider and I. Susser, 47–70. Oxford: Berg.

Lomnitz, Claudio. 2005. *Death and the Idea of Mexico.* Brooklyn, NY: Zone.

Lott, Eric. 2011. "Back Door Man: Howlin' Wolf and the Sound of Jim Crow." *American Quarterly* 63 (3): 697–710.

Loza, Steven. 1992. "From Veracruz to Los Angeles: The Reinterpretation of the *Son Jarocho*." In *Latin American Music Review* 13 (2): 179–194.

Luce, Henry R. 1941. "The American Century." *Life Magazine* February 17:61–65.

Lugo, Alejandro. 2008. *Fragmented Lives, Assembled Parts: Culture, Capitalism, and Conquest at the U.S.-Mexico Border.* Austin: University of Texas Press.

Macias, Anthony F. 2008. *Mexican American Mojo: Popular Music, Dance, and Urban Culture in Los Angeles, 1935–1968.* Durham, NC: Duke University Press.

Madison, D. Soyini. 2011. "The Labor of Reflexivity." *Cultural Studies—Critical Methodologies* 11 (2): 129–138.

Madrid, Alejandro L. 2008. *Nor-tec Rifa! Electronic Dance Music from Tijuana to the World.* New York: Oxford University Press.

Madrid, Alejandro L. 2009. *Sounds of the Modern Nation: Music, Culture, and Ideas in Post-Revolutionary Mexico.* Philadelphia: Temple University Press.

Madrid, Alejandro L. 2011. "Transnational Musical Encounters at the U.S.-Mexico Border: An Introduction." In *Transnational Encounters: Music and Performance at the U.S.-Mexico Border,* edited by Alejandro L. Madrid, 1–16. New York: Oxford University Press.

Madrid, Alejandro L. 2013. *Music in Mexico: Experiencing Music, Expressing Culture.* New York: Oxford University Press.

Maly, Michael, Heather Dalmage, and Nancy Michaels. 2013. "The End of an Idyllic World: Nostalgia Narratives, Race, and the Construction of White Powerlessness." *Critical Sociology* 39 (5): 757–779.

Marcuse, Herbert. 1977. *The Aesthetic Dimension: Toward a Critique of Marxist Aesthetics.* Boston: Beacon Press.

Martínez, Daniel E. 2016. "Coyote Use in an Era of Heightened Border Enforcement: New Evidence from the Arizona-Sonora Border Region." *Journal of Ethnic and Migration Studies* 42 (1): 103–119.

Martínez, Daniel E., and Jeremy Slack. 2013. "What Part of 'Illegal' Don't You Understand? The Social Consequences of Criminalizing Unauthorized Mexican Migrants in the United States." *Social and Legal Studies* 22 (4): 535–551.

Martínez, Daniel E., Robin C. Reineke, Raquel Rubio-Goldsmith, and Bruce O. Parks. 2014. "Structural Violence and Migrant Deaths in Southern Arizona: Data from the Pima County Office of the Medical Examiner, 1990–2013." *Journal on Migration and Human Security* 2 (4): 257–286.

Martínez, Daniel, Robin Reineke, Raquel Rubio-Goldsmith, Bruce Anderson, Gregory Hess, and Bruce Parks. 2013. *A Continued Humanitarian Crisis on the Border: Undocumented Border Crossers Deaths Recorded by the Pima County Office of the Medical Examiner 1990–2012.* Bi-National Migration Institute. Tucson: University of Arizona.

Martínez, Elizabeth. 1998. *De Colores Means All of Us: Latina Views for a Multi-colored Century.* Cambridge, MA: South End.

Martínez, Manuel Luis. 2002. "Telling the Difference between the Border and the Borderlands." In *Globalization on the Line*, edited by Claudia Sadowski-Smith, 53–68. New York: Palgrave.

Martínez, Oscar J. 1994. *Border People: Life and Society in the U.S.-Mexico Borderlands*. Tucson: University of Arizona Press.

Martínez, Oscar J. 1996. *U.S.-Mexico Borderlands: Historical and Contemporary Perspectives*. Wilmington, DE: Scholarly Resources.

Martínez, Oscar J. 1998. *Troublesome Border*. Tucson: University of Arizona Press.

Massey, Douglas S., Jorge Durand, and Nolan J. Malone. 2002. *Beyond Smoke and Mirrors: Mexican Immigration in an Era of Economic Integration*. New York: Russell Sage Foundation.

Massumi, Brian. 2002. *Parables for the Virtual: Movement, Affect, Sensation*. Durham, NC: Duke University Press.

Massumi, Brian. 2010. "The Future Birth of the Affective Fact: The Political Ontology of Threat." In *The Affect Theory Reader*, edited by Melissa Gregg and Gregory J. Seigworth, 52–70. Durham, NC: Duke University Press.

Mattingly, Doreen J., and Ellen R. Hansen. 2006. *Women and Change at the U.S.-Mexico Border: Mobility, Labor, and Activism*. Tucson: University of Arizona Press.

Mbembe, Achille. 2003. "Necropolitics." *Public Culture* 15 (1): 11–40.

McDowell, John Holmes. 2010. "Coaxing the Corrido: Centering Song in Performance." *Journal of American Folklore* 123 (488): 127–149.

Meierovich, Clara. 1995. *Vicente T. Mendoza: Artista y primer folclorólogo musical*. Mexico City: Universidad Nacional Autónoma de México, Coordinación de Humanidades.

Menchaca, Martha. 2001. *Recovering History, Constructing Race: The Indian, Black, and White Roots of Mexican Americans*. Austin: University of Texas Press.

Mendoza, Vicente T. 1947. *La décima en México: Glosas y valonas*. Buenos Aires: Ministerio de Justicia e Instrucción Pública de la Nación Argentina, Instituto Nacional de la Tradición.

Mendoza, Vicente T. 1956. *Panorama de la música tradicional de México*. Mexico City: Imprenta Universitaria, Universidad Nacional Autónoma de México.

Mendoza, Vicente T. 1961. *La canción mexicana: Ensayo de clasificación y antología*. Mexico City: Instituto de Investigaciones Estéticas, Universidad Nacional Autónoma de México.

Mendoza-Denton, Norma. 2008. *Homegirls: Language and Cultural Practice among Latina Youth Gangs*. Malden, MA: Blackwell.

Merleau-Ponty, Maurice. 1968. *The Visible and the Invisible*, edited by Claude Lefort, translated by Alphonso Lingis. Evanston, IL: Northwestern University Press.

Molina, Marco Antonio. 2010. "La improvisación en el huapango arribeño: temas y estructura de la topada." *Revista de Literaturas Populares* 10 (1–2): 183–210.

Monsiváis, Carlos. 1995. *Los rituales del caos*. Mexico City: Era.

Montejano, David. 1987. *Anglos and Mexicans in the Making of Texas, 1836–1986*. Austin: University of Texas Press.

Moraga, Cherríe. 1981. "A Bridge Gets Walked Over." In *This Bridge Called My Back: Writings by Radical Women of Color*, edited by Cherríe Moraga and Gloria Anzaldúa, xv. New York: Kitchen Table, Women of Color.

Moraga, Cherríe. 1981. "I Have Dreamed of a Bridge." In *This Bridge Called My Back: Writings by Radical Women of Color*, edited by Cherríe Moraga and Gloria Anzaldúa, xviii–xix. New York: Kitchen Table, Women of Color.

Moraga, Cherríe, and Gloria Anzaldúa, eds. 1981. *This Bridge Called My Back: Writings by Radical Women of Color*. New York: Kitchen Table, Women of Color.

Moreno Rivas, Yolanda. 1979. *Historia de la música popular mexicana*. Mexico City: Alianza Editorial Mexicana.

Nájera, Jennifer R. 2015. *The Borderlands of Race: Mexican Segregation in a South Texas Town*. Austin: University of Texas Press.

Nájera-Ramírez, Olga. 1997. "Engendering Nationalism: Identity, Discourse and the Mexican Charro." Working Paper no. 3, Chicano/Latino Research Center, University of California at Santa Cruz.

Nájera-Ramirez, Olga. 2007. "Unruly Passions: Poetics, Performance, and Gender in the Ranchera Song." In *Women and Migration in the U.S.-Mexico Borderlands: A Reader*, edited by Denise A. Segura and Patricia Zavella, 456–476. Durham, NC: Duke University Press.

Nancy, Jean-Luc. 2007. *Listening*. Translated by Charlotte Mandell. New York: Fordham University Press.

Nash, June C., and María Patricia Fernández-Kelly. 1983. *Women, Men, and the International Division of Labor*. Albany: State University of New York Press.

Negri, Antonio. 1991. *Marx beyond Marx: Lessons on the Grundrisse*. New York: Autonomedia.

Nevins, Joseph. 2002. *Operation Gatekeeper: The Rise of the "Illegal Alien" and the Making of the U.S.-Mexico Boundary*. New York: Routledge.

Ngai, Mae M. 2004. *Impossible Subjects: Illegal Aliens and the Making of Modern America*. Princeton, NJ: Princeton University Press.

Novak, David. 2015. "Noise." In *Keywords in Sound*, edited by David Novak and Matt Sakakeeny, 125–138. Durham, NC: Duke University Press.

Novak, David, and Matt Sakakeeny. 2015. "Introduction." *Keywords in Sound*, edited by David Novak and Matt Sakakeeny, 1–11. Durham, NC: Duke University Press.

Ochoa Gautier, Ana María. 2006. "Sonic Transculturation, Epistemologies of Purification and the Aural Public Sphere in Latin America." *Social Identities* 12 (6): 803–825.

Ochoa Gautier, Ana María. 2014. *Aurality: Listening and Knowledge in Nineteenth-Century Colombia*. Durham, NC: Duke University Press.

Olmos, Miguel. 2003. "La etnomusicología y el noroeste de méxico." *Desacatos* fall (12): 45–61.

Pallares, Amalia. 2014. *Family Activism: Immigrant Struggles and the Politics of Noncitizenship*. New Brunswick, NJ: Rutgers University Press.

Pallares, Amalia, and Flores-González. 2010. "Introduction." In *Marcha! Latino Chicago and the Immigrant Rights Movement*, edited by Amalia Pallares and Nilda Flores-González, xv–xxviii. Chicago: University of Illinois Press.

Paredes, Américo. 1958. *"With His Pistol in His Hand": A Border Ballad and Its Hero.*
Austin: University of Texas Press.

Paredes, Américo. 1961. "Folklore and History." In *Singers and Storytellers*, edited by
Mody Boatright, Wison M. Hudson, and Allen Mazwell, 58–68. Dallas: Southern
Methodist University Press.

Paredes, Américo. 1966. "The Decima on the Texas-Mexican Border: Folksong as an
Adjunct to Legend." *Journal of the Folklore Institute* 3 (2): 154–167.

Paredes, Américo. 1976. *A Texas-Mexican Cancionero: Folksongs of the Lower Border.*
Urbana: University of Illinois Press.

Paredes, Américo. 1993. *Folklore and Culture on the Texas-Mexican Border*, edited by
Richard Bauman. Austin: Center for Mexican American Studies, University of
Texas.

Paredes, Américo, and Richard Bauman. 1972. *Toward New Perspectives in Folklore.*
Austin: Published for the American Folklore Society by the University of Texas
Press.

Paredes, Américo, and George Foss. 1966. "The Décima Cantada on the Texas-Mexican
Border: Four Examples." *Journal of the Folklore Institute*, 3(2): 91–115.

Parra Muñoz, Rafael. 2007. "Tradición y sociedad: El devenir de las velaciones y el
huapango de la Zona Media y la Sierra Gorda." Bachelor's Thesis, Ethnohistory,
Instituto Nacional de Antropología e Historia.

Passel, Jeffrey S., D'Vera Cohn, Jens Manuel Krogstad, and Ana Gonzalez-Barrera. "As
Growth Stalls, Unauthorized Immigrant Population Becomes More Settled." Pew
Research Center, Hispanic Trends, September 3, 2014, http://www.pewhispanic.org
/2014/09/03/as-growth-stalls-unauthorized-immigrant-population-becomes-more
-settled/.

Paz, Octavio. 1961. *The Labyrinth of Solitude: Life and Thought in Mexico.* New York:
Grove.

Peña, Devon Gerardo. 1997. *The Terror of the Machine: Technology, Work, Gender, and
Ecology on the U.S.-Mexico Border.* Austin: Center for Mexican American Studies,
University of Texas.

Peña, Elaine A. 2011. *Performing Piety: Making Space Sacred with the Virgin of Guadalupe.* Berkeley: University of California Press.

Peña, Manuel H. 1985. *The Texas-Mexican Conjunto: History of a Working-Class Music.*
Austin: University of Texas Press.

Peña, Manuel H. 1991. "Class, Gender, and Machismo: The 'Treacherous-Woman'
Folklore of Mexican Male Workers." *Gender and Society* 5 (1): 30–46.

Peña, Manuel H. 1999. *Música Tejana: The Cultural Economy of Artistic Transformation.*
College Station: Texas A&M University Press.

Perea, Socorro. 1989. *Décimas y valonas de San Luis Potosí.* San Luis Potosí: Archivo
Histórico del Estado, Casa de la Cultura de San Luis Potosí.

Pérez, Gina M. 2004. *The Near Northwest Side Story: Migration, Displacement, and
Puerto Rican Families.* Berkeley: University of California Press.

Pérez-Torres, Rafael. 2006. *Mestizaje: Critical Uses of Race in Chicano Culture.* Minneapolis: University of Minnesota Press.

Plascencia, Luis F. B. 2009. "The 'Undocumented' Mexican Migrant Question: Re-examining the Framing of Law and Illegalization in the United States." *Urban Anthropology* 38 (1–2): 375–434.

Poinsett, Joel. 2002. "The Mexican Character." In *The Mexico Reader: History, Culture, Politics*, edited by Gilbert M. Joseph and Timothy J. Henderson, 11–14. Durham, NC: Duke University Press.

Powell, Philip Wayne. 1952. *Soldiers, Indians, and Silver: The Northward Advance of New Spain, 1550–1600*. Berkeley: University of California Press.

Quijano, Ánibal, and Immanuel Wallerstein. 1992. "Americanity as a Concept; or, The Americas in the Modern World-System." *International Journal of Social Sciences* 134: 549–557.

Ragland, Cathy. 2009. *Música Norteña: Mexican Migrants Creating a Nation between Nations*. Philadelphia: Temple University Press.

Ramírez, Catherine Sue. 2009. *The Woman in the Zoot Suit: Gender, Nationalism, and the Cultural Politics of Memory*. Durham, NC: Duke University Press.

Ramnarine, Tina K. 2001. *Creating Their Own Space: The Development of an Indian-Caribbean Musical Tradition*. Kingston, Jamaica: University of the West Indies Press.

Ravicz, Marilyn E. 1970. *Early Colonial Religious Drama in Mexico: From Tzompantli to Golgatha*. Washington, DC: Catholic University Press.

Redfield, Robert. 1930. *Tepoztlan, a Mexican Village: A Study of Folk Life*. Chicago: University of Chicago Press.

Redfield, Robert. 1941. *The Folk Culture of Yucatan*. Chicago: University of Chicago Press.

Redfield, Robert. 1950. *A Village That Chose Progress: Chan Kom Revisited*. Chicago: University of Chicago Press.

Redfield, Robert. 1953. *The Primitive World and Its Transformations*. Ithaca, NY: Cornell University Press.

Redfield, Robert. 1956. *Peasant Society and Culture: An Anthropological Approach to Civilization*. Chicago: University of Chicago Press.

Reuter, Jas. 1992. *La música popular de México*. Mexico City: Panorama.

Reyes, Adelaida. 1999. *Songs of the Caged, Songs of the Free: Music and the Vietnamese Refugee Experience*. Philadelphia: Temple University Press.

Rivas Paniagua, Enrique. 2003. *Nicandro Castillo: El Hidalguense*. Pachuca, Hidalgo: Consejo Estatal para la Cultura y las Artes de Hidalgo.

Robbins, Joel. 2013. "Beyond the Suffering Subject: Toward an Anthropology of the Good." *Journal of the Royal Anthropological Institute* 19 (3): 447–462.

Robinson, William I. 2003. *Transnational Conflicts: Central America, Social Change, and Globalization*. London: Verso.

Rodman, Margaret C. 1992. "Empowering Place: Multilocality and Multivocality." *American Anthropologist* 94 (3): 640–656.

Rodríguez, Russell C. 2006. "Cultural Production, Legitimation, and the Politics of Aesthetics: Mariachi Transmission, Practice, and Performance in the United States." PhD diss., University of California, Santa Cruz.

Rosa, Jonathan. 2010. "Looking like a Language, Sounding like a Race: Making Latin@ Panethnicity and Managing American Anxieties." PhD diss., University of Chicago.

Rosa, Jonathan, and Nelson Flores. 2015. "Hearing Language Gaps and Reproducing Social Inequality." In "Invited Forum: Bridging the 'Language Gap.'" *Journal of Linguistic Anthropology* 25 (1): 77–79.

Rosaldo, Renato. 1989. *Culture and Truth: The Remaking of Social Analysis.* Boston: Beacon.

Rosaldo, Renato. 1994. "Cultural Citizenship and Educational Democracy." *Cultural Anthropology* 9 (3): 402–411.

Rosas, Gilberto. 2006. "The Managed Violences of the Borderlands: Treacherous Geographies, Policeability, and the Politics of Race." *Latino Studies* 4 (4): 401–418.

Rosas, Gilberto. 2007. "The Fragile Ends of War: Forging the United States-Mexico Border and Borderlands Consciousness." *Social Text* 25 (2 91): 81–102.

Rosas, Gilberto. 2012. *Barrio Libre: Criminalizing States and Delinquent Refusals of the New Frontier.* Durham, NC: Duke University Press.

Rosenblum, Marc R., and Kate Brick. 2011. *US Immigration Policy and Mexican/Central American Migration Flows: Then and Now.* Washington, DC: Migration Policy Institute, Regional Migration Study Group.

Rothfield, Philipa. 2008. "Feeling Feelings: The Work of Russell Dumas through Whitehead's Process and Reality." *Inflexions* 2. http://www.inflexions.org/n2_rothfieldhtml.html.

Rouse, Roger. 1991. "Mexican Migration and the Social Space of Postmodernism." *Diaspora: A Journal of Transnational Studies* 1 (1): 8–23.

Rouse, Roger. 1992. "Making Sense of Settlement: Class Transformation, Cultural Struggle, and Transnationalism among Mexican Migrants in the United States." *Annals of the New York Academy of Sciences* 645 (1): 25–52.

Ruíz, Vicki, and Susan Tiano. 1991. *Women on the U.S.-Mexico Border: Responses to Change.* Boulder, CO: Westview.

Sadowski-Smith, Claudia. 2002. *Globalization on the Line: Culture, Capital, and Citizenship at U.S. Borders.* New York: Palgrave.

Saldanha, Arun. 2007. *Psychedelic White: Goa Trance and the Viscosity of Race.* Minneapolis: University of Minnesota Press.

Saldívar, Gabriel. 1934. *Historia de la música en México (épocas precortesanas y colonial).* Mexico: Impreso en los Talleres de la Editorial "Cultura."

Saldívar, Gabriel. 1937. *El jarabe: Baile popular mexicano.* Mexico City: Talleres Gráficos de la Nación.

Saldívar, José David. 1997. *Border Matters: Remapping American Cultural Studies.* Berkeley: University of California Press.

Sánchez-Tello, George B. 2012. "Jaraner@: Chicana/o Acculturation Strategy." M.A. thesis, California State University, Northridge.

Sandoval, Chela. 1991. "U.S. Third World Feminism: The Theory and Method of Oppositional Consciousness in the Postmodern World" *Genders* 10: 1–24.

Santa Ana, Otto. 2002. *Brown Tide Rising: Metaphors of Latinos in Contemporary American Public Discourse.* Austin: University of Texas Press.

Schafer, R. Murray. (1977) 1994. *The Soundscape: Our Sonic Environment and the Tuning of the World*. Rochester, VT: Destiny.

Schiller, Nina Glick, Linda Basch, and Cristina Blanc-Szanton. 1992. "Towards a Definition of Transnationalism." *Annals of the New York Academy of Sciences* 645 (1): ix–xiv.

Schmidt, Henry C. 1978. *The Roots of Lo Mexicano: Self and Society in Mexican Thought, 1900–1934*. College Station: Texas A&M University Press.

Schutz, Alfred. 1967. *The Phenomenology of the Social World*. Evanston, IL: Northwestern University Press.

Scott, James C. 1990. *Domination and the Arts of Resistance: Hidden Transcripts*. New Haven, CT: Yale University Press.

Segura, Denise A., and Patricia Zavella, eds. 2007. *Women and Migration in the U.S.-Mexico Borderlands: A Reader*. Durham, NC: Duke University Press.

Seigworth, Gregory J. 2010. "An Inventory of Shimmers." In *The Affect Theory Reader*, edited by Melissa Gregg and Gregory J. Seigworth, 1–28. Durham, NC: Duke University Press.

Serres, Michel. 1997. *The Troubadour of Knowledge*. Translated by Sheila Faria Glaser and William R. Paulson. Ann Arbor: University of Michigan Press.

Shaviro, Steven. 2009. *Without Criteria: Kant, Whitehead, Deleuze, and Aesthetics*. Cambridge, MA: MIT Press.

Sheehy, Daniel Edward. 1979. "The Son Jarocho: The History, Style, and Repertory of a Changing Mexican Musical Tradition." PhD diss., University of California, Los Angeles.

Sheehy, Daniel Edward. 1998. "Mexico." In *Garland Encyclopedia of World Music*, vol. 2, *South America, Mexico, Central America, and the Caribbean*, edited by Dale E. Olsen and Daniel Edward Sheehy, 600–625. New York: Garland.

Sheehy, Daniel Edward. 2006. *Mariachi Music in America: Experiencing Music, Expressing Culture*. New York: Oxford University Press.

Sheppard, Randal. 2011. "Nationalism, Economic Crisis and 'Realistic Revolution' in 1980s Mexico." *Nations and Nationalism* 17 (3): 500–519.

Sherzer, Joel. 2002. *Speech Play and Verbal Art*. Austin: University of Texas Press.

Silverstein, Michael, and Greg Urban. 1996. *Natural Histories of Discourse*. Chicago: University of Chicago Press.

Simonett, Helena. 2001. *Banda: Mexican Musical Life across Borders*. Middletown, CT: Wesleyan University Press.

Skinner, Robert. 2002. "Grains, Oilseeds, and Related Products." In *Effects of North American Free Trade Agreement on Agriculture and the Rural Economy*, edited by Steven Zahniser and John Link, 70–85. Washington, DC: U.S. Department of Agriculture. Retrieved from Electronic Outlook Report from the Economic Research Service, https://www.ers.usda.gov/webdocs/publications/40355/31319_wrs0201i_002.pdf?v=41471.

Slack, Jeremy, Daniel E. Martínez, Scott Whiteford, and Emily Peiffer. 2013. *In the Shadow of the Wall: Family Separation, Immigration Enforcement, and Security*. The Center for Latin American Studies, University of Arizona.

Slobin, Mark. 1993. *Subcultural Sounds: Micromusics of the West*. Hanover, NH: University of New England Press.

Spalding, Rose J. 1985. "El Sistema Alimentario Mexicano: Ascenso y decadencia." *Estudios Sociológicos* 3 (8): 315–349.

Stanford, Thomas. 1972. "The Mexican Son." *Yearbook of the International Folk Music Council* 4: 66–86.

Stanford, Thomas. 1984. *El son mexicano.* Mexico City: Fondo de Cultura Económico.

Stephen, Lynn. 2007. *Transborder Lives: Indigenous Oaxacans in Mexico, California, and Oregon.* Durham, NC: Duke University Press.

Stewart, Kathleen. 1991. "On the Politics of Cultural Theory: A Case for 'Contaminated' Cultural Critique." *Social Research* 58 (2): 395–412.

Stewart, Kathleen. 1996. *A Space on the Side of the Road: Cultural Poetics in an "Other" America.* Princeton, NJ: Princeton University Press.

Stewart, Kathleen. 2007. *Ordinary Affects.* Durham, NC: Duke University Press.

Stewart, Kathleen. 2008. "Weak Theory in an Unfinished World." *Journal of Folklore Research: An International Journal of Folklore and Ethnomusicology* 45 (1): 71–82.

Stocking, George W. 1983. *Observers Observed: Essays on Ethnographic Fieldwork.* Madison: University of Wisconsin Press.

Stokes, Martin, ed. 1994. *Ethnicity, Identity, and Music: The Musical Construction of Place.* Oxford: Berg.

Stout, Robert Joe. 2008. *Why Immigrants Come to America: Braceros, Indocumentados, and the Migra.* Westport, CT: Praeger.

Stuesse, Angela. 2016. *Scratching Out a Living: Latinos, Race, and Work in the Deep South.* Oakland: University of California Press.

Taussig, Michael T. 1993. *Mimesis and Alterity: A Particular History of the Senses.* New York: Routledge.

Taylor, Diana. 2003. *The Archive and the Repertoire: Performing Cultural Memory in the Americas.* Durham, NC: Duke University Press.

Téllez, Michelle. 2008. "Community of Struggle: Gender, Violence, and Resistance on the U.S.–Mexico Border." In "Gendered Borderlands." Special issue, edited by Denise A. Segura and Patricia Zavella. *Gender and Society* 22 (5): 545–567.

Trapero, Maximiano. 1996. *El libro de la décima: La poesía improvisada en el mundo hispánico.* Las Palmas de Gran Canaria: Universidad de las Palmas de Gran Canaria.

Trapero, Maximiano. 2001. *La décima: Su historia, su geografía, sus manifestaciones.* Las Palmas de Gran Canaria, Gran Canaria: Centro de la Cultura Popular Canaria.

Trouillot, Michel-Rolph. 2003. *Global Transformations: Anthropology and the Modern World.* New York: Palgrave Macmillan.

Turino, Thomas. 1993. *Moving Away from Silence: Music of the Peruvian Altiplano and the Experience of Urban Migration.* Chicago: University of Chicago Press.

Turino, Thomas. 2003. "Nationalism and Latin American Music: Selected Case Studies and Theoretical Considerations." *Latin American Music Review* 24 (2): 169–209.

Turkle, Sherry. 1995. *Life on the Screen: Identity in the Age of the Internet.* New York: Simon and Schuster.

Turner, Victor. 1974. *Dramas, Fields, and Metaphors: Symbolic Action in Human Society.* Ithaca, NY: Cornell University Press.

Vansina, Jan. 1985. *Oral Tradition as History.* Madison: University of Wisconsin Press.

Vargas, Deborah R. 2012. *Dissonant Divas in Chicana Music: The Limits of La Onda.* Minneapolis: University of Minnesota Press.

Vasconcelos, José. 2002. "The Cosmic Race." In *The Mexico Reader: History, Culture, Politics,* edited by Gilbert M. Joseph and Timothy J. Henderson, 15–19. Durham, NC: Duke University Press.

Vazquez, Alexandra T. 2013. *Listening in Detail: Performances of Cuban Music.* Durham, NC: Duke University Press.

Vega, Sujey. 2015. *Latino Heartland: Of Borders and Belonging in the Midwest.* New York: New York University Press.

Velázquez, Eliazar. 2004. *Poetas y juglares de la Sierra Gorda: Crónicas y conversaciones.* Guanajuato, Guanajuato, Mexico: Ediciones La Rana, Instituto de la Cultura de Guanajuato.

Vélez-Ibañez, Carlos G. 1983. *Bonds of Mutual Trust: The Cultural Systems of Rotating Credit Associations among Urban Mexicans and Chicanos.* New Brunswick, NJ: Rutgers University Press.

Vélez-Ibañez, Carlos G. 1996. *Border Visions: Mexican Cultures of the Southwest United States.* Tucson: University of Arizona Press.

Vélez-Ibañez, Carlos G. 2010. *An Impossible Living in a Transborder World: Culture, Confianza, and Economy of Mexican-Origin Populations.* Tucson: University of Arizona Press.

Vertovec, Steven. 2004. "Migrant Transnationalism and Modes of Transformation." *International Migration Review* 38 (3): 970–1001.

Vila, Pablo. 2000. *Crossing Borders, Reinforcing Borders: Social Categories, Metaphors, and Narrative Identities on the U.S.-Mexico Frontier.* Austin: University of Texas Press.

Virno, Paolo. 2004. *A Grammar of the Multitude: For an Analysis of Contemporary Forms of Life.* New York: Semiotext(e).

Wade, Peter. 2003. "Race and Nation in Latin America: An Anthropological View." In *Race and Nation in Modern Latin America,* edited by Nancy P. Appelbaum, Anne S. Macpherson, and Karin Alejandra Rosemblatt, 263–283. Chapel Hill: University of North Carolina Press.

Wald, Elijah. 2001. *Narcocorrido: A Journey into the Music of Drugs, Guns, and Guerrillas.* New York: Rayo.

Wald, Elijah. 2004. *Escaping the Delta: Robert Johnson and the Invention of the Blues.* New York: Amistad.

Watkins, Megan. 2010. "Desiring Recognition, Accumulating Affect." In *The Affect Theory Reader,* edited by Melissa Gregg and Gregory J. Seigworth, 269–288. Durham, NC: Duke University Press.

Weidman, Amanda. 2015. "Voice." In *Keywords in Sound,* edited by David Novak and Matt Sakakeeny, 232–245. Durham, NC: Duke University Press.

Weise, Julie M. 2012. "Dispatches from the 'Viejo' New South: Historicizing Recent Latino Migrations." *Latino Studies* 10 (1–2): 41–59.

Williams, Raymond. 1977. *Marxism and Literature.* Oxford: Oxford University Press.

Wise, Raul Delgado, and James M. Cypher. 2007. "The Strategic Role of Mexican Labor under NAFTA: Critical Perspectives on Current Economic Integration." *Annals of the American Academy of Political and Social Science* 610 (1): 119–142.

Woodward, Keith, and John Paul Jones III. 2005. "On the Border with Deleuze and Guattari." *B/ordering Space*, edited by Henk Van Houtum, Olivier Thomas Kramsch, and Wolfgang Zierhofer, 235–248. Aldershot, UK: Ashgate.

Zavella, Patricia. 2011. *I'm Neither Here nor There: Mexicans' Quotidian Struggles with Migration and Poverty.* Durham, NC: Duke University Press.

Note: page numbers followed by *f* and *n* indicate musical examples and endnotes, respectively.

Bartra, Roger, 47, 57, 370n10, 378n38
Bascom, William R., 384n18
Bataille, Georges, 62, 80, 128, 221–222, 230, 289
Battle of San Jacinto, 378n4
Bauman, Richard, 21, 69, 75, 82, 126
Behague, Gerard, 371n15
belonging: disassociated from racial hierarchies, 217; expressive culture and, 4; interpersonal connections and, 290; national anthem incident and boundaries of, 201; social and cultural citizenship and, 20; staking claims of, 53, 61; transnational theorists on lack of, 57; use of term, 22. *See also* citizenship
Berger, Harris M., 68, 83
Berrones, Pancho, 73, 156
Berry, Keith, 319
Bhabha, Homi K., 320, 383n14, 385n9
bifocality, 362n16
biopower and biopolitics, 249, 250–251, 270–271
bios, 221, 271
birthday party, Austin, 203–205
birthright citizenship clause, 218
Blacking, John, 371n15
Blommaert, Jan, 46
bodies: as archives of memories, 311; authoring and authorizing practices, 270–271; biopower and biopolitics, 249, 250–251, 270–271; bridging theory and practice with, 320–321; calling out and, 127; emplaced and embodied self and, 234–235; emplacement of the self across borders, 221–222; genocidal management of, 134; illegality and disposable biocommodities, 250–251; as Imaginary concept, 372n21; intimacy, unbinding, and, 80; Limón on performance and, 221; listening with whole body, 326; relationality between places and, 218–219; *saludados* and, 271–272; space of performance and, 128; watching and remembering, 235. *See also* embodiment; migrants and labor migration
Boehm, Lauren, 328
Bolton, Herbert Eugene, 361n9
Bonfil Batalla, Guillermo, 45

border, U.S.-Mexico: brutality and death, 238–239, 382n5; Doña Rosa's crossing story, 299–301; Fandango Fronterizo at Tijuana–San Diego crossing, 321; as historical site of racialized violence, 249; militarization and criminalization of, 247; as modernist reification, 317; racial ideologies and, 11–12; recognition of bonds across, 18; Ricardo's crossing story, 247; smuggling history, 214; unauthorized "wetbacks" vs. those who travel freely, 287. *See also* migrants and labor migration
borderlands: borders vs., 11; concept of, 13; disordered materialisms and racialized biopolitics in, 249–253; hybridity and, 385n9; metaphorical, vs. material conditions of bordered lives, 296; in music scholarship, 13; third spaces and, 320–321
borderland studies, 11–13, 320–321
borderlines, 10
Border Protection, Anti-terrorism, and Illegal Immigration Control Act (Sensenbrenner Bill), 279
borders: borderlands vs., 11; discursive, 10; emplacement of the self across, 221–222; as "fluid, give-and-take areas," 51; of genre, 69, 218; movement of capital vs. of migrant bodies, 54–55; physical and metaphysical, moves and flows across, 75; smaller, 2; solidarities voiced across, 61. *See also* bridging and bridges; crossing; poetic border and clandestine desires (Potosí to Tennessee); politics and poetics (verses and flows), relationship between
border studies, 11–12
"Born in the U.S.A." (Springsteen), 328–329
Bourke, Gregory, 367n18
Bracero Program, 253
Brandes, Stanley H., 294
bravata (boasting), 108–109, 114–116, 168–172, 179
bridging and bridges: Alvarez's model for, 386n3; desire and, 219; Doña Rosa's home as bridge, 297; into existence, 270; *huapango arribeño* as, 316, 320; intimacy and, 223, 230–231; Moraga and Anzaldúa's

This Bridge Called My Back, 320; poetic distance and, 233; between Potosí and Tennessee, 259; tethers among places and, 222–223; of theory and practice with body, 320–321; third spaces collapsed by, 321. *See also* crossing
Briggs, Charles L., 21, 68, 69, 75, 142
Briones, Agapito, 73, 156, 376n22
Brown, Michael, 327
"browning of America," 132
Brown is Beautiful (Olmeca), 131–132
Broyles-González, Yolanda, 44
Butler, Judith, 381n19
Byrd, Samuel K., 10–11

Cafferty, Jack, 279–280
California Proposition 187 (1994), 134
calling, the. See *destino, el*
calling out, 126–127, 164–165, 187, 288
Camacho, Lorenzo, 73
caminata (opening parade), 163
"Camino de Guanajuato" (Jiménez), 290–294
Campesinos de la Sierra, Los, 377n27
Campos, Ruben M., 290
cancionero (minstrel) tradition, 290
canciones rancheras (country songs), 38, 44–45, 72, 290–294, 385n7
canciones típicas (traditional songs), 38, 44
Cantores de la Sierra, Los, 157, 376n25, 377n26
cantos a lo divino, Plate 11
capitalism: autonomist concept of class composition, 384n20; "empire," 271, 318, 375n6; excess of performance as release from, 128; interwar period and, 137; labor-capital polarity reversal, 384n19; labor for capital and against capital, 384n2; late capitalism as death personified, 276; modernity and, 52, 366n14; self-valorization and, 383n17; valorization, capitalist, 271. *See also* labor; migrants and labor migration
Cárdenas, Lázaro, 45
Carreón, Pedro, 156
Casey, Edward S., 222, 270, 381n21
Casillas, Dolores, 10
Castillo, Simón, 73

Castro, Rafaela, 384n18
Ceballos, José, 73
Cepeda, María Elena, 378n3
Cervantes, Marco, 375n1
Charlemagne, 144, 375n11
Chavez, Leo R., 50, 217–218
Chávez, Oscar, 376n21
Chávez, Paty, 377n27
Chávez, Reina, 377n27
"Chicagoacán," 383n13
chrono-tropes, 45–46. See also *ranchero* chrono-trope
citizenship: "alien citizen" concept, 380n17; birthright citizenship clause, 218; cultural visibility and, 201; deracialized, 217; Mexicanness as impediment to, 199; postnationalism and new meanings of, 61; whiteness and, 200–201, 249. *See also* belonging
city, poetic, 263
class composition, autonomist concept of, 384n20
Cleaver, Harry, 375n8
Clifford, James, 24, 74
Coates, Ta-Nehisi, 329
comedia ranchera, 36
comités de solidaridad (solidarity committees), 188
compañeros del destino (companions of the calling), 7, 63, 80
competitive camaraderie, 118–119, 167, 179, 369n3
conjunto, 211, 213
contrapunto, 100
controversia, poetic (Velázquez and Flores Solano), 159–162
copla real, 81
Corona, Ignacio, 386n11
corporatist social programs, 188
corrido, the, 72, 211–214, 216, 219, 290, 294, 379n11
"Corrido de Kiansis, El," 213
Cortez, Gregorio, 213
Coulter, Ann, 131–132
Cowie, Jefferson R., 328
creative advance, 82, 119
Cresswell, Tim, 222
criminalization, 247, 250

troubadours: collective social location and, 142–143; competitive camaraderie, 118–119, 167, 179, 369n3; historical cohorts of, 73; interdiscursive circuits and, 155; *poesías encadenadas/enlazadas* and *poesías de esdrújula*, 106–108; positions staked in *poesías*, 108. See also *reglamento*; *topadas*
Trouillot, Michel-Rolph, 290
Turino, Thomas, 43, 214
Turkle, Sherry, 230
Turner, Victor, 384n18
Turrubiartes, Adrián, 73

unbinding, 80
United States as external other, 192
utopian performative, 143

vaivén, 97
valonas, 88–89, 333–334*f*, 335–336*f*, 372n25
valoneado, 94–95
Van Buren, Martin, 49
Vargas, Deborah R., 211, 375n1
Vasconcelos, José, 22, 47
Vazquez, Alexandra T., 58, 369n26
Vega, Carlos, 371n15
velaciones (vigils), 374n33
Velázquez, Eliazar "Chalo," 156, 374n41
Velázquez, Guillermo, *Plate 1*; about, 136; as bridge between places, 321; on changes in *huapango arribeño* over time, 76; cohort of, 73; "Como poeta trovador," 350–351, 355–357; "De la Valona al Rap," 192–193; early life, 137–140; "En Busca de Chamba," 145–148, 189–192; "En Tejas hay mucha raza," 315; "Es muy profunda su huella," 276; first *topada* in U.S., 206; Flores Solano and, 159; formation as *huapanguero*, 141–142; *fundamento* themes tested with, 144; "Gente del rancho que un día emigró," 48–49; "Los gringos no se la creen," 278; "Habrá emergencia mañana," 323–325; "Hay inquietud en la raza," 19; *huapango arribeño* workshops and, 156; Los Leones de la Sierra de Xichú and, 136, 141–142, 159, 298–299; "Las manos diestras en construir" (Velázquez), 130–131; political conscious-

ness and expression, 144–148; repressive politics of social reproduction and, 188; "Si más antes había la ignorancia," 144; in *topada*, 100–101; "Viva el huapango," 331–332*f*; Xichú festival and, 156
Velázquez, Vincent, 193–195
velorios (funeral wakes), 374n33
vernacular theorizing, 54–59
verses and flows. *See* politics and poetics (verses and flows), relationship between
verses in *son* structure, 97
versos de arte menor and *versos de arte mayor*, 88
versos de jarabe, 125–126
Veterans Day "Concert for Valor," Washington, D.C., 327–329
Victoria, Guanajuato, 29, 77, 137, 298
viejo Antonio, tale of, 196–197
vihuelas, in ensemble configuration, 72–73
Villanueva, Eugenio, 73
Villeda, Otílio, 73
violinists, 73, 104–106. See also *topadas*
Virno, Paolo, 264, 270
virtuosity, 264
voicing: concept of, 7, 20–21; embodiment and "taking place," 8; lived politics and performance, 155; of solidarities, 264–265

Wade, Peter, 47
Wald, Elijah, 296
Wallerstein, Immanuel, 366n14
Watkins, Megan, 289, 385n4
wedding *topada* in Guanajuato, Mexico, 272–275
Weise, Julie M., 253–254
wheat embargo (1983), 154–155
Whitehead, Alfred North, 82, 381n21
Whitman, Walt, 49–50
Wilson, Darren, 327
Wilson, Pete, 134
Wise, Raúl Delgado, 135
women, Xichú festival and, 157–162. *See also* gender subjectivity
Woodward, Keith, 383n12

Xichú, Guanajuato, *Plate 9*, *Plate 13*, *Plate 16*; geographic oscillation between Mexico City and, 137–142; migration from, 29; New Year *topada*, 66–67; Las Palomitas Serranas, *Plate 7*; as time, 162–163; Valentín's story, 66. *See also* Festival del Huapango Arribeño y de la Cultura de la Sierra Gorda, Xichú

Yupanqui, Atahualpa, 376n21

Zapatista National Liberation Army, 195–196
zarabanda dance, 373n32
Zavella, Patricia, 13, 56–57, 58, 301, 361n10, 368n25, 369n30
Zumaya, Esperanza, 377n27
Zuñiga, Antonio, 290